EXCAVATING
JESUS

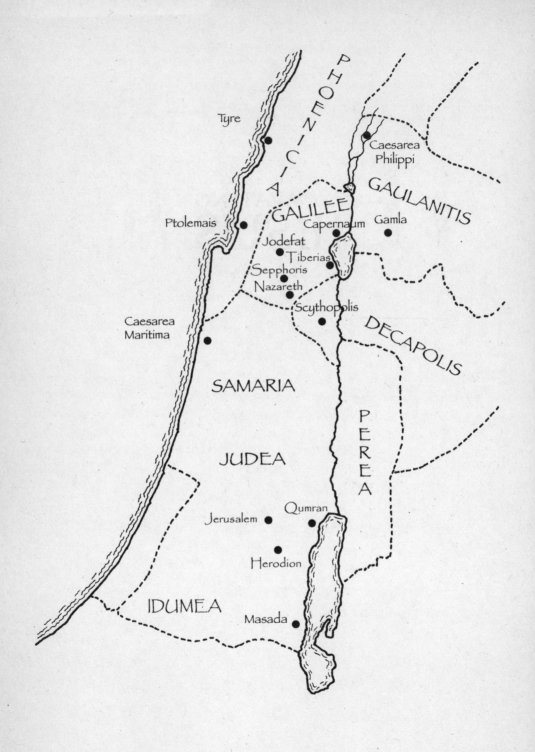

Tyre

PHOENICIA

Caesarea
Philippi

GALILEE

GAULANITIS

Ptolemais

Capernaum

Gamla

Jodefat
Tiberias

Sepphoris
Nazareth

Scythopolis

DECAPOLIS

Caesarea
Maritima

SAMARIA

PEREA

JUDEA

Qumran

Jerusalem

Herodion

IDUMEA

Masada

EXCAVATING
JESUS

Beneath the Stones,
Behind the Texts

Revised & Updated

JOHN DOMINIC CROSSAN
& JONATHAN L. REED

HarperSanFrancisco
A Division of HarperCollinsPublishers

EXCAVATING JESUS: *Beneath the Stones, Behind the Texts*. Revised and updated. Copyright © 2001 by John Dominic Crossan and Jonathan L. Reed. All rights reserved. Printed in the United States of America. No part of this book may be used or reproduced in any manner whatsoever without written permission except in the case of brief quotations embodied in critical articles and reviews. For information address HarperCollins Publishers, Inc., 10 East 53rd Street, New York, NY 10022.

HarperCollins books may be purchased for educational, business, or sales promotional use. For information please write: Special Markets Department, HarperCollins Publishers, Inc., 10 East 53rd Street, New York, NY 10022.

HarperCollins Web site: http://www.harpercollins.com
HarperCollins®, ☕®, and HarperSanFrancisco™ are trademarks of
HarperCollins Publishers, Inc.

FIRST EDITION
Designed by Joseph Rutt

Library of Congress Cataloging-in-Publication Data
Crossan, John Dominic.
Excavating Jesus : beneath the stones, behind the texts / John Dominic
Crossan & Jonathan L. Reed.—1st ed.
p. cm.
Includes index.
ISBN 0–06–061634–2 (pbk.)
1. Bible. N.T. Gospels—Antiquities. 2. Excavations (Archaeology)—Israel.
I. Reed, Jonathan L. II. Title.
BS621 .C76 2001
225.9'3—dc21 2001024960
04 05 ❖/RRD(H) 10 9 8 7 6 5 4 3 2

Dedicated
to
Annette
and
Sarah

CONTENTS

LIST OF ILLUSTRATIONS

The colored reproductions from the insert are repeated in smaller-scale black and white, but with full descriptions, at the appropriate places within the book.

FOREWORD TO NEW EDITION

It is Saturday afternoon, November 23, 2002. Toronto's sky is gloomily clouded, its temperature in the upper 30s, but any wind off Lake Ontario is mercifully absent. The sidewalks outside the Royal Ontario Museum are crowded with people and, as our taxi stops, we worry about long lines to get in, getting our tickets, getting to see the exhibit. But we soon realize that those crowds are mostly young children, some with their parents but others with organized outings, and that they are there for a somewhat different experience. The museum's McLaughlin Planetarium has a "world exclusive" on *The Lord of the Rings: The Two Towers Exhibit*, which contains "artifacts from New Line Cinema's theatrical production of *The Lord of the Rings*." The children are there for artifacts of magical fantasy and, as we nudge through their line to enter the main building, we wonder if we adults are there for an artifact of biblical fantasy. And it is rather ironic to recall as we enter the museum that *The Lord of the Rings* is not a saga of quest but of antiquest, an attempt not to find what you do not have but rather to face what is thrust upon you.

The museum's third level is dedicated to the Mediterranean World, extending from Mesopotamia and Egypt through Nubia and the Levant, and from Greece and Rome through Byzantium and Islam. Room 9 is reserved for Mediterranean World Features Exhibitions and there, in a few weeks of prodigious work, the museum's staff had managed to mount a world premiere exhibit that would normally have taken a year to prepare. The room's entrance and exit were shielded with semitransparent gauze-like screens, the walls were bright red with white lettering, and in the center, under Plexiglass, was a first-century Jewish bone box, or ossuary, with a small twenty-letter Aramaic inscription, *James, son of Joseph, brother of Jesus*. That inscription was enlarged graphically and dominated the back wall with an English translation above it and a French one below.

We were there for about two hours, watching the exhibit, watching ourselves respond, but also watching others react to what the media had called the most important archaeological discovery of Christianity. The room could hold about fifty to seventy-five people and there was a steady flow through it that whole afternoon. People moved in a clockwise circle reading the quotations and explanations on the walls before spiraling inward toward the ossuary itself. The exhibit's designers chose, most appropriately, to emphasize texts over images and it worked brilliantly. Visitors read from the New Testament and from ancient authors such as Josephus, Hegesippus, and Eusebius. They read about Jewish reburial, Aramaic scripts, and Christian interpretations of Jesus as "brother" of James and "son" of Joseph. Some viewers may already have known all that information but, lurking and listening, it was impossible not to be deeply impressed by the Royal Ontario Museum's most successful exercise in public education.

The first edition of this book established a dialectic of stone and text, an interaction of ground and gospel, an integration of archaeology and exegesis in which each discipline maintained its own full validity. Neither approach was reduced to footnote or background for the other. This revised edition changes nothing in that reciprocity. But the recently discovered ossuary, with possibly the oldest tangible evidence of Jesus, calls for a second edition using the discovery as a concentrated example, or focused symbol, for that process of integration. It is both a positive and a negative example.

After the discovery of the James ossuary and even before final conclusions are made on its authenticity, identity, and integrity, we knew we had to put it in our top ten list of archaeological discoveries for *Excavating Jesus*. But we were reluctant to lose a single one of the earlier ten so we made a virtue of necessity and combined two together. We could have combined Caiaphas and Pilate since they had cooperated for ten years and were both finally removed around the same time by their Roman superiors. But we decided on an alternative juxtaposition. The Romanization, urbanization, and commercialization of Lower Galilee focused on the Sea of Galilee in the 20s C.E. Pointedly, then, we combine both the Peter House and the Galilee Boat and call number five of our list "the Sea of Tiberias" (as it is called in John 6:1 and 21:1). Both the house and the boat reflect on the commercialization of lake fishing in different ways. That, we think, makes their combination significant. We decided to put the James ossuary in first place in our top ten list because of its importance in raising the profile of James and how he reflects on Jesus not only fraternally but theologically. And we put the James ossuary first because it underscores the importance of archaeology as a scholarly discipline and not as treasure hunting. We put it first because of the questions it raises.

There are five questions. Is the ossuary authentic? Is the inscription original? Is the family identifiable? Is the discovery important? Is the process ethical? We answer those last two immediately even if only provisionally. And these two answers will remain valid no matter what we, other scholars, or the press and public eventually decide on the first three questions.

The Discovery's Importance. The discovery is profoundly important simply because it gives a suddenly but properly high profile to James, son of Joseph, brother of Jesus. He was once well known as James the Just but has since become almost unknown in importance even if not in name. Maybe we should call him James the Lost. It is therefore about time to reconsider one who lived for over thirty years in early first-century Jerusalem accepted alike by both Christian Jews and non-Christian Jews, who disagreed with Paul and yet had Peter on his side, and whose death toppled the Jewish high priest Ananus II, who had him executed in 62 c.e. Second, when devout Jews, probably including Pharisees, protested that action, it was the Jewish ruler Agrippa II who dismissed Ananus II from office after only three months. The James ossuary reminds us how much of earliest "Christian" history involved Jewish groups in accord or discord with other Jewish groups, for example, Christian Jews in interaction with Pharisaic Jews and Sadducean Jews. Third, there was a time when James was far more important than Paul, and when James not Paul represented an ecumenical hope that ultimately failed but should be lamented none the less for that fact. Think counterfactually for a moment and mourn for what might have been. There was once a place where at least some Christian Jews and at least some Pharisaic Jews combined in opposing at least some Sadducean Jews. Once upon a time at least some might have been enough to change the future.

The Discovery's Ethics. The James ossuary has come to us through the sale of antiquities rather than excavation by archaeologists. We do not know, therefore, whether its original discovery was an unplanned finding or a planned looting, and the possibility of forgery will always haunt it. When such an artifact eventually surfaces to public awareness, individual scholars, learned societies, and museum authorities are caught in a double bind. To accept and discuss it may encourage paralegal searching, illegal looting, and unethical destruction of heritage. To avoid and ignore it may be impossible since even a refusal to discuss it is inevitably a comment upon it. We deliberately use the ossuary in this book to emphasize the difference between archaeological study and cultural looting.

Anyone can understand that the answer to our third question, the identity of the family, may never be more than a historical possibility or a statistical probability. Imagine then a different scenario. A construction crew breaks into an ancient burial cave by accident. It observes the law, stops work, and calls in the Israel Antiquities Authority. Its archaeologists find a burial site undisturbed for nineteen hundred years and in the beam of their lights are three ossuaries, one named for Stephen, another named for James, son of Zebedee, brother of John, and a third named for James, son of Joseph, brother of Jesus. In that case we would know for certain that we had the mausoleum of three Christian-Jewish saints martyred respectively in the early 30s, 40s, and 60s.

That never happened and we now have the James ossuary without context, provenance, or history. It is almost a poster warning about the destructive effects of paralegal artifact collecting, about the potential criminal sanctions for selling and buying on the illegal antiquities market, and about the moral difference between scientific archaeology and cultural looting. The James ossuary bears on its limestone sides the shadow of cultural looting rather than the patina of scientific research. Its casing was cracked in transit from Israel to Canada. But it was already cracked in transit from past to present. This discovery was cracked from the start.

Stones and Texts

Why did Jesus happen when and where he happened? Why then? Why there? Sharpen the question a little. Why did two popular movements, the Baptism movement of John and the Kingdom movement of Jesus, happen in territories ruled by Herod Antipas in the 20s of that first common-era century? Why not at another time? Why not in another place?

Imagine two ways of answering those questions: by stone *or* text, by ground *or* gospel, by material remains *or* scribal remains, by the work of the archaeologist *or* the work of the exegete. Imagine, next, every one of those four italicized *or*s replaced by equally emphasized *and*s. It is not just a case of archaeology *or* exegesis, but of archaeology *and* exegesis. Imagine, finally, those options as twin independent methods neither of which is subordinate or submissive to the other. Archaeology is not background for exegesis, and neither is exegesis decoration for archaeology. Gospel and ground must each be read and interpreted in its own way and under its own discipline. An ancient mound has its dignity and integrity with or without Homer in hand. An ancient tell has its challenge and mystery with or without Bible in backpack. Words talk. Stones talk too. Neither talks from the past without interpretive dialogue with the present. But each talks and each demands to be heard in its own way. Only after archaeology and exegesis each get their own full voice should they come together in doubled chorus and common report.

The purpose of this book is to integrate the archeology of ground and the exegesis of gospel by giving each its full explanatory power and by refusing to privilege one over the other. There is nothing new in archeologists reporting on what they have excavated. There is nothing new in exegetes describing what they have discovered. What is novel here is for a seasoned field archaeologist and an experienced Jesus scholar to work together and to do so not just on parallel tracks with alternately written chapters, but on a single track with each discipline woven into each and every chapter. How do we read stones and texts as an integrated whole?

Why, then, is the book titled *Excavating Jesus*? On the one hand, how do we justify "excavating *Jesus*"? We can certainly talk about excavating villages, towns, and cities, about digging up houses, tombs, and even boats. But who can dig up Jesus? How close could any dig ever get to his person? Is that ossuary with the James-Joseph-Jesus inscription the closest so far?

Oded Golan, a fifty-one-year-old electronics engineer from Tel Aviv, had been collecting Jewish antiquities since he was eight years old and now owns the largest private collection of such artifacts in Israel if not the world. Among three thousand or so items are thirty ossuaries including one rather ordinary one that Golan says he bought twenty-five years ago from an antiquities dealer for about $200. That, by the way, would have been in 1977, just one year before the Israeli government passed a law declaring all such artifacts state property. It came to the dealer, as Oded recalls, from Silwan, to the southeast of the Temple Mount, an area where modern homes rise above rocks pitted with ancient tombs. Even if all that hearsay is absolutely correct, the James ossuary comes to us without specific site, definite source, or certain history.

Imagine, once again, a different scenario. A homeowner digging to enlarge his Silwan basement breaks into a cave beneath it. He calls in the Israel Antiquities Authority and they discover the tomb of an extended family with parents named Mary and Joseph, adult sons named James, Joses, Judas, Simon, and married daughters named Mary and Salome. Those ordinary names on a bunch of isolated ossuaries without common provenance would not be insignificant but that precise combination *in situ* would indicate, beyond a reasonable doubt, the tomb of Jesus' family. No doubt the Israeli state would take possession of those artifacts, but the original finder, and not a later dealer or an eventual collector, should receive a very large finder's fee. That did not happen, we now have the unprovenanced bone box, and we intend both to discuss it as is and to emphasize what should have been. If it is the ossuary of James, brother of Christ the Lord, it represents the closest that archaeology has ever come to the person of Jesus. It is, in other words, as direct as we have ever been to "excavating *Jesus*" himself.

On the other hand, how can we speak of "excavating Jesus"? Granted that archaeology excavates and can excavate Jesus not just by finding a possible or even a definite fraternal ossuary but by filling out as completely as possible the social world in which he operated, why should the term "excavation" be used for texts as well as stones? Certainly texts such as the Dead Sea Scrolls of 1947 or the Nag Hammadi Codices of 1945 were found in the ground although by the random acts of shepherds and peasants rather than the exploratory probes of scientists. But when this book speaks of "excavating Jesus" not just in archeology but in exegesis, it does not intend those external textual excavations. There is something peculiarly distinctive to the gospels that justifies speaking of their internal excavation, that justifies using excavation for both archaeology and exegesis in this book, and that gives us the way, the manner, the method in which the work achieves its main purpose.

Unless a *site* had only a single layer built on bedrock and was soon abandoned and untouched thereafter by anything save time the destroyer, digging archaeologically demands careful attention to the multiple layers of habitation with later ones built upon earlier ones (the technical term for this is stratigraphy). Sometimes a *text* can be like that former case, a single layer of writing passed down untouched save for the errors of copyists, like most of Paul's letters in the New Testament. But our exegesis in this book focuses primarily on gospels and, whether those are inside or outside the New Testament, they are as multilayered as an archaeological mound. For example, when Matthew absorbs the gospel of Mark almost totally inside his own gospel, there are clearly earlier Markan and later Matthean layers in the Matthean text. If an ancient site is a series of superimposed overdwellings, an ancient gospel is a similar series of superimposed overwritings. In both cases, therefore, multiple layering is the absolutely fundamental challenge to be faced.

We could call our common work a parallel layering, an interaction between the layers of an archaeological mound and the layers of a gospel text. In both cases, for our present purpose, we must excavate down or back to the archaeological layer of Jesus' world and the textual stratum of Jesus' life. The problem of course is that, although everyone recognizes the inevitability of archaeological layering, the necessity of determining and dating the successive layers in a site, not everyone recognizes the similar inevitability and necessity, given this actual nature and relationship, to do exactly the same with the New Testament gospels.

Finally, in briefest summary, what do we get when we integrate archaeology and exegesis through a double and parallel layering? Why did Jesus happen when and where he happened?

In the generation before Jesus, Herod the Great ruled the Jewish homeland under Roman sponsorship and built magnificently in Jerusalem by expanding the Temple Mount and in Caesarea Maritima by developing a world-class port. Nothing tells so clearly that Romanization equaled urbanization equaled commercialization as the great storehouses and giant breakwaters of that all-weather harbor. In Judean Caesarea Maritima, in Samaritan Sebaste, and in far-northern Caesarea Philippi, Herod built pagan temples to the goddess Roma and divine Emperor Augustus, but he hardly touched Galilee at all compared to those other parts of his kingdom.

In the generation of Jesus, then, it fell to his son Herod Antipas to begin a more intensive Romanization, urbanization, and commercialization of Galilee, with the rebuilt Sepphoris as his first capital in 4 B.C.E. and with the newly built Tiberias as its replacement in 19 C.E. Under Antipas, then, and in proportionate imitation of his father, the Kingdom of Rome struck Lower Galilee forcibly for the first time by the 20s. But, though a veneer of Greco-Roman architecture covered the Jewish homeland and its Roman-urban commercialization redistributed wealth, archaeologists have discovered in both Judea and Galilee the persistence of the Jewish people to remain and live in ways distinct from those others with whom they dwelt in close proximity.

Next, as texts combine with stones, archaeological artifacts indicative of Jews clearly derive from a covenantal faith and a divine law that mandates justice and righteousness, purity and holiness, because the land belongs to a God who always acts from what is just to do what is right. In that law, or Torah, God says, "The land belongs to me." So how about those Herodian client-kings and their use of land? And what about the Roman Empire, which says, "The land belongs to us, we took it from you, and that's called war; or, if you prefer theology, our Jupiter took it from your Yahweh"? When, therefore, Jesus announced the Kingdom of God in the 20s in Lower Galilee, he and his companions taught, acted, and lived in opposition to Herod Antipas's localization of the Kingdom of Rome among his peasantry. We do not speak of the violent military resistance to Rome that would later leave the Temple in Jerusalem and the fortress atop

Masada in ruins to this day. That type of resistance was not present with either John or Jesus, or else Antipas would have beheaded more than John, and Pilate would have crucified more than Jesus. But even though non-violent, it certainly was resistance against the distributive injustice of Roman-Herodian commercialization—hence Jesus' emphasis on food and health—and it was enacted in the name of the covenant, the land, the Torah, and the God of Judaism.

The Top Ten Discoveries for Excavating Jesus

This book is about digging for Jesus, digging down archaeologically amidst the stones to reconstruct his world and digging down exegetically amidst the texts to reconstruct his life. It is, above all else, about integrating those twin excavations in order to locate his life in its world, to place his vision and his program in its time and place. Both types of digs involve inspection and identification, reconstruction and interpretation. Especially interpretation. We know that the stones cannot speak to us without our interpretation. But neither can the texts. Indeed, very often their interpretation is even more controversial. Neither stones nor texts speak to us directly. Both demand our respectful interpretation. What, then, by way of introduction, are the ten most important archaeological discoveries and the ten most important exegetical discoveries for this book's parallel process of "excavating Jesus"?

ARCHAEOLOGICAL DISCOVERIES

The top ten archaeological discoveries involve both specific objects and general places. The first four items listed are specific objects—with direct or indirect links to gospel texts—that also encapsulate major aspects of their contemporary worlds. The next five are pairs. That is not just to cheat and covertly expand the list to sixteen, although that is a welcome by-product. In each case the tandems point to a specific phenomenon more visible in those pairs than in either one alone: the commercialization of Lake Tiberias, the Roman-Herodian kingdom atop the Jewish homeland, the urbanization of Galilee, Jewish resistance to Rome, and Jewish village life. The last item is a set whose importance to first-century Jewish religion is internally and externally cumulative. The set's significance arises not from any single example or even from any single category alone but from the number of cases in each category and from those categories combined together.

1. The ossuary of James, the brother of Jesus
2. The ossuary of the high priest Joseph Caiaphas
3. The inscription of the prefect Pontius Pilate
4. The skeleton of the crucified Yehochanan
5. The Lake of Tiberias: Peter's House and Galilee Boat
6. Caesarea and Jerusalem: cities of Herod the Great
7. Sepphoris and Tiberias: cities of Herod Antipas
8. Masada and Qumran: monuments of Jewish resistance
9. Gamla and Jodefat: first-century Jewish villages in Galilee
10. Stone vessels and stepped pools: Jewish religion

1. *The James Ossuary.* Revealed in November 2002 and belonging to a private antiquities collector in Israel, this first-century ossuary, a box hewn of soft limestone in which bones of the deceased were reburied after the flesh decomposed, contains an Aramaic inscription of James, son of Joseph, brother of Jesus. Purchased sometime earlier from a no-longer-remembered antiquities dealer in Jerusalem, the ossuary was allegedly first found in the Arab village of Silwan, south of Jerusalem. If the inscription is authentic, then the ossuary not only once housed the bones of James the brother of Jesus and leader in the early Church, it also provides to date the earliest tangible evidence of Jesus.

2. *The Caiaphas Ossuary.* In November 1990, construction workers building a water park in the Peace Forest, south of Jerusalem's Old City between the Haas Tayelet and Abu Tor, broke through a burial cave sealed since the Roman war in 70 C.E. On an otherwise ornately decorated ossuary with an exquisitely executed pair of rosettes, the name *Caiaphas* was crudely scratched in Aramaic. His name, and family names interred with him, make it clear that the small shaft tomb was the family resting place for the high priest Caiaphas, mentioned by name in Matthew 26 and John 18 for his role in the crucifixion. This is a direct link to the gospel stories of Jesus' execution.

3. *The Pilate Inscription.* In 1962 Italian archaeologists, clearing sand and overgrowth from the ruined theater at Caesarea Maritima, longtime seat of Roman power on the Mediterranean coast, uncovered an inscription bearing the name of Pontius Pilate. Turned upside down and reused in the theater's renovation in the fourth century C.E., it was hidden and preserved up to the present. The Latin inscription boasts that Pilate had dedicated a *Tiberium,* a public structure built in honor of the Roman emperor Tiberius, just as the city itself had been built to honor his predecessor, Caesar Augustus. The inscription settled scholarly quibbles over Pilate's exact title and ruling authority by naming him a *prefect* rather than an inferior *procurator,* but was more celebrated as the first tangible witness to such a prominent New Testament figure. Indeed, it was commissioned by Pilate himself, providing another direct link to the gospels.

4. *The Crucified Man.* In June 1968 Vassilios Tzaferis of the Israel Antiquities Authority excavated some burial caves northeast of Jerusalem, at a place called Givat Hamivtar. Within the necropolis, a first-century C.E. rock-hewn family tomb with five ossuaries was discovered, one of which contained the bones of two men and a young child. The right heel bone of one of the men, 5 feet, 5 inches tall and in his mid-twenties, had been pierced by a $4^{1}/_{2}$-inch nail. A small wooden board had been nailed to the outside of his heel to prevent him from tearing his leg off the nail's small head. But the nail had bent as it was hammered into the hard olive-wood upright of the cross and could not easily be removed after his death, so it and the wooden board were still attached to his body when taken off the cross. His arms had been tied, not nailed, to the crossbar and his legs were not broken. Contrary to common practice, his body was allowed off the cross for proper family burial. The ossuary contained the name of the deceased, Yehochanan, *the Crucified Man.*

5. *The Lake of Tiberias.* First, from 1968 to 1985 the Franciscan archaeologists Fathers Corbo and Loffreda excavated a fifth-century C.E. octagonal church built on top of a fourth-century C.E. house church built on top of a simple first-century B.C.E courtyard house at Capernaum. Christian graffiti in Aramaic, Hebrew, Greek, Latin and Syriac had been scratched into the plaster of one room as early as the second century C.E. The room lacked any domestic artifacts and had been replastered several times, so the first Christian generations clearly deemed it of special significance. The excavators concluded that it was *the home of Peter,* "the house of the chief of the apostles," written about by ancient pilgrims. Second, with the

lake at its drought-caused lowest level in January 1986, a buried boat, water-logged to wet-cardboard consistency, was discovered by two members of the nearby Kibbutz Ginnosar. After an extremely difficult salvage operation and a highly successful preservation process by the Israel Antiquities Authority archaeologists, the 8-by-26-foot boat now stands in a climate-controlled facility at the kibbutz. Securely dated to around the time of Jesus from both pottery and carbon 14, seating twelve and an oarsman, it was a standard type commonly used for fishing or crossing the lake. It is now usually called the *"Jesus Boat."*

6. *Caesarea Maritima and Jerusalem.* Over twenty years of excavations at Caesarea Maritima and more than that around the Temple in Jerusalem have unearthed enough artifacts to fill museums and tax the storage capacities of the Israel Antiquities Authority. The most striking finds, however, are the enormous monumental structures built by Herod the Great (37–4 B.C.E.), the architectural legacy of his kingdom building. Caesarea Maritima, on the one hand, was transformed from a tranquil beach without a natural harbor or fresh-water source into the eastern Mediterranean's busiest and most modern port. Adorned with a magnificent temple housing statues of the emperor Augustus and the goddess Roma, the city itself was named in honor of Caesar. At Jerusalem, on the other hand, Herod beautified and expanded the Jewish Temple. He made the Temple Mount the largest monumental platform in the Roman Empire; and with massive finely cut and carefully squared stones, striking porticoes, and decorated columns, he made what ancient eyewitnesses describe as the most beautiful structure ever seen. These joint projects show both his loyalty to Rome and his dedication to the Jewish God, but above all else they were a tribute to himself and his kingdom.

7. *Sepphoris and Tiberias.* Like his father, Herod Antipas ruled as a client of Rome (4 B.C.E.–39 C.E.), not as a king, but as an inferior tetrarch, and not over all the Jewish homeland, but only over Galilee and Perea. Like his father, he built cities, but neither on the scale nor with the grandeur of his father. Herod Antipas was neither as rich nor as powerful as Herod the Great. But he urbanized Galilee with the building of Sepphoris and Tiberias, the latter named in honor of the Roman emperor. Although Tiberias today is a sprawling seaside resort that permits only limited excavation, the ancient ruins of Sepphoris lie uninhabited and have been excavated by as many as four teams over the past decades. Spectacular discoveries such as a Roman-style theater, a massive underground aqueduct,

and the Dionysiac mosaic, discoveries from throughout the Roman period, raise the question of the extent to which Antipas had earlier imposed a Greco-Roman architectural veneer onto the life of the Jewish population, and the impact of his kingdom building in Galilee. Sepphoris was, after all, only 4 miles from Jesus' hometown, Nazareth.

8. *Masada and Qumran.* Two sites off the remote and desolate western shore of the Dead Sea excavated in the 1950s and 1960s, respectively, bear witness to Jewish resistance against Rome in the first century C.E. Masada, a clifftop fortress-palace built by Herod the Great, was taken over by the Jewish Sicarii at the beginning of the revolt in 66 C.E. and fell to the Roman legions some four years after the Temple's destruction in 70 C.E. Archaeology's discovery of Roman siege works and the Jewish historian Josephus's story of the Sicarii's suicide vividly illustrate their violent resistance to Roman domination. A monastery complex built by a Jewish sect atop a marl terrace, Khirbet Qumran preserves the ruins of a different kind of resistance, communal and nonviolent, where withdrawal, study, and purity were weapons against foreign influences and moral decay. Both sites are monuments of Jewish resistance.

9. *Jodefat and Gamla.* Two villages, one atop a knoll in Lower Galilee, the other atop a ridge in the Golan Heights to the east, were destroyed by Roman legions in 67 C.E. and lay buried and undisturbed until Israeli archaeologists excavated them this past century. Aside from confirming their catastrophic ends as recorded by Josephus, Moti Aviam at Jodefat and Shmarya Gutmann at Gamla exposed frail defenses and unearthed daily life in these two Jewish towns. Neither site is mentioned in the gospels, so no commemorative church, monastery, or shrine was ever built on top of either of them. This, ironically, preserved until now an archaeological snapshot of Jewish life at the time of Jesus.

10. *Stone Vessels and Ritual Pools.* Stone vessels of varying shapes and sizes, carved or lathe-turned from soft white chalk stone, and stepped and plastered pools chiseled into bedrock, called *miqwaoth* (singular, *miqweh*) and referred to in this book as ritual baths, are both found wherever Jews lived in Galilee as well as around Jerusalem in Judea. These particular items signaled Jewishness to their contemporaries and identified them as a distinct people. Both stone vessels and ritual baths are connected to Jewish purity concerns. Neither of these artifacts is prominent in the gospels, although stone vessels are mentioned anecdotally in the story of the wedding at Cana (John 2:6). But their prevalence in the archaeological layers

of that era tells us much about what was taken for granted in the gospels concerning Jewish religion and Jewish distinctiveness at the time of Jesus.

Those ten discoveries, and all others yet to come, must be placed in their total archaeological environment. Remember, sometimes a find becomes a great discovery through the items found nearby, a tiny bronze coin beside it or several sherds of broken pottery beneath it. Such apparently valueless items, within their full comparative charting alongside all other ancient coins and ceramics, date the item in question and put it in a context that makes it not just one more discovery, but one of the top ten for the moment.

EXEGETICAL DISCOVERIES

To turn from the top ten archaeological to the top ten exegetical discoveries most significant for *Excavating Jesus* is to enter a very different world. Even if you disagree with every choice on that former list, you still have to agree that they all exist and that they can be seen today somewhere on the ground or in a museum. No matter how you might debate the meaning or interpretation of Herod's buildings, for example, you could not deny their existence. And even if you deny that a certain Capernaum structure was Peter's actual first-century house, you are arguing about or looking at a concrete place, a specific site, a ruined building. Not so at all with every item on this next list.

The first two items are clear enough. They represent a very large Jewish library and a comparatively much smaller Christian one, and they are both undeniably preserved in contemporary museums. It is also a sobering thought that, despite all the carefully planned, financed, managed, and executed digs for architectural or textual antiquities, it was not visiting scholars but Bedouin shepherds and Egyptian peasants who discovered those two hidden libraries. For many of the other items on the list, however, the very term "discovery" presents a challenge. Not only the interpretation, but also the very existence of some of the phenomena may be debated. Not everyone will accept or believe the discoveries to be true. Still, we stress these ten items because, whether one responds positively or negatively to certain ones, they will significantly determine how one excavates the textual remains for the historical Jesus.

Except for the Dead Sea Scrolls, all the following items concern texts from long after Jesus. But what one discovers and decides about them are crucial for any reconstruction of the historical Jesus himself. The final item on this list gets at a broader question of theological developments in early Christianity, namely the severe clash between James and Paul as interpreters of Jesus. While today most Christians tend to think of Paul as the normative interpreter of Jesus, in that first century even Paul himself conceded that Peter, Barnabas, and others stood not with him but with James. We must make certain, then, that we look back at Jesus not just through the eyes of Paul or even through the eyes of James but through that debate between James, along with those others, and Paul.

1. The Dead Sea Scrolls
2. The Nag Hammadi Codices
3. The dependence of Matthew and Luke on Mark
4. The dependence of Matthew and Luke on the Q *Gospel*
5. The dependence of John on Mark, Matthew, and Luke
6. The independence of the *Gospel of Thomas* from the canonical gospels
7. The common sayings tradition in the Q *Gospel* and the *Gospel of Thomas*
8. The independence of *The Teaching (Didache)* from the gospels
9. The existence of an independent source in the *Gospel of Peter*
10. The clash between James and Paul as reflected back on the historical Jesus

1. *The Dead Sea Scrolls*. These Jewish documents are the library of a sectarian group that deliberately separated itself from the priestly authorities of Jerusalem's Temple to live a communal existence in proper ritual purity and correct calendrical observance on the northwest shore of the Dead Sea. After the first discovery in 1947, the community's home was excavated at Khirbet Qumran and the library gathered from eleven caves in the cliffs behind it. Some texts were relatively complete, some were severely damaged, but hundreds were tattered into fragments numbering in the tens of thousands. The library's contents, ranging in date from around 200 B.C.E. to 70 C.E., show very fully the theory and practice of the Essenes, a sect known from several ancient writers, and they provide precious data on a specific lifestyle within the first-century Jewish homeland that is valuable as foreground for Judaism and background for Christianity.

2. *The Nag Hammadi Codices*. These Christian documents, forty-five texts in thirteen papyrus books or codices, were discovered in 1945 near

modern Nag Hammadi and ancient Chenoboskion, about 370 miles south
of Cairo. They are fourth-century transcriptions in Coptic (Egyptian written with an expanded Greek alphabet), but they contain works whose
Greek originals go back to the preceding centuries. The library's diverse
genres and theologies show an emphasis on Gnosticism (belief in salvation from human enslavement in the world of matter, as opposed to the
world of spirit, by secret knowledge, or *gnosis*) and maybe even more so on
asceticism, but they do not represent the precise ideology of any known
Christian sect. They may have been gathered together in agreement or
disagreement with their contents and thereafter buried in their sealed jar
for protection as precious to oblivion as heretical. They are extremely
important as an indication of pre-Christian Gnosticism and of the diversity within early Christianity itself.

3. *Mark, Matthew, and Luke.* Once it became obvious to scholarship that
Matthew, Mark, and Luke were so similar in sequence and content that
some sort of genetic connection had to be presumed (a first discovery), the
next step was to find the most credible trajectory for that relationship (a
second discovery). In 1789–90 Johann Jakob Griesbach suggested that
Matthew came first, Mark copied from Matthew, and Luke copied from
them both. But in 1835 Karl Lachmann proposed a different genesis: Mark
came first, and both Matthew and Luke copied from it independently of
each other. That latter alternative is today the dominant explanation, and
it is primarily the layering of Mark within Matthew and Luke that justifies
our use of "excavation" for exegesis as well as archaeology. But where else
will such textual excavation be required in gospel research?

4. *Q Gospel.* Based on those two interdependent discoveries, a third was
almost immediately added. With Mark before us, it was easy to see which
sections Matthew and Luke used. But there were too many other sections
in Matthew and Luke not in Mark, but present with sufficiently similar
sequence and content that another major source had to be postulated (a
third discovery). In 1838, Christian Hermann Weisse developed some earlier ideas of Friedrich Schleiermacher and suggested such a second source.
In 1863, Julius Holtzmann gave that source a first name. He called it "L" for
Logia, the Greek word for "sayings" (of Jesus). In 1890, finally, Johannes
Weiss gave it the name that stuck. He called it "another common source"
in Matthew and Luke (apart from Mark) and, because he was writing in
German, in which "source" is *Quelle*, the abbreviation *Q* became univer-
sally accepted.

5. *The Synoptics and John.* The consensus of scholarship about source conclusions declines steeply as one moves from Mark through the Q *Gospel* and into John. Is John dependent on or independent of the three synoptic gospels? One expert claims, maximally, that there is now "a growing consensus" for dependence, but another concludes, minimally, that in the early decades of this century the safer position was dependence, then, between 1955 and 1980, the safer position was independence, until now neither position can be safely "taken for granted." In other words, at least this: you cannot now invoke consensus on the debate, but must at least summarize the reasons for your own position. But, clearly, in terms of the excavation metaphor, it is crucially important to discover for oneself whether John is or is not dependent on the synoptic gospels. Think, for example, of the passion story: are all versions dependent on Mark alone or do we have two independent sources in Mark and John?

6. *The Gospel of Thomas.* Among the Nag Hammadi texts was a complete Coptic gospel whose Greek original had been discovered but not recognized in fragments of three different copies found around the turn of the century at modern Bahnasa (ancient Oxyrhynchus), about 120 miles south of Cairo. The *Gospel of Thomas* contains only aphorisms, parables, or short dialogues of Jesus and almost no narratives at all, especially no birth stories, miracle stories, or passion and resurrection stories. It has a distinctive theology denying any validity to a hope for the apocalyptic future, but demanding instead a return to the Edenic past through celibate asceticism. Once again, the textual-excavation question is whether it is dependent on or independent of the canonical gospels. There is probably a consensus for independence among *Thomas* experts in this country, but much less so in Europe or among New Testament gospel scholars.

7. *Common Sayings Tradition.* About one-third of the material in the Q *Gospel* and the *Gospel of Thomas* is common data. There is no evidence that either gospel is dependent on the other in terms of redactional sequence or content. Further, the order of that common tradition is so completely divergent that no common *written* source can be plausibly postulated for it. Finally, there is no particular reason why the generally orderless *Gospel of Thomas* would have changed any written source's order. Yet there are, by the most conservative estimate, thirty-seven units of tradition adopted and adapted by both gospels into their own quite different theological frameworks. This is one very significant case where a mass of "oral tradition" can be seen most clearly at work.

8. *The Teaching (Didache)*. We have many first-century letters like Paul's telling communities how they should behave, but this small text, called the *Didache*, that is, *The Teaching* or *The Instruction*, is a community rule or church order spelling out how one such early group actually lived and especially how new pagan converts had to change to join that Christian Jewish community. It was written in the second half of the first century, but early or late is disputed within that period. In 1873 it was discovered within an eleventh-century codex in a Greek monastery in Constantinople. The major issue is once again dependence or independence in relationship to the canonical gospels. This is crucially important because of a small collection of Jesus' most radical sayings that appears at the very start of the document. That minicatechism is also present in the *Q Gospel*, so stratification is once again very significant. Is either dependent on the other, or is there an earlier layer used by them both?

9. *The Gospel of Peter*. The *Gospel of Peter* is a second-century gospel known, like the *Gospel of Thomas*, from two separate discoveries. A large Greek fragment of about sixty verses, copied into a pocketbook codex between 600 and 900, was found in 1886–87 at Akmim, about 310 miles south of Cairo. Two tiny Greek fragments of under three verses, from a scroll dated to about 200, were found among those turn-of-the-century Oxyrhynchus papyri mentioned above. The present content narrates the trial, death, burial, resurrection, and apparition (presumably) of Jesus, starts and ends in mid-sentence, and is dependent on the canonical gospels. But the major question is whether it *also* contains another account that is both narratively consecutive and canonically independent. If so what is the content of that separate story?

10. *James against Paul*. What exactly was at issue and at stake in this debate? James and Paul agreed that circumcision was not to be required of male pagan converts because the final divine justification of the whole world had already begun but was an ongoing process rather than a momentary instant. They also agreed that Christian Judaism and Christian Paganism must remain a unified community. But what about kosher customs in common meals, what about purity concerns in common contacts? When Christian Jews and Christian pagans ate together should all observe Jewish kosher traditions? James said yes, Paul said no, and the key apostles agreed not with Paul but with James. Since Jesus did not decide such purity questions by the year 30, it was still being debated in the year 50.

PARALLEL LAYERING

We go back again to that term *parallel layering* for "excavating Jesus." The importance of layering for archaeological excavation is firmly established and universally accepted. As you travel the Mesopotamian plain, you can see numerous mounds, or tells, indicating superimposed layers of human habitation. They stand out noticeably against the otherwise flat monotony of the landscape. To dig away at or delve into them without a controlled examination of the layering is simply cultural looting. Unless an item you find is carefully and accurately identified within its proper historical layer, it is hardly more than an object. Recall, for example, the following two classic examples of incorrect layer analysis and, therefore, of mistaken historical conclusion.

The Treasure of Priam. At the start and end of the 1870s Heinrich Schliemann dug for ancient Troy at Hisarlik on the eastern bank of the southern approaches to the Turkish Dardanelles. He was a self-educated entrepreneurial magnate who left high school for business at fourteen and business for archaeology at forty-one. He found not one but nine cities layered on top of one another. Troy II, second from the bottom, showed signs of fiery sack, and inside a gate he discovered a cache of more than a hundred copper, silver, and gold objects. He made a sensational announcement about "the treasure of Priam" and took a famous photograph of his Greek wife, Sofia, wearing its gold ornaments. Thereafter the hoard disappeared from Greece to Germany by deceit in 1873 and from Germany to Russia by war in 1945. But none of that, or even its 1993 resurfacing in Moscow's Pushkin Museum and St. Petersburg's Hermitage Museum, could change one very simple fact.

Those nine cities ranged in date from about 3000 B.C.E. to 600 C.E. and Troy VII, dating from 1250 to 1000 B.C.E., is the most likely candidate for the Trojan War. Schliemann's identification was off by five levels and about thirteen hundred years. The city ruled by Priam and Hecuba, the city besieged by Agamemnon and Achilles, the city destroyed over a beautiful woman between two royal husbands (fiction?) or, better, over a strategic strait between two commercial seas (fact?) was, unfortunately, not Troy II, but Troy VII. How prosaic but necessary to admit that "Priam's gold" must submit to layering, to levels in dirt and debris, to precise location in place before any location in time is possible.

The Walls of Jericho. In 1907–9 a German archaeological expedition
led by Ernst Sellin and Carl Watzinger excavated at the desert oasis of
Jericho, hoping to find the city and walls that Joshua and the conquering
Israelites destroyed. Their excavations, however, came to a dissatisfying
conclusion: fallen walls were discovered, but these had been destroyed at
the end of the Middle Bronze Age (2000–1500 B.C.E.), at least two centuries too early to confirm the account in the book of Joshua. From 1929
to 1936 John Garstang set out to correct the problems he thought the
Germans had created and redug many of their trenches. Cutting through
other sections of the tell, he identified over twelve different layers dating
back to the Neolithic Age (8000–4500 B.C.E.). At the northern edge of
the mound he found what he was looking for in a level he called City IV:
a massive wall, destroyed, as he thought, in a cataclysm at the end of the
Late Bronze Age (1500–1200 B.C.E.), which was his date for the biblical
conquest. In the 1950s, the British archaeologist Kathleen Kenyon, armed
with a more careful layering method and a more accurate ceramic typol-
ogy, reexcavated the site. Garstang's walls had indeed been destroyed by
earthquake and fire, according to Kenyon, but these walls actually
belonged to fortifications from the Early Bronze Age (3200–2000 B.C.E.).
With meticulous layering precision, Kenyon showed how this Early
Bronze wall had been covered by a Middle Bronze defensive embankment,
which had badly eroded when the site was abandoned. A few Late Bronze
sherds had trickled down from above into gullies washed by rain and settled
near the Early Bronze wall, the very sherds with which Garstang dated
that wall to Jericho's destruction by the Israelites. Kenyon had the final
word: no fallen-down walls had yet been found at Jericho from the time of
Joshua. Like Priam's gold, Jericho's walls must submit to layering, to sherds
found in levels of dirt and debris, to precise location in place before any
location in time is possible.

The Layers of Gospel. All of that is clear enough and serves to emphasize the importance of correct layering for valid historical conclusions. Not
even the *Iliad* in hand can guarantee you have found Priam's treasure and
not even the Bible in hand can guarantee you have found Joshua's walls.
Layering rules in archaeological excavation. But what about layering in
exegetical excavations? Here all is much more controversial.

For some scholars exegetical layering is denied in theory and therefore
ignored in practice. For others it is affirmed in theory, but still negated by

practice. In gospel exegesis, as distinct from field archaeology, layering must be defended both theoretically and practically. It is also important, for scholarly integrity, not to take back in every specific possibility what one has affirmed as a general actuality. But that requires some explanation.

Imagine you had four witnesses in a court of law doing their best to describe accurately the accident they had seen a few weeks earlier. All are sincere, honest, impartial, and only involved as casual bystanders, accidental witnesses. There would be, of course, some discrepancies of vision and recall, but, as an attorney for defense or prosecution, you would feel most secure where all four were in closest agreement. First one: the black Explorer ran the red light right into the side of the Honda Civic. Second one: that big thing ran straight through the red light into that little car. Third one: the dark blue Expedition didn't even stop for the red light. Fourth one: those SUVs are always going too fast; this one didn't see the light, went right through it, and the other guy didn't have a chance. Consensus: the dark-colored SUV ran the red light and hit the other vehicle. No problem; all is well with the prosecution. Now imagine another scenario. One of those four informants was a reporter who got his knowledge from others directly or indirectly involved, he told the next two informants about it, and the fourth one got his data from that previous threesome. How does the prosecution's case look now? It has one not-exactly-an-eyewitness and three sincere echoes. Maybe the SUV did run the light, but maybe it did not.

Common sense notes the very large amount of agreement in sequence and content between Matthew, Mark, Luke, and even John, although the latter has always needed some qualification. Maybe John came last and, knowing what the others had said, focused on what they omitted and/or offered an even deeper interpretation than they did. But clearly, for common sense and most Christians, the work of historical Jesus study is one of organized harmony. How best do you bring together those four (or any other) witnesses into consensus? Those Evangelists were neither deceitful liars nor mistaken fools. They were, in fact, ready to die for what they believed. Gospel study, one could well conclude, is synthesis. Gospel layering, one concludes, is irrelevant.

Gospel layering has several components. Form criticism establishes the earliest formats used in transmitting the tradition (a parable, an aphorism, a dialogue, a law, etc.). Source criticism establishes who is copying from whom. Redaction criticism builds on such copying to establish the purpose for the copyist's omission, addition, or alteration. Tradition criticism uses all of the above to establish the successive layers of the tradition's development. But it is probably source criticism, above all else, that forces and grounds the problem of exegetical layering. For example, if Matthew and Luke creatively copy Mark, and if John very, very creatively copies those three earlier texts, what follows? Instead, for example, of concluding that Jesus' entry into Jerusalem the week before his death is told in all four gospels (independently), we must conclude that it is told in three superimposed layers all based on Mark (dependently). That immediately raises another question. What historical layer is Mark's account? Is it history from a layer dated to the late 20s or parable from a layer dated to the early 70s C.E.?

In this book we do not claim that everyone, even or especially the two of us who are writing it together, must agree on all such gospel layers. We do claim and we do agree that layering decisions are demanded both in archaeology and in exegesis, that disagreements about them do not negate but only emphasize their importance, and that they are correlatively crucial for excavating Jesus.

One final point on earth stratigraphy in archaeology and text stratigraphy in gospel as a prelude to the upcoming chapters. Two tendencies are at work in both those stratigraphies, whether in building stories atop Jesus' life or in building structures atop Jesus' place. One tendency is to decrease his Jewish identity; the other, to increase his social status.

On the one hand, the farther removed the layers are from the time of Jesus, the more *Christian* they tend to become. Unlike earlier gospel layers, later ones tend to distance him from Judaism and "the Jews" (so John) or use Jewish texts and interpretative devices to reinvent Judaism as Christianity (so Matthew). And later archaeological layers commemorating Jesus' life tend to efface signs of his Jewishness in the earlier ones and replace them with features from Rome or Byzantium. On the other hand, the farther removed Jesus is from his first-century Galilean context, the more elite and regal he becomes. Unlike earlier gospel layers, later ones portray him as a leisurely philosopher (so John) or a literate interpreter of scrolls and erudite partner at banquets (so Luke). And later shrines and churches in Galilee and Jerusalem efface his humble peasant beginnings in earlier archaeological layers and replace them with imperial and monumental architecture. In *Excavating Jesus*, we want to return to that earliest layer of both earth and text.

ONE

Jesus Carved in Stone

It was no way to ship an ancient artifact, authentic or not, original or not, identifiable or not, important or not. It was a 2,000-year-old ossuary, a limestone container for bones used in first-century Jewish tombs. A picture on the front page of Canada's national newspaper, *The Globe and Mail*, for Saturday, November 2, 2002, shows it being wheeled from an armored truck at the loading bay of Toronto's Royal Ontario Museum the preceding Thursday. Everything looks good at that point. You can see clearly the glassware-icon warning of the 2,000-year-old bone box's fragility and beside it twin arrows pointing "this side up." Even before that 20-by-12-by-10-inch bone box ever left Tel Aviv's Ben Gurion Airport there was a horizontal crack toward the bottom, starting on one of the larger sides and continuing all the way around the adjoining smaller one.

After overnighting in a vault for acclimatization, the package was opened early on Friday morning and immediately the scheduled press conference was postponed until 3 P.M. that afternoon. That short bottom-right crack on one of the ossuary's long sides now arched upward from a small shattered area at the start to a thin crack at the top. It also ran right through the bone box's inscription, which was, after all, the point of all the excitement over one more ossuary from the thousand or so already known from the Herodian period. The box's owner, later identified as Oded Golan of Tel Aviv, had arranged for packaging and shipping through Brinks (Israel), Ltd., as the artifact was then valued at $2 million. But, according to the Royal Ontario Museum's director of collections management, Daniel Rahimi, it was not packaged to normal museum-to-museum transportation standards. Those involve double crating with heavy packing materials in between each crate; transit damage in those cases is extremely rare.

Restoration would, of course, prove to be fully capable of stabilizing that broken area where the new and old cracks meet as well as better securing any others new or old. But, in a way, we think of that crack as a metaphor for the entire process of this ossuary's discovery. Cracked, as we said, from the start.

AUTHENTICITY AND INTEGRITY

The discovery was announced on October 21, 2002, at a press conference in Washington D.C. The media were invited and given the names and telephone numbers of a few selected scholars who had been given a one-week advance warning to expect their questions. At the conference, a packed room was briefed on the discovery of a bone box with the inscription "James, son of Joseph, brother of Jesus" from a recently disclosed private collection whose owner remained at that point anonymous. The box was dated to around 63 C.E. and was asserted to have once contained the bones of James the Just, the brother of Jesus of Nazareth, both sons of Joseph the carpenter. The press conference coincided with the release of the November/ December issue of *Biblical Archaeology Review*, whose cover announced a "World Exclusive!" feature about "Evidence of Jesus Written in Stone." The magazine told the story of how the noted epigrapher André Lemaire of the Sorbonne in Paris had visited an Israeli collector, examined the ossuary as a courtesy, and recognized its significance right away. It was, Lemaire himself argued in a well-written article, an authentic inscription; the ossuary was most likely the burial chest of James's bones, and its outside contained the earliest epigraphic record of Jesus of Nazareth. The next day newspaper headlines around the globe read "Oldest Evidence of Jesus?" or "Archaeological Evidence of Jesus?" The ossuary was shipped to Toronto's Royal Ontario Museum for an exhibit that coincided with the international meeting of religious scholars and archaeologists. The owner's anonymity was gone even before he, then known to be Oded Golan of Tel Aviv, discussed the ossuary's discovery and importance in a panel at the Royal Ontario Museum and in a seminar at the Society of Biblical Literature's annual meeting in November.

Authenticity

Many scholars greeted the new discovery with skepticism. That cynicism had nothing to do with academicians denying the Bible's historicity, but everything to do with too many "new" and "most important" archaeological discoveries turning out to be not so much inauthentic as irrelevant. From the list of new discoveries, sensational media claims, and ultimate scholarly dismissals, recall the fate of these other ossuaries before you decide on our recent most important discovery.

The (First) Jesus-Joseph Inscription. In 1931 the renowned Jewish archaeologist Eleazar Levi Sukenik delivered a lecture titled "The Jewish Tombs of Jerusalem around Jesus' Birth" to the German Archaeological Society in Berlin. In that lecture, Sukenik revealed an ossuary found in Jerusalem with the shocking inscription "Jesus, son of Joseph." The burial chest was cut from soft limestone with hammer and chisel, measured 23 inches long, 12 inches wide, and 14 inches high, and stood on low feet at each corner. An inner ledge at the top of two sides was designed to hold a now missing lid, and the ossuary was damaged in places. The front's long side resembled a triptych, with a narrow blank panel flanked by two larger square panels each containing a six-petalled rosette encircled with two concentric lines.

Inside the central panel, etched with a nail or metal tool in the Aramaic script that was the contemporary Jewish vernacular, were three graffiti-like letters, *yod*, *shin*, and *waw*, spelling out Yeshu, the common contracted form of Yeshua, or Jesus. Just above that left rosette and beneath the margins of its panel was a second, longer inscription, in the same Aramaic script and apparently by the same hand, this one reading Yeshua bar Yehoseph, or Jesus, son of Joseph.

The audience was not stunned for long. Of course Yehsua and Yehoseph were common Jewish names in the first century, Sukenik explained, and of course, as the mostly Christian audience believed, the Jesus son of Joseph of the gospels didn't leave behind bones for burial. The burial box and its inscription are now ignored in textbooks and classes on the archaeology of early Christianity. It is listed as Ossuary No. 9 among the 895 ossuaries in L. Y. Rahmani's *A Catalogue of Jewish Ossuaries in the Collections of the State of Israel,* published in 1994.

The Jesus-Invocation Ossuaries. In 1947, Sukenik published another article on Jewish ossuaries, this one titled "The Earliest Records of Christianity," which focused on two bone chests now listed as Ossuary No. 113 and Ossuary No. 114 in Rahmani's *Catalogue*. Other than those two items, that article was a mundane excavation report. It described an underground tomb in a suburban neighborhood of Jerusalem that was opened in 1945 for the first time since the Jewish war against Rome in 66–74 C.E. From a small central chamber with a low ceiling, there protruded several tunnels just large enough to fit a body (what scholars call *kokhim*, derived from Hebrew, or *loculi*, derived from Latin). Inside there was no gold, no silver, no ivory, no treasures or works of art suitable for display in a museum. Instead, the floor was scattered with the simple and ubiquitous pottery of the first century C.E., and with a single coin that dated to 42/43 C.E. Within the complex there were also fourteen ossuaries, ten decorated in the quite familiar manner and five inscribed with names—three very obviously of the deceased: Simeon Barsaba, Miriam daughter of Simeon, and Mattai— written in the common Aramaic script.

But some remarkable graffiti and inscriptions on those Rahmani-listed Ossuaries Nos. 113 and 114 inspired the article's title and drew interest from many Christians. According to Sukenik, the face of Ossuary No. 113 bore a charcoal graffito written in Greek that read "Jesus, woe" [!] and the lid of Ossuary No. 114 was incised with the Greek "Jesus, alas" [!] along with crosses marked in charcoal. These inscriptions, according to Sukenik and a group of eager Christian scholars, represented appeals to Jesus on behalf of the Christian dead, either a magical incantation or a triumphal proclamation, and their presence on ossuaries was interpreted as an expression of hope in the resurrection. Their alleged importance, of course, was that they predated 70 C.E. and were possibly from as early as 42/43 C.E.—only a decade after Jesus' death—making them the very earliest archaeological evidence for Christianity.

But. Later and more careful inspection of those ossuaries, along with consideration of the vast array of available ossuary inscriptions and their crosslike markings, dismissed those claims. The cross, it turns out, was perhaps simply the letter *tau* or a mason's mark indicating where the lid was to be positioned. The initial reading of the charcoal graffito ignored additional marks that resembled the Greek letter *delta*, and the scholarly consensus now reads the epitaph on No. 113 as Iesous Ioudou, or "Jesus, son of Judas." The "alas" on No. 114 is simply the elsewhere-attested nickname Aloth. These temporarily spectacular inscriptions simply identified the dead person, as did the names on the chamber's other ossuaries, which is always the purpose of ossuary inscriptions. No cross, no appeals to Jesus, no earliest Christian record.

The (Second) Jesus-Joseph Ossuary. When dynamite blew a hole in an ancient burial cave in 1980, salvage archaeologists from the Israel Antiquities Authority were immediately summoned to the Talpiot suburb, south of Jerusalem. Construction crews clearing the area for new apartments ceased operations, and Joseph Gath of the IAA examined a burial chamber already disturbed in antiquity. He recorded and catalogued the finds, including six ossuaries, which were then transferred to the stores of the IAA, where, identified by faded three-by-five index cards, they still sit on wooden shelves in a converted factory in the drab cement neighborhood of Romema. One or two of them have been loaned for display in the Israel Museum. Their ornamentation and decoration were absolutely common but their inscriptions were somewhat curious.

On one bone box, now listed in Rahmani as Ossuary No. 701, were the Greek words "of Mariamene, who is (also called) Mara." Mariamene is simply another form of Mariam or Mariame, our Mary. On another box, now listed in Rahmani as Ossuary No. 704, Yeshua bar Yehosef, or Jesus son of Joseph, was written in clumsily and thinly scratched letters. On another, now listed in Rahmani as Ossuary No. 705, Yoseh, a contracted form of Yehosef, or Joseph, was written in a more formal Aramaic script. The similarity of scripts and placements of the ossuaries suggests that Mary and Joseph were parents of Jesus.

Was this the family tomb of Jesus? The IAA certainly did not think it was as it wrapped up its examination and let the construction crews pour cement into the tomb for the apartment complex's foundation. A coverup? That was the gist of an article in *The Sunday Times* of London on Easter Sunday, March 31, 1996, sensationally titled "The Tomb That Dare Not Speak Its Mind." The list of names is impressive, and Joe Zias, then curator and forensic archaeologist for the IAA, was quoted in the article as saying "had it not been found in a tomb I would have said 100% of what we were looking at were simply forgeries." But, he stressed, "this came from a very good, undisturbed, archaeological context. It was found by archaeologists, read by them, interpreted by them . . . a very, very good text. It's not something that was invented."

But was it *the* Jesus, the Jesus we are excavating in this book? As *The Sunday Times* pondered the issue, it concluded by noting that no one in the archaeological community thought so, since, after Simeon, the most common male name on ossuaries is Joseph (19 of 147 names, male and

female, on known ossuaries) with Jesus almost as common (10 of 147).
And the most frequent female name after Salome is the variously spelled
Mary (20). Conservative readers that Easter morning were probably
relieved at the article's conclusion.

Scholarly consensus has relegated all those preceding discoveries to statistical patterns and sent them back to dead storage. The inscriptions are
now quietly reburied in the four hundred pages of Rahmani's *Catalogue* on
the reference shelves of research libraries. The ossuaries rest in the stores
of the Israel Antiquities Authority in Romema and are occasionally
rotated into the Israel Museum's exhibits. So when, to resume this section's beginning, scholars express hesitation or seem to dampen popular
enthusiasm over the new James-Joseph-Jesus ossuary, it has to do with history. But what are the arguments for or against the ossuary and its inscription's authenticity? Could it be a fake? Consider the following arguments.

Point-Counterpoint

The Box. There is no doubt that the ossuary box itself is authentic. It
conforms in size, craftsmanship, and style to those found around Jerusalem
from the first century c.e. The ossuary was hewn from a single block of soft
limestone—what geologists call chalk—into a chest roughly 20 inches
long, 12 inches high, and 10 inches wide, just large enough to contain the
largest human bone, the femur. It was covered with a flat lid that fits onto
thin ledges running along the long sides. It is about the size of most bone
chests that Jews of the first century used for secondary burial, or what
scholars call ossilegium, the practice of collecting the deceased's bones
into a box after the flesh has decayed.

The piece is not a work of art or even of expert craftsmanship. At first
glance it appears undecorated, except for a simple incised groove cut along
the margins of each side and the lower edge of the lid. Upon closer inspection, there appears to be at least one very faded rosette design on the back
(as one looks at it now). The external walls are rough, with chisel marks
still visible, as it was never given a polished finish. The box is slightly
larger at the top and tapers toward the base, but the corner edge of one side
is a bit shorter than the others, creating an awkwardly imbalanced trapezoidal look when viewed from two sides. With respect to its appearance, it
is like most of the thousand or so ossuaries discovered by archaeologists in
and around Jerusalem and dating to the first century c.e.: simple, aniconic,

or without image of human or beast, but with occasional geometric, architectural, or floral decorations.

The box also looks ancient, with biovermiculation stretching across wide sections and a patina covering most areas. *Biovermiculation*, a deterioration common to limestone over time, is a form of bacterial erosion that looks like tiny pits and gives the affected area an almost coral-like appearance. *Patina* is that microscopically thin weathering that forms on stone surfaces over time. In the case of this ossuary's limestone, it is a grayish-beige crystalline sheen that has an almost cauliflower-like appearance under a microscope. We are convinced, beyond any reasonable doubt, that the box and lid are authentic artifacts that come to us from two millennia ago.

The Inscription. Doubts creep in when the inscription is examined, and especially the final part of the inscription. The letters of the eight-inch long inscription were neatly cut on the right-hand side of one of the ossuary's long faces, at about the midline. The Aramaic script is mostly well executed without any spaces between words, and its first reading by André Lemaire stands without any serious challenge: Ya'acov bar Yosef akhui diYeshua, or James (Jacob) son of Joseph brother of Jesus. There were, as one would expect in antiquity's semiliterate society, considerable variations in orthography, or spelling of names. On ossuaries and in papyri from the first century and as mentioned above, sometimes Yosef (Joseph) is spelled Yehosef and sometimes Yeshua (Jesus) is contracted to Yeshu or expanded to Yehoshua. None of these differences in any way detracts from the certain reading: James son of Joseph brother of Jesus.

The problem arises when the first half of the inscription, James son of Joseph, is compared with the second half, brother of Jesus. The inscription begins with the formal script common to the first century and experts like Lemaire would date it to that century's second half. The kerning at the top of the ossuary's formal letters is typical of ones on the Dead Sea Scrolls, written in the final decades before the Roman war that led to the Temple's destruction in 70 C.E. However, some of the subsequent characters in the inscription are cursive forms of Aramaic letters, most apparent in the letter *dalet*—through which the crack now runs. And the inscription tends to slope downward a bit after "brother," with most letters at a slightly different angle and others not as deeply cut as earlier ones, most notably the *shin* of Yeshua.

If ancient inscriptions were done with typewriters, we would be certain in this case that two different machines were involved. But keep in mind that these letters were incised by hand. And most ossuary inscriptions were not executed by professionals, but etched by family or friends to identify the location of the deceased's bones, perhaps so surviving spouses or children could later be interred with them. The presence of formal and cursive scripts is not in itself sufficient to establish two hands, much less to seal the verdict of forgery, and such variations are found on a few ossuaries discovered by archaeologists. On the front of an ossuary from Jerusalem's Mount Scopus, decorated with a five-branched acanthus plant flanked by clusters of grapes, a four word Aramaic inscription has been transcribed as Yehosef bar Hananiah HaSepher, or Joseph the son of Hannania the scribe. The first word, Yehosef, is deeply engraved with distinct clarity of each letter. The second word's incisions are shallower but its letters are still clear; the third word is quite faint, and the fourth is virtually illegible with HaSepher (the scribe) no more than one scholar's guess. Do wrists simply tire the more letters they chisel on ossuaries? Possibly. Do the angles of letters simply shift because writers have to extend their hands farther over the ossuary? Maybe. But it is unsettling in our case that the cursives appear exactly at "brother of Jesus." And that is also exactly where the letters begin to slope at a slightly different angle and where many are less forcefully cut.

André Lemaire, one of the world's great epigraphers, has examined thousands of Semitic inscriptions, and he does not think the inscription is a fake. Alongside careful analysis, he also offers his instinctively immediate reaction: "When I see an inscription, either I feel at home or I don't feel at home. With this inscription, I felt at home." But Johns Hopkins University's epigrapher Kyle McCarter remarks, "We may never be absolutely certain. In the work I do, we're rarely absolutely certain about anything." A reasonable doubt?

The Patina. If ancient inscriptions are subject to human vagaries, and epigraphic judgments are subject to scholarly subjectivity, can "pure science" verify the ossuary's authenticity? Hershel Shanks, the editor of *Biblical Archaeology Review*, who broke the story, commissioned an analysis from the Geological Survey of Israel's Ministry of National Infrastructures (and not, by the way, from the experts on antiquities and forgeries at Israel's Antiquities Authority). The geologists examined six samples from the

יעקובבריוסף אחוידישוע

Ya'aqov bar Yosef akhui diYeshua
Jacob, son of Joseph, brother of Jesus (private collection, provenance unknown)

שמיברעסיא אחוידחנין

Shimi bar 'Asiya akhui diChanin
Shimi, son of Asiya, bother of Hanin (Rahmani 570, Mt. Scopus, Jerusalem)

וחוס פברחנניהסופר

Yehosef bar Chananya haSepher
Joseph, son of Hananya, the scribe (Rahmani 893, Mt. Scopus, Jerusalem)

ישועביהוסף

Yeshua bar Yehosef
Jesus, son of Joseph (Rahmani 9, provenance unknown)

ישועבריהוסף

Yeshua bar Yehosef
Jesus, son of Joseph (Rahmani 704, East Talpiot, Jerusalem)

יהודהברישוע

Yehudah bar Yeshua
Jude, son of Jesus (Rahmani 702, East Talpiot, Jerusalem)

box's chalk, six samples of the patina, or veneer, of weathering on the box's surface, and two samples from the soil with an SEM (Scanning Electron Microscope) equipped with EDS (Electron Dispersive Spectrometer). The geologists concluded that the chemical makeup of the patina was consistent with that of the ossuary. Sounds all very sophisticated.

But. Patina can be faked and has been faked. Patina is the result of a chemical process in which a thin crust is formed on an object's surface as its chemical components leech out over time and react with chemicals from its surrounding context. Forgers fake a patina in two ways. One rather crude method is by pasting a new patina on an older artifact. Another more sophisticated way is by accelerating the process that usually takes centuries with variously concocted chemical baths and reburials in wet iron-salted soils. With the former technique, the patina has a different chemical makeup and can be detected with SEM and EDS. With the latter technique, box and patina have the same chemical makeup, which is exactly what the geologists certify. In other words, their somewhat naïve method would be able to detect only foreign pigments or residue from a secondary source.

Even more puzzling in the Geological Survey's one-page report is their observation that, on the one hand, "no signs of the use of a modern tool or instrument was found" on the inscription but, on the other hand, that (parts?) of it had been cleaned. Left unanswered is by whom? When? How? Some letters had no patina, while others did, but we are not told which letters, nor are we told whether patina samples from within the letters and from within which letters were examined. Equally puzzling is the fact that the backside's rosette is faded almost beyond detection but the inscription is mostly rather deeply cut and clearly visible. The report raises more questions than it answers, but most disturbing is that the owner and the magazine presented the geologists' report as conclusive but circumvented one of the crucial steps of any scientific judgment, peer review. No other chemical or geological experts examined the ossuary, especially none familiar with forgers' techniques, and their method has not been critiqued by the appropriate specialists.

Remember this. In 1983 the J. Paul Getty Museum in Southern California purchased a *kouros*, one of those rare archaic statues of nude youths, with accompanying papers certifying it came from a private Swiss collection. But the papers turned out to be faked (a letter dated to 1952 had a postal code that didn't originate until 1972) and the statue was subjected to intense scrutiny by various scholars. Misgivings increased when another, similarly styled and certainly faked torso of a *kouros* was revealed, allegedly made in the same forger's workshop. The Getty Museum spent millions on the original statue, and again millions to acquire the fake torso and to have leading specialists stylistically and chemically analyze the *kouros*. After years of chemical analysis and debate, a colloquium was convened in 1992 at the Museum of Cycladic Art in Athens, with the world's leading art historians and archeometrists present. The published proceedings of the colloquium conclude with a somber caveat: "Stone remains the least tractable medium for technical proof of authentication." The *kouros* is still on display today, but the descriptive panel at its feet presents the stark alternatives, "Greek, 530 B.C. or modern forgery." The results of the million-dollar enterprise show that the only thing harder than proving an unprovenanced artifact's authenticity is proving its inauthenticity.

The Geological Survey's letter is almost meaningless. It simply tells us that the inscription is not a clumsy forgery. It also confirms what all archaeologists would affirm, that the box itself is from ancient Jerusalem. But it neither authenticates the inscription nor implicates it as fake. More rigorous and informed analysis is required before any conclusion deemed final can be reached. Until then, who bears the burden of proof, those who say it is real or those who say it is a fake?

The Family.   For the sake of argument, we grant the authenticity of the *entire* inscription along with the antiquity of its patina and ask the question, Is this *the* James, son of *our* Joseph, brother of *that* Jesus we are trying to excavate? The combination of names alone but especially the configuration of family relations is certainly compelling. What is the probability that this is the box that held the bones of James the Just and what is the probability that this is the earliest inscribed record of Jesus?

Here we enter the world of statistics, that place where subjective judgments are accorded rather precise figures. Here are the basic data. A study, now nearly two decades old, calculated that among all inscribed names from the Early Roman Period in Palestine, 14 percent were Joseph, 9 percent were Jesus, and 2 percent were James (Jacob). Taking these percentages, Lemaire worked with two reasonable assumptions: first-century Jerusalem had a population of 80,000 and most men had two brothers. Taking into account deaths and births over time, Lemaire calculated that there were 20 Jameses, sons of a man named Joseph, brothers of a man named Jesus, who lived during the two generations before 70 C.E.

But. A one-in-twenty chance that this is the right James is a long shot. What makes the case more likely is that, while the patronymic "son of" is standard on ossuaries, the inclusion of a fraternal relationship "brother of" is exceptionally rare. Lemaire suggests that this "probably means that the brother had a particular role, either in taking responsibility for the burial, or more generally, . . . because the brother was known." And, in this case, if it is our Jesus, also more famous and more revered. But maybe, since the purpose of ossuary inscriptions was to identify the dead, the brother's name might have been included for no other reason than to distinguish between same-named members of an extended family, to distinguish, say, grandfather James from grandson James or cousin James from other cousin James, a possibility that the knowledge of the ossuary's *original* context and accompanying ossuaries' inscriptions might have settled. Deciding whether the ossuary belonged to James the Just is as much a matter of statistics and probability as intuition and inclination.

In some ways the James-Joseph-Jesus ossuary is a litmus test for scholarly temperament and personal convictions. The old adage among field archaeologists is that you find what you want to find. Skeptics are likely to reject this inscription's authenticity or identification with James, publishers who stand much to earn are likely to accept its authenticity, and people of the Christian faith all over the world really want it to be true. Where do we stand on the issue? Why did we pick it to be our number one discovery in the top-ten list for *Excavating Jesus*? We put it first not because we affirm its authenticity, but because it underscores the integrity of archaeology. We put it number one because it is an object lesson for archaeology as a rigorous historical discipline.

Integrity

For scientific archaeology to distinguish itself from cultural looting, the magic words are the Latin *in situ*, "in place." That term applies to any artifact discovered where it had remained for centuries or even millennia before our modernity disturbed its antiquity. A find *in situ*, in a place or setting not previously disturbed and in a layer or stratum not previously touched, is an archaeological ideal not only because it ensures the artifact's authenticity, but more important because it locates the artifact within specific context, within an identifiable place in time and space, within a web of chronological and spatial relationships to other artifacts.

Ossuaries. Compare the three first-century ossuaries from our top-ten list that were discovered in Israel within the last fifty years. First, in June 1968, northeast of Jerusalem, a burial cave–complex was broken into during construction work, archaeologists were immediately notified, and everything was found as it had been for two thousand years. One ossuary contained the bones of an adult male, his child, and, probably, by accident, a bone from another male. The adult's name, scratched on the outside, was Yehochanan and his was the first crucified skeleton ever discovered in the Jewish homeland. One nail was still impaled in his right heel bone and that, indeed, gives a terrible emphasis to *in situ*. Because these finds were uncovered in a controlled excavation, much has been learned. The heel with nail was inside the ossuary, so that at least in one case, a victim of Roman crucifixion was permitted a proper family burial. And since a forensic anthropologist could analyze the victim's complete skeletal remains from the ossuary, we know that his hand and wrist bones had suffered no trauma, so that unlike in popular medieval crucifixions, his arms or hands had been tied and not nailed to the crossbeam. Furthermore, his legs had not been broken to speed his death. More important, because its excavator had photographs, field books, and catalogues, the published report was subject to cross-examination and scholarly debate.

Next, in November 1990, a similar incident happened to the south of Jerusalem. Construction workers again broke into a burial chamber, archaeologists were again notified, but they found that the tomb had been looted by grave robbers in antiquity and also disturbed by the discoverers before they arrived. Inside the burial chamber was a beautifully decorated ossuary containing the bones of four young children, one male youth, an adult female, and a 60-year-old male. Scratched on the ossuary was the name of that adult male, Yehosef bar Caiapha, known in the New Testament by that unusual name Caiaphas and in Josephus as Joseph Caiaphas. It was his ossuary, his and his family's bones, and all were still basically *in situ*. Because the bones of those inside this single ossuary and the surrounding ossuaries could be analyzed, considerable data has been added to our knowledge of infant mortality rates, life spans, and common diseases in that first century. And because glass, lamps, and pottery were still in the chamber, the chronological span of the burial can be determined, and some coins not only date the burial but provided some surprises, to be discussed in Chapter 7. And more important perhaps to many, the bones of the deceased were given a proper and dignified re-reburial by Jewish authorities.

Finally, in October 2002, not a discovery but a press conference announced another important ossuary. In terms of the interaction of archaeology and exegesis for *Excavating Jesus*, it may well be the most significant of the three bone boxes, but nothing about its discovery was exactly ideal. It had apparently been looted earlier from a tomb south of Jerusalem and sold to a private antiquities collector who did not notice the implications of its Aramaic inscription: James, son of Joseph, brother of Jesus. The dealer and the date of purchase are uncertain (but the owner is emphatic that it was pre-1978). A few scraps of tiny bone fragments still inside the ossuary when the owner purchased it are now sealed in Tupperware inside his freezer.

To repeat ourselves, and to do so emphatically, that ossuary's mode of arrival on the scene was far from the archaeological ideal. Neither were those of the Dead Sea Scrolls and the Nag Hammadi Codices, the mid-twentieth century's great manuscript discoveries. They were found by chance and sold by middlemen rather than discovered or at least investigated *in situ* by archaeologists. Like those manuscripts, the ossuary is now here and its presence demands discussion. For that very reason, in one sense, it is the perfect focal point for this book. It is one single artifact that brings together archaeology and exegesis. It is also one single artifact that emphasizes how such objects are of value only when embedded among all those other discoveries that give it full context and final meaning.

Laws. For all these reasons, most Mediterranean and Middle Eastern countries have strict laws against buying and selling ancient artifacts and especially against their export. Now fortunately gone is the normalcy of colonial looting, which condoned disassembling the Miletus gate in Turkey and reassembling it in Berlin or the removal of the Elgin Marbles from the Athens Acropolis and the Rosetta Stone from the Nile Delta to their present display in London's British Museum. The UNESCO Convention sought to prohibit and prevent the illicit import, export, and sale of ancient artifacts that are part of a people's cultural heritage, and it was ratified by the United States in 1982. Across the world, professional archaeologists and members of scholarly societies denounce the direct or indirect participation in buying or selling illegally excavated or imported artifacts. The policy of the American Schools of Oriental Research, the scholarly society of Syro-Palestinian and biblical archaeologists, states the key reason succinctly: "Trade in antiquities, especially illicit trade, encourages the looting of archaeological sites and thus is a direct cause of the destruction of sites and the loss of the information they contain."

But Israel, perhaps because of the popularity of collecting among former statesmen such as Moshe Dayan or Jerusalem's Mayor Teddy Kollek, tries to keep the black market above ground by licensing a limited number of strictly controlled antiquities dealers. Since 1978, these eighty-some authorized sellers can legally obtain artifacts, but only by purchasing them from old collections or by importing them from abroad. They are forbidden from acquiring clandestinely and illegally excavated artifacts. Nevertheless, according to the director of the theft prevention unit, Avni Ganor, "90 percent of what they offer for sale comes from freshly pillaged graves." If the Israel Antiquities Authority knows or suspects that an artifact was looted, it can confiscate it, especially anything it deems of national or historical value.

Ethics. Collectors of antiquities are supplied by dealers. Buyers attract sellers, demand creates supply. That coin, lamp, or pot purchased in Jerusalem's Old City by tourists (all allegedly discovered before 1978 and legally obtained), and those statues, mosaics, or ossuaries (likewise allegedly discovered before 1978) acquired at exorbitant prices in Los Angeles or London auction houses, generate an industry. The reality, of course, is that not all of the artifacts were discovered prior to the almost universally enacted laws against looting. As everyone knows, the lure of easy money leads many people to poke around beneath their houses, dig about their backyard fields, or worse, track the movements of archaeologists and then at night or after the excavation season pillage through the site with metal detectors and picks, a danger with which most field archaeologists are familiar and anticipate by hiring guards or by concealing finds.

Archaeologists. Here are some examples of what archaeologists must do to protect their sites, and the cat-and-mouse games the IAA plays with gangs of grave robbers, dealers, and their go-betweens. First is the archaeologist. In 1987, a stunningly beautiful portrait of a woman was found on a mosaic floor in Galilee's Sepphoris. Since a mosaic medallion had been cut out and lifted from a nearby national park earlier, the excavators covered this new mosaic with sheets and two feet of sand to conceal or at least make theft cumbersome. The next season, student volunteers spent nearly a week reexcavating the mosaic. In 2000, a whole jar was found embedded among the Iron Age layers at Ein Zippori in northern Israel. A student volunteer and a staff member guarded it the entire day and slept nearby at night in its cattle-field site. The director was not so concerned to protect the pot for its value, but to preserve it *in situ*, to keep it in its proper layer and examine its contents in that original context. The next day, meticulous excavation clarified whether the jar was on, in, or under which beaten earth layer, and whether the jar was used to store water or grain, or for infant burial. That jar is a reminder that the context of an artifact tells the archaeologist much more about the ancient world than the artifact alone ever can.

Inspectors. In May 1998 the Israel Antiquities Authority's Unit for the Prevention of the Theft of Antiquities boarded a ship in the port of Ashdod to foil smugglers from shipping a nearly 500-pound stone from Bethlehem's Church of the Nativity. The stone was crated and labeled with the address of a prominent antiquities gallery in Strasbourg, France. In December 1999, a villager from the Hebron area was caught trying to sell a massive collection of looted artifacts to an authorized dealer in Jaffa. Agents confiscated over seven hundred items pillaged from tombs around Jerusalem, including spearheads, golden jewels, and marble statues, as well as rare silver coins minted during the first Jewish revolt against Rome when the Temple in Jerusalem was destroyed, coins that have netted nearly a quarter-million dollars in upscale auction houses. The thief faced a maximum of two years in prison, the dealer was not charged, and potential collectors were merely disappointed.

Collecting items like the James-Joseph-Jesus ossuary is not benign. It's not a hobby like collecting stamps or pressing leaves. This we guarantee. Now that the ossuary has been insured for two million dollars, gangs of semiprofessional tomb raiders have doubled their efforts and at this very moment are at work scavenging through Jerusalem's neighborhoods and the Judean countryside, and fakers in workshops are etching Peter, John, Stephen, Jude, or whatever Christian saint or martyr they can think of, onto stone boxes old or new.

Science. Our reservations about collecting antiquities are not just legal or moral but also intellectual. Collecting rests on the desire to personally own something of artistic or historical value from antiquity. Likewise our reservations about media coverage of archaeology have to do with their emphasis on aesthetically pleasing finds or on discoveries they think will answer complex questions with a yes or a no. Does this excavation prove the Bible false? Does that artifact prove the Bible true? Does the James-Joseph-Jesus ossuary back up the biblical account? These are conceptually immature and sensationally announced views that belong to the early part of the last century and have no place in serious archaeological dialogue.

Think, for a moment, about all the information relating to ossuaries that scholars were instantly able to offer after the discovery of the James ossuary was made public:

- they are typically Jewish
- they were put in shaft tombs
- they were used primarily in and around Jerusalem
- they emerge around 20 B.C.E.
- their origin coincides with stonemasons' work on Herod's Temple Mount
- they replaced the practice of depositing bones in pits
- they were not used exclusively for individual burials but often contained skeletons of several people
- they went out of use almost entirely after 70 C.E.
- their use continued modestly in Galilee into the second century

None of this information is mentioned in any ancient literary text; we know it only from the meticulous, cooperative, and careful work of archaeologists over the past century. We know all these things because many sites have been carefully excavated. After burials are discovered, professional archaeologists first photographed the ossuaries *in situ*, then carefully removed, registered, and relayed them to storage where they await analysis and cross-examination by other specialists. Surrounding artifacts such as pots, lamps, and ointment vials are assigned registration numbers and charted on site plans, and then the burial cave's debris is removed layer by layer and is sifted for coins, potsherds, bone fragments, and other tiny artifacts that are meticulously catalogued in field books by place numbers. Finally, forensic anthropologists examine the bones for demographic information before passing them on for reburial.

Once this data has been published, any qualified scholar can compile the data and analyze patterns with their various chronological and geographical variations and developments. Then, in dialogue or often heated debate, a scholarly consensus is slowly developed, perhaps to be modified as new discoveries are published. And this consensus can be discussed with scholars working in Greece and Rome, Turkey and Egypt.

The intellectual problem we have with the James box and its "discovery" is that the archaeological process has been circumvented while its presentation to the public has reduced it to an arbiter of faith over unbelief. The tragedy is not that the box is now cracked but the that its discovery was cracked from the very beginning.

THE BROTHER OF JESUS

If we had only the writings of the first-century Jewish historian Josephus we would know about John the Baptist, Jesus the Christ, and James the Brother, but we would not know that, for example, Peter or Paul ever existed. And, if we calculated comparative importance by amount of space, the ranking would be, first, James with 27 lines of Greek in the *Jewish Antiquities* 20.199–203, then John with 24 lines in 18.116–19, and finally Jesus with 13 lines in 18.63–64. James, in other words, gets twice the space of his brother Jesus (even including Christian additions about the latter). If, therefore, you ever imagined finding a tomb or an ossuary from one of that Josephan triad, James would have been your best guess. Now that an ossuary has been found that may once have contained the bones of James the brother, what do we know about that individual? And more important, how do we evaluate the various and competing early Christian texts about that James? The archaeologist distinguishes the layers in the ground and looks for clues in the pattern of artifacts. Similarly, the exegete must distinguish the various layers in the text and look for clues on the purpose of traditions.

Identity

Whether as Semitic Ya'akov, Greek Jacobus, or Latin Jacomus—those names we anglicize as Jacob or James—two must be carefully distinguished from the several in the New Testament. They are:

James,   son of Zebedee,   brother of John
James,   son of Joseph,   brother of Jesus

Around the end of the first century C.E., the writer of the Gospel of Luke records in his second volume, Acts of the Apostles, that the Roman-appointed ruler of Palestine, Herod Agrippa I, executed "James, the brother of John" (Acts 12:2). Both James and John had been identified as "sons of Zebedee" in his Gospel (Luke 5:10). Agrippa also imprisoned Peter at that same time in 41 C.E., and, when he escaped, Peter said, in Acts 12:17, to "tell this to James," clearly not the just-executed James but another with the same name. Luke never identifies this second James any further but his authority is indicated as recipient of that message and we conclude that he is the same James who later acts most authoritatively in Acts 15:13 and 21:18. Furthermore, the earliest gospel, Mark, identified a James in first place among the four brothers of Jesus (Mark 6:3), and Matthew 13:55 followed Mark in that listing, but Luke omitted it entirely. In summary, then, you would know from Luke that there was a second and very important James but you would never know from either of Luke's volumes that James was in fact the brother of Jesus.

On the other hand, none of Paul's letters in the New Testament dating to the 40s and 50s ever mentions James, son of Zebedee, brother of John. But in 1 Corinthians 15:5–7 Paul distinguishes risen apparitions "to Cephas [Semitic for Peter]," then to "the twelve," then "to James, then to all the apostles." Note, by the way, that the Twelve are a narrower group within the wider circle of apostles—Paul does not equate and delimit them as the Twelve Apostles. In Galatians 1:19 Paul describes his first visit to Cephas in Jerusalem and says that he "did not see any other apostle except James the Lord's brother." Thereafter, in Galatians 2:9, he cites "James and Cephas and John" as acknowledged pillars of the Jerusalem community and, finally, in Galatians 2:12 he mentions "certain people who came from James" to Antioch. We conclude that Paul is always speaking there of the James he had initially identified as the brother of Jesus.

We conclude that the authoritative James of Luke's later Acts of the Apostles is that same authoritative James of Paul's earlier epistles, namely, James the brother of Jesus. Those texts establish, in fact, both identity and authority, with the following section confirming that latter point.

Authority

1 Corinthians 15. At the start of this chapter Paul gives all the traditional apparitions of the risen Lord in one continuous list. But 1 Corinthians 15:5–7 mentions, as just noted, that he "he appeared to Cephas, then to the twelve," and, "he appeared to James, then to all the apostles."

But, prior to Paul's comprehensive and consecutive listing, did those twin sentences recall competing traditions or, better, competing versions of the same tradition? First to receive a risen apparition meant first in authority. In other words, for some communities, Peter was "first," for others, James was.

Gospel of Thomas. The original of this gospel dates from the second half of the first century, is independent of our four New Testament gospels, and was discovered among the Nag Hammadi Codices, found in Egypt in 1945. As that title indicates, it is presented under the authority of the apostle known since John 20 as Doubting Thomas. But James, identified here as "the Just," is given as a presumably pre-Thomas authority in Saying 12:

> The disciples said to Jesus: We know that you will depart from us; who is it who will be great over us? Jesus said to them: No matter where you are, you are to go to James the Just, for whose sake heaven and earth came into being.

Without any rejection of that high praise, the very next Saying 13 establishes Thomas's authority and emphasizes it over against both Peter and Matthew. Presumably, the authority of James was not rejected but simply replaced by Thomas's (after the former's death?).

Gospel of the Hebrews. This is a gospel for Greek-speaking Jews centered probably at Alexandria, independent of our four New Testament gospels, known only from patristic citations rather than manuscript fragments, and dated anywhere from the late first to sometime in the second century. In the seventh of those citations, James's authoritative importance is grounded in the claim that he was the first to whom the risen Lord appeared:

> And when the Lord had given the linen cloth to the servant of the priest, he went to James and appeared to him. For James had sworn that he would not eat bread from that hour in which he had drunk the cup of the Lord until he should see him risen from among them that sleep. And shortly thereafter the Lord said: Bring a table and bread! And immediately it is added: he took the bread, blessed it and brake it and gave it to James the Just and said to him: My brother, eat thy bread, for the Son of man is risen from among them that sleep.

Those texts agree with Luke's Acts of the Apostles and Paul's letter to the Galatians on the authority of James. In fact, his importance is found at every layer of the Christian tradition, from the very early layer of Paul, through the later canonical Acts and the noncanonical gospels of Thomas and of the Hebrews, and into the latest writings attributed to him among the Nag Hammadi Codices such as the *Apocryphon of James* or the *First* and *Second Apocalypse of James*. Such texts may not reflect the theology of the historical James but they certainly confirm James's authority across geography and chronology in early Christian theology.

Martyrdom

Josephus. In 62 C.E., during the administrative interim between Festus's death in office as Roman governor of the Jewish homeland and his replacement by Albinus, Herod Agrippa II dismissed Joseph, son of Simon, as high priest and appointed Ananus, son of Ananus, in his place. *Jewish Antiquities* 20.200 describes what happened:

> Ananus thought that he had a favorable opportunity because Festus was dead and Albinus was still on the way. And so he convened the judges of the Sanhedrin and brought before them a man named James, the brother of Jesus who was called the Christ, and certain others. He accused them of having transgressed the law and delivered them up to be stoned. Those of the inhabitants of the city who were considered the most fair-minded and who were strict in observance of the law were offended at this.

Those "offended" complained to both Herod Agrippa II and Albinus with the result that Ananus was deposed after only three months in office. That is a quite extraordinary story.

First, the younger Ananus "followed the school of the Sadducees," according to Josephus, and the latter's expression, those who were "strict in observance of the law," probably meant the Pharisees. Second, the family of Annas, or Ananus, produced eight high priests (himself, five sons, one son-in-law, and one grandson) across a cumulative forty years between 6 and 66 C.E. Theirs was, in other words, an extremely important high-priestly family. Third, James had lived in Jerusalem for at least thirty years without incurring anti-Christian persecution and his execution toppled an Ananite high priest. James was clearly important not just to Christian

Jews but also to non-Christian Jews and presumably to Pharisaic Jews in Jerusalem.

Hegesippus. The fourth-century church historian Eusebius of Caesarea cites that stark factual account of James's execution from Josephus:

> So they killed him, seizing the opportunity for getting their own way provided by the absence of the government, for at that very time Festus had died in Judaea, leaving the province without governor or procurator.

But he also includes a more theologically laden and fictionally expanded version from the second-century Christian writer Hegesippus. That author makes four main points about James. First, he insists on his ascetic holiness, lifelong abstinence, and nickname of James the Just. Second, he mentions his great success at winning converts to Christian Judaism so that "many even of the ruling class believed." Third, the "Scribes and Pharisees" grew afraid that "the entire people" would convert so they asked James to speak against Jesus from the Temple's parapet at Passover. Fourth, James did exactly the opposite so that "many were convinced, and gloried in James's testimony, crying: 'Hosanna to the son of David.'" Finally, therefore,

> The Scribes and Pharisees . . . went up and threw down the Righteous one . . . and began to stone him, as in spite of his fall he was still alive . . . [until] one of them, a fuller, took the club which he used to beat out the clothes, and brought it down on the head of the Righteous one. Such was his martyrdom.

Although Hegesippus theologically fictionalized that execution, he at least knew James had been stoned by Jewish authority. Similarly, he may also have been correct on James's renowned holiness even if it, too, is told with an overenthusiastic imagination. That would at least explain a standing among pious non-Christian (Pharisaic?) Jews adequate enough to have James's execution topple an Annanide high priest. Notice, by the way, that the fictional account in Hegesippus blames the "Scribes and Pharisees" for the death of James. Yet the historically accurate account in Josephus puts those zealous for the law (Pharisees?) on the side of James and a Sadduceesan high priest against him. That fits into the contemporary tension between Pharisees vs. Sadducees within Judaism and it reminds us, once again, that lethal opposition to earliest Christian Judaism came precisely from the house of Annas.

Opposition

The most significant point about James, however, is not his authority within early Christianity. Nor is it his martyrdom, which like his brother's, was due to his opposition of the high priests. The most significant point about James is his opposition to Paul. This is already evident in Paul's letter to the Galatians. It is, on the one hand, programmatically absent from Luke's Acts and represents one of those basic locations where one should not collate and combine Paul *and* Luke, not collapse these distinct layers into one single layer, but separate and distinguish the earlier Paul *over* the later Luke. It is, on the other hand, fictionally expanded and fantastically heightened in a still later layer, the second-century source within the Christian novel known as the *Clementine Recognitions*. This raises a very important question for excavating Jesus textually. What happens if you look at Jesus through his brother James rather than, or at least as well as, through his apostle Paul?

Paul and Luke. There was, Luke and Paul agree, a crucially important debate in Jerusalem around the year 50 C.E. on whether male pagan converts to Christianity would have to be circumcised before they could be accepted into full and equal membership alongside male Jewish converts who were, of course, already circumcised. They also agreed that the source of the affirmative, or restrictive, position (*yes* to male pagan circumcision) came from "certain individuals," as Luke puts it in Acts 15:1, or from "false believers," as Paul puts it in Galatians 2:4. That difference is a good indication, by the way, of their divergent narrative tones: for Luke, all is irenic consensus; for Paul, all is polemical tension. They further agree that the final decision was in the negative (*no* to male pagan circumcision). Finally, they agree that James was quite important in the entire proceedings. Luke records that Peter, Barnabas, and Paul spoke first, and James last. But it is James who concludes that "I have reached the decision that we should not trouble those Gentiles who are turning to God" by demanding that their males be circumcised (Acts 15:19). Paul again concurs that "when James and Cephas and John, who were acknowledged pillars, recognized the grace that had been given to me, they gave to Barnabas and me the right hand of fellowship, agreeing that we should go to the Gentiles and they to the circumcised" (Gal. 2:9). But granted those general and important agreements, everything else is specific and is in equally important disagreement.

Acts 15 vs. Galatians 2. In the later Acts 15, Luke speaks of *one* single debate, at *one* time in Jerusalem, and with *one* result, complete harmony on both that first original subject (*no* to circumcision traditions for pagan male converts) and also a second and added subject (*yes* to kosher regulations for all converts). In *the earlier* Galatians 2, Paul, on the other hand, speaks of *two* debates, at *two* times in Jerusalem (2:1–10) *and* Antioch (2:11–16), and with harmonious consensus on the first subject but severe discord on the second one.

On the former subject, there was, as just mentioned, agreement by all (save, presumably, Luke's "certain individuals" and Paul's "false believers"?). That position would have been acceptable to somebody like James because one strand of Jewish tradition held that God would bring the Gentiles into full community with Jews at that ideal utopian or eschatological moment in the future when God finally made the earth divinely just. Gentiles would then be converted not to Judaism, with male circumcision, for example, but to the God of the entire world. Jews and Gentiles would then feast together with that God on a pure, just, peaceful, and fruitful earth. It was a vision of God's eventual justification and pacification of a violent earth *not by* the Great Final War at Mount Megiddo (Armageddon) in which evildoers would be finally slaughtered *but by* the Great Final Banquet on Mount Zion in which evildoers would be finally converted. Recall, for instance, the rhapsodic images of Micah 4:1–4 and Isaiah 2:2–4 on cosmic peace:

In days to come the mountain of the Lord's house shall be established as the highest of the mountains, and shall be raised up above the hills. Peoples shall stream to it, and many nations shall come and say: "Come, let us go up to the mountain of the Lord, to the house of the God of Jacob; that he may teach us his ways and that we may walk in his paths." For out of Zion shall go forth instruction, and the word of the Lord from Jerusalem. He shall judge between many peoples, and shall arbitrate between strong nations far away; they shall beat their swords into plowshares, and their spears into pruning hooks; nation shall not lift up sword against nation, neither shall they learn war any more; but they shall all sit under their own vines and under their own fig trees, and no one shall make them afraid; for the mouth of the Lord of hosts has spoken.

And, that cosmic peace is celebrated at a cosmic banquet hosted by God in Jerusalem according to Isaiah 25:6–8:

On this mountain the Lord of hosts will make for all peoples a feast of rich food, a feast of well-aged wines, of rich food filled with marrow, of well-aged wines strained clear. And he will destroy on this mountain the shroud that is cast over all peoples, the sheet that is spread over all nations; he will swallow up death forever. Then the Lord God will wipe away the tears from all faces, and the disgrace of his people he will take away from all the earth, for the Lord has spoken.

Against that background and within precisely that irenic tradition of eschatological apocalypticism, James and all the others (save for some dissident holdouts?) agreed that circumcision was not mandatory for male pagan converts to Christian Judaism.

Galatians 2:11–17. It was, however, on that second subject that Luke and Paul disagree both profoundly and directly. Paul sets this second debate not at Jerusalem but later at Antioch. *What was at stake was no more and no less than the present and future unity of the new community.* Would there be two separate, unequal, and maybe even inimical wings to that new Christian community, a Christian Jewish one observing kosher regulations and a Christian pagan one not doing so? And that question was especially acute because a united community of Jews and Gentiles eating together would have to go one way or the other. Either all together would observe kosher, with Christian pagans conceding to Christian Jews, or all together would avoid kosher, with Christian Jews conceding to Christian pagans. The whole problem, of course, arose only where such joint assemblies were already taking place or might eventually do so.

That second subject was not about circumcision. That was already conceded by James at Jerusalem and was not being retracted by James at Antioch. And neither was it about Christian pagans observing kosher all by themselves in, say, Ephesus, Corinth, or Rome. *It was precisely and accurately about and only about common meals when Jewish and pagan converts ate together in religious assembly.* Here is Paul's account of the debate, dispute, or row, at Antioch in Galatians 2:11–16:

> But when Cephas came to Antioch, I opposed him to his face, because he stood self-condemned; for until certain people came from James, he used to eat with the Gentiles. But after they came, he drew back and kept himself separate for fear of the circumcision faction. And the other Jews joined him in this *hypocrisy*, so that even Barnabas was led astray by their *hypocrisy*. But when I saw that they were not acting consistently with the truth of the gospel, I said to Cephas before them all, "If you, though a Jew, live like a Gentile and not like a Jew, how can you compel the Gentiles to live like Jews?" We ourselves are Jews by birth and not Gentile sinners; yet we know that a person is justified not by the *works of the law* but through *faith in Jesus Christ*. And we have come to *believe in Christ Jesus*, so that we might be justified by *faith in Christ*, and not by doing the *works of the law*, because no one will be justified by the *works of the law*.

Centuries of Christian commentary have presumed that Paul was obviously right in that debate. We propose that he was not.

First, non–circumcision for male pagan converts was worth an absolute non-negotiable position and James had agreed to that position at Jerusalem. Without that agreement Christian paganism would have died at birth if not conception. Second, and only as second, could a further question arise, namely, in joint (eucharistic?) meals between Christian Jews and Christian pagans, will unity be maintained by common kosher or common nonkosher custom? Third, read again Paul's accusation against Peter. We interpret that sentence to mean that Peter, a Christian Jew, had been observing the common nonkosher solution when eating with Christian pagans. And so, apparently, were (several, many, all?) other Christian Jews at Antioch. But now they have agreed to James's demand for the common kosher solution. Such a change from nonkosher for all to kosher for all, Paul twice condemns as *hypocrisy*. The assembly's response to Paul is not given but, no doubt, they would have said that, no Paul, it is not hypocrisy but simply *courtesy*. Fourth, this is a pragmatic question against which Paul mounts an in-this-case irrelevant argument. Had Peter and the others ever believed that kosher was still mandatory for their salvation, they could not so easily have omitted it.

The question at Antioch was not fundamentally different from modern, believing Christians observing all Jewish customs while eating in a Jewish home or praying in a Jewish temple. It would not be a question of communal hypocrisy but of ecumenical courtesy now, and it would also have been a question of communal unity then. Finally, to this pragmatic question Paul introduces "works of the law" three times and opposes to them "faith in Christ" three times. Paul's antithesis of faith and works might be theologically justifiable in the abstract but for that pragmatic question at Antioch it was irrelevant in the concrete. Does anyone believe that James, Peter, Barnabas, and all the others (save Paul) had opted for justification by "works of the law" rather than "faith in Christ"? Paul's position (at least as recorded to the Galatians) was akin to machine-gunning butterflies. James, Peter, Barnabas, and all the others who agreed with him, were right at Antioch. Paul was wrong at Antioch.

Romans 15 and Acts 21. There is one final New Testament indication of James's authority in Jerusalem and here, once again, Paul and Luke differ profoundly but now indirectly. Before, but especially after, the Jerusalem decision on circumcision, the group's unity was an obvious and fundamental problem. And Paul was very aware of it. That was why he agreed enthusiastically and followed up conscientiously on the common decision to take up a collection from Christian pagans for those Christian Jews known as "the poor" in Jerusalem (a common-life community like at Qumran?). After James and the Jerusalem "pillars" accepted the noncircumcision of male pagan converts, "they asked," he said in Galatians 2:10, "only one thing, that we remember the poor, which was actually what I was eager to do." But, while Paul discusses that collection repeatedly in his letters, Luke's Acts never mentions it at all. There are, however, sections in that book that make sense only if Luke (or at least his sources) knew about it and presumed its existence and operation.

Paul discusses his plans for delivering the collection to Jerusalem in Romans 15:25–27, 30–31 and he acknowledges two dangers that may well destroy its function as a unifying process between Christian Jews and Christian pagans:

At present, however, I am going to Jerusalem in a ministry to the saints; for Macedonia and Achaia have been pleased to share their resources with the poor among the saints at Jerusalem. They were pleased to do this, and indeed they owe it to them; for if the Gentiles have come to share in their spiritual blessings, they ought also to be of service to them in material things. . . . I appeal to you, brothers and sisters, by our Lord Jesus Christ and by the love of the Spirit, to join me in earnest prayer to God on my behalf, that I may be rescued from the unbelievers in Judea, and that my ministry to Jerusalem may be acceptable to the saints.

The external danger was opposition from non-Christian Jews and the internal danger was rejection by Christian Jews. Both happened. And knowing they both might happen, Paul still accompanied the collection instead of sending it with community representatives. For Paul, the unity of the community's twin wings was important enough to accept the risk of martyrdom. But in Acts 21:17–25, although he never mentions any collection, Luke tells, in effect, how both of Paul's fears were realized at Jerusalem. James and the Christian Jewish community placed a condition on the collection's acceptance and, when Paul followed it, he was attacked by non-Christian Jews in the Temple. Here is their condition:

When we arrived in Jerusalem, the brothers welcomed us warmly. The next day Paul went with us to visit James; and all the elders were present. After greeting them, he related one by one the things that God had done among the Gentiles through his ministry. When they heard it, they praised God. Then they said to him, "You see, brother, how many thousands of believers there are among the Jews, and they are all zealous for the law. They have been told about you that you teach all the Jews living among the Gentiles to forsake Moses, and that you tell them not to circumcise their children or observe the customs. What then is to be done? They will certainly hear that you have come. So do what we tell you. We have four men who are under a vow. Join these men, go through the rite of purification with them, and pay for the shaving of their heads. Thus all will know that there is nothing in what they have been told about you, but that you yourself observe and guard the law. But as for the Gentiles who have become believers, we have sent a letter with our judgment that they

should abstain from what has been sacrificed to idols and from blood
and from what is strangled and from fornication."

That text is cited as one further indication of James's authority in
Jerusalem and of the continuing tension, carefully muted by Luke in Acts
21 as earlier in Acts 15, between James and Paul. The latter was now in a
terrible double bind. One alternative was to refuse James's condition,
accept the collection's rejection, and acknowledge Christianity's split condition. The other was to follow James's condition, deliver the collection
and thereby emphasize unity, but risk the charge of hypocrisy that he himself had once leveled at Peter.

Epistle of James. The "James" of this New Testament epistle is not identified any further but he is almost certainly the ossuary's James, James the
Righteous or Just One, James, the son of Joseph, the brother of Jesus. That
"Epistle *of*" could mean anything from personal authorship through developed teaching to fictional attribution. Each position is defensible but none
is absolutely provable. For here and now, we emphasize only one point. If
you tried to imagine the theology of James from *a careful examination of the
layers composed of* Luke's Acts, Paul's Galatians, and Josephus's *Jewish
Antiquities*, you could easily come up with something like the content of
the epistle attributed to him.
    Paul insisted in Galatians 2:11–17, as just seen, on justification through
faith in Christ rather than in works of the law, an argument simply irrelevant to the pragmatic problem at Antioch, which was about maintaining
unity rather than obtaining justification. James does not respond, in his
2:14–19, that justification comes from works rather than from faith or
from either alone (would any Jew have ever argued those positions?), but
he argues that it comes from faith and works together, from faith operating
through works, from faith manifested by works, from faith's inability to be
separated from works.

What good is it, my brothers and sisters, if you say you have faith but
do not have works? Can faith save you? If a brother or sister is naked
and lacks daily food, and one of you says to them, "Go in peace; keep
warm and eat your fill," and yet you do not supply their bodily needs,
what is the good of that? So faith by itself, if it has no works, is dead.
But someone will say, "You have faith and I have works." Show me

your faith apart from your works, and I by my works will show you my faith. You believe that God is one; you do well. Even the demons believe—and shudder.

Faith and works are like twin sides of the one coin, distinguishable but not separable, a dialectic, not a dichotomy. It is quite possible to argue that James and Paul meant different things by their common terms, faith and works, by their common use of Abraham as model, and by their common citation of Genesis 16:5 ("Abraham believed God, and it was reckoned to him as righteousness"), James 2:23, Galatians 3:6, and Romans 4:3. It is also quite possible, therefore, to claim that James 2:14–19 is arguing past Paul's position but, then, so was Paul arguing past that of James and everyone else in Galatians 2:11–17. We have, once again, to imagine how differently we would see the situation at Antioch if we imagine that, not Paul, but James (and everyone else) had the better case.

Clementine Recognitions. This is a second-century source contained in the first book of a fourth-century Christian novel called the *Clementine Recognitions*. It is another version of that story from Hegesippus but there are two major expansions. First, individual members of the Twelve speak about Jesus before both the people and Caiaphas in the Temple at Passover and James "ascends" the steps as the climactic last to bear witness. He speaks for a week and persuaded "all the people and the high priest that they should hasten to receive baptism" (1.69.8). Second, a murderous intervention prevents that general conversion. "A certain hostile man" entered the Temple and "began to murder. . . . Much blood flowed. There was a confused flight, during which the hostile man attacked James, and threw him headlong from the top of the steps. As he believed him to be dead, he was not concerned to beat him further" (1.70.1, 6, 8). That "hostile man" is never identified directly by name but he is definitely Paul himself since "the hostile man had received authority from Caiaphas the high priest to pursue all who believe in Jesus and travel to Damascus with his letters, so that there also by using the help of unbelievers he might bring ruin on the faithful" (1.71.4). That, of course, is intended to recall the description of Paul from Luke's Acts 9:1–2.

You will notice that the text makes three very serious accusations against Paul. One is that, but for his intervention, all the people and all the priests were about to convert to Christianity. Another is that he himself murdered and incited others to murder Christians in the Temple. A final one concerns James. This extremely tendentious, utterly libelous, and completely fictional account knows about James's "thrown-down" martyrdom but manages both to say and not to say that Paul killed him. We are not told anything about James after that point so one could easily presume that what Paul believed was correct and that James was dead, murdered by Paul. And that is what the text intends us to think.

Three major themes, then, appear and develop concerning James the Just of Jerusalem, son of Joseph, brother of Jesus. They move in the layers both inside and outside the New Testament. And in both places they move from fact to fiction and from history to theology along tracks of ideological acceptance or rejection. The first theme, James's authoritative importance, appears in 1 Corinthians 15:7, the *Gospel of Thomas* 12, and the *Gospel of the Hebrews* 7. The second theme, James's martyrdom, develops from Josephus to Hegesippus. The third theme, the opposition between James and Paul, is absent from Luke's Acts, where everyone agrees with James, but is present in Paul's Galatians, where everyone agrees with James *except Paul.* Opposition continues, concerning faith and works, Abraham and Genesis, in the Epistle of James, and it climaxes as libelous fiction in the *Clementine Recognitions*.

Once those textual layers are carefully distinguished and their literary purposes clearly emphasized, we can see them as disputes within Christian Judaism, debates growing ever more bitter between proponents of James and of Paul, but never as Christianity against Judaism. That is exactly the same context in which we see Jesus in this book. His is one of the options within his contemporary Judaism, an option disputing with and struggling against other ones in the crucible of that fateful first century.

STONE AND TEXT, ARCHAEOLOGY AND EXEGESIS

There remain these five questions about the James ossuary. Is the ossuary authentic? Is the inscription original? Is the family identifiable? Is the discovery important? Is the process ethical? That final question is a first, last, and abiding one. Hopefully, then, media publicity and popular excitement about the James ossuary may raise general awareness about the legal, ethical, and historical problems of unprovenanced artifacts.

It should be possible eventually to answer those first two questions beyond a reasonable doubt. The third one is more difficult. If that ossuary is judged authentic and the inscription judged original, is that family of

Joseph, James, and Jesus the same as the New Testament one? That can scarcely ever be certain beyond a reasonable doubt. At best, using the difference between the certitude required for civil as distinct from criminal judgment, we could conclude that the preponderance of evidence indicates a positive answer. But at its very best that could never be more than a statistical argument, a good probability, unless, of course, the actual tomb were relocated and further evidence were then forthcoming.

For the moment, however, let us grant that the ossuary is what it is claimed to be by its owner. And, of course, that will have to be reviewed in the future if the Israeli government takes possession of the ossuary and reports on its authenticity. Granted, for the moment, authenticity, originality, and even identity, what is its importance? And, we would emphasize, that question may still stand even if the final judgment on those first three questions turns out to be decidedly negative. Fakes can also teach very important lessons and raise very important questions. In terms of this book, then, what is its importance for archaeology and exegesis?

First, with regard to the interaction of those twin disciplines, this ossuary is a condensed symbol of the entire process. Without all that archaeology already knows about first-century Jewish primary and secondary burial customs, without all those tombs already found and ossuaries already catalogued, what meaning would this single, isolated box have for anyone? What on earth is it? An ancient filing cabinet, maybe? Without all that we know of a James, son of Joseph and brother of Jesus, from inside and outside the New Testament, from fact and fiction, history and legend, that inscription would mean nothing now to anyone. Maybe, it simply identifies the filing cabinet's owner? But, granted all that archaeology and exegesis already knows about ossuaries and Jameses, the discovery is a striking example of the disciplinary convergence between ground and gospel, stone and text.

Second, with regard to archaeology, the ossuary became badly cracked in transit from Tel Aviv to Toronto. But everything about the discovery was already badly cracked in any case. It is an isolated artifact of unknown provenance and any information about its history may be invented at best and self-serving at worst. Maybe the Israeli Antiquities Authority will be able to trace its path from source to museum. Maybe, if judged authentic and valuable, it will generate search-and-destroy missions all over ancient burial sites around Jerusalem. All of that serves only to emphasize the legal and moral difference between artifact collecting, or cultural looting, and

controlled search, or scientific archaeology. The James ossuary is a magnificent example of how not to discover something. That is, unfortunately—
no matter the final judgment on its validity—its major archaeological
importance.

Third, with regard to exegesis, if the emphasis is placed *on Jesus*, the discovery does not tell us anything we did not already know nor will it likely
change the interpretation of what we already think. If it were absolutely
authentic and identifiable, you could take it as archaeological proof,
alongside the textual evidence from the earliest pagan, Jewish, and
Christian sources, that Jesus existed. Beyond that, what? The New
Testament already said Jesus was a son of Joseph and that James was a
brother of Jesus. The ossuary's inscription repeats that information. Those
who have always read the text as meaning that Joseph was the birth-father
and James the blood-brother of Jesus will read the stone that same way.
Those who have always read Joseph as stepfather and James as stepbrother
of Jesus or Joseph as uncle and James as cousin of Jesus will read the stone
along those same lines. Nothing will change there.

What if, however, we take the emphasis off an exclusive focus on Jesus
and place it *on Jesus and James?* They were both martyred, Jesus around 30
and James in 62 c.e. But think now of the contrasts. Jesus was executed by
collaboration of the high priest Caiaphas and the Roman governor Pilate.
Nothing happened to either of them for that incident although both were
later deposed for malpractice in office by Roman authority in 36–37 c.e.
James was executed by the high priest Annas, or Ananus II, for which he
was immediately deposed by the Jewish king, Agrippa II, and the Roman
procurator, Festus. And both of those high priests were from the powerful
Anninide dynasty. Those two very different martyrdoms warn us to be
extremely careful to keep Jesus within Judaism and Judaism within the
Roman Empire. It is not a crude case of Christianity against Judaism but of
an intra-Jewish debate where Christian Judaism was but one among the
varied options of first-century Judaism responding from ancient tradition
to contemporary imperialism. The James ossuary, be it ultimately judged
authentic or inauthentic, reminds us that the historical James is very
important for understanding the historical Jesus. *How do we see the historical Jesus when James is considered to be his brother's keeper?*

Finally, what if we place the emphasis entirely on James? It is, after all,
his bone box. Then everything changes a little and it should do so even if
this ossuary is ultimately judged a whole or partial fake. What about James

the Forgotten? What about the opposition between James and Paul? What if we were to judge James right and Paul wrong at Antioch and thereafter? How does that change our view of earliest Christianity? Here then is the important question long present in our texts but raised anew and emphasized now by this ossuary's existence, especially for this present book: *How do we see the historical Jesus when James rather than Paul is considered to be his better continuation?*

TWO

Layers upon Layers
upon Layers

Modern Nazareth is a thriving tourist and pilgrimage city. Known as the hometown of Jesus, tourists flock there to see where Jesus grew up and to eat the best falafel in Israel. Sightseers haggle with vendors hawking trinkets and crafts in the market, and pilgrims stream into the church that commemorates the spot where the archangel Gabriel revealed to Mary Jesus' divine conception. Inside the modern church complex, in Franciscan custody, contemporary mosaics from around the globe portray Mary and the infant Jesus in the native dress and with the facial features of the country that commissioned them. Those representations surround the austere and imposing Basilica of the Annunciation, built in the 1960s atop an ancient grotto, presumably where Gabriel spoke to Mary. Inside the Basilica, stone walls and stained glass protect orderly chant, quiet meditation, and fragrant incense from the scenes outside, scenes not always serene or irenic.

Nazareth is a loud and noisy city, chaotic and bustling, a mix of Palestinian Christians and Muslims in a large lower city, and Jews of Russian, Ethiopic, and other origins in the upper city, called Nazeret Ilit. Earlier a remarkable model of peaceful coexistence, after the broken peace process Nazareth was marred by violence and arson. A year earlier the construction of a new mosque next to the Basilica of the Annunciation spurred tensions between Christians and Muslims, conflicts exacerbated by accusations of Israeli mismanagement and daily protests. Israel's Ministry of Justice just completed a large glass, metal, and concrete structure to administer judgments and render verdicts. Built in modern architectural style on top of a knoll, it overlooks the lower city's rooftop clutter of antennae and satellite dishes, drying laundry and water tanks.

Jackhammers pound and drills hum at construction sites everywhere, although the new megahotels anticipating a surge in visitors following the year 2000's papal pilgrimage stand mostly vacant today. John Paul II's visit did stimulate municipal action to allocate funds for the expansion and repavement of the main street that winds through downtown Nazareth so that, where cars once double-parked and choked traffic in exhaust and bottlenecks, cars and vans now triple-park and do the same.

Modern Nazareth is a unique city, a place that must be seen, smelled, and experienced. Its sounds and sights are part Middle Eastern, with Arabic calls to prayer and male heads wrapped in *kefilas*; part Israeli, with *Egged* tourist buses, cell phones, and skullcaps; part European and Japanese, with Mercedes taxis and Isuzu pickup trucks, brown Franciscan habits and Fuji film; and part American, with Kentucky Fried Chicken restaurants and boys in Lakers jerseys.

Twenty-first-century Nazareth contrasts starkly with first-century Nazareth. Twenty centuries of history separate the former from the latter, and layers upon layers of occupational debris are stacked atop the ancient site. Twenty centuries of architectural construction, renovation, and demolition have obliterated much of the first-century Jewish hamlet. To get a glimpse of Jesus' Nazareth, you have to cut through many layers superimposed on it. But as you get closer, pay careful attention to the complex layering. The closer you get to the first century, the more difficult it is to distinguish earlier from later, but the more crucial becomes that separation, lest evidence from the later second, third, or fourth centuries be mistaken for that from the earlier first-century village. An archaeological sketch of first-century Nazareth begins with those later layers not only because that is how the archaeologist's spade and trowel expose them, but also so that they can be clearly delineated from the earlier layers. Later deposits need to be peeled off cautiously, their debris must be sifted carefully for first-century artifacts uprooted from their context, and the later structures' impact on those underneath must be assessed. To expose first-century Nazareth, continuities and discontinuities between earlier and later layers must be discerned in a complex multi-layered excavation. We begin therefore, with Nazareth's broader Galilean context and an overview of the historical periods that shaped its archaeological characteristics.

Byzantine Period (mid-fourth to seventh century C.E.***).*** The stratigraphic layers from this period in Galilee were profoundly affected by the
emperor Constantine the Great's conversion of the Roman Empire to
Christianity. In subsequent centuries, this fueled a steady influx of pilgrims, imperial finances, and architects, who transformed the Jewish
homeland into the Christian Holy Land with churches, shrines, and
monasteries. Galilee's Jewish population responded with more elaborate—
but mostly internal—artistry in synagogues. But the period is characterized by a gradual decline in the material culture's quality: houses are less
well constructed and local pottery is coarser and less well fired.

Middle and Late Roman Periods (second to mid-fourth century C.E.***).***
The layers of these periods are characterized by Galilee's incorporation
into the Roman province of *Palestina*. After the two Jewish wars with
Rome in 66–74 and 132–35, numerous refugees from Judea and Jerusalem
migrated to Galilee, and Rome permanently stationed a legion nearby to
prevent further unrest. Two forces were at work in these layers: first, there
was considerable population growth and the synagogue developed as the
replacement of the Temple in Jewish religion. And second, Roman policy
accelerated urbanization to facilitate control and taxation; as a result, public architecture at larger sites was redeveloped, and international trade
increased.

Early Roman Period (mid-first century B.C.E. ***to first century*** C.E.***).***
Herod the Great's Roman-sponsored kingdom building (37–4 B.C.E.)
dominates this layer across the Jewish homeland, sometimes called the
"Herodian Period." His son Herod Antipas urbanized Galilee (4 B.C.E.–39
C.E.) and introduced Greco-Roman urban architecture there with the
building of Sepphoris and Tiberias. But there and elsewhere Jewish self-
expression in domestic life is common and widespread. Towns and villages
share a simple architecture, but well-fired pottery was being produced at
several kilns. Some evidence of trade and luxury items is found in the
cities or isolated wealthy houses in towns. At the end of this period, many
sites are destroyed in the first Jewish revolt against Rome.

Late Hellenistic Period (second to mid-first century B.C.E.***).*** The
Late Hellenistic Period in Galilee is characterized by significant Jewish
settlement under the Hasmonean rulers (the so-called Maccabees, who

reestablished an independent Jewish kingdom and ruled it from Jerusalem). Most of Galilee's Roman-Byzantine sites were first settled at this
time, and in addition to simple villages several Hasmonean military forts
and outposts helped carve out and protect a Jewish territory surrounded by
rural gentile populations and larger pagan and Hellenized cities. During
this period Galilee was sparsely populated and somewhat isolated, and
ample land was available for farming.

Reconstructing first-century Nazareth is not just an archaeological
enterprise limited to sorting out artifacts from the above mentioned layers.
Centuries of architectural construction, renovation, and demolition at
Nazareth were accompanied by centuries of intellectual construction projects—theological, dogmatic, and ideological—that have been superimposed on Jesus. Before general life in Jesus' Galilee can be imagined, and
before his particular life can be reconstructed, modern notions projected
onto the past need to be deconstructed. Common preconceptions about
Nazareth from upper-class biases in the literary sources must be taken into
account, and dogmatic assertions about Jesus from some Christian theologies must be taken to task. Two points stand out. First-century Nazareth
was a *peasant* village in an agrarian society. And first-century Nazareth was
a *Jewish* village adhering to the Temple-oriented Judaism of its day. *Jesus,
then, was a Jewish peasant.*

ANYTHING GOOD FROM NAZARETH?

In John's gospel, the soon-to-be disciple Nathanael quips, "Can anything
good come out of Nazareth?" when others tell him they have found "him
about whom Moses in the law and also the prophets wrote" (1:45–46). His
retort, insulting to be sure, is surprising insofar as anyone had actually
heard of Nazareth. Outside the gospels and the early Christian texts that
rely on them, there are no pre-Constantinian citations referring to
Nazareth. It is never mentioned by any of the Jewish rabbis whose pronouncements are in the Mishnah or whose discussions are in the Talmud,
even though they cite sixty-three other Galilean towns. Josephus, the
Jewish historian and general over Galilee during the first Jewish revolt in
66–67 C.E., refers to forty-five named sites there, but never to Nazareth. It
is unknown in the Christian Old Testament. Even though Zebulun's tribal
allotment in the Bible catalogues some fifteen Lower Galilean sites in
Nazareth's vicinity, it is not counted among them (Josh. 19:10–15). It was
absolutely insignificant.

TWENTY-FIRST-CENTURY NAZARETH. *The Christian pilgrimage city of Nazareth sprawls today over the ruins of the first-century village and hometown of Jesus. Seen here from atop the Nazareth Ridge, the city center is dotted by holy sites and dominated by the massive Basilica of the Annunciation (1). It was built by the Franciscan order in the 1960s atop an earlier Crusader church and Byzantine shrine on the spot commemorating Gabriel's revelation to the Virgin Mary. Beside it, the Church of St. Joseph (2) covers an underground chamber hailed in recent centuries as the workshop of Joseph. Ancient terraces along the slope in the foreground (3) and tombs cut in antiquity into the surrounding hills in the background delineate the modest size of Jesus' hometown.*

It's no surprise that Nazareth is never mentioned. Writing in antiquity was an upper-class activity, so that references to Nazareth increase dramatically after Christianity rose to political power in the fourth century C.E. Those who had learned to read and write in antiquity were the rulers, the wealthy, or their scribes, so that the histories, biographies, and narratives surviving from the past were mostly penned or dictated by powerful men. They were interested primarily in public persons and political conflicts. These very few atop the social pyramid cared little about the vast majority of people and what went on in small towns, rural villages, or countryside hamlets like Nazareth, unless they caused trouble or threatened stability and income.

Peasant Life.   The peasantry, by contrast, had little time to learn how to write and had less interest in reading the upper classes' writings. They were interested primarily in working the land, both to pay their taxes and to survive on what was left. Self-sufficiency was their goal and polycropping their method. Polycropping, or scattering their plots and diversifying their crops, held many advantages for peasant families. Diversification minimized the consequences of a single-crop failure, important in a world where famine was never more than a drought or a bad harvest away. Diversification also spread labor demands more evenly over the seasons. If one could grow one's own food, it would cut down reliance on others, especially the patronage of the urban elite and wealthy landowners who usurped land, and it would minimize haggling with shrewd merchants in the markets.

A peasant's diet was meager; the staples were bread, olives, olive oil, and wine. Bean or lentil stew that included a few seasonal vegetables was sometimes ladled on pita bread, and nuts, fruits, cheese, and yogurt were welcome additions. Salted fish was occasional and meat was rare, reserved only for special celebrations. Most skeletal remains predictably show iron and protein deficiencies, and most had severe arthritis. A case of the flu, a bad cold, or an abscessed tooth could kill. Life expectancy, for the luckier half who survived childhood, was somewhere in the thirties. Those reaching fifty or sixty were rare.

Parents were anxious to have carefully balanced families: enough sons were needed to work the fields, but too many meant land would be carved up in inadequate inheritances or younger sons would be pushed off the land. Daughters were needed for domestic work, but too many meant dowry requirements might quickly exhaust the family's assets, while unmarried women might slowly drain them. Landless men, younger sons, or men born out of wedlock could try to eke out a living as craftsmen, fishermen, day laborers, soldiers, or could turn to banditry; women without the protection of a father, husband, or brother would beg or whore. Upward mobility was unknown, social movement was as a rule downward, and most peasants lived perilously close to the edge.

Life was predominantly local. Travel was dangerous. People moved about little, and when they did, say, go to the city for festivals or markets, family members or friends accompanied them with clubs and staffs. Some Galileans might make the lengthy pilgrimage to Jerusalem by traveling with clan members for protection or joining caravans with hired guards.

Trade was dangerous and impractical. Bulky items required a slow and hungry ox and cart, which made imports rare and very expensive. Even a few small objects from afar—lamps, perfume, glassware, plates—were signs of wealth.

Literary Evidence. Prior to Rome's conversion, the literate elites and politically powerful in the empire knew nothing about Nazareth. It was only locally known. The very few elites who did know about it, like some administrators in Herod Antipas's capital, Sepphoris, some 4 miles to the north, could not have cared less about it. Unless tax quotas were not met or feuds could not be settled, this small Jewish hamlet merited no attention. A story is told by the fourth-century church historian Eusebius about the grandsons of Jude, the brother of Jesus, who were brought before the Roman emperor Domitian (81–96 C.E.). He interrogated the members of Jesus' family, who presumably had remained in Nazareth:

> Denounced as being descendants of David, the officer led them before Caesar Domitian, for he feared the coming of the Christ just as Herod had. He asked them if they were descendants of David, to which they confessed. Then he asked them how much they possessed and how much money they controlled. They said that between the two of them they possessed nine thousand denarii, half each, and they said that they did not have this in cash but that this was only the value of their twenty-five acres of land, on which they paid taxes and lived on by manual labor. Then as testimony of their labor they showed him their hands and hardness of bodies, with callused hands from incessant work. . . . Upon this Domitian did not condemn them but despised them as worthless, released them, and ordered an end to the persecution against the Church. (*Ecclesiastical History* 3.20)

Peasants before the emperor. They had no cash, they had little land, they paid their taxes and eked out a living, their bodies bore the scars of hard work, and they were despised. This was the world of Jesus the peasant.

Though cloaked in obscurity during earlier times, after Constantine's conversion and throughout the Byzantine Period, Nazareth attracted the attention of Christian pilgrims as Jesus' hometown, of imperial architects as a construction site, and of authors as the setting for Jewish-Christian tensions. The fourth-century Christian theologian Epiphanius reports the following about Joseph of Tiberias, a Jew converted under Constantine's rule who gained permission and funds to build churches in Galilee:

> Joseph sought only this favor from the emperor, that he be entrusted to build for Christ—by royal decree—churches in the cities and villages of the Jews, where no one had ever built them, since among them were neither Greeks, nor Samaritans, nor Christians. This was especially the case in Tiberias, in Diocaesarea also called Sepphoris, in Nazareth, and in Capernaum, where they saw to it that those of other races do not live.

Nazareth appears about a century later in a text from 570 C.E., with the words of a Christian pilgrim from Piacenza anticipating an outbreak of religious intolerance. He reports, from his visit to Jesus' hometown, that the synagogue there "as yet *still* belonged to the Jews." Half a century later, in 629 C.E., the emperor Heraclius expelled all Jews from holy sites, including Jewish Nazareth. And Nazareth had indeed been Jewish, though so much of the literary evidence for Nazareth is Christian, written in either Greek or Latin by people from outside Galilee.

Epigraphic Evidence.   The only epigraphic evidence for Nazareth comes from a Jewish synagogue inscription, written in Hebrew. A small dark gray marble fragment from a third- or fourth-century C.E. synagogue plaque was discovered at Caesarea Maritima in 1962, containing the earliest occurrence of the name Nazareth in a non-Christian source. This fragment and two others unearthed with it preserve a list of the traditional locations where Jewish priests resettled after the Roman emperor Hadrian banned all Jews from Jerusalem in 135 C.E. Of the twenty-four priestly families who had earlier rotated their weekly service in Jerusalem's Temple, the eighteenth priestly family, which went by the name of Hapizzez, resettled in Nazareth. This inscription underscores Nazareth's Jewish character inasmuch as it was considered an appropriate home for refugee priests.

Jewish Religion.   By the Middle Roman Period, the refugee priests who settled in Nazareth were no longer central to Jewish religion. After the destruction of the Temple, rabbis in the synagogue began to replace priests as the center of Jewish religious life. Their focus was on reading the scriptures and especially on interpreting Mosaic law and applying it to daily life. In Jesus' day, however, these roles were reversed: the Temple in Jerusalem and its priesthood dominated Jewish religion; rabbis, among whom the Pharisees were the most influential, were secondary. In fact a large measure of their prestige was as interpreters of the law as it related to the Temple, priests, and purity. Some of the Pharisees were scholar-scribes, wealthy enough and situated in urban settings with enough support and leisure to read and write. They were popular with the people and prominent in the communal gatherings, which had yet to develop the full liturgy and service of the later synagogues. At Jesus' time, synagogues were communal gatherings at which marriages were sealed, town meetings held, circumcisions performed, scriptures translated out loud from Hebrew into the vernacular Aramaic, elders consulted, and traditions discussed.

Galileans were somewhat removed from the Temple, a distance that may have been spiritual as well as geographical. It's possible that in Galilee synagogue meetings had gained more importance for religious life than in Judea, and they—the Galileans and their meetings—certainly were suspect by Judeans. But whether Judean and right in the shadow of the Temple or Galilean and far from it, the main bearer of Jewish tradition was the extended family: at birth and death, on the Sabbath, at seasonal celebrations and daily meals, fathers and grandfathers, mothers and grandmothers passed on their traditions. This was the world of *Jesus the Galilean Jew*.

From Constantine the Great to the present, the written evidence portrays Nazareth as the setting for political conflicts and religious disputes. Yet prior to the conversion of the empire, no evidence suggests that it was torn by political strife—it was absolutely insignificant. And no evidence suggests that it was torn by religious discord—it was entirely Jewish.

THE ARCHAEOLOGICAL LAYERS OF NAZARETH VILLAGE

Not surprisingly, the most substantial layers at Nazareth are large-scale Christian construction projects commemorating Jesus' and his parents' lives. Hewn stones and other building blocks from monumental edifices, erected when Christian power or influence, wealth or population held sway in the land, cover traces of a humble Jewish settlement. Three layers stand out. One is from the twentieth century, when pilgrimage developed into a tourist industry. Another is from the Crusades, when Christian monks, clerics, and a bishop lived in Nazareth under the protection of the

Knights Templar. A final one is from the Byzantine Period, when the first shrines, basilicas, and monasteries were built under imperial patronage.

The most recent constructions on land in Franciscan custody allowed archaeologists to carry out excavations in the heart of Nazareth. The rebuilding and renovation in the 1930s of the Church of St. Joseph exposed numerous subterranean features, and in the 1960s Bellarmino Bagatti conducted large-scale excavations in and around the massive Basilica of the Annunciation prior to its construction. Under these modern structures, a large Romanesque church and the bishop's palace built by the Crusaders were found, which in turn covered an older Byzantine church and monastery. Each of these layers—modern, Crusader, and Byzantine—cut through earlier ones, in some places to bedrock in search of solid foundations, at other times reshuffling earlier layers to fill in subterranean caves or pits as a foundation.

As the modern structures were built, fill was removed and crevices in bedrock exposed, and artifacts from earlier centuries were unearthed for the first time. A set of ornate capitals was discovered that was carved by French workmen and hidden since 1187, when Sultan Saladin expelled Christians from the Holy Land. They depict scenes from the lives of the apostles, but the apostles look European not Semitic, their accessories appear medieval not ancient, and their clothes are regal not peasant. What was to be the most magnificent Crusader church constructed in the Holy Land was unfinished and abandoned, to be completed only some eight centuries later in the twentieth century.

Underneath the unfinished Crusader church, the outlines of an earlier Byzantine church and monastery were found. The church's focal point was the so-called Grotto of the Annunciation, where plaster and stone etched with Christian symbols, prayers, and invocations were discovered, some of which might even predate the Byzantine church. Its construction during the Byzantine Period was monumental and imperial. Hundreds of dislodged mosaic stones—mostly white and black mosaic stones, or *tessarae*—were found all around the grotto, as were pieces of painted plaster, or fresco. The church was frequently renovated, as patrons from afar made generous donations to replaster the walls or repave the mosaic floors. Some recorded their generosity in stone. In one corner of a white mosaic, cut with black squares and lozenges containing equal-armed crosses, an inscription reads: "Gift of Conon, Deacon of Jerusalem." Another mosaic floor, still in place and intact, dates to the fifth century C.E. It was deco-

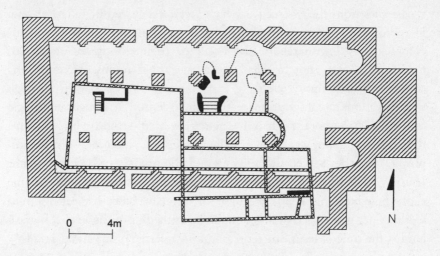

0   4m

N

CHURCH OF THE ANNUNCIATION, CRUSADER (single-hatched), BYZANTINE (cross-hatched), AND ROMAN (black) STRATA (AFTER BAGATTI)

rated with a red-and-black tessaraed wreath or crown in three concentric circles with what look like ribbons hanging from the base. In its center was a monogram cross very similar to the *chi-rho* abbreviation for *Christos* and the symbol that Constantine saw in a vision and carried on his military standards against the rival emperor Maxentius at the battle of the Milvian Bridge on October 28, 312 C.E.

The mosaic's symbol of Christian triumph was built on top of two meters of debris, within which an earlier structure's architectural elements were found: two unadorned capitals, several crudely hewn column shafts, and five column bases, as well as arch imposts, cornices, thresholds, and doorjambs. These *may* have been the remains of a Jewish synagogue atop which the church was imposed, as reported in the itineraries of some Christian pilgrims. Their style is typical of Jewish synagogues in the third century C.E. and later in Galilee and their workmanship more akin to that of the Late Roman Period; none of the ceramic material accompanying them in the fill suggests a date earlier than the third or fourth century. Even if it were a synagogue, it could not have been from the time of Jesus, but from centuries later, when synagogues were being built across Galilee.

In fact, not a single synagogue from the first century or earlier has been found in Galilee. Only one synagogue from a Jewish village or town has been found from the time of Jesus, at Gamla in the Golan. Two other likely synagogues from the first century have been excavated in Judea, at the Herodion and Masada, but both were structures built into earlier Herodian complexes by Jewish rebels who occupied them during the revolt in 66–74. They were not originally synagogues, but rooms converted for communal use by those rebels.

Excavations and inscriptions testify to first-century synagogue buildings in the Jewish diaspora at urban sites across the Mediterranean basin and in the Near East. They were usually called, in Greek, *proseuche*, or "house of prayer," and they served the religious and communal needs of expatriate Jews. With the Temple far away and priests and sacrifices a remote concept, these buildings kept Jewish identity alive at Sabbath meetings in a world of pagan civic religion and imperial cults. But in the Jewish homeland at the time of Jesus, the term *synagogue* referred primarily to a *gathering*, and less so to a *building* with an accompanying, well-defined liturgy. The architectural and liturgical features developed in a more standardized form in Roman Palestine only after the destruction of the Temple in the Middle and Late Roman Periods, when Jewish religion began to focus on scrolls and rabbis. There certainly were *synagogues* (the *knesset* of the Mishnah) in the villages of Galilee at the time of Jesus, *gatherings* of Jews for communal and religious purposes, but who knows what their architectural form looked like. Not all would have been in structures like the one at Gamla. Perhaps many gatherings took place in the village square, and others in courtyards or rooms of a villager's large house, each of which would be indistinguishable to archaeologists in their function as a synagogue. Perhaps some larger villages or towns in Galilee had proper synagogue buildings in the first century, either modest structures built at communal expense or more conspicuous structures built with the aid of patrons' donations, but they are somewhat elusive in the archaeological record or, apart from Gamla, yet to be found by archaeologists.

In places like Nazareth there were no doubt synagogues in the sense of village gatherings and assemblies. But the only evidence for a synagogue-as-building at Nazareth postdates Jesus by some two centuries. The synagogue *building* that Jesus might have visited cannot be discussed with any archaeological credibility, since there is no evidence whatsoever for any public architectural structure in the hamlet from Jesus' time or before. But that conclusion from archaeological layering raises an interesting problem in exegetical layering.

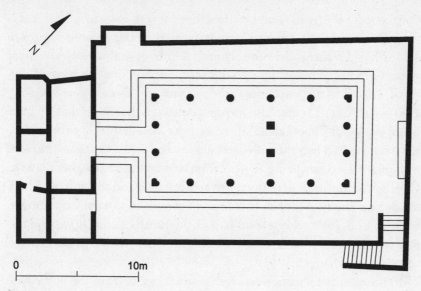

THE FIRST-CENTURY SYNAGOGUE AT GAMLA (AFTER MAOZ)

IN THE SYNAGOGUE AT NAZARETH?

The story of Jesus' rejection at Nazareth in Luke 4:16–30 advances through five consecutive steps: synagogue situation, scriptural fulfillment, initial acceptance, eventual rejection, and, finally, lethal attack.

In the synagogue situation Luke seems to presuppose not just synagogue-as-gathering, but synagogue-as-building. In the scriptural fulfillment Luke's Jesus enters the synagogue, reads a section from the prophet Isaiah (61:1–2), and announces that he is its fulfillment, he himself is the promised one anointed by the Spirit of God to bring good news to the poor, to proclaim release to the captives, to give sight to the blind, and to let the oppressed go free. Those phrases echo the commands of Torah, the imperatives of divine law in places like Deuteronomy 15, Exodus 21, and Leviticus 25. In the Sabbath Year, every seventh year, remission of debts and freedom of enslaved debtors were commanded. In the Jubilee Year, every fiftieth year, a return of all expropriated peasant lands and rural houses was commanded.

In the initial acceptance, after Jesus announces that magnificent vision as fulfilled among them "today," their immediate reaction is this: "All spoke well of him and were amazed at the gracious words that came from his mouth. They said, 'Is not this Joseph's son?'" (4:22). The first half of that verse is very positive and, within that context, the second half reads more like amazed wonder than incipient rejection. But that all changes in 4:23–29, and it seems deliberately provoked by Jesus himself, who, as it were, turns from present Jews to distant Gentiles. First, he himself suggests: "Doubtless you will quote to me this proverb, 'Doctor, cure yourself!' And you will say, 'Do here also in your hometown the things that we have heard you did at Capernaum.'" That suggests a challenge they themselves have not made. Then the provocation gets worse. Jesus cites two ancient examples of God turning, as it were, from Israelites to pagans, from Jews to Gentiles. In the first half of the ninth century, God had the prophet Elijah assuage the famine not of an Israelite, but of a pagan woman, according to 1 Kings 17:8–16. In the second half of the ninth century, God had the prophet Elisha cure the leprosy not of an Israelite, but of a pagan general, according to 2 Kings 5:1–14.

In the eventual rejection and lethal attack, we find out the immediate result of Jesus' provocative examples. "When they heard this, all in the synagogue were filled with rage. They got up, drove him out of the town, and led him to the brow of the hill on which their town was built, so that they might hurl him off the cliff. But he passed through the midst of them and went on his way" (4:28–30). In that case, Jesus' turn from Jews to Gentiles is cause rather than effect of eventual rejection and lethal attack.

This is the crucial layering question. Is that story a later-layer creation in the gospel of Luke or an earlier-layer incident in the life of Jesus? In other words did Luke himself invent that incident at Nazareth? Notice, by the way, that the incident is recorded only in Luke, although it is undoubtedly his own very creative and particular expansion of the general story in Mark 6:2–4.

The main argument for a Lukan creation is that Luke placed this story as programmatic overture to his twin-volume composition, which our present New Testament has renamed and separated as the gospel of Luke and the Acts of the Apostles. Luke's two-volume gospel tells how the Holy Spirit took Jesus from Galilee to Jerusalem in the first volume and then the church from Jerusalem to Rome in the second one. It took two volumes to announce the Lukan good news that the Holy Spirit had moved headquarters from east to west and that Rome had replaced Jerusalem.

In the course of those two volumes, and most especially in the context of the second one, Luke explains how Christianity began as a Jewish message to fellow Jews, how most Jews rejected it, and how, only then and therefore, Christianity turned to pagans in replacement. That, by the way, is simplification at best, distortion at worst, and it often strains against the very stories Luke tells to exemplify it. In any case, to sustain his principle of first Jews (rejection) and then Gentiles (replacement), Luke has Paul start always and everywhere at each city's Jewish synagogue in the Acts of the Apostles. That, actually, contradicts the agreement made at Jerusalem that Peter would lead the mission for Jews and Paul that for Gentiles, as emphasized in Galatians 2:7–9. It also contradicts Luke's own accounts in which there is often confusion between Jewish rejection preceding as a condition or following as a result from pagan inclusion. Did Christianity turn to pagans because of Jewish rejection or did Jewish rejection ("jealousy") derive from pagan acceptance? That ambiguity stalks the Lukan Paul in Acts and began with the Lukan Jesus in Luke 4:16–30. The rejection in that story was created precisely as advance warning for that future one or, to repeat from above, as programmatic overture to Luke's twin-volume gospel.

That Lukan story, complete with its ambiguity concerning Jewish rejection as cause or effect of Gentile mission, is an inaugural model for what will happen to Paul wherever he goes in the Jewish diaspora. For example, those five stages repeat themselves with Paul at Pisidian Antioch, today in west-central Turkey, or Thessalonica, today in northeastern Greece. Here, for example, are the parallel sequences in tabular summary:

Literary Elements	Jesus in Luke 4:16–30	Paul in Acts 13:14–52	Paul in Acts 17:1–9
synagogue situation	4:16–17	13:14–16a	17:1–2
scriptural fulfillment	4:18–21	13:16b–41	17:2b–3
initial acceptance	4:22	13:42–43	17:4
eventual rejection	4:23–28	13:44–49	17:5
lethal attack	4:29–30	13:50–52	17:5b–9

Notice how, with Paul as with Jesus, there is a blur at the heart of the story as initial acceptance changes to eventual rejection. In Acts 13:42–45:

As Paul and Barnabas were going out, the people urged them to speak about these things again the next sabbath. When the meeting of the synagogue broke up, many Jews and devout converts to Judaism followed Paul and Barnabas, who spoke to them and urged them to continue in the grace of God. The next sabbath almost the whole city gathered to hear the word of the Lord. But when the Jews saw the crowds, they were filled with jealousy; and blaspheming, they contradicted what was spoken by Paul.

And again in Acts 17:4–5a:

Some of them were persuaded and joined Paul and Silas, as did a great many of the devout Greeks and not a few of the leading women. But the Jews became jealous, and with the help of some ruffians in the marketplaces they formed a mob and set the city in an uproar.

It was all about jealousy, but jealousy over what? Why would Jews in a diaspora city be jealous over pagans converting to some form or even any form of Judaism? "Jealousy" is surely not an adequate explanation. There is, of course, no problem with the presence of Jewish synagogue buildings in those diaspora cities, but Luke has simply retrojected his own later experience of them back into the Palestinian locale, earlier time, and humbler place of Jesus' Nazareth.

Luke also presumes that a tiny hamlet like Nazareth had both a synagogue building and scrolls of scripture. The first presumption is most unlikely and, as noted above, no evidence for a first-century synagogue building was discovered at Nazareth. The second presupposition is questionable—scrolls were mostly an urban privilege and, most likely, lectionary readings came later. A third presupposition, that there was some nearby cliff from which a miscreant could be hurled to death, is simply false.

But, more important, Luke also presumes that Jesus is not only literate, but learned. He does not simply "begin to teach" (Mark 6:2), he "stood up to read" (Luke 4:16). Luke, himself a learned scholar, takes it utterly for granted, as do many modern scholars, that Jesus was literate and learned. That is very unlikely. The best general work on ancient literacy in the Mediterranean basin concludes about a 5 percent literacy rate. The best specific work on ancient literacy in the Jewish homeland concludes about a 3 percent literacy rate. In that world, as mentioned earlier, literacy was the prerogative of elite aristocrats, trained retainers, and scribal experts. If Jesus was an illiterate peasant, as one would expect from his Nazareth origins, that does not mean he could not think, does not mean he did not know his tradition, and does not mean he did not teach. It just means he did not read. It just means he was more likely to concentrate on the core of his tradition than on its footnotes.

In any case, those later Lukan stories about Paul help us understand the Lukan story about Jesus. That story is not only *in*, it is also *from* a later layer of the Jesus tradition. It is, in other words, an incident created by the evangelist Luke himself. It is, as presented, not history from Jesus' past in the Jewish homeland of the late 20s, but parable for Paul's future in the Jewish diaspora of the early 50s.

All of that serves to vindicate the importance of layering analysis not just in an archaeological mound, but also in a gospel text. Luke is not telling a lie and does not intentionally defame the people of Nazareth. He retrojects the serious and even lethal opposition to Paul in the later Jewish diaspora onto the earlier experience of Jesus in the Jewish homeland. But it is still a very dangerous parable, for one might well wonder something like this. Even granting some provocation on the part of Jesus, he was still summarizing scriptural content. What sort of people were those inhabitants of Nazareth who, all together, decided to kill him for that? And could one move from "all Nazareth" to "all Israel"? Exegetical layering matters just as does archaeological layering.

NAZARETH AT THE TIME OF JESUS

Nazareth's monumental architecture, its ashlars and arch keystones hewn by skilled stonemasons, mosaic floors and frescoed walls, stone columns and pediments are clearly later, the result of Jesus' association with Nazareth, not indicative of Jesus' Nazareth. Across that ancient Nazareth inhabited in earlier times, including each of the areas excavated by the Franciscans, there is no evidence for public architecture of any kind whatsoever. None of the evidence beneath the modern, Crusader, or Byzantine strata from pits, crevices, or debris packed together for their foundations, suggests that first-century Nazareth was anything other than a modest village void of public architecture. The massive layer representing the Christian construction of *terra sancta*, Holy Land, rests atop a frail and elusive layer representing a simple Jewish peasant life: excavations underneath later Christian structures uncovered no synagogue, but also no fortification, no palace, no basilica, no bathhouse, no paved street, nothing. Instead, olive presses, wine presses, water cisterns, grain silos, and grinding stones scattered around caves tell of a population that lived in hovels and simple peasant houses.

First-century Nazareth was a small Jewish settlement with no more than two to four hundred inhabitants. Like the rest of Galilee, which lay relatively uninhabited until the Late Hellenistic Period, Jews settled it under Hasmonean expansionist policies. There is some evidence, mostly ceramic, not architectural, for its occupation in the Middle Bronze and Iron Age, but without continuity to the time of Jesus. The Assyrian Empire under Tiglath Pileser III invaded the Northern Kingdom of Israel in 732 B.C.E. and devastated as well as depopulated Galilee, including Nazareth. Other than a few way-stations along roads, Galilee was virtually uninhabited from the eighth to the second century B.C.E., when Jews repopulated it.

Alexander the Great's sweep across the eastern Mediterranean broke Persian hegemony, and after Alexander's death, his generals carved up his kingdom, with Palestine becoming a buffer zone between the Ptolemaic dynasty in Egypt and the Seleucid dynasty in Syria. After these dynasties were weakened by a succession of wars with each other, a power vacuum was created in the second century B.C.E. This period witnessed considerable movement of peoples, including the movement of Jews into Galilee. Elsewhere, the Syro-Phoenicians extended their control along the Palestinian coast and moved inland to the Huleh Valley. The Itureans, a more nomadic and pastoral people, moved from the Ante-Lebanon toward the northern Golan. Neither group's pottery or housing styles have been uncovered in Galilee, but beginning in the late second century B.C.E., numerous settlements appear across Galilee with coins from the Jerusalem-based Hasmoneans in their foundations and with a material culture similar to that of Judea. Pottery forms and types were similar; both Judea and Galilee used stone vessels; villages contained stepped, plastered pools, or ritual baths; the people's diets avoided pork; and they practiced secondary burial as bones were gathered into ossuaries, or bone boxes.

The people of Nazareth at the time of Jesus were Jews, very likely the descendants of Hasmonean colonizers or Jewish settlers who migrated there over a century earlier. The spot was ideally situated, somewhat secluded and nestled in a bowl atop the Nazareth Range, which separates the Nahal Zippori and Beit Netofah Valley to the north from the much larger Jezreel Valley to the south. The latter was a vast and fertile plain that was alternatively part of royal estates ("king's land") or controlled by the Hellenistic city of Scythopolis, formerly Beth-Shean, the largest city in the area. Under later Roman rule Scythopolis was combined with several cities east of the Jordan River into the semi-autonomous Decapolis region.

An upward incline from the Jezreel Valley to Nazareth limited travel to winding footpaths, lessening Nazareth's interaction with the large royal estates or Scythopolis's countryside toward the south. Travel along the range's east-west axis was more inviting, possibly on well-beaten paths, since Galilee's major road went from Tiberias on the Sea of Galilee to Ptolemais on the Mediterranean along the Beit Netofah Valley, just north of Sepphoris. The site of Sepphoris was some 4 miles from Nazareth, about an hour-and-a-half walk away along a short climb over the hill's crest, a steep descent, and then a sloping incline.

The Hasmonean authorities had fortified the site of Sepphoris to overlook the valleys and control the trade routes, and the Romans, recognizing its strategic importance, appointed one of the Jewish councils there when they came on the political scene in 63 B.C.E. After Herod the Great's death in 4 B.C.E., some Jews rallied at Sepphoris against foreign rule and taxation, but were quickly crushed by the Syrian-based Roman legate. Subsequently, Herod Antipas rebuilt it into Galilee's largest city and made it the first capital of the lands he inherited from his father. At the time of Jesus, Nazareth was in the shadow of Sepphoris and under Herod Antipas's political control.

Nazareth's position in the hills south of Sepphoris was well suited for the Mediterranean dietary triad of grain, olive, and grape, the hallmark of an ancient site's agricultural objective of self-sufficiency. The south-facing slopes over which the village's houses spread were ideal for viticulture; vines with deep blue grapes were grown on trellises or on the ground and seasonally cut back with pruning hooks, then harvested and trampled in rock-cut basins scattered on the hills. The ravines in the slope and the rockier ground were suitable for clusters of trees whose olives were gathered, crushed with large grinding stones, pitted, and pressed for oil. The fields on the slopes could grow the various grains—wheat, barley, and millet, whose chaff was separated on threshing floors with winnowing forks and whose kernels were ground in family courtyards. The alluvial soil spreading south of the village was sufficiently fertile for vegetables and legumes. Terraces built and irrigated along the steeper slopes maximized the grain harvests and could also support fig and pomegranate trees. An adequate but not perennial water source was located at the western edge of the village, now called the Well of Mary, and trickled along the length of the village, giving the people of ancient Nazareth the ability to grow their own food.

The village in the first century was small. The area within which the Franciscan excavators found evidence from the Roman Period was limited to the vicinity around the two churches and toward the Well of Mary. The discovery of many underground tombs, chiseled in typical Jewish fashion into the soft limestone bedrock, helps delineate the village's perimeter to the west, east, and south, since burial was customarily outside of inhabited areas. Steep ravines and ancient terraces on the northern slope confined the ovoid-shaped settlement. It would have been 2,000 feet at its greatest east-west length and around 650 feet at its greatest north-south width, though the actual area inhabited in the first century was much less, perhaps only around ten acres. The site's agrarian character necessitated ample space between the houses for livestock and their enclosures, as well as gardens and orchards or communally shared agricultural facilities, yielding a relatively low population density. Nazareth would have had a population of around two to four hundred in antiquity, that is to say, several extended families or clans.

There's not much evidence for first-century Nazareth's houses, an absence indicative of their modesty. Had their roofs been tiled, their walls constructed with nicely hewn limestone, their floors fitted with flat stone pavers or mosaics, their walls plastered or frescoed, they would have been apparent to the Franciscan excavators. Instead, we must assume that they were—like homes in other villages of the Galilee and Golan—simply constructed with unhewn fieldstones, which were stacked atop each other, held together by smaller stones packed into the interstices, and smeared with clay, mud, or even dung mixed with straw for insulation. Floors were of packed dirt or beaten earth. The absence of arches, girders, and roof tiles implies that the roofs were thatched, with wooden ceiling beams supporting a thick bed of straw or reeds, which protected the beams from dampness and was itself covered with packed mud for insulation. Many of the houses had subterranean cavities. There were bell-shaped cisterns for storing water to compensate for the lack of a perennial spring, other plastered cisterns would have been used to store grain, and many dwellings were built around caves that were used for living space. Such was the case at the Grotto of the Annunciation, whose original use was domestic.

There is no way of knowing, by the way, whether this was, in fact, Mary's house. The many constructions around the grotto and the invocations etched in plaster show that it was revered by Christians from the third or fourth century on, but whether it accurately marks a spot where Mary lived is pure speculation. But the spot is important, if not for the reasons pilgrims suppose: the semi-troglodyte dwelling underscores the humble status of the first-century hamlet. Lots of Nazareth houses incorporated caves into their dwellings, thereby taking advantage of temperate conditions, dry and warm in the rainy winters, cool and pleasant in the hot summers.

The small finds and artifacts in the fill of these subterranean cavities prior to the Byzantine Period, along with the artifacts deposited in the hamlet's tombs, are unanimously modest. Only a handful of coins—bronze, not silver—have been found in the tombs, and very few contained decorative items—mostly cheap jewelry—unlike other burial sites nearby or in Judea. Very little glass from before the Byzantine Period has been found at Nazareth, whether cups or chalices, ointment bottles or perfume vases, and bronze or other metal cups and bowls are absent. The pottery from the Late Hellenistic and Roman Periods is almost entirely locally made and utilitarian—decorated or even simple serving bowls are rare. The assemblage consists of coarse cooking pots, casserole dishes, water jugs, and storage jars. Imported amphorae with stamped handles from the Greek isles of Rhodes or Knidos, which have been discovered at larger cities like Scythopolis or coastal Caesarea, as well as in Herod's Judean palaces, are absent at Nazareth. So are imported fine-wares, lustrous plates and bowls from kilns in Cyprus and North Africa, which do appear here in later periods when Christian pilgrimage to the Holy Land brought both wealth and goods to Nazareth. Then, instead of wine amphorae, cross-stamped serving plates were common.

All the archaeological evidence from the Roman Period points to a simple peasant existence at Nazareth. It also points to a *Jewish* Nazareth. Each of its many tombs is like those typically Jewish burial chambers discussed in chapter one: initial burial was in so-called *kokhim* or *loculi*, body-length shafts cut at right angles into the walls of the tomb chamber, which was often sealed with a large stone rolled into place. Unlike in Jerusalem and its environs where ossuaries were the norm, in Galilee, for the most part, bones from which the flesh had decayed were gathered into one of the shafts or a separate pitlike repository. Two stepped, plastered pools, or ritual baths (*miqwaoth*), were also found by the Franciscan archaeologists at Nazareth. Used for ritual-purity immersion by Jews, they are found at virtually every Jewish site in Galilee, the Golan, and Judea. Although one likely dates to the third century C.E. and was near the area where fragments of that possible later synagogue were found, the other was probably a shared facility used by the villagers. Several fragments of stone vessels from the Roman Period, carved from soft limestone or chalk and typical of Jewish homes in Judea and Galilee, were also discovered at Nazareth.

The tiny village of Nazareth, off the main road, over the hill but still within walking distance of the city of Sepphoris, was Jesus' home. The peasant families there hoped to eke out a living, pay their taxes, have enough left over to survive, and avoid attention from officials. The families there were also observantly Jewish as can be seen from the archeological data. Presumably, therefore, they also circumcised their sons, celebrated Passover, took a day from work on the Sabbath, and valued the traditions of Moses and the prophets.

THE EXEGETICAL LAYERS OF NAZARETH STORY

No individuals, professional or nonprofessional, would look at modern Nazareth and think it told them anything about the hamlet where Jesus lived. There, the need for discerning layers is self-evident to anyone. Somewhere down there, below cars and buses, houses and hotels, lies hidden a tiny two-thousand-year-old village. What we glimpse beneath a modern church only confirms the difficult reconstruction facing our contemporary imagination. Allowing, of course, for all the obvious differences between layers of ground and layers of text, do gospel stories about Nazareth also demand a parallel excavation to distinguish earlier and later strata, or can it be presumed that they are always Layer I, as it were? One case was examined above, and it was proposed that the synagogue story in Luke 4 was not the earliest layer from the life of the historical Jesus, but a later layer from the pen of the historical Luke. Before moving now to a second and even more complicated example of exegetical layering within a story, a reminder may be useful.

Recall those first top ten textual discoveries discussed in our Introduction. Because of them and despite all sorts of continuing debates, there is now a massive consensus that the words and deeds attributed to Jesus in our New Testament gospels fall into major layers built successively one

RECONSTRUCTION OF FIRST-CENTURY NAZARETH. *The hometown of Jesus was a Jewish peasant village with some two hundred inhabitants in the first century. Like most Galileans, the people of Nazareth eked out a living off the land. The ridge's sunny southern slopes were ideal for vineyards, where wine presses (1) and collection vats (2) were cut right into bedrock, shown here with pruning hooks (3) and Galilean-made storage jars (4) uncovered at Nazareth. Vegetables, legumes, and grains were spread along a dale irrigated by a spring (5), today commemorated as the Well of Mary, and olive trees were cultivated on the slopes of the rockier soil, where also pigeons were raised in towerlike columbaria (6). The Jewish village lay in anonymity until the conversion of the Roman Empire to Christianity made it a popular pilgrim destination.*

upon (that is, over, under, around, and through) another. Think of them as, first, the *original* layer, coming from Jesus' own words and deeds in the 20s; next, as the *traditional* layer, coming from the tradition's adoption, adaptation, and creation of those materials in the 30s, 40s, or even later; and, finally, as the *evangelical* layer in the gospels we now possess from the 70s through the 90s. Note that, as mentioned at the end of the Introduction, it is not just a question of being later than an earlier text, but of being directly dependent upon it. Obviously, all dependent texts are later, but not all later texts are dependent.

The First Layer. Layer I contains materials that go back to the historical Jesus in the late 20s. It is always, of course, a scholarly reconstruction, a decision through explicit theory, disciplined method, and public debate on what in the Jesus tradition goes back to Jesus himself. In this book we will concentrate not just on isolated units from that proposed first layer but on the major earliest "chunks" to see if and how they fit with the situation of the late 20s in Antipas's territories. We emphasize that such layering presumes prior conclusions about the nature and relationship of the gospels as good news for a community's life.

The Second Layer.   Layer II contains materials either adopted from that earlier layer or else created by and within the ongoing tradition. It too involves scholarly reconstruction and includes such items as the following: when Paul, writing in the 50s, identifies something explicitly or implicitly as pre-Pauline tradition, that pushes such materials back toward the 40s or even 30s. Also, tradition found in two independent sources, such as the Q Gospel, also from the 50s, and any other independent gospel, be it inside the New Testament as with Mark, or outside the New Testament as with the *Gospel of Thomas* or the *Didache,* points back to earlier layers. Such double and independent vectors point back to oral or written materials from the 30s or 40s and possibly from the historical Jesus himself.

The Third Layer.   Layer III is crucial because it contains three internal sub-layers, or levels. (In an archaeological mound these could be designated as Stratum IIIa, IIIb, and IIIc.) The first level of Layer III contains the Q Gospel and Mark, spanning the late 50s to the early 70s. The second level, most probably dependent on those two preceding gospels, contains Matthew and Luke, from the 80s. The third level, quite possibly dependent on Mark, Matthew, and Luke, is the gospel of John. That canonical process is, by the way, our most secure evidence for layering as a gospel phenomenon.

Finally, of course, any other texts, such as the *Gospel of Peter,* must be studied in similar fashion. What internal layers are discernable within it and where do such layers intersect with the three major ones just mentioned?

Beneath those three distinct layers is an even more basic one. It is less a layer than a matrix, an environment, a tradition interacting with a situation. Think of this parallel. Below the archaeological strata of an ancient mound lies the bedrock, the foundation, the ground. It is not just a passive given, but much more like an ever active presence. The topography of Jerusalem, for example, was not just ground, but destiny, whether for military defense or sacred edifice. So also with those three exegetical layers. Beneath them as ground and always interacting with them as presence is Jewish experience as an ancient and venerable tradition that struggled hard against the overweening pride of Greek cultural internationalism and the overwhelming arrogance of Roman military imperialism. In this book, we will be especially concerned with the dialectic between that ground and the original layer of the textual tradition, with understanding the historical Jesus as he lived in the false quiet immediately after horror's prelude in 4 B.C.E. and decades before horror's consummation in 66–74 C.E.

Separating the overlaid levels in a text is sometimes little more than an interesting exercise. It may establish accuracy rather than importance. With Luke 4:16–30 above, the conclusion was not just that early first-century Nazareth had no synagogue building, no scrolls of Law and Prophets, no literate and learned peasants, no nearby cliff, but also, and more important, no murderous inhabitants. Jesus' home villagers had never attempted to kill him. That story came, not from the original level of Stratum I, but from the Lukan level of Stratum IIIb. That conclusion was worth the trouble, not only for historical accuracy, but also for the honor and dignity of a tiny Jewish hamlet in a small country long, long ago. Jesus did not grow up in a village of killers.

After those villagers in Luke, here are two other cases involving the Nazareth of Jesus. One concerns his family, and especially James, in Mark. The other concerns his parents, and especially Mary, in Matthew. In that second and much more involved case, watch how stories, other stories, and counterstories interact together and build narratives layered with textual interaction. The result is a narrative intertextuality as dense and diverse as any archaeological stratigraphy.

A Brother in Disbelief?

In a passing remark, unfortunately terse and unfortunately influential, John 7:5 said of Jesus that, "not even his brothers believed in him." That indictment includes James the Just of Jerusalem, James the brother of Christ the Lord, James the center of the ossuary debate. If James did not believe in Jesus, one might explain his conversion from the risen apparition mentioned by Paul in 1 Corinthians 15 and noted in the preceding chapter. But the noncanonical *Gospel of the Hebrews* 7 said nothing about prior disbelief. There, to the contrary, James was at the Last Supper and had so believed in the eventual resurrection of Jesus that he "had sworn that he would not eat bread from that hour in which he had drunk the cup of the Lord until he should see him risen from among them that sleep." Once again, then, the question of textual layers and gospel strata arises: Is John 7:5 Layer I from the time and history of Jesus or Layer IIIc from the time and theology of John? And, since John's comment is so short, that points the question back to two longer narratives in Mark on which John may well be dependent: Do Mark 6:1–6 and 3:19–35 represent Layer I from Jesus in the late 20s or Layer IIIa from Mark in the early 70s?

Labor Against Wisdom. The story in Mark 6:1–6 says that those who heard Jesus "in his own country," that is, Nazareth, did not believe in him but dismissed him with disdain:

> They said, "Where did this man get all this? What is this wisdom that has been given to him? What deeds of power are being done by his hands! Is not this the carpenter, the son of Mary and brother of James and Joses and Judas and Simon, and are not his sisters here with us?"

That text, of course, is where we find Jesus' named brothers and unnamed sisters. James is mentioned first among those six or more siblings. But "they said" in that dismissal refers to the "many in the synagogue who heard him." The connotation in that sneer is that both Jesus' occupation and Jesus' family are so insignificant that the hearers "took offense at him." Absolutely nothing there tells us that Jesus' own family, let alone James, disbelieved in him. It is the villagers, not the family, that are specifically cited as unbelievers. But, of course, that later text in Mark 6 must be read along with this earlier one in Mark 3.

Blood Against Faith. What we have in Mark 3:19–35 is a classic case of what scholars call a Markan intercalation or, more colloquially, a Markan sandwich. This is a literary device intended to make a theological point and it works like this. A first incident begins (unit A1), a second incident interrupts (unit B), and the first incident is then finished (unit A2). The function of the dualism is to create a dynamic interaction so that each event comments on the other and the reader has to ponder how exactly the interpretive dialectic works. For example: Jesus' truthful and courageous confession in Mark 14:55–65 is framed within Peter's untruthful and cowardly denial in Mark 14:54 and 14:66–72. This the intercalation (or sandwich) in 3:19–35:

> (A1)   Mark 3:19–21   the family of Jesus
>   (B) Mark 3:22–30   the scribes from Jerusalem
> (A2)   Mark 3:31–35   the family of Jesus

What is the point? That internal section in 3:22–27 is about as inimical as possible. In it "the scribes who came from Jerusalem" declare that Jesus is possessed and exorcizes demons only under demonic influence. He mocks them in rebuttal by declaring that Satan must then be divided and destroyed, but also accuses them of the unforgivable sin against the Holy Spirit because "they had said, 'He has an unclean spirit.'" Now, in dialectic with that attack from others and rebuttal by Jesus, read those frames concerning his family.

But those most inimical scribes are now framed by an equally inimical family, and the purpose of the Markan intercalation is precisely to create that effect. The opening frame of the family unit in 3:19–21 says that,

> Then he went home; and the crowd came together again, so that they could not even eat. When his family heard it, they went out to restrain him, for people were saying, "He has gone out of his mind."

Note that, in the ancient world, insanity and possession are very close to one another so that, in effect, Mark makes the scribal and familial opposition almost synonymous. And the closing frame of the family unit in 3:31–35 comes immediately after Jesus' indictment of the scribes who said he had an unclean spirit in 3:27. But, apart from the opening family frame, the closing family frame is far less inimical:

> Then his mother and his brothers came; and standing outside, they sent to him and called him. A crowd was sitting around him; and they said to him, "Your mother and your brothers and sisters are outside, asking for you." And he replied, "Who are my mother and my

brothers?" And looking at those who sat around him, he said, "Here are my mother and my brothers! Whoever does the will of God is my brother and sister and mother."

In itself, all that story does is exalt faith over blood and extol theological over biological kinship. But when 3:19–21 prefaces 3:31–35, it reads as if family and Jesus reject one another. Notice, by the way, that in 3:31–35 *mother and brothers* (thrice) is expanded by Mark into *mother, brothers, and sisters* (twice). That makes it impossible not to combine in one's mind the *mother, brothers, and sisters* of 3:31–35 and 6:1–6. When all of that is read in sequence and combination, the clear impression is that Jesus' family (mother, brothers, and sisters) thought he was insane rather than divine.

Here is how, by contrast, another gospel tells that same story of the family's arrival and Jesus' reaction to them. It is from the *Gospel of Thomas* 99, a text not present in the New Testament but discovered in 1945 at Nag Hammadi in Upper Egypt.

> The disciples said to him, "Your brothers and your mother are standing outside." He said to them, "Those here who do what my Father wants are my brothers and my mother. They are the ones who will enter my Father's kingdom."

That, of course, also exalts faith over blood, and theology over biology, but there is no hint of any insanity problem and no mention of the sisters.

Our conclusion is that the whole indictment of Jesus' family for disbelief (and worse, for their suspicion of his insanity) is not from Jesus' Level I in the late 20s but from Mark's Level IIIa in the early 70s. Indeed, it fits with a major emphasis in Mark's theology, namely, that those closest to Jesus failed him most dismally: his fellow villagers, his family, his disciples, and even the Twelve, but especially Peter, climaxing with his denial at the trial of Jesus. The point is not that among Jesus' family, James, for example, was an unbeliever or was converted from unbelief, but rather that Mark's gospel records part of that opposition to James that we saw stretching from Paul's Galatian epistle to the *Clementine Recognitions* in the preceding chapter. Far from being an unbeliever in Jesus, James was an important enough believer to have begotten all of that intra-Christian opposition to his faith, his authority, and maybe even his fraternal relationship with Jesus.

A Mother in Adultery?

Sometime just before 180 C.E. a Greek philosopher named Celsus wrote a polemical critique of Christianity called *On the True Doctrine* in which he defended the truth of classical paganism. His original book is lost and known only from a detailed Christian rebuttal, *Against Celsus*, written by Origen of Alexandria in the middle of the next century. This is Celsus's scathing commentary on the conception of Jesus:

> Let us imagine what a Jew—let alone a philosopher—might put to Jesus: "Is it not true, good sir, that you fabricated the story of your birth from a virgin to quiet rumors about the true and unsavory circumstances of your origins? Is it not the case that far from being born in royal David's city of Bethlehem, you were born in a poor country town, and of a woman who earned her living by spinning? Is it not the case that when her deceit was discovered, to wit, that she was pregnant by a Roman soldier named Panthera she was driven away by her husband—the carpenter—and convicted of adultery? Indeed, is it not so that in her disgrace, wandering far from home, she gave birth to a male child in silence and humiliation? What more? Is it not so that you hired yourself out as a workman in Egypt, learned magical crafts, and gained something of a name for yourself which now you flaunt among your kinsmen?"

That accusation is *in* a layer even later than the third, or *evangelical*, layer seen above in discussing Luke 4:16–30. But the question is, once again, does it come *from* the much later layer or is it found there from the earliest one? What, in other words, does it tell us about the conception of Jesus?

Celsus's accusation is not just later than but dependent on the third, or *evangelical*, layer as represented by Matthew's gospel. The crucial clue is not the mention of a Bethlehem birth, found also in Luke, or even of Egypt, found only in Matthew. It is in that identification of "her husband—the carpenter." Mark 6:3 had called Jesus himself "the carpenter," but, in copying from Mark, Matthew changed that to "the carpenter's son" (13:55). He probably found that occupation unsuitable for Jesus, as did Luke, who omitted it completely. But that helps us to see that Celsus's knowledge of Jesus' conception comes specifically from Matthew and nowhere else. But it does not seem to come thence directly. Notice that he "imagines" it as coming from a Jewish opponent of Christianity and, indeed, that criticism is well known within later Jewish tradition. Most likely, therefore, its origins were within intra-Jewish polemics between non-Christian Jews and Christian Jews. In other words, the claim of virginal conception was not a cover-up for adulterous conception made by Christian Jews. It was exactly the opposite. The accusation of adulterous conception was a rebuttal of virginal conception made by non-Christian Jews.

Consider such polemics for a moment before proceeding. In the ancient world, rhetoricians attacked philosophers and philosophers attacked one another, pagans attacked Jews and Jews attacked one another, Jews attacked Christians and Christians attacked one another. Their name-calling was termed *vituperatio*, and we recognize it today as character assassination, negative campaigning, and polemical advertising. In all such strife, accuracy and truth yield swiftly to libel and slander. Christian Jews called non-Christian Jews nitpickers, legalists, hypocrites, and "whitened sepulchers." Non-Christian Jews called Jesus a demoniac, a Samaritan, a glutton, and a drunkard. That is simply name-calling, not character description. There should be no more historical discussion of the Pharisees as hypocritical than of Jesus as possessed. But there is also another process called story-mongering. It is, in its own way, far nastier than simple name-calling, but no more accurate, then or now. And that is what we are encountering in the present case. Story and claim beget antistory and counterclaim.

From Moses to Jesus

The accusation of Celsus may strike many Christians as profoundly offensive. But we must remember that Joseph was the first one to imagine that Jesus' conception was 'adulterous and Matthew was the first person to recount that suspicion in his own gospel. Matthew's infancy story of Jesus is told primarily from the viewpoint of Joseph, just as Luke's is told from that of Mary. For example, in Matthew it is Joseph who receives the annunciation, not Mary as in Luke. But, although Matthew's Joseph raises the question of adultery, there is nothing whatsoever about such a possibility in the birth story of Luke 1:26–38. Luke, like Matthew, knows that Mary was engaged to Joseph. But then in Luke, and only in Luke, the angel announces to her that she will conceive the Son of God by overshadowing of the Holy Spirit. In Luke, the reader is allowed to presume, and must presume, that she went and told Joseph what had happened and that he believed just as fully as she did. But that is not Matthew's account. Here, instead, is how he tells that incident, in 1:18–25:

> When his mother Mary had been engaged to Joseph, but before they lived together, she was found to be with child from the Holy Spirit. Her husband Joseph, being a righteous man and unwilling to expose her to public disgrace, planned to dismiss her quietly. But just when he had resolved to do this, an angel of the Lord appeared to him in a dream and said, "Joseph, son of David, do not be afraid to take Mary as your wife, for the child conceived in her is from the Holy Spirit. She will bear a son, and you are to name him Jesus, for he will save his people from their sins.". . . When Joseph awoke from sleep, he did as the angel of the Lord commanded him; he took her as his wife, but had no marital relations with her until she had borne a son; and he named him Jesus.

As far as we can tell, Galilean custom was more strict than Judean on sexual relations for a couple between the initial engagement, which established a legal right, and the final ceremony, which established a common home. But even in Galilee, villagers would have presumed that Mary's pregnancy came not from fornication or adultery, but from a slightly ahead-of-time marital consummation. Apart from Mary, only Joseph knew whether that could have been the explanation. Note, by the way, that, with adultery only affecting a husband's rights, Mary could not have committed adultery unless Joseph already had marriage rights over her.

Jesus' Conception in Matthew. But here is a simple question. Why on earth did Matthew tell the story that way? Why raise the specter of adultery even for a moment? Since they were already officially engaged, pregnancy, even if not exactly proper before Mary's move from her father's to her husband's home, would make nobody save Joseph suspect adultery. Eyebrows might rise and tongues might wag, but little else would happen, and it certainly would not make Jesus' conception adulterous. Even if Joseph divorced Mary and said nothing, neighbors would not necessarily presume adultery. And even if he claimed it, he might not be legally believed. Around the year 200 C.E., for example, the Jewish legal codification in the Mishnah recorded the following debate: "If a man says, 'This my son is a bastard,' he may not be believed. Even if they both said of the unborn child in her womb, 'It is a bastard,' they may not be believed. R. Judah says: They may be believed" (*Qiddushin* 4:8).

So why even raise the issue? Does Matthew know historical details that Luke does not know? Does he have special information about what went on, and went on for only a short time, in Joseph's mind? Or does Matthew have narrative purposes that Luke does not have? It is necessary to look very closely at the conception of Jesus as represented by Matthew. Otherwise, we must conclude that he has unnecessarily raised a possibility that has survived from ancient tradition to modern scholarship. But was Mary an adulteress and Jesus a bastard in historical reality, that is to say, in the first and original layer? And, if not, to repeat, what is Matthew doing in that infancy story and why does he raise, even as mistake and even for a moment, the possibility of divorce because of presumed adultery?

Moses and Jesus in Matthew.   At the start and end of Jesus' public life, Matthew places him on a mountain in Galilee. His final words to the disciples are given on "the mountain to which Jesus had directed them" (28:16). His inaugural words to them are what we call the Sermon on the Mount and what Matthew would probably have called the Renewed Law on the Renewed Mount Sinai. Jesus "went up the mountain" (5:1), said that he came "not to abolish the law or the prophets but to fulfill them" (5:17), and did so by intensifying the law to an ideal perfection in six striking antitheses. Reiterating an opening refrain, "You have heard that it was said to those of ancient times. . . . But I say to you . . . ," he forbade anger, lust, divorce, oaths, violence, and demanded universal love (5:21–48). Matthew's gospel sees Jesus as a new and even more ethically intransigent Moses atop a new and even more morally demanding Mount Sinai. With such a gospel, the content of its birth-story overture is already established. Matthew designed an infancy narrative, a birth story for Jesus, on the deliberate model of Moses.

Moses' Conception in Tradition.   Over a thousand years before the time of Jesus, Pharaoh had decreed, according to Exodus 1–2, that all newborn Jewish males must be killed to control the number of Jews on Egypt's northeastern frontier. Moses was already conceived and, after his birth, he was saved by Pharaoh's daughter, who reared him as an Egyptian. None of that looks particularly promising as a model for the infancy parallelism of

Moses and Jesus required for Matthew's overture to his gospel. But the Exodus story is so minimal that any decent storyteller would want to answer at least two obvious questions. Is it not a little too coincidental that Moses just happened to be born at that unfortunate moment of general male infanticide? Is it not strange that those Jewish parents did not choose divorce, separation, or at least celibacy to prevent male infanticide and female enslavement? Already by the first century C.E., popular expansions of Moses' birth story moved in to fill out those details, and that process of expansion would continue across the first millennium within Jewish tradition.

In that tradition such rewriting of a scriptural story could come from *haggadic midrashim*, commentaries both explaining and expanding narratives from the Hebrew scriptures, and/or from *targumim*, Aramaic commentaries translating, explaining, and expanding such tales. Ordinary people would know the original story primarily or exclusively as it was filtered through those continuing developments. For our present purpose, we focus on two sources that can be dated securely to the late first century, but, of course, they are transmitting rather than creating what they record. The *Jewish Antiquities* by the historian Josephus and the *Biblical Antiquities* by an anonymous author (called Pseudo-Philo because it was preserved among the works of the Alexandrian-born Jewish philosopher Philo) record the early stages of what would eventually become a small cottage industry of narrative improvements on that birth story of Moses. Think of that process as ongoing software upgrades, as it were, and notice that they focus around two points, the king's decree and the father's decision.

The King's Decree. First, with regard to Pharaoh's command. It was not, those expansions insist, that Moses just happened to be born after that degree of genocide was promulgated. One of Pharaoh's advisers warned of danger for Egypt from a soon-to-be-born Jewish child who would both threaten them and save his fellow Israelites, according to Josephus's *Jewish Antiquities*:

> While they were in this plight, a further incident had the effect of stimulating the Egyptians yet more to exterminate our race. One of the sacred scribes—persons with considerable skill in accurately predicting the future—announced to the king that there would be born to the Israelites at that time one who would abase the sovereignty of the Egyptians and exalt the Israelites, were he reared to manhood,

and would surpass all men in virtue and win everlasting renown. Alarmed thereat, the king, on this sage's advice, ordered that every male child born to the Israelites should be destroyed by being cast into the river. (2.205–6)

In other words, the general male infanticide is intended specifically to kill Moses-to-be. He is now at the center of the story and not just an accidental casualty of more general processes. Moses-to-be was the occasion and not just the accident of that general slaughter. Versions of that tradition known only in later texts have Pharaoh dreaming of a lamb outweighing all of Egypt and, in the morning, calling together his advisers for interpretation.

You can see immediately how much better the popular version is than the scriptural one for Matthew's purpose. Herod the Great is the new Pharaoh the Oppressor. Both receive learned advice about the soon-to-be-born child. Herod gets it from "all the chief priests and scribes of the people" in Matthew just as Pharaoh got it from "one of the sacred scribes" in Josephus. Both determine on a general male infanticide to destroy the destined child, be it Moses or Jesus.

The Father's Decision. Second, with regard to Amram's action. Once again the account in Exodus is skeletal at best. After Pharaoh's decree "a man from the house of Levi went and married a Levite woman" in Exodus 2:1 and Moses is conceived. Only later in 6:20 are they named as Amram and Jochebed. That is, once again, not very promising for a Moses-Jesus parallel. But, once again, the popular accounts are much more helpful for Matthew's purpose. Anyone reading that Exodus sequence of extermination decree and marriage ceremony might ask the obvious question: Why risk infanticide for males and servitude for female infants? Why marry or conceive? Why not separate or divorce? Both Josephus and Pseudo-Philo know traditional answers to those questions, and the difference between them indicates a fairly rich tradition already at work on the subject.

In Josephus's *Jewish Antiquities,* Amram and Jochebed are already married and pregnant when Pharaoh's decree is promulgated:

Amaram(es), a Hebrew of noble birth, fearing that the whole race would be extinguished through lack of the succeeding generation, and seriously anxious on his own account because his wife was with child, was in grievous perplexity. He accordingly had recourse to prayer to God. . . . And God had compassion on him and, moved by his supplication, appeared to him in his sleep, exhorted him not to despair of the future, and told him that . . . "This child, whose birth has filled the Egyptians with such dread that they have condemned to destruction all the offspring of the Israelites, shall indeed be yours; he shall escape those who are watching to destroy him, and, reared in a marvelous way, he shall deliver the Hebrew race from their bondage in Egypt, and be remembered, so long as the universe shall endure, not by Hebrews alone but even by alien nations." (2.210–11)

We can now begin to understand why Matthew must tell the infancy story from the viewpoint of Joseph and not of Mary. He is watching consistently the Mosaic parallelism with its emphasis on the father, Amram, and not on the mother, Jochebed.

In Pseudo-Philo's *Biblical Antiquities*, Amram's role is very much expanded. He and Jochebed are not yet married when the decree is promulgated and the question is whether any future marriages should take place under the threat of infanticide. Amram refuses celibacy, separation, or divorce as a solution, but now it is Miriam, sister of Moses-to-be, who has the revelatory dream:

Then the elders of the people gathered the people together in mourning [and said] . . . "let us set up rules for ourselves that a man should not approach his wife . . . until we know what God may do." And Amram answered and said . . . "I will go and take my wife, and I will not consent to the command of the king; and if it is right in your eyes, let us all act in this way." And the strategy that Amram thought out was pleasing before God. And God said . . . "He who will be born from him will serve me forever." And Amram of the tribe of Levi went out and took a wife from his own tribe. When he had taken her, others followed him and took their own wives. . . . And this man had one son and one daughter; their names were Aaron and Miriam. And the spirit of God came upon Miriam one night, and she saw a dream and told it to her parents in the morning, saying: I have seen this night, and behold a man in a linen garment stood and said to me, "Go and say to your parents, 'Behold he who will be born from you will be cast forth into the water; likewise through him the water will be dried up. And I will work signs through him and save my people, and he will exercise leadership always.'" And when Miriam told of her dream, her parents did not believe her. (9.2–10)

The theme of continuing or not continuing marriage is a new element in that text. But now the revelatory dream is to Miriam directly and to her parents only through her. In both cases, however, the dream's content is the same: Amram and Jochebed are to be the parents of the destined and endangered child. Versions of that tradition known only from later texts have Amram and Jochebed divorce along with all the others, and it takes Miriam's dream to command them back to their marriage bed for the conception of Moses.

Two Parallel Infancy Stories. Imagine yourself within Matthew's mind composing a birth story for Jesus on the model of those popular Mosaic accounts current in and even before such securely first-century works as Josephus and Pseudo-Philo. You have successfully handled the Pharaoh/ Herod parallelism. But you must also handle the Amram/Joseph parallelism. That must involve paternal hesitation, be it of doubt and perplexity or separation and divorce. Also, there must be a revelatory dream to resolve that problem. Finally, there must be a declaration to the parents that the destined child is "theirs." Read, once again, what Joseph did in that earlier citation of Matthew 1:18–25. His private presumption of adultery (others would presume a too-early marriage consummation) sets up the problem. The dream reassures him both about Mary and about her son who "will save his people from their sins" as Moses would "deliver the Hebrew race from their bondage in Egypt."

We conclude that Matthew himself created that fictional or parabolic account of the birth of Jesus, that he did it quite deliberately to make him a divinely destined fulfillment of Moses, but that, in the very process of that parallelism, he himself raised the question of adultery, which would haunt his story from antiquity to modernity. Matthew's creative composition is a third, or *evangelical*, layer and it begot, as a very obvious rebuttal, an immediate counterstory in a post-Matthean layer. Imagine the normal name-calling of infighting between factions of the same religion. *Pro-Jesus Jews:* "He was born of God by a virgin mother without any human father." *Anti-Jesus Jews:* "If Joseph is not his father, Mary is an adulteress, and Jesus is a bastard. You say virginal conception by divine power. We say adulterous conception and not just by a sinful fellow Jew, but by a pagan, a Roman soldier." Point and Counterpoint. Story and Counterstory.

SON OF MARY, SON OF JOSEPH, SON OF GOD

The James ossuary identifies that individual as "son of Joseph, brother of Jesus," and, although it is not said, one would presume Jesus was also the son of Joseph. But no new information was thereby carved in stone. We already knew from the New Testament itself that Jesus had brothers and sisters, with James named first among them. And we also knew that Jesus was "the carpenter's son" in Matthew 13:55 or "son of Joseph" in Luke 4:22 and John 6:42. As one interprets the text, so, no doubt, will one interpret the stone. But, once again, the very presence of the ossuary forces us to raise some old questions and rethink some old solutions.

We could say, as has been said since the fourth century to preserve particular theological views about Mary's virginity, that James is the younger blood brother or older half brother or even first cousin of Jesus. We could say that Joseph is only the guardian or stepfather of Jesus. That would reconcile that "son of Joseph" in Luke 4:22 with this earlier text in Luke 1:35: "The angel said to her [Mary], 'The Holy Spirit will come upon you, and the power of the Most High will overshadow you; therefore the child to be born will be holy; he will be called Son of God.'" But here is the more basic question: For the ancients and/or for the moderns, can a child be both biologically the son of Joseph and theologically the Son of God? In other words, is Son of God any more or less metaphorical than Word of God or Lamb of God as a title for Jesus? Each announces a special, particular, and unique relationship between God, Jesus, and Christians, but while each of them is real, none of them has to be literal. And if the title is not literal but metaphorical, then the conception story that turns it into narrative is not literal but parabolical. There is, then, no contradiction between Jesus as biologically the son of Joseph and also theologically the Son of God. And one relationship is no more or less real than the other. That, at least, would explain why only Matthew and Luke but not Paul, Mark, John, or anyone else in the New Testament mentions that conception story, but all consider Jesus to be Son of God. But why do Matthew and Luke not only accept the title Son of God but develop it into a conception parable? And, especially, why is that conception parable about a virgin?

In the biblical tradition, predestined children—children marked with a divinely foreseen destiny—were born to aged and infertile parents and not to young and virginal mothers. The classic model was Isaac, born to the barren and aged Abraham and Sarah. When God promised them a son, both laughed at the idea. In Genesis 17:17, "Abraham fell on his face and laughed, and said to himself, 'Can a child be born to a man who is a hundred years old? Can Sarah, who is ninety years old, bear a child?'" And in Genesis 18:11–12, "Abraham and Sarah were old, advanced in age; it had ceased to be with Sarah after the manner of women. So Sarah laughed to herself, saying, 'After I have grown old, and my husband is old, shall I have pleasure?'" That is the traditional biblical and Jewish pattern for such a divinely controlled conception.

On the one hand, it might seem that a young and virginal conception is an even greater miracle, an even greater sign of God's intervention, than an aged and infertile one. That is certainly how Luke 1–2 contrasts and exalts the virginal conception and birth of Jesus over that of John the Baptist, conceived by infertile and aged parents. In 1:7 the latter's parents had "no children, because Elizabeth was barren, and both were getting on in years," and in 1:18, "Zechariah said to the angel, 'How will I know that this is so? For I am an old man, and my wife is getting on in years.'" It would seem that virginal conception overpowers aged conception, even granted that both involve divine intervention. Jesus is far, far greater than John, even or especially from their comparative conceptions.

On the other hand, an aged and infertile conception is publicly visible, legally provable, and commonly checkable. Nobody can debate the fact of an aged and infertile conception and birth and it demands some extraordinary explanation. But a virginal conception depends, positively, on the mother's word and, negatively, on the father's assurance. It tempts the obvious rebuttal of adultery or fornication. So why would anyone think it a greater claim, a more magnificent divine intervention? Is it not simply a much more easily dismissible assertion? Why choose the biblical novelty of direct divine conception rather than the biblical tradition of indirect divine conception?

One obvious answer is that the virginal conception was created as a fulfillment of Isaiah 7:14, a text cited explicitly in Matthew but present only implicitly if at all in Luke. The Greek translation of that Hebrew verse says, "behold, the virgin will have in (her) womb and will bear a son and will call his name Immanuel." That meant, in Hebrew certainly and even in Greek probably, that its promise would be fulfilled within a year, that is, within the time span when some young virginal woman now getting married would bear and name a child. It did not mean that she would remain a virgin in that process but simply that she would start it as one. In other words, early Christian-Jewish exegetes may have used Isaiah 7:14 and taken "virgin" literally, but they were hardly forced to do so by the text itself. Something else must have been at work, something that made Christian-Jewish exegetes think about direct divine conception and then go looking for a biblical text to vindicate that most-unbiblical idea.

In the biblical tradition, as just seen, the divinely controlled births of specially predestined children were normally indicated by the unexpected pregnancies of infertile and/or aged couples. But in Greco-Roman tradition, from Alexander to Augustus, they were indicated by an earthly individual being overshadowed by heavenly power, that is, by human and divine interaction. This, for example, is the divine conception of Octavian, who would become eventually Caesar Augustus, Lord and Savior of the Roman Empire, according to Suetonius's *The Lives of the Caesars: The Deified Augustus* 94.4:

> When Atia had come in the middle of the night to the solemn service of Apollo, she had her litter set down in the temple and fell asleep, while the rest of the matrons also slept. On a sudden a serpent glided up to her and shortly went away. When she awoke, she purified herself, as if after the embraces of her husband, and at once there appeared on her body a mark in colors like a serpent, and she could never get rid of it; so that presently she ceased ever to go to the public baths. In the tenth month after that Augustus was born and was therefore regarded as the son of Apollo. Atia too, before she gave him birth, dreamed that her vitals were borne up to the stars and spread over the whole extent of land and sea, while Octavius dreamed that the sun rose from Atia's womb.

Writing in the second century, Suetonius attributes the story of that conception in the winter of 62 B.C.E. to an Egyptian source from around 30 B.C.E. It arose, in other words, in the Eastern world soon after Octavian's victory over his rivals Antony and Cleopatra off the coast of Actium in northwestern Greece. It arose, in other words, in the Eastern world at the time of Augustus's first ascendancy.

Jesus' conception story in Matthew and Luke indicates some common tradition before either of them and that base narrative moves in the world of story and counterstory but now Jesus' conception is exalted over that of Augustus. We have moved out of the Jewish world of aged and infertile parents, of indirect divine intervention, and into the Greco-Roman world of earthly females and heavenly males, of direct divine intervention. In Matthew, Luke, and even before them, Jesus is Lord, Savior, Son of God, and has usurped Augustus's titles. But Atia was not a virgin; she already had a firstborn daughter about a half dozen years before Octavian. So, while Isaiah 7:14 was helpful in making this all seem somewhat biblical, prophetic, and foreordained, it was more likely that exaltation over Augustus was determinative for its creation.

If you take Jesus' conception story literally, take Augustus's literally. If you take Jesus' conception story metaphorically, take Augustus's metaphorically. Wherever you place one on a spectrum from 100 percent literal to 100 percent metaphorical, place also the other at the same location (and do not cheat). The final point is this: from his very conception, Jesus is placed on a collision course with Augustus in a story that comes not from a historical event in Level I, but from a theological parable in Level II, a narrative from anytime after Jesus publicly proclaimed the Kingdom of God in opposition to the kingdom of Caesar.

THREE

How to Build
a Kingdom

Before beginning to build a kingdom, you must know what kind of kingdom you want to build. Or can it be taken for granted that there is only one type, one model, one scenario? Is a kingdom always about power and glory, force and violence? Is it about the very few controlling the very many? Is an agrarian kingdom about protection given to peasants in exchange for the surplus extracted from them? Is it, in other words, about protecting them from somebody else who would do the same thing to them? Is it always, at best, about the mailed fist in the velvet glove? Is it always, at worst, about the mailed fist in the mailed glove? Is there only a kingdom of power and violence, everywhere? Or is there a kingdom of justice and nonviolence, anywhere?

A CLASH OF KINGDOM TYPES

Neither Herod the Great and Herod Antipas, on the one hand, nor John the Baptist and Jesus, on the other, had to imagine, proclaim, and construct their very different kingdoms as if from scratch, as if without types and models from long before. Here, as almost a random example, is a paradigmatic clash of two kingdom types, a clash that took place well over half a millennium before that first common-era century.

In the first half of the eighth century B.C.E., Jeroboam II ruled the Kingdom of Israel, which, along with the Kingdom of Judah, formed the northern and southern halves of what had been the single kingdom of David and Solomon in the glory days of the tenth century. Jeroboam II reigned for around thirty years, a long time in a world where the average life expectancy was just about that same span. Archaeologists excavated his capital, Samaria, in 1908–10, 1931–35, and 1965–68. The first dig, by Harvard University, discovered sixty-three potsherds with black-inked Hebrew inscriptions detailing taxes of oil and wine sent to the royal store-rooms from the surrounding countryside. The second dig, a joint expedi-tion of Harvard University, Hebrew University, and three different British institutions, discovered many ivory plaques and hundreds of ivory frag-ments in the royal palaces. They combined Egyptian mythology, Phoeni-cian artistry, and, sometimes, Hebrew lettering. Palace and countryside, then, taxes and ivories.

Those excavations and especially those ivories told of a powerful monarch, a splendid court, and a luxurious aristocracy. If only material remains but no textual remains spoke to us of Jeroboam II's Samaria, we might still wonder about it. They were imports from Egyptian artistry, but it was freedom from Egyptian oppression that was still celebrated in Israelite covenant and cult, song and story, festival and remembrance. What, one might wonder, had Israel to do with Egypt, Samaria with Phoenicia? But we do have texts, and they record another and very differ-ent view of Samaria's boom years. They give an opposing vision on how to build a kingdom.

Those exquisite ivory miniatures dug up in the 1930s were mentioned by Amos, an eighth-century shepherd-seer from Tekoa in Judah, a lower-than-peasant prophet who came north amidst Jeroboam II's prosperity with prophetic accusations, dire warnings, and promises of unrelenting doom. "I will tear down the winter house along with the summer house; the houses adorned with ivory will be destroyed and the mansions demol-ished," God declares (3:15). And: "You put off the evil day and bring near a reign of terror. You lie on beds inlaid with ivory and lounge on your couches" (6:3–4). What, for Amos, was wrong with Jeroboam II's way of building the Kingdom of Israel? Watch four crucial themes.

Commerce and Poverty.   The theme of oppressing the poor repeats like a drumbeat throughout the oral oracles of Amos now gathered in the book that bears his name. But in 8:4–6 it is combined with the theme of com-mercialization. "Hear this, you who trample the needy and do away with the poor of the land, saying, 'When will the New Moon be over that we may sell grain, and the Sabbath be ended that we may market wheat?'—skimping the measure, boosting the price and cheating with dishonest scales, buying the poor with silver and the needy for a pair of sandals, selling even the sweepings with the wheat." Expensive imports from abroad meant intensive commerce at home.

Poverty and Justice.   It is not just that everyone is poor and that poverty is bad. It is that luxury increases at one end of society by making poverty increase at the other. The rich get richer as the poor get poorer. "They sell the righteous for silver, and the needy for a pair of sandals. They trample on the heads of the poor as upon the dust of the ground and deny justice to the oppressed" (2:6–7). "You trample on the poor and force him to give you grain. . . . You oppress the righteous and take bribes and you deprive the poor of justice in the courts" (5:11–12). "You have turned justice into poison and the fruit of righteousness into bitterness" (6:12). Justice equals righteousness; to do what is just equals to do what is right. And that righteous justice is not just individual but structural, not just personal but systemic, not just retributive but distributive.

Justice and Worship.   The themes of justice and worship come to a surprising climax in these most famous verses, more often quoted than deeply understood: "I hate, I despise your religious feasts; I cannot stand your assemblies. Even though you bring me burnt offerings and grain offerings, I will not accept them. Though you bring choice fellowship offerings, I will have no regard for them. Away with the noise of your songs! I will not listen to the music of your harps. But let justice roll on like a river, righteousness like a never-failing stream!" says the voice of God (5:21–24). That is not a simple case of oracle against cult, prophet against priest, let alone southern Jerusalem shrine against northern Bethel shrine. But how was Amos so sure that God wanted justice and righteousness rather than sacrificial offering and festal song?

Worship and Covenant.   Imagine the confrontation described in 7:10–17 between Amos, prophet of Tekoa, and Amaziah, priest of Bethel, "sanctuary of the king and temple of the kingdom." Amaziah warned Jeroboam II that Amos was "raising a conspiracy against you in the very heart of Israel." Imagine the differing views behind this non–meeting of minds. *Amaziah:* "God demands worship and we obey." *Amos:* "God demands justice and you do not obey." *Amaziah:* "What you call injustice, we call commercial prosperity; what you call unrighteousness, we call business acumen." *Amos:* "You cannot worship a God of justice in a state of injustice." *Amaziah:* "Leave the temple, prophet, while you are still alive to do so."

What exists behind that interchange are two radically divergent ways of imagining a kingdom. For shorthand, we call Jeroboam's model a *commercial kingdom* and Amos's model a *covenantal kingdom*. But, of course, it is never just a matter of names and titles. It is content, very, very specific content that counts in the end. What does your kingdom do to a world that belongs to God? How do you distribute the material bases of life in a world not your own? Who owns and who runs it? Think of those two kingdom types as ideal extremes between which a spectrum of kingdom realities could be imagined, but the core clash, tension, or dialectic is always there in Israelite and Jewish history. In a commercial kingdom the land that belongs to humanity must be exploited as fully as possible. In a covenantal kingdom the land that belongs to divinity must be distributed as justly as possible. Is there still commerce within covenant? Of course. But that is not the question. Is there still covenant within commerce? That is the question.

TYPE 1: A COMMERCIAL KINGDOM

Look down this hierarchy from top to bottom: from the Roman Empire of Caesar Augustus, through the Jewish kingdom of Herod the Great, to the Galilean-Perean tetrarchy of Herod Antipas. In reverse, from bottom to top: Antipas to Herod to Augustus. The Herodians are not greater than the Romans in anything, but they are miniatures of them in everything. Romanization meant urbanization, which meant commercialization. Watch, then, how, first, Herod the Great built a Roman full-kingdom and, after him but imitative of him, his son Antipas built a Roman bit-kingdom on Jewish soil.

Herod the Great as King and Master Builder

In 40 B.C.E., a generation before Jesus, Herod the Great destroyed the final resistance in Galilee to his newly established kingdom. The son of an official from converted Idumea in the native Jewish ruling house of the Hasmoneans, Herod had positioned himself as a consistent supporter of Rome during the dynastic struggles between the Hasmonean prince-brothers Antigonus and Hyrcanus. Recognizing Rome's inevitable dominance on the geopolitical scene, he pursued a series of relationships with its officials that led him before the Roman Senate in 40 B.C.E. to petition for control over the Jewish homeland. The Senate bestowed upon him the title King of the Jews and gave him authority to rule the territories of Idumea, Judea, Samaria, and Galilee as a client of Rome. But his brother had just been murdered by adversaries, his family was besieged at Masada, and most of the territories promised him by Rome, including their capital Jerusalem, were in the hands of his Hasmonean rival Antigonus, who was backed by the powerful Parthian Empire. His was a kingdom promised, but not fulfilled.

After returning from Rome, Herod first freed his family besieged in the fortress atop Masada, and then began in Galilee a violent struggle to obtain his kingdom. According to Josephus, he captured the Hasmonean garrison town of Sepphoris in Lower Galilee during a snowstorm, and from there began to root out all opposition to his rule. He laid siege to the last remaining opponents in the Arbel cliffs overlooking the northwest shore of the Sea of Galilee—he set fire to their caves, swung his soldiers down on cradles from an overhang above, and pulled them to their death with grappling hooks. With Galilee pacified, he then moved southward to Judea and Jerusalem, taking three years to secure his kingdom.

Herod then set about constructing his kingdom architecturally as energetically as he had set about conquering it militarily. He was one of antiquity's most prolific builders, whose projects dotted the entire eastern Mediterranean and dominated his kingdom's landscape and whose ruins left a lasting mark in the archaeological record. He built a monumental and colossal kingdom. Herod's projects combined elements from his local Hasmonean predecessors, from eastern Mediterranean Hellenistic city-states, and from Roman technology and style to create a unique set of structures. They were built at times possibly for the sake of architecture itself, at times probably for the sake of his people, but always and certainly for his own need, desire, and rule.

Watch how his architectural feats tell the story of his rule, and how their style betrays his persona and character as a king. His first projects were a series of royal residences, including the oasis-compound at Jericho, the terrace palace at Masada, and the complex called the Herodion, each of which was fortified; the last two were nearly impregnable. He was both paranoid and opulent, building these early residences with security as much as luxury in mind. After completing several residence-fortresses throughout his kingdom and, with his rule now secure, he embarked on two immense projects—the city of Caesarea with its harbor Sebastos, and the Temple Mount in Jerusalem. That port city is commonly called Caesarea Maritima to distinguish it from Caesarea Philippi, built later by his son Philip at the source of the Jordan River. On the one hand, Caesarea Maritima's construction opened up Herod's kingdom to the wider Mediterranean world and oriented it geographically, culturally, politically, and commercially toward Rome, initiating ties on a larger scale than previously possible. On the other hand, the massive Temple project in Jerusalem gave his Jewish subjects one of the largest and most spectacular sacred precincts of the ancient world. Note, underlying these two projects, the tension or even schizophrenia of his rule as both *Roman client-king* and *King of the Jews*.

The city of Caesarea and its port Sebastos were the most ambitious and daring projects ever attempted in the eastern Mediterranean. Obviously, and as confirmed from ancient literary texts, their very names paid tribute to the ultimate source of Herod's power, Caesar Augustus, born Octavius. The city took its name from the titular Caesar, the port took its name from his title *Sebastos*, Greek for the Latin *Augustus*, and gigantic statues of both the emperor and the goddess Roma were enshrined in the city's most prominent structure, an enormous temple welcoming ships and travelers. Thanks to archaeological excavations, we know that the port city's construction was about more than nominal tribute to Caesar and Rome—tribute in the form of taxes funneled through it from Herod's entire kingdom to Rome, with ample riches staying in the city. Agricultural produce flowed into the city from the countryside, and, alongside grain, wine, and olive oil, currency also made its way to the city as Herod monetized the economy. The wealth flowing into Herod's treasury and the coffers of his ruling elite funded the construction of a lavish urbanization at Caesarea, and the initial investment of the port paid dividends by realigning trade routes from the East through his kingdom and by tapping into the lucrative Mediterranean sea routes. Herod transformed the Jewish homeland into a commercial kingdom.

Every summer for decades, teams of American and Israeli archeologists along with an army of international volunteers have descended on the seaside resort of Caesarea to excavate and record the layers of the site, from the moat and walls of the Crusader city through the churches and synagogues of the Byzantine Period, to the marble columns of the Roman city down to its very Herodian foundations. The structures, artifacts, and

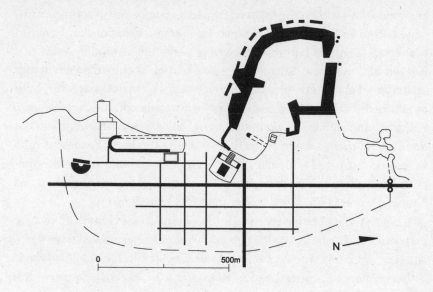

HEROD THE GREAT'S CAESAREA MARITIMA (AFTER NETZER)

mass of finds from this lowest layer reveal how expensively and expansively Herod built his kingdom's capital city. He opened his kingdom to the west, and his city told Rome what it wanted to hear. And in the aesthetic-architectural dialect of the day, he told his subjects what they better understand.

The arrangement, style, and materials of his newly constructed city and harbor announced three things. First, Caesarea Maritima heralded Herod's *imposition of order* on his kingdom, an order that conveyed a sense of his power and ability to control both nature and society. Second, Herod displayed *a predilection for façades*, declaring the city's wealth and at the same time delineating the social order. And third, Herod *reinforced the social hierarchy* of his kingdom at Caesarea. The imposition of order and the erection of façades along with specific public structures announced and reinforced, atop the social pyramid, first Rome, then Herod, and finally his ruling elite. Those three interrelated areas furnish Herod's blueprint for *how to build a kingdom*.

The Imposition of Order at Caesarea. Herod the Great ordered the landscape subdued and society regularized. The site Herod selected on the coast had neither a natural harbor nor a suitable water supply. No matter.

He imposed his will on the topography and terrain by constructing an artificial harbor and by bringing in water on a high-level aqueduct from distant springs. For his harbor, breakwaters were built extending some 800 feet out into the open sea, and half a mile of mole sheltered an anchorage of almost 40 acres. The breakwater piers were 130 to 200 feet wide, built by setting hydraulic concrete in casings with a mix containing *pozzolana*, volcanic sand shipped in from the Bay of Naples, then floating them out and sinking them section by section to secure the harbor's substructure. Perhaps constructed with the aid of architects and master builders imported from Italy, the project nevertheless displayed logistical prowess and financial power behind it that were markedly Herodian.

Though the harbor has received its due attention for Herod's innovative and daring engineering, equally important but often overlooked is his imposition of order onto society by laying out Caesarea in a carefully planned orthogonal grid. As with the ideal Roman city, he bisected Caesarea with two major thoroughfares, the north-south *cardo* and, perpendicular to it, the east-west *decumanus*. These led from the main city gates and opened directly onto a plaza adjacent to the temple of Augustus and Roma. Through these carefully planned avenues, the flow of traffic was guided toward public spaces and appropriately propagandistic landmarks designed to foster shared social experiences and create social cohesion. At the same time, a strategy for excluding unwanted people was at work in the city gates and grid; the former controlled entrance into the city, and the latter was used to impede passage to restricted areas, such as the Herodian palace.

Some specific buildings also underscored social control, such as the freestanding theater and amphitheater in the city's southwestern zone. Built from the ground up, access and egress could easily be guarded at portals, the so-called *vomitoria*, located at ground level. Developed in Rome under Julius Caesar and Augustus at the Forum Iulium and the Circus Maximus in response to the mob violence and riots during the civil wars, this new architectural form joined the semicircular seating area, or *cavea*, to the stage of the theater, creating easily controlled bottlenecks.

A Predilection for Façades at Caesarea.   The Roman historian Suetonius quotes the emperor Augustus as saying of Rome that, "I found the city made of brick and I left it made of marble." Herod's patron was well known for wanting to play his part right and for putting up a good front, a feature he accentuated architecturally in further promoting a series of Greek architectural features in Rome. Similarly, Herodian architecture was preoccupied with appropriate façades—the substructures of his projects were not always tight-fitting, some were merely functional, and even a few shoddily constructed, but they were always covered with suitable façades and arranged to accentuate shape, proportion, and vistas. Caesarea was a city of mosaic floors, plastered and frescoed walls, marble sheeting, red roof tiles, and columns, lots of columns, mostly of local stone, that were stuccoed and fluted with molded plaster.

Previously in the eastern Mediterranean and the entire Near East, massive columns had been featured in temples and smaller columns reserved for the sheltered promenades, or *stoa*, in more Hellenistic cities. But at Herod's Caesarea, Roman-style architecture spread columns throughout and created vistas across the city, shrouding the entire city in a civic-religious aura. Under Augustus, marble became the architectural code for Roman rule in the provinces. And Caesarea's marble, which increased dramatically in the late first and early second century after quarries and their trade were organized into an imperial system, symbolically linked Rome with the provinces, Augustus with Herod the Great.

The Reinforcement of Hierarchy at Caesarea.   Rome and its emperor stood at the top the architectural hierarchy at Caesarea. Put yourself in its midst. From everywhere in the city or port you could see the temple to Roma and Augustus. Rising to a height of 80 to 110 feet and built on top of an artificial platform, the temple towered over the city. Put yourself on your way there. It was the first landmark you could reconize on your approach to the city by land or sea. Its polished white stone glistened in the sunlight. Seat yourself in the theater or along the eastern tiers of the amphitheater. This temple dominated the scenery. In it were housed two massive statues, the goddess Roma as Hera Argos and the emperor Augustus as Zeus Olympios, described by Josephus but yet to be discovered. But other bronze and marble limbs and torsos from slightly later periods have been found at Caesarea. The life-size cuirassed torso of Trajan (98–117) and a headless seated Hadrian (117–38 C.E.) offer concrete evidence of the imperial cult and emperor worship there.

This is the context in which the Pilate inscription discovered in 1962 by Italian archaeologists from Milan must be understood. The fragmentary inscription, written in Latin on a stone that had been flipped and reused as part of the theater's renovation in the fourth century, reads:

PONTIUS PILATE INSCRIPTION FROM CAESAREA MARITIMA
(collection of the Israel Antiquities Authority, photograph copyright the Israel
Museum, Jerusalem)

. . . this Tiberium, Pontius Pilate, prefect of Judea, did (or erected) . . .

Too many commentators stress that the inscription's importance lies in
proving the veracity of the gospels on the existence of Pilate, an obvious
point that few had ever doubted. Many others cite the inscription's significance in clarifying his title, which had been debated as governor, procurator, or prefect, a point of Roman legal minutiae and of little general interest.

Discussions along these lines mute the message that the inscription and the building (the *Tiberium*) dedicated to the emperor Tiberias announced: *Rome Rules!* Written in Latin, a language few there could understand much less read, the structure and its inscription nevertheless communicated even to the dullest mind that Rome and its representatives stood at the top of the social pyramid and held absolute control over the land.

Herod the Great stood a close second on the social scale, a position he conveyed in the setting and style of his seaside palace. At Caesarea's foundation, Herod sponsored games and athletic competitions in the theater and amphitheater built in a southwestern zone of the city. Herod's promontory palace encroached into this area otherwise set aside for athletic events and entertainment, blurring the lines between private and public. The theater was intentionally aligned off the city grid. If you sit in the theater, you face Herod's palace squarely, which hovers over the low stage platform, or *scaenae frons*, and appears as part of the stage's scenic backdrop. You and each of the spectators know who sponsored the event—think of it as an ancient subliminal commercial. A major exit on the curved southern end of the amphitheater opened onto a vestibule-like garden next to the palace. Very likely a separate exit led visiting dignitaries or local elites directly to the palace, while others were funneled past the gardens back into the city's center. Herod accentuated his role as benefactor and patron by linking the palace with places of public spectacle, a piece of subtle propaganda.

The theater further delineated a rigid social stratification. If you were rich, you entered one way and sat in one section. You had privileged seating apart from the many. Your seat was nearest the stage, had a backrest, and may even, as at Neapolis, have had your family name permanently chiseled into it. You entered exclusively and separately through side entrances along the stage, and upon entry you could gaze at the masses for whom you were part of the pageantry. They streamed and elbowed out the back through the *vomitoria*, which were guarded as a measure of crowd control. The theater, and in similar ways the nearby amphitheater, visibly magnified class distinctions and reinforced the social hierarchy.

How did Herod the Great finance his kingdom? Where did the money come from, how were the workers paid and the materials afforded? Trade and tariffs from the harbor certainly helped, but agriculture was the base of the Roman economy, and land the measure of wealth. Ancient cities' architecture was built with agricultural wealth from peasant labor, and

Herod needed a lot of wealth for his city and kingdom. Polycropping and self-sufficiency on family farms gave way to monocropping on estates and royal lands and to an asymmetrical exchange of goods. Landholding patterns changed and tenancy increased to create economies of scale. Coinage and currency increased in the local economy to facilitate taxation to the coffers of Herod and Rome, which funded the architectural grandeur of Caesarea. The kingdom was commercialized, not in the sense of a mercantile state, but in efficiently moving goods and money from the land to the city. Luxury increasing at one end of society made labor and poverty increase at the other. Expensive architecture in the city meant intensive agriculture in the country. Countryside and city, then, taxes and marble.

Herod Antipas as His Father's Son

Galilee was passed over in the architectural blueprint of Herod the Great's kingdom. He built along the coast and in the north at Banias, in Jerusalem and all across the Judean desert, and he even sponsored projects in faraway Mediterranean cities. But he ignored Galilee.

Sepphoris and Tiberias.   Herod's contested will apportioned his kingdom to three of his sons after his death in 4 B.C.E., with Galilee going to Herod Antipas along with Perea, on the eastern side of the Jordan. Like his father's reign, Antipas's rule in Galilee had a violent beginning. Roman legions, under the Syrian-based legate Varus, crushed an uprising at Antipas's first capital, Sepphoris, just before Caesar Augustus confirmed the will in Rome. In that confirmation Augustus refused to give Herod's title, King of the Jews, to either Antipas or his brother Archelaus. But Antipas the *tetrarch* (ruler of a quarter-kingdom) survived while Archelaus the *ethnarch* (ruler of the people) was sent into exile in 6 C.E. As long as Augustus was alive, Antipas stayed prudently quiet. It would seem, however, that he always hoped to become, one day, King of the Jews by Roman appointment.

In 14 C.E. Augustus died and Tiberius, finally, took over the empire. Then, and only then, did Antipas make his move. First, he built a new capital named for the new emperor, Tiberias, and minted his first coins. The foundation was around 19 C.E. But he himself was the son of Herod and his Samaritan wife Malthace, so a Hasmonean connection was needed. Sometime in the late 20s C.E. he rejected his Nabatean wife and

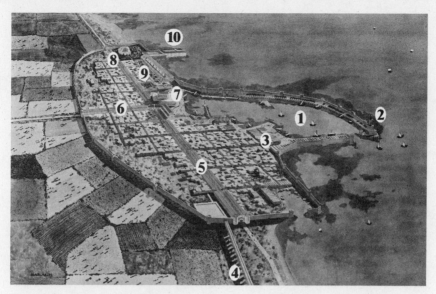

RECONSTRUCTION OF FIRST-CENTURY CAESAREA MARITIMA *Herod the Great, King of the Jews 37–4* B.C.E., *opened his kingdom to the wider Roman world by constructing Caesarea Maritima and its massive harbor. Breakwaters extended into the sea (1) and a lighthouse (2) guided ships into the port, where giant storehouses held wares and produce (3). Because the city had no water source, an overland aqueduct (4) brought in fresh water from afar. Built on a rigid orthogonal grid, the city's main thoroughfares, the so-called* cardo *(5) and* decumanus *(6), led to a massive temple dedicated to the goddess Roma and Caesar Augustus (7), after whom the city was also named. At Caesarea's southern end, excavations have uncovered a theater (8), an amphitheatrical hippodrome (9), and Herod the Great's lavish palace (10). Though Jesus never visited Caesarea, Paul later set sail from Caesarea on his voyage to Rome.*

married Herodias, wife of his half brother Philip. She was a granddaughter of the executed Hasmonean Mariamne and daughter of the executed Hasmonean Aristobulus. Considering Antipas's political and populist intentions for that marriage, you can understand how little he would have tolerated John the Baptist's criticism of its illegitimacy. You can also understand how palace and desert, Antipas and John are set up as opposites in Luke 7:24–25. But, in any case, Antipas was never destined to become King of the Jews. That title fell to Herod Agrippa I, and Antipas, like Archelaus before him, died far away in exile.

Still, earlier, when all looked possible, Antipas built a totally new city on the western shore of the Sea of Galilee, in a previously uninhabited spot or, more precisely, atop an ancient graveyard, according to Josephus. One might well wonder, in view of Antipas's carefully aniconic coinage, which showed respect for Jewish imageless traditions, whether this was factually true or a reflection of opposition to the new foundation. In any case, modeling his father, Herod Antipas built a new Roman-style city and harbor, named it after the new Roman emperor, and thereby sought to urbanize his kingdom, link it up with the broader world, and vie for the title of king. That, after all, is how his father had built his kingdom.

Since the mid-1980s, four different excavation teams have been working at Sepphoris, and though Tiberias today is a thriving tourist city, bits and pieces of that ancient city have been excavated over the years. At Sepphoris, spectacular finds typical of a Roman-style city and with ample pagan iconography have been unearthed, such as a villa with Dionysiac themes, a mosaic floor with pagan Nile river scenes, and even a Jewish house of study featuring the signs of the zodiac. But a careful look at the layering shows that these pagan and mythological themes are all from the Late Roman and Byzantine Periods, well after the stationing of Roman troops in nearby Maximianopolis in the second century, after which Jews were adapting and in some ways also accommodating to Hellenistic and Roman ideas and motifs for their own purposes. In earlier layers, however, in particular from the time of Antipas, all evidence points to an as yet aniconic Jewish population and a cautious Antipas who heeded the religious sensibilities of his Jewish subjects. The first coins Herod Antipas struck at Sepphoris and Tiberias show the tightrope he walked between trying to build a Jewish kingdom in the Roman world: they avoided his image and, instead, bore representations such as reeds, palm branches, and palm trees, symbols that were appropriately Jewish, but not necessarily foreign to the wider Greco-Roman world.

Two inscriptions from Sepphoris, one written on a potsherd, or *ostracon*, and the other on a lead weight, provide specific examples of how the Jewish city coped with and adapted to foreign influences. The first-century B.C.E. storage-jar fragment had '*pmlsh* painted in red Hebrew block letters, a translation of the Greek *epimeletes*, "manager, overseer, or treasurer." The jar had contained grain, olive oil, or wine that was taxed in kind and handed over to the *epimeletes*, who wrote in Hebrew letters, but had adopted a Greek administrative title. The lead weight, dating to the first century C.E., lists on one side in Greek letters the amount of the weight, the standard Latin measure of a half *litra* (36 ounces), and is surrounded by schematic drawings of a colonnaded street signifying the market, or *agora*. The other side lists in Greek letters the distinctly Jewish names Justus and Simeon, two market inspectors, or *agoranomoi*, who sold permits, ensured quality, or controlled weights. The weight combines a Roman/Latin measure, Greek script, and evidence of Jews controlling important administrative matters in Sepphoris.

One inscription from Tiberias, on a lead weight decorated with a wreath and palm branch, provides an example of how the Herodian family even adopted Roman names. Dated to the thirty-fourth year of Herod Antipas's rule (29/30 C.E.), the piece of lead had been weighed and inscribed in Greek by an *agoranomos* identified as "Gaius Julius." That is a Roman name to be sure, but it refers most likely to Herod Agrippa I, brother-in-law of Antipas and later King of the Jews. Educated in Rome, he was appointed by Antipas as market inspector in Tiberias, according to Josephus, and, like other scions of Herod, he had adopted a Roman name. Since Julius Caesar had granted Antipater, Herod the Great's father, Roman citizenship, those of the Herodian house were called *Iulii*, and the praenomen Gaius was commonly adopted as well. An interesting artifact, then: the lead weight of a Jewish king-in-waiting who wrote in Greek and used a Latin name from the imperial Roman family.

Since the cities of Tiberias and Sepphoris, unlike Caesarea, were inhabited primarily by Jews and were in almost exclusively Jewish Galilee, Herod Antipas built them without many of the trappings of the classical pagan city such as statues or pagan temples. But he covered Sepphoris and Tiberias with a Greco-Roman architectural veneer, which made them not only the first large cities in Galilee, but complete novelties in their style, in which traces of the same aesthetic-architectural themes found at Caesarea are apparent. His kingdom, in other words, was adapted from his father's blueprint.

The Imposition of Order at Sepphoris and Tiberias. Like Herod the Great's Caesarea, Antipas's inaugural project in his aspiring kingdom left traces in the archaeological record. Sepphoris was earlier a Hasmonean outpost settled by Jews in the Late Hellenistic Period with a population of around one thousand. No widespread evidence of destruction has been found attributable to the Roman legate Varus, whom Josephus says burned the city to the ground and sold its inhabitants into slavery in 4 B.C.E. (*Jewish War* 2.68–69; *Jewish Antiquities* 17.288–89). His tendency to accentuate Roman might and the repercussions of rebellion seem to have led him to exaggerate the fate of Sepphoris, but his description of Antipas's rebuilding it into the "ornament of all Galilee" (*Jewish Antiquities* 18.27) resonates with the archaeological record. Archaeologists have discerned considerable building activity around the turn of the common era, when the city grew in population to between eight and twelve thousand. At the same time, a rigid orthogonal grid was imposed on the plain just east of the acropolis, bisected by two perpendicular streets, the north-south *cardo* and east-west *decumanus*, a similar but miniature version of Caesarea. On the western slope of the acropolis, a massive retaining wall, an alley and street, and several domestic units have been excavated that were all laid out on parallel lines. At Sepphoris, the grid conformed somewhat to the contours of the land, but went askew as one ascended the acropolis. At Tiberias, the main thoroughfare made a bend along the shore's contours.

Predilection for Façades at Sepphoris and Tiberias.   As for façades, Sepphoris and Tiberias had what Galilean villages did not: white plastered walls, frescoes, mosaics, and red roof tiles. And structures were built and arranged to accentuate shape, proportion, and vistas. At Tiberias, a monumental gate from the time of Antipas has been discovered on the southern edge of the city. Facing the springs at Hammath Tiberias, the massive gate had two round towers some 23 feet in diameter made of local basalt squarely hewn into ashlars. Two niches and two pedestals for columns with rhomboids in relief flanked the entry, decorations suggesting the entire structure was as much ornamental and symbolic as it was defensive. Oddly enough, the only walls found date to the Byzantine Period; none from the first century have been found. Perhaps the earlier walls were obliterated when the later ones were built on top of them, leaving no traces for archaeologists. Or perhaps, as strange as it may seem today, the gate served no defensive purposes whatsoever, but was purely monumental, symbolic, and freestanding. But it marked in from out, urban citizens from rural peasants.

With or without city walls, the imposing façade of the city gate at Tiberias opened onto a *cardo* that ran through the entire city. Best preserved from later periods, dark gray basalt pavers laid diagonally in herringbone style covered a 40-foot-wide street, flanked by 16-foot-wide colonnades on either side supported by granite columns, which led into

FIRST-CENTURY CITY GATE AT TIBERIAS (AFTER FOERSTER)

small cubicle-like shops. Similarly at Sepphoris, a *cardo* with a width of 44 feet was one of the most imposing features on the grid. Local stone pavers, also laid in herringbone style, covered a sewage system and were sturdy enough to survive five hundred years of wagon wheels cutting deep ruts into their surface. The street was lined on each side with rows of columns that cordoned off roofed sidewalks, originally paved with simple white mosaics and lined, as in Tiberias, with shops. All of the columns, however were of local limestone or granite, not expensive imported marble, and the ashlars of the shops' façades show no evidence of marble sheeting, but were simply plastered over with whitewash and shaped with stucco, ranking it on a lower level of urban elegance.

The Reinforcement of Hierarchy at Sepphoris and Tiberias. To date no clear evidence for Antipas's palaces has been found at either Sepphoris or Tiberias, though Josephus describes how the lower classes stormed one at Tiberias in the first Jewish revolt, and certainly Antipas would have built palatial structures in both his cities to set his residence above all others.

An impressive structure has been excavated in the lower market at Sepphoris, however, a basilica dating to the first century. Although that term today refers to a type of church, in antiquity basilica, or royal building, was a Roman architectural form used for official and administrative purposes. *Basileia* is the Greek word for "kingdom," so think of *basilica* as Rome's kingdom in architectural miniature and symbolic presence. In its design, the basilica had a central nave and two aisles separated by columns with cross beams on top that could support a wide roof. Under its roof, subjects would focus on the podium and semicircular apse, whose acoustics permitted royal pronouncements or imperial judgments to be heard. At Sepphoris, the basilica covered an area of 115 by 130 feet and its porches another 80 by 130 feet. It had a mosaic floor, frescoed walls, and marble-lined pools. It served as an administrative building, very likely a court, and possibly as an upscale market, an imprint of the ruling elite.

At Tiberias, a small section of an as yet unexcavated theater has been discovered, and one of the most debated discoveries at Sepphoris is the theater on its northern slope overlooking the Beit Netofah Valley. Some scholars argue that this theater illustrates Antipas's Romanizing policies and the Hellenistic character of the city at the time of Jesus, and some have even suggested that Jesus might have visited the theater and adopted the use of the term *hypocrite*, a Greek term for those actors who wore masks on stage, from visits to the theater. The ceramic evidence used to date the theater, however, is in dispute, and the theater may well date to the late first century C.E., decades after Jesus and Antipas.

Even if the theater was built after Herod Antipas's rule and Jesus' ministry, it tells us about the character of Sepphoris. This theater was modest compared to others in the eastern Mediterranean, with a diameter of over 200 feet and a seating capacity of just below four thousand, much less than the theater at Caesarea. And, rather than being constructed from the ground up, as was typical of Roman-style theaters, its builders took advantage of the topography and chiseled the lower portions of the auditorium's seating into a natural cavity on the northern slope of the acropolis. The structure's interstices were composed of fieldstones and packed dirt, with only a façade of well-hewn limestone ashlars. Costs were cut by building the lower auditorium into the hill and by using fresco and stucco instead of real marble and fluted columns, and all of that covered up less than ideal workmanship.

As an aside, if the theater—of Sepphoris, Tiberias, or elsewhere—is of relevance to the Jesus traditions, it is neither as a source for the word *hypocrite* nor as a vehicle for classical Greek culture in Galilee. Provincial theaters usually provided baser forms of entertainment like jugglers and acrobats, mimes and pantomimes, farces and vulgar spectacles. Rather

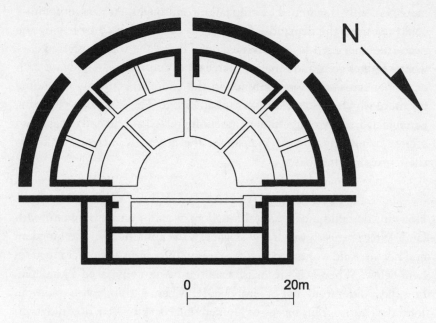

FIRST-CENTURY THEATER AT SEPPHORIS (AFTER MEYERS, NETZER, AND MEYERS)

than being the conduit of *haute culture*, the theater's hierarchical seating symbolized the Roman Empire's rigid class distinctions and encapsulated Galilee's social pyramid, divisions under attack in the egalitarian teachings of Jesus.

Sepphoris was rebuilt and Tiberias was newly built. New architectural styles, larger structures, and expensive materials were introduced into Galilee by Herod Antipas, yielding two miniature Caesareas, just as that city itself was Rome in miniature. Both Galilean cities differed markedly from the surrounding towns and villages. Though Herod Antipas was cautious of being too novel or too foreign and avoided direct confrontations with Jewish sensibilities, the obvious means of funding his kingdom's construction need to be emphasized. Like coastal Caesarea's, these cities' buildings were made with wealth generated from agriculture derived from peasant labor. But unlike coastal Caesarea, Galilee was not on an international trade network, placing even more strain on its fields, vineyards, and olive trees. More productive agricultural methods were called for, fewer fallow years permitted, and more intensive labor required. Polycropping waned as monocropping increased, leaving peasants even more perilously threatened by crop failure or drought. As peasant families could not meet the demands of taxes or became indebted by buying the necessities they used to grow, possession of their land was transferred elsewhere. Estates grew and tenancy increased as economies of scale for cash crops were created. More currency in the Galilean economy facilitated taxation, which funded Antipas's urbanization. The kingdom was being commercialized. Architectural grandeur increased at one end of Galilean society by making poverty increase at the other. Countryside and city, then, taxes and frescoes.

TYPE 2: A COVENANTAL KINGDOM

How do you build a covenantal kingdom, a realm under covenant with God? What, beneath words and slogans, is the content of such a kingdom and how, beyond words and slogans, does it differ from any other kingdom here below? When, within Jewish tradition, Amos envisaged a kingdom, how did it differ from that of Jeroboam II? When, within Jewish tradition, John the Baptist or his successor Jesus envisaged a kingdom, how did it differ from that of Herod the Great or his son Antipas?

Kingdom and Land

Two short scriptural verses, one in the Law and the other in the Prophets, both placed on the lips of God, are basic for understanding the covenantal kingdom, the rule of God over a people, in a land, upon this earth. In Leviticus 25:23 God commands that "the land shall not be sold in perpetuity, for the land is mine; with me you are but aliens and tenants." And in Isaiah 5:8 a woe or curse is announced against those "who join house to house, who add field to field, until there is room for no one but you, and you are left to live alone in the midst of the land!" There are four presuppositions, call them mythological or ideological, theological or philosophical, behind those aphorisms.

First, God is just. Second, the land of Israel belongs to that just God. Third, the land was originally distributed fairly and equitably among the tribes, clans, and families of Israel. Fourth, the Law decrees against and the Prophets inveigh against the inevitable human drive for fewer and fewer people to have more and more land and for more and more people to have less and less land. Neither Law nor Prophets proclaims bright, shining manifestos about equality, but both strive to control and curtail the steady growth of inequality. Land is the material basis of life itself and cannot be

RECONSTRUCTION OF FIRST-CENTURY TIBERIAS. *Like his father, Herod the Great, Herod Antipas built a new seaside city and named it in honor of the Roman emperor. Not on the Mediterranean but the Sea of Galilee, not the capital of a kingdom but only of a tetrarchy, or quarter kingdom, not for Caesar Augustus but for his son Tiberius Caesar, the city was Caesarea Maritima in miniature minus the pagan elements. Since today Tiberias is a thriving tourist city, only bits and pieces of the ancient Jewish city have been excavated, like the corner of a theater (1), as yet to be stratigraphically dated, the initial portion of the cardo (2), and the southern city gate (3), though no accompanying first-century city walls have been found, shown here under construction with cranes (4). Pieces of a later basilica (5) and market area near the harbor have also been excavated. The palace (6) is known from Josephus's writings and alluded to in Luke 7:25, though according to the gospels Jesus never visited Tiberias, perhaps to avoid a direct confrontation with Antipas.*

treated like any other commercial commodity. It involves God in a very special way on two separate but connected fronts.

Buying and Selling Land.   Tenant farmers and resident aliens, recall Leviticus above, cannot sell land that does not belong to them. The classic paradigm here is the story of Naboth, who owned a vineyard, and Ahab, who ruled Israel about one hundred years before Jeroboam II, as told in 1 Kings:

Naboth the Jezreelite had a vineyard in Jezreel, beside the palace of King Ahab of Samaria. And Ahab said to Naboth, "Give me your vineyard, so that I may have it for a vegetable garden, because it is near my house; I will give you a better vineyard for it; or, if it seems good to you, I will give you its value in money." But Naboth said to Ahab, "The Lord forbid that I should give you my ancestral inheritance." Ahab went home resentful and sullen because of what Naboth the Jezreelite had said to him; for he had said, "I will not give you my ancestral inheritance." (21:1–4)

Ahab's reaction shows him to be a moderate monarch, but his queen is Jezebel, daughter of the king of Tyre. She comes from a different religion with a different economic theology. She believes in free trade, has Naboth murdered, and gives the contested vineyard to her husband. Naboth was not seeking to insult the king, but to remain faithful to the ancient and conservative covenantal theology that saw the land as belonging to God, and he refused to treat it like any other commercial commodity, buying and selling it at will.

Mortgaging and Losing Land.   If you could not sell your land, you could still lose it in one other way. You could go into debt using your land as collateral, default on repayment, and lose the land to foreclosure. Not buying or selling, not stealing or robbing, just indebting and foreclosing. So the Law has a lot to say about debt. Once again, it does not forbid it, but attempts to control or curtail its worst results, in five major ways.

By *Forbidding Interest*. Interest is forbidden among Israelites, whether taken before or after the loan, whether taken on money or goods. "If any of your kin fall into difficulty and become dependent on you, you shall support them; they shall live with you as though resident aliens. Do not take interest in advance or otherwise make a profit from them, but fear your God; let them live with you. You shall not lend them your money at interest taken in advance, or provide them food at a profit" (Lev. 25:35–37).

By *Controlling Collateral*. Collateral should not involve oppressive actions or demands. "No one shall take a mill or an upper millstone in pledge, for that would be taking a life in pledge. . . . When you make your neighbor a loan of any kind, you shall not go into the house to take the pledge. You shall wait outside, while the person to whom you are making the loan brings the pledge out to you. If the person is poor, you shall not sleep in the garment given you as the pledge. You shall give the pledge back by sunset, so that your neighbor may sleep in the cloak and bless you; and it will be to your credit before the Lord your God" (Deut. 24:6, 10–13).

By Remitting Indebtedness. Debt could still build up, slowly but surely, to an amount that could never be paid off. But not forever, at worst for seven years. "Every seventh year you shall grant a remission of debts. And this is the manner of the remission: every creditor shall remit the claim that is held against a neighbor, not exacting it of a neighbor who is a member of the community, because the Lord's remission has been proclaimed" (Deut. 15:1–2).

By Liberating Enslavement. Similarly, individuals or families who were sold into slavery for debt must be released after seven years. "If a member of your community, whether a Hebrew man or a Hebrew woman, is sold to you and works for you six years, in the seventh year you shall set that person free. And when you send a male slave out from you a free person, you shall not send him out empty-handed. Provide liberally out of your flock, your threshing floor, and your wine press, thus giving to him some of the bounty with which the Lord your God has blessed you" (Deut. 15:12–14).

By Reversing Dispossession. Finally, there was the extreme case of dispossession, as land became indebted, foreclosed, and lost to its original owner. But, just as those two preceding solutions took place every seventh year, so this one took place every fiftieth year, the Jubilee Year. "You shall hallow the fiftieth year and you shall proclaim liberty throughout the land to all its inhabitants. It shall be a jubilee for you: you shall return, every one of you, to your property and every one of you to your family" (Lev. 25:10). That restoration applied only to rural properties and not to urban ones. God protected the peasantry not as a preferential option for the poor, but as a preferential option for justice. Not "preference," actually, because it could not be otherwise?

Maybe some or all of that is theoretical rather than practical, ideal rather than real, but it is deeply imbedded in covenantal law, in the Torah, by which a people were to live in a land under a God of justice and righteousness. It represented what a covenantal kingdom might look like, and it distinguished the boom kingdom built by Jeroboam II from that demanded by Amos in the name of God, and the boom kingdom built by Herod Antipas from that proclaimed by Jesus in the name of the same God.

Kingdom and Eschaton

The oracles of Amos were rendered swiftly and terribly accurate when, under Sargon II in 721 B.C.E., the Assyrian Empire came down like a wolf on the fold, destroyed Samaria, and dispersed ten of the original twelve tribes forever. Those who collected and preserved his prophetic indictments could not end them without this more positive finale, this glimmer of hope:

> The time is surely coming, says the Lord, when the one who plows shall overtake the one who reaps, and the treader of grapes the one who sows the seed; the mountains shall drip sweet wine, and all the hills shall flow with it. I will restore the fortunes of my people Israel, and they shall rebuild the ruined cities and inhabit them; they shall plant vineyards and drink their wine, and they shall make gardens and eat their fruit. I will plant them upon their land, and they shall never again be plucked up out of the land that I have given them, says the Lord your God. (9:13–15)

That text promises restoration for a devastated land and a dispersed people, and it does so in a rhapsodic description of overflowing fertility in field and vineyard along with an unqualified pledge of dispossession "never again." But, and this is the most important point, if that vision were to come true, would those lost tribes return to the rich kingdom built by Jeroboam II or the just kingdom demanded by Amos?

Such hopes and promises are often called *eschatological*, but that term should not be understood from its later Christian meaning in which this material world is replaced by a spiritual one, this earthly world here below is replaced by a heavenly one there above. In ancient Israelite or Jewish texts eschatological language refers to a divinely established Utopia (from the Greek, "no place") or, better, Eutopia (from the Greek, "good place"), in which God puts an end to this world of injustice and unrighteousness, here below, and replaces it with a world of justice and righteousness, here below. It does not repeal creation by cosmic destruction, but destroys evil by cosmic transformation. The eschatological kingdom is the covenantal kingdom brought to its ultimate perfection and ideal consummation, but *here below, upon this earth.*

The prophets Amos and Micah both came from Judean peasant villages, both excoriated society for systemic and distributive injustice, one north, one south, and both had their ferocious indictments collected later into books in which they were glossed with eschatological hope. But Micah now contains an oracle far more ecstatic and rhapsodic than Amos's appended finale. Here is a vision of God's eschatological future, of God's earthly Eutopia, now present in both Micah (4:1–4) and his contemporary Isaiah (2:2–4):

> In days to come the mountain of the Lord's house shall be established as the highest of the mountains, and shall be raised up above the hills. Peoples shall stream to it, and many nations shall come and say: "Come, let us go up to the mountain of the Lord, to the house of the God of Jacob; that he may teach us his ways and that we may walk in his paths." For out of Zion shall go forth instruction, and the word of the Lord from Jerusalem. He shall judge between many peoples, and shall arbitrate between strong nations far away; they shall beat their swords into plowshares, and their spears into pruning hooks; nation shall not lift up sword against nation, neither shall they learn war any more; but they shall all sit under their own vines and under their own fig trees, and no one shall make them afraid; for the mouth of the Lord of hosts has spoken.

The content of that vision is as magnificent as the timing of its consummation is vague. The eschatological vision appended to Amos spoke of "on that day" and "the time is surely coming." The eschatological vision appended to Micah spoke of "in days to come" and "in that day." Like our contemporary "we shall overcome," the certainty of its *what* and *that* is not accompanied by an equal certainty of its *how* and *when*. But there is something even more striking about the eutopic ideal in that text.

Attacks on religious syncretisms, political alliances, and economic processes that negated Yahweh as a God of justice and righteousness were always dangerous, but also at least meaningful in dealing with indigenous Israelite kings. But what about those imperial monarchs who had destroyed Israel, the Northern Kingdom, at the end of the eighth century and controlled Judah, the Southern Kingdom, after the end of the seventh? What about the Assyrians, Neo-Babylonians, Persians, Greeks, Greco-Egyptians, Greco-Syrians, and, finally, the Romans? What did they care about village custom or divine covenant?

It was not just a question of chauvinism, xenophobia, or exclusivism. It was not just a question about the pagans as abstract entities known theoretically, but about the empires, the nations, the Gentiles whom the Israelites knew practically as oppressive forces. If the covenantal kingdom was less and less a reality and colonial status more and more an experience, how would Yahweh as God of justice and righteousness handle those imperial nations, handle the Gentiles, in establishing the eschatological kingdom that would finally realize that covenantal one as divine Eutopia, here below, upon this earth?

We have just seen one answer in that oracle added in both Micah 4:1–4 and Isaiah 2:2–4. Those warlike and conquering empires would be converted to Yahweh as God of justice and peace. They would not become Israelites, but both Gentiles and Israelites would live together under God. So also for Jews and Gentiles much later in a prophecy from the mid-second century B.C.E. There, in *Sibylline Oracles*, God will "raise up a kingdom for all ages among men," and "from every land they will bring incense and gifts to the house of the great God." Then, the "prophets of the great God will take away the sword" and "there will also be just wealth among men for this is the judgment and dominion of the great God" (3:767–95).

You can trace that positive vision of a cosmic conversion to justice and peace amidst fields unbelievably toil-free and/or animals unbelievably pacific across the entire Jewish tradition that wrestled with the problem of eschatological Gentiles. But, alongside that positive vision of eschatological justice, there is also a negative one of eschatological vengeance. "On that day" those marauding nations, the imperial gentile kingdoms, will be totally subjected to Israel or will be completely exterminated.

Those twin responses to oppression, conversion *or* extermination, justice *or* revenge, are not reconciled, but simply left side by side within the tradition. But both, we emphasize, are there, for example, in those same two texts cited above. "In that day," God says in Micah, "in anger and wrath I will execute vengeance on the nations that did not obey" (5:10, 15). Those enemies will "be trodden down like the mire of the streets" and they "shall lick dust like a snake, like the crawling things of the earth; they shall come trembling out of their fortresses; they shall turn in dread to the Lord our God, and they shall stand in fear of you" (7:10, 17). Similarly, in *Sibylline Oracles*, that other, negative side is also present: "All the impious will bathe in blood. The earth will also drink of the blood of the dying; wild beasts will be sated with flesh" (3:695–97).

No doubt those twin solutions could be combined, as in *2 Baruch*, written around the end of the first century C.E.: "He will call all nations, and some of them he will spare, and others he will kill. . . . Every nation which has not known Israel and which has not trodden down the seed of Jacob shall live. . . . All those, now, who have ruled over you or have known you, will be delivered up to the sword" (72:2–6). More often, however, they are simply left there, side by side even in the same text, the positive solution of conversion and the negative one of extermination. The end is always, as the pre-Maccabean text *The Book of the Watchers* says in *1 Enoch*, to "destroy injustice from the face of the earth . . . to cleanse the earth from all injustice" (10:16). But there is also the question of means, even of divine means. And here, especially, the end does not justify the means.

Kingdom and Apocalypse

The convenantal kingdom's sublime perfection is the eschatological or eutopian kingdom and the eschatological kingdom's imminent advent is the apocalyptic kingdom. They are on a continuum from ideal good (convenant) to perfect best (eschatology) and from distant hope (eschatology) to proximate presence (apocalypse). The further the present kingdom of God deviated from normal good, the more some people looked to ideal best. The further that ideal best deviated from present now, the more some people looked to future soon. An apocalypse is a *revelation* about that *ending* of evil and injustice as coming soon, very soon, right now almost. Without that continuity from covenantal to eschatological Kingdom of God, the content of an apocalyptic kingdom becomes an open question or an empty expectation. Compare, for example, the different final kingdoms announced in these following instances.

First, in the mid-170s B.C.E. Aemilius Sura described this sequence of five empires: "The Assyrians were the first of all races to hold world power, then the Medes, and after them the Persians, and then the Macedonians. Then through the defeat of Kings Philip and Antiochus, of Macedonian origin, followed closely upon the overthrow of Carthage, the world power passed to the Roman people." The sequence of four past empires and a climactic fifth one was already known in the ancient world, but to claim Rome as the fifth one was just the Roman option, historically quite defensible but not universally acceptable.

Next, in the mid-160s B.C.E. the apocalypse in the biblical book of Daniel also spoke of four kingdoms and a climactic fifth one. The four are now the Neo-Babylonians, the Medes, the Persians, and the Greeks. In Daniel those four great empires come out of the roiling sea's primordial chaos like ferocious wild beasts: a lion, a bear, a leopard, and a "fourth beast, terrifying and dreadful and exceedingly strong. It had great iron teeth and was devouring, breaking in pieces, and stamping what was left with its feet. It was different from all the beasts that preceded it" (7:7). The fifth kingdom appears when "one like a human being" comes before God, the Ancient of Days, or Lord of Time (7:13). (The Semitic male-chauvinistic phrase "a son of man" is equivalent to our English male-chauvinistic phrase "a member of mankind." Both mean a human being, a person.)

The beastlike ones come from the disorder of the sea; the humanlike one comes from the order of heaven. "Their dominion was taken away" and, instead, "dominion and glory and kingship" over "all peoples, nations, and languages" was given to "the people of the holy ones of the Most High" as an "everlasting kingdom" (7:14, 26–27). Whether the humanlike one is the corporate personification or angelic representative of God's people, theirs is clearly the fifth kingdom. Notice, however, that, although it is clearly antithetical to the earlier foursome, its details are not spelled out and presume a whole tradition about the eschatological and the covenantal kingdom.

If the apocalyptic kingdom is an ideal society, a perfect world, a divine Eutopia in imminent advent here below on earth, not all would necessarily agree on its details. All might agree on the restoration of Israel or the return of the lost tribes. All might agree on justice and peace, piety and holiness, fertility and prosperity. All might agree as long as those hopes remained unspecified. But, even within Judaism, female and male, slave and free, poor and rich, peasant and aristocrat would surely have had divergent emphases and priorities for a divine kingdom here below. What *was* the content of God's kingdom to be built on earth?

Consider one example. The apocalyptic scenario in *Sibylline Oracles* 2:196–335 is dated to the Augustan age at the turn of the common era. It is, as it were, a full-service Jewish apocalypse. First, the whole world will be engulfed in "a great river of blazing fire." Second, there will be a universal judgment at "the tribunal of the great immortal God." Third, that will include the dead, who "will be raised on a single day" when "Uriel, the great angel, will break the gigantic bolts, of unyielding and unbreakable steel, of the gates of Hades." Fourth, "all will pass through the blazing river and the unquenchable flame" so that "all the righteous will be saved, but the impious will then be destroyed for all ages." Fifth, that latter destruction is then exemplified in excruciating detail. Sixth, the former salvation is for those lifted from "the blazing river" and it is, of course, salvation within a perfect world and an ideal society. "The earth will belong equally to all, undivided by walls or fences. It will then bear more abundant fruits spontaneously. Lives will be in common and wealth will have no division. For there will be no poor man there, no rich, and no tyrant, no slave. Further, no one will be either great or small anymore. No kings, no leaders. All will be on a par together." Seventh, here is the final element. "To these pious ones imperishable God, the universal ruler, will also give another thing. Whenever they ask the imperishable God to save men from the raging fire and deathless gnashing he will grant it, and he will do this. For he will pick them out again from the undying fire and set them elsewhere and send them on account of his own people to another eternal life with the immortals in the Elysian plain." In that irenic scenario, evildoers are first consigned to a hell-like location, but they could be freed thence by request of those "concerned with justice and noble deeds."

Focus, for a moment, on those last two elements. Would everyone have imagined or agreed with that sixth point? Maybe, all would agree as long as it was wishful future thinking. Or would they? Was such radical egalitarianism acceptable to the aristocracy even as abstract ideal? Or, again, would everyone have imagined or agreed with that seventh point? That Jewish apocalypse received this gloss by a Christian scribe in one manuscript tradition: "Plainly false. For the fire which tortures the condemned will never cease. Even I would pray that this be so, though I am marked with very great scars of faults, which have need of very great mercy. But let babbling Origen be ashamed of saying that there is a limit to punishment." That Jewish scenario of separate but equal Eutopias is closer to the positive ideal of the Gentiles' conversion rather than to the negative one of extermination. Radical human equality? Radical divine mercy?

Along that divine continuum from covenantal through eschatological to apocalyptic kingdom, along that continuum of hoped-for justice and longed-for righteousness here below, it is not the beautifully vague and general scenarios that would cause internal tension, but the specific details, the practical results, and the socioeconomic implications. How exactly did the kingdom of Jeroboam II differ from that of Amos, the kingdoms of Augustus and Tiberius or Herod and Antipas differ from those of John the Baptist and Jesus of Nazareth? How did Sepphoris differ from Nazareth, Tiberias from Capernaum?

THE KINGDOM OF GOD
AT CAPERNAUM?

Herod the Great and Herod Antipas were two rulers with two kingdoms, each inaugurated by violence and each marked by construction projects. But, although the former succeeded in leaving a lasting imprint on the land, the latter was eventually exiled, leaving behind only second-rate architectural remains. The finds from the ruins of Caesarea in the kingdom built by Herod the Great astound their excavators each and every excavation season, while the layers of Antipas's Tiberias and Sepphoris are more elusive and less spectacular. Jesus' kingdom, by contrast, left behind no structures whatsoever, no inscriptions, no material artifacts. Nevertheless, archaeologists can help understand his program by examining the context in which he proclaimed and lived the Kingdom of God. And even if he never set foot in the city of Caesarea or any other large urban site such as the cities of the Decapolis, and even though the two Galilean cities of Sepphoris and Tiberias are never mentioned in the gospels, the character of all those cities in the first century is crucial to historical Jesus research for two reasons.

One is that they provide a point of comparison for the sites that are mentioned in the gospels. To understand the site of Nazareth, for example, we need to compare Nazareth with Capernaum, Capernaum with Sepphoris or Tiberias, Sepphoris or Tiberias with Caesarea Maritima or Jerusalem. Another and even more important reason is that they may provide an answer to why John and Jesus happened when and where they happened. Why did the Baptism movement of John and the Kingdom movement of Jesus happen in the territories of Herod Antipas in the late 20s, not beforehand and not afterward? Does the Romanization of Lower Galilee begun by Antipas with the reconstruction of Sepphoris in 4 B.C.E. and climaxed with its replacement as his capital by Tiberias in 19 C.E. have anything to do with those popular religio-political movements in the following decade? Is it significant, for example, that Jesus and the Kingdom of God are associated not with either Sepphoris or Tiberias, but with Capernaum? And how is that association to be understood? Turn, then, to Capernaum, the village, after Nazareth, most associated with Jesus, but with a picture of Herod the Great's master project of Caesarea Maritima and his son Antipas's second-rate cities of Sepphoris and Tiberias always in mind.

The First-Century Jewish Village of Capernaum

Population. First-century Capernaum was a modest Jewish village on the periphery of Antipas's territory relying chiefly on agriculture and fishing. An oppressive heat hovers over Capernaum during the long summers, the fields nearby are rocky and difficult to work, and in Jesus' day it was off any major trade route. It was not a sought-out spot, but a good place to get away from, with easy access across the Sea of Galilee to any side. It was also only a short distance from the territory of Herod Philip, a fairer and more moderate ruler than his half brother Antipas, according to Josephus. In both area and population, first-century Capernaum was dwarfed by Caesarea and was much smaller than Sepphoris and Tiberias. They covered areas of around 100 to 150 acres and had populations of eight to twelve thousand, but Capernaum was much more modest at around 25 acres and one thousand inhabitants. Capernaum was a step up from Nazareth, but many, many steps down from Sepphoris or Tiberias, and not steps but worlds below Caesarea.

Buildings. Like most Jewish villages in Galilee, including the hamlet of Nazareth, first-century Capernaum lacked the Greco-Roman architectural features that were part of the common urban parlance. Only the later Byzantine layer has a synagogue and church, but the earlier dearth of civic buildings underscores the village's provincial character. It didn't have a gate marking the entrance to the town like Tiberias, and there weren't any defensive fortifications or walls. There were no civic structures providing entertainment, such as a theater, amphitheater, or hippodrome as enjoyed by the urban elites at Caesarea and elsewhere, nor was there a public bathhouse or latrine for their convenience. There is not even evidence of a basilica structure used either for judicial matters, general assemblies, or commercial activities. Those, most likely, would have been dispensed in the open areas or along the lake. The archaeological excavations to date have uncovered no overtly pagan artifacts associated with shrines or temples at Capernaum, and there are no indications that there were statues or any other kind of iconography. The village had no constructed *agora*, or market, with shops or storage facilities. Market days were held in tents or booths on the open unpaved areas along the shore and outside private houses whose owners hawked their wares or sold their catches.

Streets. Just as important as the lack of public buildings for assessing Capernaum at the time of Jesus is its lack of centralized planning. It was not on an orthogonal grid and had no perpendicularly intersecting thoroughfares. Archaeologists have found no trace of a *cardo maximus* or *decumanus*, those crossed main streets that were hallmarks of Roman Period urban planning. None of the streets were paved with stone slabs. None were adorned with columns or porticoes. None were wider than 6 to 10 feet, more alleys and passageways than streets. None had channels for running water. Sewage was simply tossed in alleyways made of packed earth and dirt, dusty in the long hot seasons, muddy in the short wet seasons, but smelly in all seasons. None of the building materials associated with urbanism and wealth greeted ancient visitors to the site: there were no plaster surfaces, no decorative frescos, no red granite from Aswan, no white marble from Turkey, no marble of any kind, no patches nor even tessarae stones, and no red ceramic roof tiles in Roman Period contexts.

Capernaum's layout was organic rather than orthogonal. Even though the Franciscan excavators have referred to the various domestic units as *insulae*, they were certainly not the apartment structures planned on an orthogonal grid like those in Rome's port city of Ostia. They were a series of rooms clustered around a single enclosed courtyard belonging to an extended family. A close look at the excavators' plans shows that the fifth-century C.E. synagogue and complex around St. Peter's House, to be described below, imposed the most orderly perpendicular blocks onto the town's plan. The rest of the excavated walls are somewhat uneven, determined by makeshift growth of houses around central courtyards instead of a rigid grid imposed from above. You could easily manage your way around Capernaum by keeping to the spacious shoreline, or you could cut through the village in spaces left between clusters of courtyard houses. Passageways and streets ran in slightly crooked and curved lines with wider spots used to work on a boat, hang and mend fishing nets, or set up goat and sheep pens. Unlike Caesarea, Sepphoris, or Tiberias, the village of Capernaum had no axial ordering, no enclosing walls or imposing façades, no structures arranged to create vistas.

Inscriptions. No first-century C.E. or earlier public (or private) inscriptions have been found at Capernaum, betraying its modest stature (and illiteracy?). Public inscriptions were an important aspect of Greco-Roman city life, and proclamations of this or that benefactor were incised on all sorts of public surfaces: pavements, columns, fountains, and statues—they were the "billboards" of ancient city life. Individual expenditure on public building projects left its mark on stone in the ubiquitous honorific inscriptions unearthed in cities across the Mediterranean littoral, such as Pilate's at Caesarea. People paid to see their names in stone. There's nothing like it at first-century Capernaum or other Galilean villages.

Houses.   Keep in mind this description of Capernaum's houses for contrast with that of the Herodian palaces and urban villas in Chapter 3. And think of their description as at the opposite end of the spectrum from the Herodian commercial kingdom. Capernaum's houses are like the ones found in other Jewish villages in eastern Galilee and southern Golan, where local dark basalt furnished the building materials, along with some crooked wood beams, straw or reeds, and mud. The houses were built without the benefit of a skilled craftsman's techniques or tools, though an experienced elder from the village probably assisted in the design, lent some rudimentary tools, and performed the more difficult tasks, and members of the household, friends, and neighbors provided the labor.

The construction quality was low, in contrast to the tightly fitting Herodian bossed masonry, well-planned *opus quadratum* technique, or header-stretcher ashlar construction, to be seen in more detail in the next chapter. Walls were built atop basalt boulder foundations; the surviving lower courses were two lines of unhewn fieldstones with smaller stones, mud, and clay packed into the interstices; and instead of plaster or fresco, the walls' faces were smeared with mud or dung and straw, with insulation instead of aesthetics in mind. A few of the walls were thick enough to support a second story, but if they did, those stories would have been frail, in need of constant repair, and prone to occasional collapse. None of the roofs have survived intact, but the lack of stones shaped as arches, vaults, or rafters, coupled with the complete absence of roof tiles, means that the houses were covered with thatched reeds, as they are described in Jewish rabbinic literature. Wooden ceiling beams supported a thick bed of reeds that protected the timbers from dampness, and the whole was covered with packed mud for additional insulation. Such a roof is assumed when Mark recounts the healing of the paralytic at Capernaum, where his stretcher bearers "dug through the roof" (2:4) before they lowered him to Jesus. A generation later, miles away and a social stratum higher, Luke edits Mark to read that they lowered him "through the tiles" (5:19), a statement inapplicable to Capernaum, but certainly appropriate to Luke's more urban environment and upper-class audience, who lived under roof tiles.

Unlike aristocratic villas, Capernaum's houses were not laid out with an axial arrangement that afforded a glimpse from the entrance, through the atrium, to the *triclinium*, or formal dining room, but, instead, several abutting rooms centered around a courtyard. Along with an enclosure wall, these working rooms, storage facilities, and sleeping quarters cloistered the courtyard, so that, unlike the atrium house, visibility to the interior was obstructed. Most of these complexes had only one entrance; one found almost intact at Capernaum had a hewn threshold and ashlar doorjamb with some kind of locking mechanism for a wooden door, but it was nowhere near the sturdiness and size of the monolithic door frames at Sepphoris, much less those in any of Herod's palaces. The few windows in the walls were set rather high, designed for lighting and ventilation rather than for scenic vistas, as were those in Herodian palaces or other aristocratic villas. The inhabitants cared more about security and a sense of seclusion from outsiders and street life. So they restricted access to the courtyard and placed their windows high enough to conceal their lives. Once inside the complex, internal doorways to the various rooms were crudely made of fieldstones, with simple wood beams framing the entry and lacking any apparent closing mechanism—they may simply have been covered with straw mats or curtains.

The walls and rooms formed an enclosure that shielded the courtyards at Capernaum from view, courtyards that had no signs of wealth or luxury items for show. The courtyard was the scene of vibrant family life and work activities, as numerous artifacts indicate. It functioned, in a way, analogous to the modern living room, kitchen, and dining room, as well as a workshop, garage, and storage area wrapped into one. Fragments of clay ovens, gray ash, and grinding stones remain from the women who made bread from grain on a daily basis. Some courtyards even had substantial agricultural implements, such as large mule- or ox-turned grinders and olive presses, which were perhaps shared by several families. In the typical Galilean village from the Roman Period, table scraps were simply tossed onto the courtyard floor and later treaded into it. Larger courtyards had a portion fenced off for goat pens. Chickens roamed the entire lot. Fishhooks and net weights were found strewn around and testify to the time when fishers tried to keep their tackle functioning and boats afloat.

Rooms. The material remains inside the rooms from Early Roman layers at Capernaum bespeak a simple existence of fishers or farmers. There were no luxury items or other indications of wealth. No stamped handles from imported wine amphorae were found in these contexts, nor were any tiny *unguetaria* containing fine oils or perfumes excavated, and even the simplest glass forms are lacking.

Numerous stone vessels have been uncovered by the excavators, but these are mugs, cups, or basins that were either handmade or turned on a small lathe, not the more expensive vessels turned on a large lathe. The lamps from the first century were almost exclusively simple, undecorated Herodian types; virtually no imported or finely decorated lamps were found. The very few lamps of somewhat finer quality bore no mythological, pagan, or erotic motifs common on lamps found along the coast and at larger cities, but bore only simple floral decorations. In the same way, the pottery was entirely locally made, much of it apparently manufactured at the Upper Galilean village of Kefar Hananya, and consisted of cooking pots, casserole dishes, water jars for storage, and jugs, Serving vessels, bowls, and cups are less frequent, and fine wares imported from afar for dining are nearly nonexistent in Early Roman contexts. Only a few fine wares have been found, cups or bowls that were locally made but that imitated imported ceramic wares from world-famous manufacturing sites.

Boats. Capernaum's inhabitants took advantage of fishing in the lake. At a later period, a more robustly built but simple quay lined the shore. Earlier the water lapped up against the irregular shore, with some jetties and breakwaters made of stacked fieldstones jutting out into the lake. That is hardly a "harbor" in the sense of Caesarea's monumental all-weather port.

Certainly fishing provided sustenance and work for a good portion of the inhabitants of Capernaum, but their houses alone make clear that the fishing "industry" was no financial bonanza. Thanks to the discovery in 1986 of a fishing boat from the first century, more details of boat making and fishing on the Sea of Galilee have come to light. During a dramatic drop in the Sea of Galilee's water due to severe droughts, two brothers from the Kibbutz Ginnosar noticed the outlines of a boat buried in mud near ancient Magdala, and rescue operations began to recover and restore the boat before the rising water level covered it once more. Nearly two thousand years ago, the dilapidated 8-by-26-foot boat was stripped of its reusable parts and

THE FIRST-CENTURY GALILEE BOAT
(courtesy Yigal Allon Museum, Kibbutz Ginnosar)

pushed offshore to sink. That covered it with silt and mud, encasing it in an anaerobic state and protecting it from bacteria and decay.

The hull's construction and materials tell the story of an experienced boatwright with sparse resources. The craftsman lacked suitable raw materials for his craft, but was experienced, clever, and determined enough to keep the vessel afloat for some time. It was originally constructed from timbers salvaged from other boats as well as from inferior wood locally available. The forward keel was the only part of the boat made from appropriate wood, a piece of Lebanese cedar that had served the same function on an earlier boat—the cut marks from those earlier joints were still visible. Most of the planks were from low-quality lumber that no Mediterranean boatwright would have considered using, such as pine, jujube, and willow. The hull's strakes and planks were joined with mortise-and-tenon joints, locked together with carefully measured oak pegs, around which pine resin somewhat sealed the wood; a frame hammered in with iron nails and staples stabilized the hull; and the whole underside was smeared with a bitumen pitch.

Over time, however, the materials betrayed the boatwright as tenons snapped, timbers sprang, and pegs rotted. Stripped of its sail, anchor, and reusable parts, including even nails, the hull was floated away from the shore, where it quickly sank. Simple open and closed cooking pots and an undecorated local lamp date the boat to the first century, which carbon-14 dating on the wooden planks confirmed. Lacking proper materials, fishers on the Sea of Galilee worked hard to keep their vessels afloat, using this and that scrap of wood to replace rotting planks and eking out a living by casting or dragging their nets along the shoreline. Herod Antipas's commercial kingdom didn't launch a fishing or mercantile fleet on the lake.

Later Kingdom Building at Capernaum

Herod the Great's kingdom and Herod Antipas's tetrarchy imposed a Roman veneer onto Jewish Galilee and changed economic structures, which ultimately led to two Jewish wars against Rome. Thereafter, Rome abandoned the use of client-kings and settled for direct rule and a legionary presence. Roads were built and improved throughout the Jewish homeland in order to integrate it better into the Roman East's road network and to facilitate the imperial campaigns against the last great enemy of Rome, the Parthians on the far eastern reaches of the empire. Traces of Galilee's incorporation into Roman imperial kingdom building have also been found at Capernaum.

A Roman Bath. Excavated in the late 1980s on the Greek Orthodox patriarchate's portion of Capernaum's ruins, a small bathhouse suggests initially some connections with a gospel story. Built in typical Roman legionary style, the bathhouse stood on what was then the easternmost outskirts of town. The 26-by-56-foot building was constructed to standards unlike any other at the site: a brick-and-tile system with flues underneath was covered by a thick waterproof mortar-and-concrete floor; the walls were constructed of uniformly cut stones, in carefully leveled courses and with ample mortar. The bathhouse's division into four chambers—a *frigidarium*, or cold-water room, *tepidarium*, or warm-water room, *caldarium*, or hot-steam room, and *apodyterium*, or changing room—is like any other row-type bathhouse of the Roman legions on the western borders in Britain and Gaul during the second century C.E.

Such a bathhouse, however, does not imply that public bathing in Roman urban style was practiced by the villagers of Jesus' Capernaum. It indicates, instead, the presence of a Roman occupying force that wanted to bathe there in Roman style. And it has no connections with the story

RECONSTRUCTION OF FIRST-CENTURY CAPERNAUM. *The site most frequently associated with Jesus' ministry in the gospels was a medium-sized Jewish village. Capernaum took advantage of fishing on the lake and fertile lands nearby and housed a population of around a thousand. The boat in the foreground (1) is a plank-by-plank rendition of that accidentally discovered first-century vessel now housed in the Yigal Allon Museum at Kibbutz Ginnosar, and the storage jar (2) is based on one found inside the boat. Fishers typically dragged nets from several boats or cast circular nets from a single boat (3); the nets needed frequent mending, as shown here on the anchorage (4), made from simple local basalt stones stacked into breakwaters, a far cry from the harbor at Caesarea Maritima. Without any significant public architecture, vendors, fishers, and farmers lined Capernaum's open shoreline to hawk their wares or socialize (5).*

of the Capernaum centurion in the *Q Gospel* at Matthew 8:5–13 = Luke 7:1–10 and in John 4:46–54. Ceramic sherds taken from the structure by its excavator, Vassilios Tzaferis, of the Israel Antiquities Authority, confirm its date to the Middle Roman Period. The bathhouse dates then to the second century, when Roman legionaries were stationed permanently in Galilee after the revolt of 132–35 C.E. The official, called a "centurion" in Luke (from the Greek *hekatonarchos,* "ruler of one hundred") should not be mistaken for a Roman centurion presiding over a legion's contingent. John's story simply calls him a *basilikos* ("royal official") and those earlier mentioned inscriptions from Sepphoris and Tiberias show that Antipas readily adopted Greek and Roman terminology for his officials. Most of his officials were Jewish, though Luke and maybe even John presume some gentile mercenary from a foreign land serving in this border town. Under Antipas's rule there were no permanently stationed Roman officials in Galilee.

A Roman Milestone.   Evidence for legionary presence from around the same period has been found in the form of a milestone near Capernaum. Roman legions, who served also as engineers, were busy at work in Galilee and elsewhere in the East constructing the Roman road system at the directive of the emperor Hadrian. He wanted travel in the East to be easier and quicker for his legions who were fighting the Parthians or might need to quell another Jewish uprising. The Roman milestone, in Latin, bears the emperor Hadrian's name:

IMP(erator)
C[A]E[S]AR DIVI
[TRAIA]NI PAR(thici)
F(ilius)[DIVI NERVAE][N]EP(OS)TRAI
[ANUS][HA]DRIANUS AUG(ustus)

Translation: "The Emperor Caesar, son of the divine Trajan who conquered the Parthians, grandson of the divine Nerva, Trajan Hadrian Augustus."

Two centuries after the second Jewish war against Rome (132–35 C.E.), its supremacy would be reasserted again over Galilee and Capernaum, but now with the proclamation of Christian victory. At Capernaum, however, as in the rest of Galilee, the Christianization of public space did not go unopposed. Although it had been the site of most of Jesus' life, teachings, and miracles, three centuries later very few Christians lived in Galilee, which was still overwhelmingly Jewish. Many Christian pilgrims passed through it, however, as it was dotted with important destinations on itineraries to the Holy Land. Archaeological excavations in Galilee have uncovered a tight network of imperially sponsored Christian structures from the Byzantine Period, pilgrim sites such as the Grotto of the Annunciation in Jesus' hometown Nazareth, the shrine at Cana commemorating the water turned into wine, and the monastery complex at Kursi, where the legion of demons had been exorcised. But just as many archaeological remains point to a flourishing of Jewish self-expression, and even of resistance to and defiance of Christian imperialism, in the form of synagogues, mosaics, and art.

A Jewish Synagogue.   The ruins at Capernaum on the northern shore of the Sea of Galilee testify to the competition between church and synagogue. Archaeological excavations conducted there during the past century on land in Franciscan custody have uncovered a fifth-century octagonal church built to venerate the house of St. Peter, "the prince of the apostles," and have exposed a synagogue nearby—a response by the Jewish villagers to the foreign religion's incursion.

In the fifth century when the octagonal church announced Christianity and empire in the village's public space, the people of Capernaum countered with an architectural statement of their own, Jewish and indigenous. They constructed, just a block north of the church, a magnificent limestone synagogue, dated to the fifth century by ceramic evidence and numerous coins under its floors. This synagogue was one of the largest and most well built of the Byzantine Period, somewhat surprising given the modest nature of the site. Its walls, pavers, and columns were made of white limestone brought in from farther west in Galilee and contrasted starkly with the dark gray buildings made from the local basalt stone native to the Sea of Galilee's surroundings. With its façade and entrance facing Jerusalem, the main room was flanked by two tiers of seats on the eastern and western sides and divided by two rows of columns with ornately decorated capitals. Otherwise, the decorations were somewhat simple and rather provincial: some rosettes and garland streams, as well as a menorah, several stars, including what looks like a Star of David, and a depiction of the Ark of the Covenant or portable Torah shrine.

Ironically, the funds with which the synagogue was built may have come through wealth generated from Christian pilgrims. Two dedicatory inscriptions were found inside the synagogue, one on a column and one on a lintel, as by this century the practice of commemorating gifts in stone was well established in the Jewish community. The former is in Greek, somewhat of a rarity, and the latter is in Aramaic, as were most contemporaneous synagogue inscriptions. They contain the names of Jewish patrons who sponsored and craftsmen who built the synagogue: Herod (son of?) Halphai, and Chalfo, son of Zebida, son of John. These Jewish names, of course, sound vaguely similar to those found in the gospels, whose associations with Capernaum some four centuries earlier were memorialized in the nearby church.

But does the synagogue itself have any connections to the gospel stories? It is *possible*, but very unlikely. The Franciscan excavators have suggested that some Early Roman walls under the fifth-century C.E. limestone synagogue represent the foundations of the earlier synagogue. But that a synagogue building stood in Capernaum in the first century cannot be confirmed by these one or two short walls from that time, which are indistinguishable from the other first-century domestic walls at the site. Nor can the gospel references to a *synagogue*, where Jesus exorcised demons (Mark 1:21) and taught (John 6:59), be used as proof that this is the synagogue. As mentioned in Chapter 1, the term *synagogue* refers primarily to a *gathering* and only secondarily to a *structure* during the Early Roman Period. Only Luke's story of the Capernaum "centurion" presumes a synagogue *structure* at Capernaum, an edifice built with the centurion's benevolence (Luke 7:5).

But Luke narrates events from a viewpoint outside Palestine, where Jewish diaspora communities more clearly used this term for an actual structure, and at a much later period, when the classical synagogue structure was developing. Luke, remember, was also wrong about the roofs at Capernaum, the synagogue at Nazareth, and the scrolls read by Jesus. But this does not undermine the validity of Luke's message—that he thinks there was a synagogue-as-building shows only that he envisioned the events as occurring in an environment similar to his and his audience's. And it also shows that he presumes a righteous Gentile would take seriously his patronal responsibilities and build a synagogue, like that later God-fearing and alms-giving centurion named Cornelius described by Luke in Acts 10. But Jews in Galilean villages at the time of Jesus met in synagogues-as-gatherings, maybe at times in an open square, a large house's courtyard, a village elder's residence, and, in larger villages or towns, in modest structures no longer identifiable as synagogues by excavators. The issue of a building at Capernaum was surely incidental to Luke, and to speak about the "synagogue of Jesus" at Capernaum has no archaeological credibility.

A Christian Church. That fifth-century synagogue faced the fifth-century octagonal church, which was built atop a fourth-century building centering on a single room, itself part of a private house from the first century

B.C.E. Presumably it belonged to Peter's family and was where his mother-in-law was healed from a severe fever according to Mark 1:29–31. It actually is one of the very few credible localizations of a New Testament tradition.

The Archaeology of Peter's House. Franciscan archaeologists, conducting excavations around the site between 1968 and 1985, uncovered three distinct layers, or strata: the octagonal fifth-century church (which the excavators call Stratum III), a fourth-century house-church and shrine (Stratum II), and a simple courtyard house occupied from the first century B.C.E. (Stratum I).

Stratum III was constructed in concentric octagons, the inner of which could be entered from several sides and whose ceiling was supported by eight columns. The porticoed space between the two octagons was covered with mosaic floors decorated with simple geometric designs and lotus-flowered borders. The central room of the fifth-century church had also been set apart in the fourth-century Stratum II, when a quadrilateral wall of roughly 80 by 80 feet marked off the block as some kind of sacred precinct. A ceiling supported by a central arch covered the central room at that time. This room had been the focus of attention for some time, possibly as early as the second century C.E. The floor and walls of this room were repeatedly plastered in contrast to the remaining walls and floors of the complex, and hundreds of graffiti-like inscriptions—in Greek, Syriac, Hebrew, and Latin—had been etched into its surfaces.

Although much of the graffiti is altogether illegible and some of it is apparently quite ordinary or even profane, some of the phrases etched into the plaster appear to have been from the hands of visitors to the room and of Christian pilgrims from far afield. Though much of the overly tendentious and pious transliterations of the Franciscan excavators, involving theories of a thriving Jewish-Christian community and including elaborate speculations on acrostics and symbolism, are not persuasive, these graffiti are important. The very fact that the room was plastered and graffitied, makes it totally unlike any other in Capernaum, or elsewhere in Galilee, and demonstrates that this one-time room in a private residence was held in special regard by many people only a century after Jesus' activities in Galilee. And note how they wrote. They did not inscribe as Pilate had at Caesarea, dedicating an imperial Roman building in official Latin, nor as Antipas had at Tiberias, appointing his brother-in-law with an imperial Roman name in Greek; rather, they indecipherably scratched and scrawled with knives and rocks into plaster.

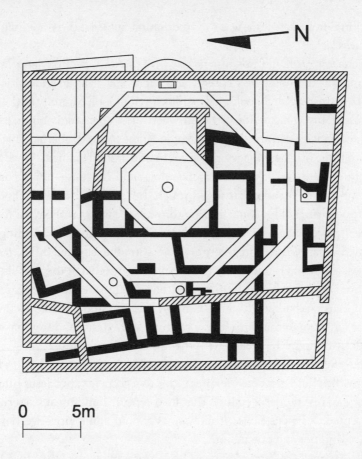

St. Peter's House and Church, fifth century (white), fourth century (hatched), first century (black) strata (after Corbo)

Although the house-become-octagonal-church and the magnificent synagogue point to the clashing visions over identity and rule in fifth-century Galilee, they tell us little about Capernaum at the time of Jesus. Whether or not the level and scratched inscriptions of the so-called "sacred area" *(insula sacra)* verify that the house belonged to Peter is not the most important point. Even if the center of the octagon marks the right spot (where Jesus healed? where Jesus ate?), and even if archaeology could authenticate Peter and Jesus' presence there, we would no better understand Jesus, his proclamation of the Kingdom of God, and the kind of kingdom he was building among his followers. For Christian pilgrims past and present, the *where* is understandably important, but the pressing question is not *where* Jesus was in Capernaum, but *what* the Capernaum of Jesus *was like*.

Archaeology should not just be used to carefully peel off later layers, determine if the house was Peter's, and then offer it as an illustration or visual aid. Instead, archaeology should be used to look carefully at the *kind* of house it was, compare it to other first-century Capernaum houses, examine the character of the village as a whole, and contrast Capernaum's character to those of other villages and cities in and around Galilee. As we have tried to show so far, combining archaeology and exegesis—doing parallel layering—is not just about cutting through the layers of the texts to find the authentic sayings of Jesus and cutting through the layers of the ruins to find the real places where Jesus stayed. Instead, it extends to examining the archaeological record of first-century layers in all excavated cities, towns, villages, and hamlets, including those never mentioned in the gospels, like Sepphoris and Caesarea Maritima, so that the broader social context in which Jesus was building his kingdom can be understood. And the content of that kingdom in the earliest text stratum of the Jesus tradition has to fit interactively and dynamically with the archaeological context.

The goal may not be to find a "holy site," or "sacred area," but it's hard to deny the allure of a possible direct link to a gospel text or Jesus himself. In any case, even or especially if that first-century building at Capernaum is accepted as Peter's house, there are two final ambiguities we have to raise, one minor and one major.

The Ambiguity of Peter's House. The minor ambiguity is this. In 30 C.E. Herod Philip elevated the lakeside fishing village of Bethsaida to city status and renamed it Julias in honor of Augustus's wife and Tiberius's mother, Livia Julia. It is called "the city of Andrew and Peter" by John (1:44). But in Mark 1:29 Jesus "entered the house of Simon and Andrew," healed Simon's mother-in-law, and, thereafter, "she began to serve them." There is, obviously, no problem with imagining Simon Peter and Andrew as having moved from Bethsaida to Capernaum or even as maintaining a house in each place. But, when a mother-in-law (ad)ministers to guests, it is her home, it is her daughter's home, and it is, because and only because of that, her son-in-law Simon Peter's home. Peter, most likely, was living with his wife's family. Maybe, therefore, we might speak more accurately not of Peter's, but of Peter's wife's home at Capernaum.

The major ambiguity is this. Matthew is especially interested in correlating Jesus' dwelling places with prophetic promises. First, in 2:23, Jesus left

Bethlehem, presumably his parental home for Matthew, unlike Luke, and "made his home in a town called Nazareth, so that what had been spoken through the prophets might be fulfilled, 'He will be called a Nazorean.'" Second, in 4:13–16, Jesus "left Nazareth and made his home in Capernaum by the sea [i.e., the lake], in the territory of Zebulun and Naphtali, so that what had been spoken through the prophet Isaiah might be fulfilled: 'Land of Zebulun, land of Naphtali, on the road by the sea [i.e., the Mediterranean], across the Jordan, Galilee of the Gentiles—the people who sat in darkness have seen a great light, and for those who sat in the region and shadow of death light has dawned.'" Did Jesus make his "base" at Peter's (wife's) house in Capernaum and, if he did, what did "base" mean?

Matthew probably got the idea of Capernaum as Jesus' home base from Mark, where, however, the ambiguity is more emphasized than eliminated. On the one hand, Mark 2:1 describes Jesus as being "at home" in presumably Peter's (wife's) house at Capernaum. But is he visiting or based in that house? The question arises from Mark's description of the inaugural day at Capernaum in 1:16–38. Powerful teaching and healing sends Jesus' fame throughout Galilee and brings post-Sabbath crowds to the house. Any Mediterranean reader would have expected Jesus to settle down there and let Peter, his family, and his village broker him to the surrounding countryside. But, instead, according to 1:35–38, "in the morning, while it was still very dark, [Jesus] got up and went out to a deserted place, and there he prayed. And Simon and his companions hunted for him. When they found him, they said to him, 'Everyone is searching for you.' He answered, 'Let us go on to the neighboring towns, so that I may proclaim the message there also; for that is what I came out to do.'"

Two points. In Mark, Jesus prays in Capernaum at the start and in Gethsemane at the end of his public life. He prays when his will is tempted to deviate from the divine will, either in life or in death. And to settle down at Capernaum and let all come to him is against the geography of the Kingdom of God. That is why Jesus "came out" from Peter's (wife's) house. It could not be his "home base" as if the Kingdom of God could, like the kingdoms of Caesar Augustus at Rome, of Herod the Great at Caesarea, or of Herod Antipas at Sepphoris and then Tiberias, have a dominant center, a controlling place, a local habitation and a name.

Neither Matthew nor Luke knows what to make of Mark's phrase about "coming out" and each solves it in a different way. Matthew copies all the other incidents from Mark's inaugural day at Capernaum, but he omits completely any mention of a dawn prayer and a "coming out." Luke accepts the unit from Mark, but changes its final phrase from Mark's "for that is what I came out to do" into his own alternative "for I was sent for this purpose" (4:43).

That first-century Capernaum house may well have been where Jesus visited and stayed as a guest. But it was not the "home base" of the Kingdom of God. That could be neither with his family at Nazareth nor with Peter at Capernaum, because, unlike the commercial kingdoms it opposed, this covenantal kingdom could not have a dominant place to which all must come, but only a moving center that went out alike to all.

The Irony of Peter's House. The irony is that a house where Jesus may once have shared a simple meal in private space with the family of Peter's in-laws was ultimately transformed into a place of public pilgrimage under Roman imperial protection and patronage. The irony is that, earlier, Jesus' covenantal Kingdom of God and Herod's commercial Kingdom of Rome were on a collision course with one another, but, later, the development of Capernaum looked more like the latter than the former.

Early first-century meals in Capernaum or similar villages were not a show for others, but a family affair. Unlike in the wealthy urban villas or royal palaces with elegant dining rooms, the villagers shared their meals in one of the larger rooms in the short rainy and cold season and in the shaded portions of the courtyard during hot summers. They ate their meals not on plates, but on bread, onto which they ladled olive oil, lentils, beans, or vegetables in stew form, sharing olives and perhaps a bit of cheese or fruit. Fish, salted, dried, or grilled on a spit, was sometimes available. Wine—local to be sure—supplied a portion of the daily caloric intake and took the edge off a hard day's work. None of Capernaum's domestic units had a setting that was marked off in any way architecturally with plastered or frescoed walls, not to mention mosaic floors; indeed, not a single tessara has been found in first-century domestic contexts.

But if plaster and fresco were lacking in Capernaum's first-century courtyard houses, it was precisely their presence in the "sacred area" of the *insula sacra* from the later Roman and Byzantine strata that caused it to differ so markedly from the other rooms and led to its identification as non-domestic space, a house-church or a shrine. This room, once private and ordinary, was first plastered, then had Christian graffiti etched into it, and ultimately was transformed into public space with monumental characteristics. The octagonal basilica with columns, mosaics, and precinct walls was separated off as sacred space. The once private and secluded space became designated public and imperial space, with access through a series of partitions in three concentric circles: the outer precinct wall, the middle portico, and the inner columnar wall.

Those architectural changes at the site in the subsequent stratigraphy correspond with a shift in the ceramics. Elegant fine wares, from well-known kilns in Africa and Cyprus, dramatically increase in the Byzantine stratum's ceramic profile at Capernaum. As Christian pilgrims traveled to the Holy Land, they may have brought with them fine wares from their homeland as offerings, or more likely infused sufficient cash into the regional economy to enable some locals to afford fine wares from afar. A significant number of sherds were from fine clay expertly fired into expensive plates, many of which were stamped with crosses. There were fewer cooking wares at Capernaum's *insula sacra* reflective of simple families preparing and sharing meals, but the presence of lamps and of elegant fine wares for serving increased. The concentration around the *insula sacra* of these plates along with more cups implies that the Eucharist, or Lord's Supper, was celebrated there. What was once the setting for menial work, family activities, and simple meals was, under Christian imperial sponsorship, absorbed into a civic life that the social elites dominated through financial patronage and priestly hierarchy.

This chapter raises a fundamental question that reappears at the start of the next one and returns at the end of the last one. If life in the Kingdom of God as lived by Jesus and his companions was opposed to that in the tetrarchal Kingdom of Antipas around it, the royal Kingdom of Herod before it, and the imperial Kingdom of Augustus or Tiberius above it, how did all of that relate to the Christian Kingdom of Constantine? In the next chapter, for example, family picnics, simple, communal, and religious, are transformed into civic and symbolic acts under priestly leadership, hierarchical control, and royal patronage, first by Herod with a temple and then by Philip with a city. If a Herodian edifice covered a site long sacred to paganism and Pan, how exactly did that differ from a Constantinian edifice covering a Christian site long sacred to Peter?

FOUR

Putting Jesus in His Place

Tell me, said the anthropologist, how you eat and I will tell you how you live; show me your table and I will know your society. How do you dine with your God? Are the seating arrangements and food distributions open or regulated, egalitarian or hierarchical? And, if hierarchical, on what norm is that hierarchy established? How do you dine with your king? Are the invitations universal or particular, for all alike or for the very special few? And, once again, what criteria establishes you among those very special few? How do you eat with Augustus and/or Herod and/or Antipas in the Kingdom of Rome? And how, above all, do you eat and drink with Jesus of Nazareth in the Kingdom of God?

IN THE SHRINE OF A GOD

Sacrificing and offering edible gifts to the gods, eating with them, and even eating the gods were commonplace in antiquity. Archaeologists have uncovered traces of sacred meals and ritual dining in the form of inscriptions, altars, butchered animal remains, cooking pots, and serving vessels at shrines across the Mediterranean.

One of the most pleasant settings with striking scenery for such rites was at Banias, located on a plateau at the southern base of Mount Hermon around a cave near one of the sources of the Jordan River, nearly 30 miles from Capernaum and the Sea of Galilee. The lush and verdant area around this grotto and spring was associated in antiquity with the god Pan, half-man and half-goat in form, the companion of woodland nymphs, the riotous but lyrical deity of forests, mountains, and streams. Along a slender terrace, wedged between precipitous cliffs above and pools with a stream flowing from the springs below, lies a spot that had attracted locals and visitors alike. Shaded by both steep cliffs and ample foliage and cooled by the water gushing from the springs, the site served as a sanctuary of the nature god Pan during the Hellenistic and Roman Periods; the grotto itself was called the *Paneion* in Greek, and the surrounding area *Panias*, arabicized today as Banias. It was initially a natural shrine in a bucolic and rural setting until Herod the Great built the *Augusteion*, a temple dedicated to Caesar in front of the grotto. Later, Herod's son Philip elaborated the sanctuary complex and founded his capital city south of the springs with the name *Caesarea Philippi*.

Pan's Shrine

Excavations undertaken around the temple complex and among the ruins of the city of Caesarea Philippi tell the story of the site's rise and fall. Detailed stratigraphic examination of the architecture and analysis of the ceramic remains shed light on the practice of ritual dining at the sanctuary. There were no architectural structures whatsoever during the earliest phase of the cult site, but Andrea Berlin's thorough study of the site's pottery shows that, during the Hellenistic Period, people went to the site and left behind traces of their visits in the form of sherds from cooking pots, casserole dishes, bowls, and saucers. Some of the vessels they took there broke, and these pieces were swept off the terrace in antiquity. A large number of Hellenistic sherds present without any contemporary architecture tells of visitors congregating around the cave over the course of two centuries prior to the common era. What they were doing is clear from the kinds of vessels they left behind. Of the some 250 Hellenistic diagnostic sherds—pieces big enough to identify securely and date by form and type—virtually none were from lamps or storage vessels, otherwise common components in domestic and public spaces excavated by archaeologists. Instead, the diagnostic sherds are evenly split between serving vessels and cooking vessels, many of which showed fire marks. The central activity around the Pan grotto was the preparation and consumption of food and drink.

The fabric and ware of the potsherds also tell us where the pilgrims came from. Almost 90 percent of the wares were locally made. Some of them were the brownish pink, heavily tempered, and coarsely made wares of the Itureans, but the majority of them were the so-called spatter-painted wares of the Syro-Phoenicians. The Itureans, a pastoral and seminomadic pagan group with origins in Lebanon, also inhabited the northern Golan in the Hellenistic Period, and the Syro-Phoenicians were Greek-speaking pagans from the northern coast around Tyre and Sidon who had made incursions inland as far as the Huleh Valley. The few nonlocal pieces were semifine wares from the coast, along with two wine amphorae from the Greek islands, each commonly found at Syro-Phoenician sites.

In short, during the Hellenistic Period the shrine was a local sanctuary attracting pagan visitors from the immediate surroundings; visitors who brought offerings and meals in simple local wares. They left behind neither impressive gifts nor signs of wealth. This evidence looks much like ritual dining, but as Berlin puts it, the sherds there "could also be interpreted, more informally, as picnicking." Sacred meal or picnic? Perhaps both, though the archaeologist is hard-pressed to distinguish between such meals or know the visitors' attitudes, except that they took the time to prepare food, eat it, and leave behind vessels around the cave at Banias. The next layer at the site is from the Early Roman Period and, with all the architectural components of a sanctuary, more clearly ties the ceramic remains to cultic meals and offerings.

Herod's Temple

Herod the Great acquired the territory around the springs midway through his reign as a reward for his loyalty to Caesar Augustus. In return, according to Josephus, Herod promptly erected a temple around the cave, dedicated it to Augustus, and called it the *Augusteion*. Until recently, rocks and boulders fallen from the cliff covered the site, but archaeologists digging through the debris have uncovered evidence for this very temple. Three walls, two perpendicular to the cliff-face, and a façade were built atop a 30-by-60-foot platform carved outside the cave. They were constructed with squarely hewn limestone ashlars in *opus quadratum* technique, perhaps by the same Italian architects whom Herod commissioned for his palace at Jericho. On the interior of the walls, mortises once held marble plaques, and a series of circular and rectangular niches were carved to house miniature statues. The temple had no back wall, but opened onto the grotto; in essence, the constructed portion of the temple served as the forecourt, while the cave itself was marked off as the inner sanctum. The *Augusteion* retained the natural character appropriate to Pan, but added a façade and architectural veneer appropriate to the cult of the Roman emperor.

The James Ossuary
(courtesy Biblical Archaeology Society, Washington, DC)

Twenty-First-Century Nazareth

Reconstruction of First-Century Nazareth

Reconstruction of First-Century Caesarea Maritima

Reconstruction of First-Century Tiberias

The First-Century Galilee Boat
(courtesy Allon Museum, Kibbutz Ginnosar)

Reconstruction of First-Century Capernaum

Reconstruction of a First-Century Courtyard House at Capernaum

Reconstruction of Late Roman Dionysos Villa at Sepphoris

Masada's Northern Palace
(photograph copyright Baron Wolman)

Reconstruction of the Destroyed Town of Gamla

Reconstruction of a Wealthy Priest's Home in Jerusalem's Upper City

Reconstruction of the Temple Mount Looking Toward the Mount of Olives

Reconstruction of the Herodion

Reconstruction of the Church of the Holy Sepulcher

The Temple Mount in Jerusalem
(photograph copyright Baron Wolman)

Philip's City

After Herod's son Philip inherited this area, he made it his capital and built there a Greco-Roman-style administrative city just below the Paneion in 2 B.C.E. As was the custom among the Herodians, he named it in honor of the Roman emperor, but called it Caesarea Philippi to distinguish it from his father's Caesarea on the coast. The area changed from being an isolated shrine to an urban site with a sanctuary. Pan's complex was expanded during and after Philip's reign, with an open-air shrine built on a promontory around a newly carved artificial cave, called the "Cave of Pan and the Nymphs" in a later inscription from the mid-second century C.E. Other elements were also added to the complex: a Temple of Zeus and Pan, another open-air shrine now called the "Nemesis Court," a long narrow building with three halls abutting the cliff, and a stagelike structure called the "Temple of Pan and the Goats" by its excavators.

During the three centuries following Philip's reign, many Greek inscriptions were chiseled into the cliffs and onto the buildings. Some examples. From the base of the niche just above the artificial cave: "The *priest* Victor, son of Lysimachos, dedicated this goddess to the god Pan, lover of Echo." From near the open court: "For the preservation of our *lords* the *emperors,* Valerios [Titi]anos, *priest* of the god Pan, dedicated the Lady Nemesis and her shrine which was made by cutting away the rock underneath [. . .] with the iron fence, in the month of Apellaios." On the cliff-face above the Nemesis shrine next to an undecorated niche: "Agrippas, son of Markos, *ruler,* in the year 223, having received divine instructions in a dream, dedicated the goddess Echo, together with Agrippias, his spouse, and Agrippinos and Markos and Agrappas, *civic council members,* and Agrippine and Domne, their children."

Architectural changes at the site in the subsequent stratigraphy correspond with a shift in the ceramic profile. Herodian sponsorship of the site not only established permanent religious structures at Banias, it also changed the ceramic evidence left behind. Different kinds of visits to the site are apparent from the Early Roman diagnostic sherds that had been swept off the structures and wedged into soil pockets around the rim of the terrace. Of the 457 Early Roman diagnostic sherds, 141, or almost a full third, are from oil lamps, in contrast to only 7 lamp sherds from the Hellenistic Period. The dramatic increase in lamps shows that many visitors made shorter stays and left inexpensive and less time-consuming offerings. The continued presence during the Early Roman Period of

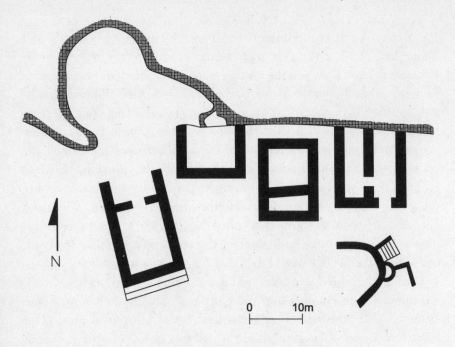

N

0   10m

THE SANCTUARY OF PAN AT CAESAREA PHILIPPI (AFTER MAOZ)

cooking vessels, many of which were charred, and of serving vessels, both
drinking cups and bowls, shows that the sanctuary of Pan continued to be
used for meals and offerings, a common Syro-Phoenician pagan practice.
But now many citizens of Caesarea Philippi would briefly stop off at the
shrine, drop off a lamp along with a prayer, while others still picnicked and
lingered for longer periods.

The Early Roman ceramic profile shows an increase in imported wares.
Over half of the lamps found were manufactured in Italy, Cyprus, or Syria.
A significant percentage of the pottery sherds were fired at kilns outside
the immediate environs. Some were from nearby Upper Galilee or from
along the Syro-Phoenician coast, along with a few fine wares from some
distance away. These imported lamps and sherds do not mean that pilgrims
from Asia Minor, Italy, or Cyprus were now visiting the sanctuary, but that
some of the locals who lived at Caesarea Philippi were able to afford more
elegant imported wares. In other words, the shrine began to attract a more
upper-class clientele.

As the complex reached its architectural apex from the end of the first
century through the second century C.E., the volume of ceramic evidence

bottomed out. The drop in diagnostic sherds, from 251 Hellenistic ones, to 457 Early Roman ones, to just 52 Middle Roman ones, corresponds with a fundamental change in the ceramic forms. Almost all of the Middle Roman sherds were from forms of lamps or table vessels; only a single sherd was from a cooking vessel. Preparing meals at the site and offering them to Pan or his consort had virtually ceased, and there is no more evidence for eating or picnicking around the grotto. Architecturally, however, the shrine was at its most impressive, built under official Herodian sponsorship and later receiving imperial backing and the patronage of the urban elites, as the epigraphic evidence indicates. Locals no longer came to linger, eat, and offer at the shrine, which had taken on the character of an official civic cult. By the second century C.E. the shrine at Caesarea Philippi had become an architectural showcase, a medium for the wealthy to display their munificence and generosity. The abrupt drop in Middle Roman ceramics does not mean that the shrine was abandoned or that visits decreased. It indicates that families, friends, or fellow worshipers no longer offered sacrifices, ate cultic meals, or picnicked there. What began as the setting for family meals and full-day picnics of ordinary people came under the imperial control of a priestly hierarchy and was absorbed into a civic life dominated by social elites who were patrons of the temple. The supreme irony is that, as mentioned earlier, what happened to Pan's shrine at Caesarea Philippi under pagan imperial patronage would also happen to Peter's house at Capernaum under Christian imperial patronage.

IN THE PALACE OF A KING

While Syro-Phoenicians and Itureans from towns and villages around the source of the Jordan were going out into nature to eat meals, wealthy citizens and ruling families across the Roman world were bringing elements of nature into their dining rooms. Those formal dining rooms were called *triclinia* (singular *triclinium*), and that title tells us two very specific details about them. First, there were three (hence *tri*) favored dining couches, a middle one for the host and others to right and left for his honored guests. Second, the host and his most important guests reclined (hence *clinia*)—they did not sit up on chairs as we do—and therefore they required servants and attendants for the meal. To recline, in other words, is a statement of social class.

In country villas, windows and entrances of *triclinia* opened up to spectacular views of nature, whether shorelines, forests, or oases. In wealthy urban residences, nature was brought into view by landscaping the peri-style courtyard with gardens and pools. Motifs from nature and bucolic scenes were also brought inside the *triclinia* through floral, faunal, and mythological themes drawn on the walls or set in mosaics. Somewhat iron-ically then, as Herod the Great and his successors were reducing oppor-tunities for dining in nature by the common people at Banias, they were re-creating this very ambiance in their banquet halls. At the same time as Herod was building temples at Banias and elsewhere, his banquet halls mimicked aspects of public space through the use of the carefully spaced columns, mosaics, and marble he introduced into his palaces. Wealthy cit-izens across the Mediterranean were consciously privatizing architectural features that had been part of the Hellenistic *polis*'s public life, elevating their homes into the civic realm and marking off in particular the *triclin-ium* as prestigious space. Using characteristics typically reserved for public architecture lent their homes a monumental stature and with clever use of space and decoration reinforced their status atop the social pyramid, as did their ostentatious display of wealth.

Archaeological excavations have shown that some of these dining habits had penetrated into the upper social strata of the Jewish homeland under the Herodians. This style of wealthy dining common across the Roman world is characterized by three elements. First, it brought the illu-sion of nature into the *triclinia*. Next, it adopted elements of public archi-tecture. Finally, it underlined the host's position at the top of the social hierarchy. Each of those trends is clearly visible in the unique palaces of Herod the Great, the oasis-palace at Jericho, the northern cliff-palace at Masada overlooking the Dead Sea, the fortress-palace of the Herodion in the Judean desert, and the seaside palace at Caesarea Maritima.

Masada on the Mountain

In the 1960s, the famous Israeli archaeologist and statesman Yigael Yadin excavated Herod the Great's palace on Masada's northern edge, including a *triclinium* on the lowest terrace boasting a spectacular view of the Dead Sea and the Judean desert. The discovery of several half-column drums with slots for window posts, as well as actual windowsills, shows that the *triclinium* opened up toward the north to provide a breathtaking view of the rugged landscape. Protected from the sun blazing down from the south, guests enjoyed not only the shade, but also a stunning panorama as the Judean hills met the Transjordan plateau at the Rift Valley. Even in such a

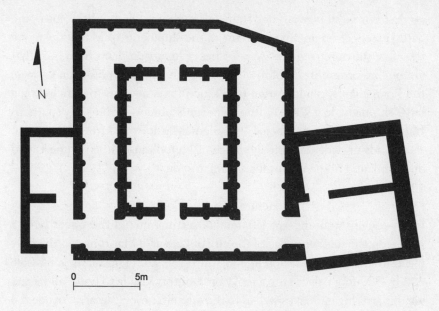

The Triclinium at Masada's Northern Palace (after Foerster)

remote setting, the host entertained his guests in a regal manner. Though it was far off the coast and nearly inaccessible, rendering the import of heavy marble columns impossible and even marble sheeting improbable, guests were surrounded with façades that mimicked these finer building materials: column drums of local stone were finished with stucco fluting and topped with molded Corinthian capitals, and walls were smoothly plastered and painted to imitate marble sheeting. Diners ate on couches resting on a waterproof mosaic floor, which servants could easily wash off with water—scraps were customarily tossed on the floor by the guests.

By laying out the hall in two concentric colonnaded squares, an ambulatory portico was created reminiscent of the civic architecture of the *stoa's* covered walkways or even of a temple precinct. On the inner square, pilasters, columns half embedded in the wall, along with frescoes creating the illusion that the columns were detached from the wall, gave visitors a sense of dining in a monumental setting, re-creating an aura not unlike a meal or offering at a temple. That the guests dined in a divine manner is clear—the dishes were expensive fine wares and the food was exotic. Much of the pottery unearthed in the excavations around the northern palace was the finest available plates and shallow bowls. Painted lettering on sherds from storage jars and stamped amphorae handles list some of the dates, places of origin, and contents of the shipments to Masada. Among the more surprising imports were a series of luxury products from Italy that are unique or rare in Palestine, including preserved apples from Cumae, the Pompeiian specialty *garum* (fish sauce), and ample wine, including a large shipment in 19 B.C.E. from vineyards around Brindisi in southern Italy and a rare vessel labeled "excellent Massic wine" from Campania. Such finds provide tangible evidence of Herod's taste for the finest food and drink and his penchant for dining in style.

Caesarea on the Coast

In an equally stunning but less remote setting, Herod the Great built a palace on the southern edge of the city of Caesarea Maritima. At the only place where Caesarea's shoreline juts into the sea, Herod built a massive 200-by-300-foot palace atop a rocky promontory visible to both sailors and visitors arriving by boat as well as to the inhabitants of Caesarea. Inside the colonnaded peristyle courtyard was the focal point of the massive palace, a large 60-by-120-foot pool cut into the rock. This was sealed by Herod with hydraulic plaster to hold fresh water brought from inland and manually conveyed to the pool, rather than saltwater from the Mediterranean. Even though centuries of waves have badly eroded the structure, the pool's depth is still preserved at over 3 feet. In addition to serving an aesthetic function, the pool probably functioned as a swimming area for athletic amusement. Herod the Great, in the tradition of the earlier Jewish Hasmonean kings, made swimming pools and baths an important component of his palaces not only here, but also at Jericho, the Herodion, and even atop Masada. Evenly spaced rectangular cavities were cut into the ground around the pool to serve as planters for trees, hedges, or flowers, encasing the pool with a garden. The pool and garden were surrounded by a colonnade and a spacious walkway, presumably at one time floored with mosaic or marble arranged in geometric patterns of variously shaped pieces. The main room of the palace was a *triclinium* situated on the western side of the building between the pool and the sea. As at Masada, Herod visually connected his dining room with nature, externally by having a sweeping vista of the Mediterranean Sea and dinnertime sunsets to the west, and internally by overlooking the lush garden and pool to the east.

Covering nearly an acre, Herod's palace was monumental, built to proportions otherwise reserved for civic structures. Yet he wisely avoided

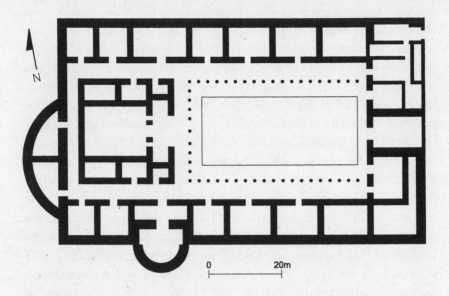

HEROD'S PROMONTORY PALACE AT CAESAREA (AFTER NETZER)

megalomania, so that his palace did not surpass the temple to Rome and Augustus, which, along with the harbor, dominated the architectural landscape. Dwarfing other residences, however, Herod's palace approached the scale of public structures while employing similar building techniques, materials, and style, so that it resembled civic and public rather than domestic and private space. Despite a sophisticated ambiguity and interplay between public and private, the promontory palace sent a clear message of Herod's position in the social hierarchy. He put his palace not within the city's domestic quarters, but as a component of the entertainment complex in the southwestern portion of the city. As mentioned in the last chapter, the large amphitheater was built along the shore perpendicular to the palace at its southern end. Farther to the southeast, the theater, built along with the temple askew to the city's grid, squarely faced the promontory palace, which made the latter part of the former's stage scenery.

Herod's well-planned city may have copied arrangements at Alexandria and Rome, where the ruling house encroached into the civic life and subtly reinforced the social hierarchy. At Caesarea, Herod masterfully configured space for his own purposes. If you were one of that city's average citizens, a laborer, a sailor, or a visiting peasant at the theater and amphitheater, you were dispersed swiftly with the mass of spectators through one of the numerous exits, or *vomitoria*. But if you were one of its privileged citizens or visiting dignitaries, you left on the curved southern end of the amphitheater or next to the theater's stage, which opened onto a vestibule-like garden leading directly to the palace. Within the palace, the elites would find their social place and rank by how many partitions and boundaries they crossed. Some came only as far as the large audience hall attached to the palace and its peristyle courtyard. Others, more privileged, were admitted into the promontory palace itself, perhaps held up at the vestibule or maybe let into the garden and pool area. But only a very few were treated to a meal in the *triclinium* at the westernmost end. The entire palace structure, from the vestibule-like gardens outside, to the audience hall of the upper courtyard complex, to the atrium garden and pool, to the flanking rooms, to the *triclinium* itself, articulated quite clearly the existing social strata. It's tempting to think of the various components as reflecting the continuum from public to private, but the sequential thresholds were not closed off visually; each was visible from every station, so that the status of individuals, as they either ascended or descended the social ladder, was publicly announced.

IN THE VILLA OF AN ARISTOCRAT

Herod the Great's ostentatious banquet settings, his bold palaces, and clear delineation of the social hierarchy are prominently featured in the archaeological record, and though we can assume that his son Antipas mimicked this pattern, the remains he left behind are more elusive. The first encounter with Antipas in Mark's gospel locates him with his elite retainers in a banquet setting, and it is after that meal's entertainment that John the Baptist's head was served on a platter (6:14–29). But first-century layers at neither Sepphoris nor Tiberias furnish clear evidence for Antipas's palaces, let alone for their *triclinia*. And that, of course, is what we would like to describe next.

Instead, and perforce, we will go atop the Sepphoris acropolis, look at a later aristocratic villa, and try to imagine an Antipas *triclinium* between it and those *triclinia* just seen in Herod the Great's palaces. Even if from a later than first-century layer, we use it to emphasize the social purpose of such formal dining rooms across the entire Roman world and during the entire Roman Period. Our example is Sepphoris's so-called Dionysos Villa dating to the Middle and Late Roman Periods.

The villa was built on top of Sepphoris's acropolis in the latter part of the second or early third century C.E. In order to accommodate the extent of the house's layout, some 75 by 130 feet, a platform had to be constructed by leveling off bedrock on its western side and hauling in fill on its southern side. In the process, traces of any earlier structures (perhaps an earlier palace?) were obliterated when the terrain was flattened. As in other public structures of the period, the villa walls were constructed with large, well-fitting limestone ashlars, which presumably supported a second story. Resembling that of other houses of wealthy and influential citizens throughout the Roman world, the villa's axis ran architecturally and visually from the entrance, through a peristyle courtyard, to the *triclinium*.

The garden in the peristyle courtyard had a small fountain or pool that brought a touch of nature into the midst of an urban setting. Some of the villa's interior walls had frescoes with floral designs to continue visually the garden's growth inside the surrounding rooms. The *triclinium*'s mosaic floor used artistic stonework to create a rather romanticized bucolic and rustic ambiance. A colorful U-shaped band depicted peasants in a procession bringing the agricultural fruits of their labor—no hint there of expropriated surplus! That band surrounded a central rectangle composed of panels celebrating the joys of the vine and the life of Dionysos, the wine god and close associate of the goat-god Pan. Little in the mosaic reflects cultic elements and the room is not associated with Dionysiac rituals or mysteries. Instead, the central panel emphasizes the mosaic's theme by depicting a drinking bout between the strong-man Herakles and the wine-god Dionysos. In flanking panels, Dionysos is declared the victor as he reclines in his chariot and casts a glance toward the next panel, where a puking Herakles is being helped by a male satyr and a female maenad. Other panels rejoice in the fruit of the vine and show the trampling of grapes and a village festival. Some panels recall legends of Dionysos, such as the washing of Dionysos by the nurses who hid him for safety, his revealing of the vine's mystery to the shepherds, and his marriage to Ariadne. Interspersed with medallions, bucolic processions portray peasants joyfully handing over their harvest, including clusters of grapes, fruit, chickens, and ducks. Facing the host's seat is a portrait of a beautiful woman (Ariadne or the matron of the house?), which the excavators dubbed "the Mona Lisa of the Galilee." Male eyes looked on female face, aristocratic eyes gazed on peasant produce. All was serenely happy and socially complacent from those privileged viewpoints.

Diners were surrounded by bucolic scenes that urged a festive atmosphere. They could gaze out toward the peristyle garden for a glimpse of nature and even out through the garden's entrance to the street, where the excluded were regularly visible. The use of columns in the atrium, along with mosaic floors, frescoed walls, and marble—even if only painted pseudo-marble—suggested a civic aura. The small fishpond or fountain, however diminutive compared to Herod's pool at the promontory palace in Caesarea, evoked an air of public life at the baths, around a fountain (*nymphaeum*), or inside a sacred precinct.

The Dionysos Villa was set apart visually, with its red-tiled roof and white-plastered walls, and, placed atop the acropolis, it put the owner's wealth and status on display to the entire city. As at Herod's palace in Caesarea, a theater flanked the mansion at Sepphoris, and its owner was very likely a sponsor of theatrical spectacles. Dionysos was, after all, not only the god of wine, but also the patron of theaters and actors. The layout of the house likewise betrays the owner's interest in publicizing his opulence. The peristyle house's view, from the entrance through the atrium garden to the *triclinium*, conspicuously displayed the owner's wealth to the passersby. The very design of a peristyle house reinforced the social hierarchy by framing the insiders' meals with mosaic floors, frescoed walls, and fluted columns. That clearly delineated inside from outside and insiders from outsiders. The few reclined and were served with food and drink; the many could pass and see, but could not enter or participate, except as servants, entertainers, or retainers.

The social hierarchy was further reinforced among the elites invited into the *triclinium*. The 18-by-23-foot mosaic, of exceptional artistic quality, was composed of over twenty different-colored tessarae and divided the room into separate zones. There was a U-shaped area with white tessarae and "gamma" marks to locate the placement of the three main couches. This layout privileged the centrally placed host with his guests of honor to right and left. Their couch locations were clearly demarcated, and they were given much more emphasis and space. And, of course, since guests *reclined* on those couches, they had to be *served* by multiple attendants. The remaining diners crowded around the white tessaraed areas in descending social order. That is, for example, the procedure imagined in Luke 14:7–11, where the guest first sits at the back and is then called up beside the host for special honor.

IN THE HOUSES OF ELITES

The Dionysos Villa is clear evidence for aristocratic Roman-style domestic architecture at Sepphoris by the third century. But, even though that is long after the time of Jesus, some of those features had made inroads much earlier at the time of the city's rebuilding under Herod Antipas. Here are two examples of such first-century houses, elegant to be sure, but not quite up to the standards of that third-century villa.

An Enclosed-Courtyard House

One example, excavated in the early 1990s by Eric and Carol Meyers, of the Sepphoris Regional Project and Duke University, and labeled Unit II, was an enclosed-courtyard house built atop the western domestic quarters. The family's daily activities were somewhat shielded by the layout around the courtyard, which was not in peristyle format. But, on the inside, the owners marked their prominence on the social scale by adopting decorative elements such as fresco, mosaic, white plaster, and red roof tiles.

The walls were well constructed in evenly shaped, regular-sized limestone ashlars and stood upon solid bedrock with boulder foundations. The 2-foot thick walls, carefully arranged in header-stretcher technique, could have easily supported a second story. Some rooms in the house were covered with *al secco* fresco, a cheap and simple technique in which plaster was painted after it had dried. The designs were simple floral or geometric patterns as well as green and red rectangles of imitative marble paneling similar to those in Herod's palace at Masada. The frescoed rooms had smooth plaster floors, as did the courtyard, and patches of mosaic tessarae were discovered removed from their original context in the fill of another room whose Early Roman phase was destroyed beyond recovery. The kitchen area and several other rooms, however, had only beaten earth floors.

In addition to the fresco and mosaic, several other artifacts reflect the first-century inhabitants' wealth. Fragments of an expensive, molded glass cup, a hanging lamp, and an incense bowl are among the finds from the Early Roman strata, as are finely carved bone pins and a makeup spatula. The inhabitants were not, of course, as wealthy or ostentatious as Herod the Great or Antipas. Their cosmetic items were bone and not ivory, they had no imported wines, and their ceramics were mostly common table wares made in Galilean villages, though a few sherds of expensive *terra*

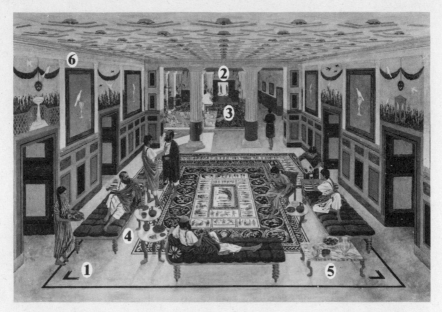

RECONSTRUCTION OF THE LATE ROMAN DIONYSOS VILLA AT SEPPHORIS. *Named after a mosaic depicting the wine god and celebrating the joys of wine, the villa housed one of the leading citizens of Sepphoris, the one-time capital of Galilee built by Herod Antipas. Although the villa dates to over a century after Jesus, it illustrates wealthy dining in the Roman world, with guests seated in the triclinium in hierarchical arrangement around three couches, indicated by the "gamma" marks on the side (1), the very arrangement presumed in Jesus' teachings in Luke 14. The villa's axial arrangement emphasized distinct private and public realms: outsiders (2) could see in through the peristyle atrium (3) and knew that they were excluded, an arrangement that also flaunted the owner's wealth, illustrated here by imported serving vessels (4) and fine glass bowls and decanters (5). The frescoed wall (6) and molded ceiling are analogous to those of other wealthy houses across the Roman world.*

sigillata serving plates were also found. But they lived at the top of Sepphoris's acropolis and the top of Galilee's social pyramid.

A Peristyle-Courtyard House

Still at Sepphoris, just across the street to the north, an equally wealthy and contemporary house shows that some Jewish families in the first century were not only incorporating architecturally decorative elements, they were also displaying their wealth in ostentatious Roman fashion. This house, built with a peristyle courtyard that provided axial visibility into the atrium, was first excavated in 1931 by Leroy Watermann, of the University of Michigan. He thought it a Christian *basilica* because of its use of columns, mosaic floors, plastered walls, and fresco. He also assumed that the cavities carved into bedrock were catacomb-like features from the time when Christianity's "rites were practiced in secret." Recently, however, James F. Strange, of the University of South Florida Excavations, further excavated this complex and determined that it was, in fact, a villa, and that several of the chiseled cavities were *miqwaoth,* or Jewish ritual baths.

Watermann's misidentification was not just a case of an earlier generation's romantic and adventurous quest for the sensationally religious. The original design of the house and the owner's intent introduced elements of public space into this private house: pillars, axial arrangements, well-dressed limestone ashlars, white plaster, some fresco, and mosaic floors with black-and-white geometric designs and borders. What conclusively established its identification as a villa was Strange's discovery of its kitchen and the identification of several *miqwaoth,* which were also commonly found at other houses in Sepphoris. Further, both excavators found numerous domestic artifacts: cooking wares, bone hairpins, kohl makeup applicators, loom weights, and basalt grinders.

The *Pax Romana* Comes to Galilee

These two houses show how aware wealthy Sepphoreans were of Roman architectural styles prevalent in the broader Mediterranean world. And they show how eager they were to obtain some of the symbols of the empire's social elite, like frescoes, mosaics, and luxury imports. They show that only the upper stratum of Galilean society was ready to accept and able to afford the Roman system of openly flaunting one's social rank. Prior to Antipas, the Jewish Hasmoneans had no known palaces in Galilee, and Herod the Great first built his palaces in secluded spots, at Masada, Jericho, and only later in cities like Caesarea and Jerusalem, but he never built any in Galilee. Only under Antipas, who certainly built palaces at Sepphoris and Tiberias, did the Galilean urban elites introduce pronounced social stratification. To be sure, there were a few such houses in the larger towns of Galilee, like one found at Jodefat just across the Beit Netofah Valley and one at Gamla in the Golan, but these were rather exceptional and not as common as in the Galilean cities.

The introduction and diffusion of wealth in Galilee was not just a personal matter, but a social process, since the display of luxury items marked one's place within the social hierarchy. The value of these goods was proportionate to their relative inaccessibility among the lower social strata, and display, rather than just possession, created their value. Also, of course, that increase in luxury and conspicuous consumption had to be funded by increased productivity and profitability from the surrounding countryside, one way or another.

What did the peasantry think about Antipas's Sepphoris, rebuilt in 4 B.C.E. to be, in Josephus's phrase, "the ornament of all Galilee," and of Tiberias, built in 19 C.E., to be its replacement capital for Antipas's domain? Maybe this gives us some idea. In his *Life*, Josephus described what the peasants (he called them "the Galileans") actually wanted to do while he was attempting to train them in 66–67 C.E. for the inevitable legionary reprisals at the start of the first revolt. In what follows, notice the repeated mention of *hatred, detestation*, and *extermination*:

> I marched with such troops as I had against Sepphoris and took the city by assault. The Galilaeans, seizing this opportunity, too good to be missed, of venting their *hatred* on one of the cities which they *detested*, rushed forward, with the intention of *exterminating* the population, aliens and all. Plunging into the town they set fire to the houses, which they found to be deserted, the terrified inhabitants having fled in a body to the citadel. They looted everything, sparing their countrymen no conceivable form of devastation. . . . As, however, they refused to listen to either remonstration or command, my exhortations being overborne by their *hatred*, I instructed some of my friends to circulate a report that the Romans had made their way into another quarter of the city with a large force . . . that . . . I might check the fury of the Galilaeans and so save Sepphoris. . . . Tiberias, likewise, had a narrow escape from being sacked by the Galilaeans . . . loudly denouncing the Tiberians as traitors and friendly to the king [Agrippa II], and requiring permission to go down and *exterminate* their city. For they had the same *detestation* for the Tiberians as for the inhabitants of Sepphoris. (374–84)

Romanization meant urbanization meant commercialization and, especially with the establishment of Tiberias by the early 20s C.E., the new *Pax Romana's* economic boom struck Lower Galilee fully and forcibly. If we think of covenant rather than commerce, would an Amos have said anything very different to Antipas at Tiberias in the first century than he said to Jeroboam II at Samaria in the eighth century long before? Be that as it may, in the later 20s C.E. we find two popular movements, the Baptism movement of John and the Kingdom movement of Jesus operating in the territories of Herod Antipas. Why then? Why there? Was it coincidence or resistance?

IN THE KINGDOM OF GOD

It was obvious, from Chapter 1, that ancient invective was every bit as nasty as its modern equivalent. Its capacity for name-calling and story-mongering was just as mean as our own. Sometimes, however, then and now, you can retain the descriptive *what* even as you discount the accusatory *why*, you can accept the basic action described (e.g., "preached") and still ignore the evil motivation alleged (e.g., "for personal gain"). In criticisms lodged against John the Baptist or Jesus, for example, we have to separate description (what they were doing) from accusation (why they were doing it). Furthermore, when opponents looked at the Baptist movement of John and the Kingdom movement of Jesus, they judged that both protagonists were strange, weird, and deviant, and also that they were not only differently but even oppositely so. And, strange as it might seem to us, the items they chose on which to focus that divergence both from normalcy and from one another were food and drink, eating and dining.

Accusing John about Food

After a scholarly consensus agreed that Mark's gospel was the primary source for both Matthew and Luke, it was obvious that those two had used some other major source as well. They had too many similarities, in both general sequence and specific content, that were not present in Mark and that could not be explained by sheer coincidence. That other source was called Q (short for *Quelle*, the German word for "source") but, since that describes its use rather than its identity, we acknowledge its own integrity by calling it the Q Gospel. It is only there that the twin accusations against John and Jesus are preserved at Matthew 11:16–19 = Luke 7:31–35.

The context is a counteraccusation by Jesus claiming that his opponents are like stubborn children refusing to play along with either sad

games or glad games, refusing both those opposed alternatives for suggested playacting. It is in that rebuttal that their own accusations are
repeated. First, "John the Baptist has come eating no bread and drinking
no wine, and you say, 'He has a demon.'" Second, "the Son of Man has
come eating and drinking, and you say, 'Look, a glutton and a drunkard, a
friend of tax collectors and sinners!'" In each of those accusations it is necessary to distinguish the former part, the *description*, from the latter part,
the *accusation*, that is, to separate out the actual basis grounding the attack
and giving it whatever credibility it could have, at least among opponents.

The description of John as fasting is easy to understand and quite
believable. We know about him from two major sources and both agree on
his nickname, the Baptizer or Baptist, and on his execution by Herod
Antipas. But they agree on very little else.

Josephus says nothing about the desert, the Jordan, or the forgiveness of
sins while discussing John in his *Jewish Antiquities* (18.116–19). John's
baptizing, he says, was a secondary purification of the body after, and only
after, purification of the soul was already achieved. It was "a consecration
of the body implying that the soul was already thoroughly cleansed by
right behavior." And that latter meant "to practice justice toward their fel-
lows and piety toward God." But despite that absolutely innocent program
and without any further explanation, Josephus has Antipas behead John as
a preemptive strike "before his work led to an uprising." But why would
Antipas even suspect such an eventuality from a gathering of saints?
Something is missing between that summary description of a life, and a
death. Something is left out. Something is deliberately left out? What is it?

If we only had Josephus, we would know very little about first-century
messianism or apocalypticism. Instead, he gives us this completely tendentious interpretation of those concepts and expectations. Apart, he
says, from the three older and more normal Jewish philosophical schools,
the Essenes, Pharisees, and Sadducees, there was a more recent and upstart
school he calls only the "fourth philosophy." Its slogan was, "No Lord but
God," it refused submission to Rome, it led the people eventually into the
disastrous war of 66–74 C.E., and it had profoundly messianic and/or
apocalyptic roots. Josephus, however, does not tell us about those roots
because, as he says, those messianic prophecies and apocalyptic expectations referred not to any Jewish figure, but to the advent of Vespasian's
Flavian dynasty as that new imperial family displaced the Julio-Claudian
line of Augustus. "What more than all else incited them to the war [even

as the Temple burned in 70 C.E.] was an ambiguous oracle . . . found in their sacred scriptures, to the effect that at that time one from their country would become ruler of the world. This they understood to mean someone of their own race, and many of their wise men went astray in their interpretation of it. The oracle, however, in reality signified the sovereignty of Vespasian who was proclaimed Emperor in Jewish soil" (*Jewish War* 6.312–13).

Other Jews had earlier incarnated the hoped-for Davidic messiah in pagan rulers, in a Persian monarch in the sixth century or an Egyptian pharaoh in the second century B.C.E., but to find him in the Roman emperor whose son Titus had just burned down the Temple was much more of a stretch. In any case, and against that Josephan theology, John the Baptist is safely protected from any messianic or apocalyptic association. But, of course, such an association is exactly what he receives in our other source about him, the New Testament itself.

In the gospels, as against Josephus, John is located in the desert at the Jordan, and his baptism is for the forgiveness of sins. In the gospels, John's baptism is not like the ordinary Jewish purification rites to be discussed in the next chapter, which were never administered by another and especially not by one particular person. Furthermore, his message is apocalyptic—it is about the imminent advent of the avenging God, and he is there to prepare the way. The *Q Gospel* has John announce, in Matthew 3:7–10 = Luke 3:7–9, "You brood of vipers! Who warned you to flee from the wrath to come? . . . Even now the ax is lying at the root of the trees; every tree therefore that does not bear good fruit is cut down and thrown into the fire."

How, then, can one prepare for such divine vengeance, prepare especially to avoid it? You must, said John, become the pre-purified people of that purifying God. How? By reenacting the Exodus, by crossing from the eastern desert over the Jordan into the Promised Land. You must, above all else, leave behind your sins in the cleansing waters of the river. In that way, a critical mass of holy people would be established and then, when the avenging God arrived, evildoers would be destroyed, but those holy ones would be saved. And, maybe it would only be after that critical mass was established that the awaited apocalypse of vengeance and deliverance would occur.

What John is doing is reenacting the Exodus, taking penitents from the desert, through the Jordan, into the Promised Land, to posses it in holiness once again. It is both preparation and proleptic anticipation of the long-awaited and now imminent apocalyptic consummation. It is an action that starts what it symbolizes. He is both similar to and also different from that later prophet, "the Egyptian," who led an unarmed throng from the desert, across the Jordan, and toward the walls of Jerusalem, which, like those of Jericho before Joshua, would tumble to the ground at their arrival. But, just as Josephus sanitized John for his Roman readers, so did the gospels for their Christian readers. He becomes, once again, not religio-political, but religio-spiritual. Desert and Jordan become accidental or neutral backdrops. John prepares not for the advent of God, but for the arrival of Jesus.

When both those sources are combined and their divergent biases understood, John appears clearly as a prophet of imminent apocalyptic consummation who both spoke and acted on that dangerous boundary between passive and active expectation. Mark 1:6 mentions his dress and diet: "John was clothed with camel's hair, with a leather belt around his waist, and he ate locusts and wild honey." That parallels Josephus's description of his own mentor Bannus, "who dwelt in the wilderness, wearing only such clothing as trees provided, feeding on such things as grew of themselves" (*Life* 11). Whether you interpret that as asceticism accepted and/or civilization rejected and/or purity intensified, it explains John's "eating no bread and drinking no wine." Location and action, dress and diet form a coherent whole. But that only emphasizes the problem in understanding the corresponding description of Jesus. Not eating or drinking was extraordinary enough for comment or criticism. You can see, even if not agree, with how opponents got from accurate description to invidious accusation. John was obviously an ascetic prophet of imminent apocalypse. Name-calling, after all, works best when it is based on something. But what about Jesus?

Accusing Jesus about Food

Recall the content of those twin accusations from the *Q Gospel* against both John and Jesus cited earlier. Both concern food (too little or too much), but Jesus is indicted for his habits in both diet and company. John, that attack said, was possessed. Most exegetes do not take that comment seriously; they do not usually debate whether John did or did not have a demon. They recognize it as invective, vituperation, name-calling, character assassination. With Jesus, however, it is a little different. There is no serious discussion of the first accusation: was he or was he not a glutton and a drunkard? That, once again, is recognized as nasty name-calling. But the second accusation has, unfortunately, not been handled in the same way. And since Jesus' dining style involves both diet and company, we look first at that second accusation, the one in which he is called a "friend of tax collectors and sinners."

What did the term "sinners" mean in its first-century context? It did not mean all those who ignored somebody else's stricter purity rules. It did not mean "so-called sinners," those who were poor or suffering and who, therefore, must have sinned and were now being punished for it by destitution or disease (the Job fallacy). It certainly does not indicate all those who were repentant "sinners." It means the deliberately, continuously, and obstinately wicked. The term "tax collectors" or "toll collectors" indicates those who collaborate with the local or imperial oppressors and/or operate with excessive force, bribery, or corruption. Put together, the phrase "tax collectors and sinners" denotes those who are morally and occupationally wicked, those who are irrevocably evil.

Consider these two similar phrases. Matthew, wishing to designate a community member to be avoided at all costs, says "let such a one be to you as a Gentile and a tax collector" (18:17). The set phrase indicates persons to be absolutely avoided, not ones to be visited, befriended, and converted. Another verse, on the other hand, announces that "John came to you in the way of righteousness and you did not believe him, but the tax collectors and the prostitutes believed him; and even after you saw it, you did not change your minds and believe him" (21:32). Another set pair of proverbial malefactors is used here, comprising both genders, but it now designates the successfully converted, not the irredeemably lost. Such phrases are, in other words, especially useful for name-calling. To call Jesus "a friend of tax collectors and sinners" is to dismiss him absolutely and denigrate him completely. It is like the use of "fellow travelers, pinkos, and commies" in the American 1950s.

The accusation of association with "tax collectors and sinners" was not only remembered in that *Q Gospel* text, where its nonliteral, name-calling origins are clearly evident. In other texts it is taken literally, but Jesus is then defended from immorality by claiming that such contact was only for conversion. In those cases the defense is specifically against Pharisees or others who criticize Jesus' action. One example is Jesus' eating with Levi along with "tax collectors and sinners" in Mark 2:13–17. But that is explained because Jesus "came not to call the righteous, but sinners" (2:17) and, lest there be any misunderstanding, "to repentance" is added in Luke (5:32). Another example, besides Levi at Capernaum, is Zacchaeus at Jericho, "a chief tax collector [who] was rich" (Luke 19:1–10). Jesus is the "guest of one who is a sinner" but, thereafter, Zacchaeus gives half his possessions to the poor and repays defrauded accounts fourfold. "Today salvation has come to this house, because he too is a son of Abraham. For the Son of Man came to seek out and to save the lost." The problem is, of course, that if salvation and conversion resulted from such contacts, approval—not criticism—would have been inevitable for Jesus. What Jewish individual, group, or sect would have criticized Jesus for converting sinners to saints, vice to virtue, or Gentiles to Judaism?

Here, then, is the problem. Granted that Jesus did not eat freely with irrevocably evil people and granted that he was no more a gluttonous drunkard than John was a possessed madman, what physical basis begot those accusations against him? What exactly does his "eating and drinking" entail? How is that description, completely apart from any accusation, even meaningful? Jesus eats and drinks. So what? Indeed, even if one took that accusation as literally accurate, how do you get from excessive eating and drinking to death on a Roman cross?

Paul's Refusal of Jesus' Command

If you only had that comparison of John and Jesus in the Q Gospel's twin accusations, you might presume that Jesus is criticized simply for being different from John. He is accused of not being an ascetic, which the martyred Baptist clearly was. In Mark 2:19–20, for instance, right after that defense of Jesus for "eating with tax collectors and sinners" in order to call them to repentance, Jesus' disciples are criticized for not fasting like the disciples of John and the Pharisees. Is that all there is to it—that Jesus is not a fasting ascetic? That he eats normally? And so do his companions? If Mark and the Q Gospel belong to the third layer's first level, is there anything in earlier levels on Jesus and food? And do those levels help us understand that description of Jesus as eater and drinker? We return once again to the intricacies of exegetical layering.

The material in Paul's letters is from the most securely dated layers in the Jesus tradition. In the winter of 53–54 C.E., for example, Paul wrote to the community at Corinth and gave his "defense to those who would examine" him concerning "food and drink" (1 Cor. 9:3). The accusation is not that Paul is taking undue advantage of their hospitality, but that, to the contrary, he is not making the expected use of it. He admits that, "the Lord commanded that those who proclaim the gospel should get their living by the gospel," but he also concedes that, "I have made no use of any of these rights" (9:14–15).

It is not immediately clear why Paul refuses to follow at Corinth what he admits is a command from Jesus himself, which others are obeying. He is not against taking financial assistance from his communities on principle. "You Philippians indeed know that in the early days of the gospel, when I left Macedonia, no church shared with me in the matter of giving and receiving, except you alone. For even when I was in Thessalonica, you sent me help for my needs more than once" (Phil. 4:15–16). He refers, in fact, to that very instance in writing to Corinth: "I robbed other churches by accepting support from them in order to serve you. And when I was with you and was in need, I did not burden anyone, for my needs were supplied by the friends who came from Macedonia. So I refrained and will continue to refrain from burdening you in any way" (2 Cor. 11:8–9). Later he tells the Romans that he expects them to speed him on his way to Spain (Rom. 15:24), and that probably meant travel subventions and not just farewell waves from the Ostian port of Rome.

Maybe those financial gifts were acceptable because they were *from* one community but *for* another? Maybe, more likely, there was some special trouble with accepting financial aid at Corinth? Instead of the radical egalitarianism cited by Paul concerning Jew and Gentile, slave and free, male and female (Gal. 3:28), there were well-to-do members of the Corinthian community, probably freed slaves, who were operating according to the standard patronal hierarchies of normal Greco-Roman tradition. That seductive subversion of Christian equality caused problems in their celebration of the Lord's Supper (1 Cor. 12), and it probably forced Paul to decline a mode of hospitality more hierarchical than egalitarian, more a matter of control than of assistance.

In any case, and for whatever reason, Paul declines financial assistance or household hospitality from the Corinthians, but admits they are criticizing him correctly for not following the general apostolic custom derived from Jesus' own command. On that latter point he is not acknowledging some private revelation, but admitting what is common tradition. In other words, if you think of Pauline tradition as the second layer of the tradition, that command from Jesus is from the first layer, from the historical Jesus himself. But what exactly does it mean? Jesus commanded hospitality? Who didn't? Jesus commanded wages? Who didn't? Jesus himself ate and drank. Who didn't? What exactly is at stake here and why is there so much fuss about food all across the Jesus tradition?

A Program of Reciprocal Sharing

We presume here the validity of two scholarly judgments, the existence of the Q Gospel and the independence of the Gospel of Thomas. Once those are accepted as operational theories, the presence of thirty-seven similar units distributed quite divergently in both gospels indicates a store of oral tradition from which they are both independently drawing. Those scholarly conclusions were cited, as you will recall, among the most important textual "discoveries" for excavating Jesus in this book's Introduction. From within that specific oral tradition, which we call the Common Sayings Tradition, we take one specific unit for present emphasis. It is the admonition about *Mission and Message*, and here are its versions in *Thomas*, Mark, and the Q Gospel.

In the *Gospel of Thomas* 14 Jesus commands, "When you go into any region and walk about in the countryside, when people take you in, eat what they serve you and heal the sick among them." Notice that rural rather than urban situation, the implicit possibility of nonacceptance, and the reciprocity of eating and healing.

In the Q Gospel, the situation is more complicated, since both Matthew and Luke are reading twin versions, one in the Q Gospel and the other in Mark 6:7–13. The standard scholarly judgment is that Matthew 10:7–15 integrated both sources together while Luke kept them separated, with Luke 9:1–6 from Mark and Luke 10:4–12 from the Q Gospel. Here are those two texts, from Mark and the Q Gospel:

Mark 6:7–13: He called the twelve and began to send them out two by two, and gave them authority over the unclean spirits. He ordered them to take nothing for their journey except a staff; no bread, no bag, no money in their belts; but to wear sandals and not to put on two tunics. He said to them, "Wherever you enter a house, stay there until you leave the place. If any place will not welcome you and they refuse to hear you, as you leave, shake off the dust that is on your feet as a testimony against them." So they went out and proclaimed that all should repent. They cast out many demons, and anointed with oil many who were sick and cured them.

THE NAG HAMMADI CODICES
(reproduced with permission, copyright the Institute for Antiquity and Christianity, Claremont, California)

Q Gospel *in Luke 10:4–12*: Carry no purse, no bag, no sandals; and greet no one on the road. Whatever house you enter, first say, "Peace to this house!" And if anyone is there who shares in peace, your peace will rest on that person; but if not, it will return to you. Remain in the same house, eating and drinking whatever they provide, for the laborer deserves to be paid. Do not move about from house to house. Whenever you enter a town and its people welcome you, eat what is set before you; cure the sick who are there, and say to them, "The kingdom of God has come near to you." But whenever you enter a town and they do not welcome you, go out into its streets and say, "Even the dust of your town that clings to our feet, we wipe off in protest against you. Yet know this: the kingdom of God has come near." I tell you, on that day it will be more tolerable for Sodom than for that town.

Apart from the general contact between those two texts and the subject of food, there are four other reasons for selecting that unit from the Common Sayings Tradition for privileged emphasis here. First, since the unit derives from Jesus, concerns food and eating, hospitality and reciprocity, it links directly with the command of the Lord that Paul declines to follow in 1 Corinthians 9. Maybe, here, in other words, we can see the content and purpose of that command?

Second, a parallel unit appears in Mark, and that combination of Paul, the Common Sayings Tradition, and Mark is a heavy weight of independent attestation and deserves special attention. Third, scholars sometimes debate whether the words or deeds, the sayings or actions of Jesus should receive primary or even exclusive emphasis. This unit cuts across that often dreary dichotomy, because it contains words about deeds, sayings about action, and, as such, it emphasizes their mutual dependence and reciprocal importance.

Fourth, this unit indicates a signal distinction between the Kingdom program of Jesus and the Baptist program of John, a distinction that was crucial for their divergent destinies. John was nicknamed "the Baptist" by both Josephus and the New Testament. You did not baptize yourself and you were not baptized by others—you were baptized by John himself. Hence that specific nickname. Irrespective of what that baptism meant, it made John so important that his execution doomed his movement to a slow but inevitable demise. It would be almost impossible for there to be a Baptist movement without John the Baptist.

In the unit to be considered now, Jesus tells his companions to go out and do exactly what he himself was doing. Further, they are not told to do it in his name. In modern jargon, John created a Baptist monopoly, but Jesus created a Kingdom franchise. That did not make inevitable the continuation of his movement after his own execution, but it ensured that his own execution would not be his movement's inevitable termination.

Healing and Eating.   Healing and eating form the first and most important of several paired items we are using to discuss those mission directives of Jesus. As a reciprocal combination it is explicitly present in both versions of the Common Sayings Tradition, but in Mark that reciprocity is only implicit. Eating is there all right, but only indirectly (staying in a house), and healing is described rather than commanded. But that close reciprocity presumes two classes in conjunction, itinerants and householders, the destitute and the poor. But each has something to offer the other: one has spiritual gifts (healing) and the other has material gifts (food to eat). That juxtaposition involves a close reassociation and free redistribution of spiritual and material needs at the base of peasant society.

Dress and Interdependence.   Dress and interdependence are not present in the Common Sayings Tradition, but only in the Q *Gospel* and Mark. Yet, on the one hand, this pair is very intimately linked with those former elements, and, on the other, Mark is already softening the Q *Gospel's* injunctions. For example, the do-not-wear-sandals of the Q *Gospel* in Matthew 10:10 = Luke 10:4 becomes the you-can-wear-sandals of Mark 6:9. But it is hard to imagine a greater symbol of indigence than to be without any protective foot coverings. Similarly, the disciples are to travel without a knapsack, almost a contradiction in terms. If they are beggars, how are they to carry alms? Precisely. That lack sends a message of interdependence between itinerants and householders. Itinerants depend on householders for food and lodging, not just for charity and handouts.

Are Jesus' companions sent out to individual courtyard homes like those at Nazareth and Capernaum or to the public squares of towns and cities like those of Sepphoris and Tiberias? *Gospel of Thomas* 14 mentions the "country" rather than the town/city and only hints at the dialectic of acceptance or rejection ("when people take you in"). In Mark only "house" is mentioned, but both acceptance (6:10) or rejection (6:11) are explicitly noted. In the Q *Gospel* there is an interweave of "house" and "town/city" along with acceptance and rejection. Thus, in Luke, you have house acceptance (10:5–6a, 7) and house rejection (10:6b), followed by town/city acceptance (10:8–9) and town/city rejection (10:10–11). Matthew 10:14 recognizes the problem of that disjunction and solves it with "town/city or village" in 10:11 and "house or town/city" in 10:14. All in all, the original layer of that unit most likely emphasized houses and later developments and experiences widened it to towns/cities. Recall, for example, the curses uttered against Chorazin and Bethsaida, but most especially against Capernaum in the Q *Gospel* at Matthew 11:20–24 = Luke 10:13–15. Probably then Jesus' earliest companions had far better success with individual courtyard homes in small hamlets than with the more public arenas of large villages or small towns (so-called cities).

The Challenge of Itinerancy and Commensality
The surface of that program is relatively clear. Itinerancy, for example, is not just about vagrancy, about a kingdom of beggars. It is the refusal to settle down in a central place and have all come to you there, the refusal to give the Kingdom of God a specific geographical center. Commensality

RECONSTRUCTION OF A FIRST-CENTURY COURTYARD HOUSE AT
CAPERNAUM.   *The simple peasant life of a Galilean family centered around the
courtyard, where children played, livestock were kept, and family members worked
and ate. This rendition is based on the so-called House of St. Peter excavated by
the Franciscans, upon which an octagonal basilica was later built in the fifth
century* C.E. *Though most storage rooms (1) or units that surrounded the
courtyard were single-storied, we render one here as two-storied, built with local
basalt stones and smeared with mud and straw for insulation (2). Walls were made
of stacked fieldstones packed with smaller stone rubble, and roofs (3), which
provided additional space to dry fish (4) or sleep (5), were made of thatch and mud
as presumed in Mark 2, where friends of the paralytic "dig through" the roof to
lower him to Jesus. An intergenerational group of women (6) is shown here milling
grain into flour and baking bread in a clay oven.*

is not a matter of charity, of almsgiving, of a handout at the door. It is
about the just sharing of food as the material basis of life, of life that
belongs to God. Itinerancy and commensality are a mutuality forged at the
peasants' level of society. They sought to restore that society, fractured by
Herodian Romanization, urbanization, and commercialization, from the
bottom upward, and they did so as constitutive of the Kingdom of God, a
divine realm in confrontation with the narrower realm of Antipas within
the wider realm of Caesar. But both those aspects of the Kingdom's program require deeper investigation.

Itinerancy.   Jesus' itinerancy was not just a radical condition of mission, a demand that all of his companions leave familial home forever and live off the roads. From the very beginning that juxtaposition of healing and eating, of itinerants and householders, created a dialectic at the heart of the Kingdom that requires special consideration. When the historical Jesus first sent his companions out to do exactly what he himself was doing, was he breaking apart perfectly happy families or picking up the debris of shattered ones?

First, the fastest way to break up families is to advocate divorce, to separate wife and husband and thereby leave the children homeless. But Jesus forbade precisely that in his *Against Divorce* saying, according to Paul in 1 Corinthians 7:10–11, the Q Gospel in Luke 16:18 = Matthew 5:32, and in Mark 10:11–12 = Matthew 19:9. Those quotations in Paul, the Q Gospel, and Mark indicate a most likely origin from the historical Jesus in the first layer of the tradition.

Second, the *Peace or Sword* aphorism present in the Common Sayings Tradition, that is, the *Gospel of Thomas* 16 and the Q Gospel in Luke 12:51–53 = Matthew 10:34–36, also points back to the historical Jesus in that first layer. But that puts the axis of separation not between husband and wife, but between parents and children, with the emphasis on married children. That axis is exactly where separations would occur as extended families were forced to work outside the common farm for survival under increased commercialization.

Roman urbanization and Herodian commercialization brought the *Pax Romana's* economic boom to Lower Galilee, but that dislocated the ancient safety nets of peasant kinship, village cohesion, and just land distribution. It did not, of course, impoverish the entire area. It enriched it (for whom?), but it also involved profound changes and dispossessions as smaller farms were amalgamated into larger holdings and freehold farmers were downgraded into tenant farmers or day laborers. It created the type of situation imagined in the parable of the vineyard laborers in Matthew 20:1–15. The householder could go into the marketplace morning, midmorning, noon, as well as early and late afternoon and still find laborers available. High unemployment kept them there all day, they could even be blamed for their unemployment ("lazy"), and, at sunset, the master could be personally good with their wages. But what about the structural and systemic justice of that overall situation?

It is precisely such dispossessed peasants, the newly rather than the permanently destitute as it were, that become the itinerants of the Kingdom program. It is to those that Jesus can say, also from that Common Sayings Tradition in the *Gospel of Thomas* 54 and the *Q Gospel* at Matthew 5:3 = Luke 6:20: "Blessed are the destitute." That is a more correct translation than "Blessed are the poor." The *poor* are the peasantry in general, those who still hold on to their family farms. The *destitute* are those who have lost such holdings or were forced to work outside them as well as on them just to survive. You could say that itinerancy was making a virtue of necessity, but it would be more accurate to say that, since the necessity was unjust in the eyes of God, virtue was on the side of the dispossessed.

Originally, then, Jesus' itinerancy had nothing to do with asceticism, with a voluntary abandonment of normal family, home, and possessions. But at a very early stage of the Jesus tradition, voluntary asceticism began to replace involuntary dispossession, a tendency apparent in both the *Gospel of Thomas* and the *Q Gospel*. Many of those well-known sayings about abandoning goods or hating parents eventually came to be interpreted as demanding a life of ascetic negation. Those who, following and repeating such sayings, left goods and families voluntarily created serious tensions with householders, like those in the *Didache*'s community who responded with the admonition neither to judge nor to imitate them (11:11). But we think that in the earliest layers, Jesus' itinerancy was not an attempt at a new and individual asceticism, but a cry for an ancient and corporate justice.

Purity.   Before moving from itinerancy to commensality, some background on Jewish purity codes is necessary, since debates and invectives about those rules by Jews *within* Judaism became debates and invectives by Christians *against* Judaism. Polemical caricatures of Pharisaic Jews by Christian Jews, of Essene Jews by Pharisaic Jews, or of Sadducean Jews by Essene Jews are fights from inside and not from outside the family. But because of pervasive and long-standing Christian misunderstandings, usually coupled with false accusations of Pharisaic legalism, the Jewish concept of purity and the purity system in the Second Temple Period need historical clarification and not mindless repetition.

First, the Jewish concepts of pure and impure, clean and unclean cannot be equated with virtue and vice, good and evil. Instead, purity is a symbolic framework connected with the Temple, the divine presence there, and, more broadly, with the experience of bodily life and bodily death. Most things that make one impure through contact are related to death: human corpses, animal cadavers, even dead reptiles or insects, semen, since it implies a loss of a life-giving force, and blood, which is associated both with draining of a life force and death itself. Burying one's dead is a scriptural obligation, procreation is a mandate in Genesis, and a woman's menstrual flow is unavoidable and natural. None of these is a sin or in any way a moral lapse. Think of it this way: after coming into contact with the human realm of death, one needs simply to wash and wait before one is able to approach the divine realm of life. This is a concrete and bodily way of acknowledging that God is the author of life, is holy, and is set apart. Only if moral lapses are committed were sacrifices or offerings required in addition to purifying and waiting, but purity in and of itself is the symbolic system reminding Israel of its imperative to "choose life . . . so that you might live in the land that the Lord swore to give to your ancestors, to Abraham, to Isaac, and to Jacob" (Deut. 30:19–20). Washing was to be done not in drawn water, but in "living water," in a spring or river or lake; the *miqweh,* or ritual bath, used rainwater as a substitute in towns or houses without a convenient source nearby. The washing and waiting was not viewed in any of the Jewish literature as magical—no incantations or prayers were recited, and the act was not therapeutic in the sense that it healed or cured a person. It was more like a confession, a declaration of faith, an act of divine respect, a regular bodily reminder that bodily life belonged to God.

Second, the Torah, or covenantal law, was about holiness, about how to be a holy people of a holy God in a holy land. Holiness involved both justice and purity, not justice alone, not purity alone, but both together and in that order. It was, to repeat, not about purity *only,* but it was about purity *also.* It was usually easy to distinguish, if not always to separate, justice from purity. Sometimes, however, it was difficult even to make such a separation.

Think, for example, of the Sabbath. Was that about justice or ritual or both? Read the full content of these two legal commandments establishing its meaning and purpose:

Exodus 23:12: Six days you shall do your work, but on the seventh day you shall rest, so that your ox and your donkey may have relief, and your homeborn slave and the resident alien may be refreshed.

Deuteronomy 5:12–15: Observe the sabbath day and keep it holy, as the Lord your God commanded you. Six days you shall labor and do all your work. But the seventh day is a sabbath to the Lord your God;

you shall not do any work—you, or your son or your daughter, or your male or female slave, or your ox or your donkey, or any of your livestock, or the resident alien in your towns, so that your male and female slave may rest as well as you. Remember that you were a slave in the land of Egypt, and the Lord your God brought you out from there with a mighty hand and an outstretched arm; therefore the Lord your God commanded you to keep the sabbath day.

It is almost impossible even to distinguish, let alone separate, distributive justice from ritual observance in those texts. It is not just rest *for* worship but rest *as* worship. Animal and human, slave and free, parent and child must receive alike a day of rest. No matter how different all else may be, the symbolic stasis of equal rest is commanded for all. It is, after all, quite possible to have a ritual observance of divine justice itself.

Third, there is one common feature between laws about justice and codes about purity: they both focus on the body. Justice is not about mental ideas or even spiritual intentions; it is about how each and every body gets fair and equitable access to the material basis of life, to that unavoidable foundation without which full human life is not possible. In other words, the Torah's sense of divine justice, of God's distributive justice, is not about land or food so much as about life itself. Purity's emphasis on the body reminds one permanently that justice's demands also involve an emphasis on bodily life.

Fourth, purity codes and purification rituals include, in the widest sense, one's bodily *state* and, in the narrowest sense, one's bodily *diet*. In what follows on commensality, we are speaking primarily about that latter aspect, about purity with regard to food. In the next chapter we look at purity in the wider scope of pure or impure state, not just a pure or impure diet.

Commensality.   In the *Mission and Message* saying cited earlier, the version in *Gospel of Thomas* 14 reads, in full: "When you go into any region and walk about in the countryside, when people take you in, eat what they serve you and heal the sick among them. After all, what goes into your mouth will not defile you; rather, it's what comes out of your mouth that will defile you." That seems to put commensality in deliberate contrast with or opposition to purity concerns about what should or should not be eaten. In other words, a (or the?) major feature in the Kingdom of God program from the historical Jesus in the tradition's first layer was an attack

THE TITLE (last) PAGE OF
THE GOSPEL OF THOMAS
(reproduced with permission,
copyright the Institute for
Antiquity and Christianity,
Claremont, California)

on Jewish purity concerns at least with regard to food. There are, however, three problems with that interpretation.

First, if the nonobservance of (at least) food purity rules was that clear from the historical Jesus, why does Acts 10–11 need a solemn revelation to Peter denying any food distinctions of clean versus unclean? In 10:12–15 God tells Peter thrice that, with regard to "all kinds of four-footed creatures and reptiles and birds of the air . . . what God has made clean, you must not call unclean." Then, in 11:6–10, that is all repeated in full once more as Peter retells it to the other apostles. So, we hear once again that, with regard to "four-footed animals, beasts of prey, reptiles, and birds of the air . . . what God has made clean, you must not call unclean." An announcement, given three times by God is told twice by Luke. That rhetorical overkill indicates new revelation from God rather than old revelation from Jesus.

Second, in the middle of the first century there were debates at Jerusalem over whether pagan converts to Christian Judaism needed to be circumcised (no) and at Antioch over whether meals involving Jewish and pagan converts should observe kosher (yes). But neither in Paul's rather polemical account in Galatians 2 nor in Luke's more irenic version in Acts 15 does anyone cite the historical Jesus on either subject. In Galatians 2:11–14, for example, the combined Antioch community shifted from nonkosher to kosher meals at James's insistence. Paul disagreed with everyone else about that move, but he never cited any command or custom of Jesus in his own defense.

Third, in the last quarter of that same century, two gospels could disagree rather absolutely on that very same subject of clean versus unclean, pure versus impure with regard to diet.

Mark 7:15 repeats that same saying about *Inside and Outside* appended to the *Mission and Message* unit in *Gospel of Thomas* 14 earlier. But to explain it he adds three contextual comments. It needs to be privately explained to the disciples in 7:17–23. It receives the explicit Markan gloss asserting, "(Thus he declared all foods clean)." It immediately precedes a sojourn by Jesus in pagan territory, a sort of proleptic Gentile mission. That is all clear enough, but is it the first or the third layer of gospel tradition, is it from Jesus or from Mark?

That Markan phrase about Jesus declaring "all foods clean" is omitted at the parallel place in Matthew 15:17–18. That is only to be expected after Jesus said earlier in Matthew 5:17–18, "Do not think that I have come to abolish the law or the prophets; I have come not to abolish but to fulfill. For truly I tell you, until heaven and earth pass away, not one letter, not one stroke of a letter, will pass from the law until all is accomplished." Mark and Matthew, in other words, pull the historical Jesus in opposite directions on the subject of food purity and impurity, and that could still be done as late as the 70s and the 80s.

The obvious conclusion from those three items is that the earliest layer furnished no clear attitude *for* or *against* food purity rules from the historical Jesus. He, in other words, observed exactly the same rules about food purity as did other Galilean peasants of his time and place. But, if his emphasis on food was not concerned with purity, with what was it concerned?

Commensality without Itinerancy.   We argued earlier that, whatever the final judgment on the authenticity and identity of the James ossuary, its public presentation and scholarly discussion are very important to highlight properly the importance of Jesus' brother James. And that importance reflects backward on the itinerancy and commensality of Jesus as his basic vision and fundamental program for the Kingdom-of-God movement.

According to the *Gospel of Thomas* 12 as cited in our first chapter, Jesus placed his brother in charge once he himself had departed: "No matter where you are, you are to go to James the Just, for whose sake heaven and earth came into being." James was clearly not another itinerant but was in some specific location, known, attainable, but unnamed. Both Luke, from Acts 12:17 through 15:13 to 21:18, and Paul, from Galatians 1:19 to 2:12, agree on the authority of James and his location in Jerusalem. And they may both agree on something else about James but each gives us only half of the full picture.

Luke speaks of the Jerusalem community as radically egalitarian. According to Acts 2:44–45: "All who believed were together and had all things in common; they would sell their possessions and goods and distribute the proceeds to all, as any had need." And again, according to Acts 4:32–35:

> Now the whole group of those who believed were of one heart and soul, and no one claimed private ownership of any possessions, but everything they owned was held in common. With great power the apostles gave their testimony to the resurrection of the Lord Jesus, and great grace was upon them all. There was not a needy person among them, for as many as owned lands or houses sold them and brought the proceeds of what was sold. They laid it at the apostles' feet, and it was distributed to each as any had need.

Luke then continues with a positive example in the case of Barnabas's donation and a counterpointed negative example in the case of Ananias's and Sapphira's deceit. It is possible to dismiss that as Lukan romanticism but several reasons point in the opposite direction. First, on the level of Lukan theology, he never mentions a similar lifestyle elsewhere, so it is not one of his standard motifs. He tends to gloss over disagreements (or

deceits) and he admits it here. He notes that communalism was voluntary
and not required of all. Second, on the level of contemporary history, he
notes that the Jerusalem community's lifestyle was similar to that of the
Qumran community. According to the Dead Sea Scrolls' *Rule of the
Community*, after one year in that community, the initiate's "wealth and
his belongings will also be included in the hands of the Inspector of the
belongings of the Many. And they shall be entered into the ledger in his
hand but they shall not use them for the Many . . . until he completes a
second year." Only after that second probationary year was the final and
available-for-use "placing of his possessions in common." Furthermore, "if
one is found among them who has lied knowingly concerning goods, he
shall be excluded from the pure food of the Many for a year and shall be
sentenced to a quarter of his bread" (1QS 6). Third, on the level of apocalyptic eschatology, there is a vision of radical egalitarianism in an early
first-century description of God's perfect community here below upon a
perfected earth. At that imminent time, according to the *Sibylline Oracles*
2:319–24,

> The earth will belong equally to all, undivided by walls
> or fences. It will then bear more abundant fruits
> spontaneously. Lives will be in common and wealth will have no
>   division.
> For there will be no poor man there, no rich, and no tyrant,
> no slave. Further, no one will be either great or small anymore.
> No kings, no leaders. All will be on a par together.

All in all, then, we take Luke's account as basically accurate. The Jerusalem Christian-Jewish community practiced voluntary communalism in
a share-community that programmatically resisted the normalcy of greed-
community in its contemporary incarnation as Sadduceean collaboration
with Roman imperialism. James was the head of this group and that
explains his title as James the Just. It also explains his reputation for sanctity among Christian Jews. Recall Hegesippus from our first chapter. His
account of James's sanctity and martyrdom contained both accurate
details and incredible elements or, better, a basically correct story overlaid
with heavy polemical, apologetical, and theological layers. But, as you will
recall, even his religiously motivated account of Paul's "murder" of James
reflected knowledge of James's actual martyrdom. Similarly with James's

sanctity. The details are clearly overdone, to put it mildly, and the examples are mostly overimaginative, but behind and beneath them is the fact of James's holiness. On that basic point, Eusebius's *The History of the Church* 23 cites Hegesippus's claim that James "was often found on his knees beseeching forgiveness for the people, so that his knees grew hard like a camel's from his continually bending in worship of God and beseeching forgiveness for his people." Whatever about James's knees, we accept James's sanctity as history. Finally, it also explains why his execution was so opposed by non-Christian Jews so zealous for the Law that they had the high priest Ananaus II deposed for James's death.

In summary, therefore, James was urban where Jesus was rural, and James was nonitinerant where Jesus was itinerant. But James's communalism and commensality were an absolutely valid continuation of his brother's vision and program for the Kingdom of God. They were but divergent share-communities like the Qumran group in the *Rule of the Community* and those other non-Qumran Essene groups in the *Damascus Document*. As observant of God's divine justice, they were thereby resistant to Rome's imperial injustice.

FROM LAND TO WORLD AND FOOD

Recall what was said in the last chapter about the covenantal Kingdom of God, about the justice and righteousness of God in the Law and the Prophets, about the just distribution of land and, therefore, about the Torah's attempt to control the spread of debt. Land, as the material basis of life, could not be bought and sold like any other commodity. It belonged to God in a way so special that its equitable distribution was not just a human virtue, but a divine necessity. "The land shall not be sold in perpetuity, for the land is mine; with me you are but aliens and tenants" (Lev. 25:23). From that basis about the *land* in Torah one could go, almost necessarily and inevitably, in two different directions, expanding from that focal point to *world* and contracting from it to *food*.

Land and World

However specifically that divine sovereignty was aimed at the particular land of Israel, it also held for the entire world with regard to the justice and righteousness of God. In Psalm 82, for example, God sits down as the Supreme Divinity to judge all the other divinities who are in charge of the nations and in control of the earth. Here is the indictment: "How long will you judge unjustly and show partiality to the wicked? Give justice to the weak and the orphan; maintain the right of the lowly and the destitute. Rescue the weak and the needy; deliver them from the hand of the wicked" (82:2–4). Those accused divinities do not even seem to comprehend the situation or to understand the indictment. It is as if they never knew that justice was part, or even the principal part, of their job description: "They have neither knowledge nor understanding, they walk around in darkness." But the results of their failure are catastrophic: "All the foundations of the earth are shaken" (82:5). A failure to administer the world equitably and justly does not simply displease the Supreme God; it rocks the very foundations of creation. This justice is not a human idea or even a divine commandment. It is that alone on which and by which the world moves in security as the just possession of a just God.

Two footnotes to that expansion from land to world. One is this. When we Christians read of "justice and righteousness" in our Old Testament, we often hear it as speaking of retribution and punishment. But in that psalm, for instance, the emphasis is not on personal and retributive justice, but on structural and distributive justice. Those failed divinities are not actually punished by the Supreme God. Here is the only result, the only "punishment" for their failure to maintain justice across the world. "I say, 'You are gods, children of the Most High, all of you; nevertheless, you shall die like mortals, and fall like any prince'" (Ps. 82:6–7). Divinities of power eventually die as the power that upheld them falters and fails. The phalanxes of Greece are gone and so is Zeus. The legions of Rome are gone and so is Jupiter. But can a God of justice ever die?

Or, again, when the last line of Psalm 82 cries, "Rise up, O God, judge the earth; for all the nations belong to you," it is certainly not an appeal for punishment against the speaker or even, although it might be much more acceptable, against the speaker's oppressors. It appeals to God alone for a fair shake, an equitable deal, a just decision in a world where such was almost impossible to discover. Recall Jesus' admonition in Matthew 5:25–26: "Come to terms quickly with your accuser while you are on the way to court with him, or your accuser may hand you over to the judge, and the judge to the guard, and you will be thrown into prison. Truly I tell you, you will never get out until you have paid the last penny." That is exactly how the peasantry of the ancient world thought about human justice: stay away from the courts or you will remain embroiled until your last penny is taken from you in useless bribes. If you do not find distributive justice here below, you yearn for a God who will administer it fairly and equitably.

The other footnote is this. We Christians usually translate the New Testament word *agape* as "love" and interpret it to mean charity or alms-giving. It would be better to translate it not as the rather vague term "to love," but as the much more precise term "to share." That is, of course, "to share" on the presumption that we are not so much generously sharing what is ours as equitably distributing what is God's. And that means, very simply, that justice in the Christian Old Testament is exactly the same as *agape*/love in the Christian New Testament.

Land and Food

Actually, however, it is not the land itself, but the food it produces that is the material basis of life. The just distribution of land is about the just dis-tribution of food. That is why those visions of the eschatological and/or apocalyptic Kingdom of God imagine not more and more land, but more and more fertility. That incredible future fertility is depicted in texts three hundred years apart, in a text from before the Syrian persecution and the revolt of the Maccabees to a text after the Roman war and the destruction of the Temple. In *The Book of the Watchers* at *1 Enoch* 10:19: "Every seed that is sown on her [the newly righteous earth], one measure will yield a thou-sand [measures] and one measure of olives will yield ten measures of presses of oil." And in *2 Baruch* 29:5–6: "The earth will also yield fruits ten thou-sandfold. And on one vine will be a thousand branches, and one branch will produce a thousand clusters, and one cluster will produce a thousand grapes, and one grape will produce a cor of wine." That eschatological world, that divine Eutopia on earth, would be a perfect Mediterranean superplentitude of cereal, oil, and wine. Land without food would be certainly inadequate. Food without land would be perfectly adequate.

Why do we find a shift in emphasis from distributive justice with regard to land to distributive justice with regard to food at the time of Jesus? It would be nice to think that he was so prescient that he foresaw the later Christian move from a rural to an urban environment, that he was pre-paring the way for life in the cities of the Mediterranean rather than on the farms of the Galilee. The proclamation that God's renewed creation demanded necessarily a just distribution and a communal sharing of food was utterly appropriate among unlanded urban artisans, freed slaves, and their first-generation freeborn children. But Jesus' emphasis on food rather than on land indicated not so much future knowledge as present necessity. It indicated that the situation by the late 20s at least in Lower Galilee was too far gone to change the distribution of land from the bottom upward. That was the Kingdom of Antipas. Even to suggest the just distribution of land let alone to attempt its implementation, would almost inevitably have involved violent revolution. All that was still possible was to attempt the redistribution of eating and healing, of the material and spiritual bases of life, from the bottom upward. That was the Kingdom of God. On earth.

The fundamentally Jewish vision and program of Jesus in the tradition's first layer is land as food and justice as *agape*. And the fundamentally Jewish basis for that is a theology of creation that not only asks who *made* the world, but who *owns* it. We humans, after all, have never suggested that we created the earth, but we normally presume that we own it.

FIVE

Jewish Resistance to Roman Domination

Remember two crucial points throughout this chapter. One is that, in any situation of discrimination or oppression, overt resistance is but the iceberg tip beneath which covert resistance moves stealthily, but steadily. Another is that whenever we cite disjunctive options such as resistance or nonresistance, violence or nonviolence, read disjunction but hear spectrum. Those disjunctions emphasize not just themselves, but all the combinations and permutations in between them. Without imagining extremes, however, it is difficult to see the spectrum of options or analyze the range of possibilities confronting individuals and groups in a century that opened in 4 B.C.E. with two thousand rebels crucified in Jerusalem and ended with five hundred a day crucified there in 70 C.E.

RELIGION AND POLITICS, COLONY AND EMPIRE

We have thousands of coins from archaeological digs and looted sites across the Jewish homeland in the common era's first century. Originally those coins were not only a means of commercial exchange, they were also the only mass medium of information in the ancient world.

A coin of Julius Caesar shows his spirit ascending cometlike to take its place among the eternal deities. A coin of Augustus Caesar calls him *divi filius*, son of a divine one, son of a god, son of the aforesaid comet. A coin of Tiberius Caesar hails him as *pontifex maximus*, supreme bridge builder between earth and heaven, high priest of an imperial people. A silver denarius was a day's pay for a laborer and, if a day laborer meant somebody who worked every day rather than somebody who looked for work every day, it would have been a very good salary. Imagine this situation. If, after three days of hard work, a day laborer held those silver denarii in his hand, how would he, could he, should he distinguish between politics and religion in the Roman Empire?

Think some more about Augustus Caesar. He was four ways divine, almost a case of transcendental overkill. He was divine from a millennium-old tribal origin at the time of the Trojan War, a descendant of the divine Aphrodite-Venus and the human Anchises, as seen in Virgil's *Aeneid*. He was divine from a conception through Apollo and Atia, as seen at the end of this book's first chapter. He was divine by an adoption from Julius Caesar, as just seen on his own coinage. In case all of that was not enough, he was deified personally and directly by a senatorial decree upon his death in 14 C.E. How exactly did one distinguish between politics and religion in such adulation? Could you oppose Augustus politically but not religiously, religiously but not politically? Indeed, from Augustus's own viewpoint, why would anyone want to oppose the *Pax Romana*, his new world order of political reformation and moral rearmament, his hard roads free of bandits and his sea lanes free of pirates, his cities linked by common culture and economic boom, and his legions guarding the periphery behind which only western barbarians howled and eastern Parthians prowled?

Rome, and Rome alone, had built a kingdom and only it could approve how to build an underkingdom, a minirealm, a subordinate rule. How did you separate religion and politics in building a kingdom, with Rome or against Rome? Whose was the kingdom, the power, and the glory in that difficult first-century situation?

By that century, the Jewish homeland had been held by Greek cultural imperialism for over three hundred years and by Roman military imperialism for under one hundred years. This chapter is about responses to those twin imperialisms. We do not presume that every Jew thought only about resistance or that those who did thought about it in the same way. On the subject of imperial control, pagan domination, and social oppression there was always a spectrum of Jewish opinion, just as there was on any other important subject. Indeed, only a spectrum of spectra would do complete justice to a first-century Judaism, neither monolithic nor univocal, but ancient and traditional, as it confronted overweening cultural condescension and overwhelming military might. But we have chosen to focus here on reaction to imperialism and resistance to oppression for one main reason.

The Jewish homeland was under imperial control for about five hundred years before the Romans arrived. After the Babylonians destroyed the First Temple and deported the Jewish leadership, the land was successively controlled by the Persians, the Greeks, the Greco-Egyptian Ptolemies, and the Greco-Syrian Seleucids. In all that time there was only a single revolt, and that was under the supreme provocation of a foreign religious persecution that resulted in a century of Jewish rule by the Hasmonean Maccabees. But in the first two hundred years of Roman rule there were four major revolts against its presence: in 4 B.C.E., in 66–74 C.E., in 115–17 C.E., and in 132–35 C.E. After those revolts were over, direct Roman governance was established, the Second Temple was leveled, Egyptian Judaism was destroyed, and Jerusalem was officially a pagan city forbidden to Jews. Response to imperialism is at least one very important spectrum to consider for the first century in the Jewish homeland and, within that continuum of reaction, the first and most intransigent options were between nonresistance or resistance.

OPTIONS FOR NONRESISTANCE

Think of colonial nonresistance as passive or active, as consciously minimal or deliberately maximal cooperation. Think of the latter as treason at worst or collaboration at best and know, of course, that the difference between traitors and collaborators can be vague and slippery in practice. And, apart from abstract options, think about Tiberius Julius Alexander or Flavius Josephus in the first century.

Traitors

Tiberius Julius Alexander, son of a famously wealthy financial officer in Roman Alexandria and nephew of the philosopher Philo, was born a Jew, but rejected Judaism for Roman paganism. Thereafter, successively and successfully, he was in charge of Palestine, Egypt, and the emperor's Praetorian Guard in Rome. He was a crucially first governor to proclaim allegiance to the imperial claims of Vespasian in 69, and he was a ranking officer among the advisory staff of Vespasian's son Titus at the siege and destruction of Jerusalem and its Temple in 70 C.E. His was a great Roman career but, from a Jewish viewpoint, was it treason and apostasy? In the earlier *Jewish War* Josephus praised him without any hint of criticism, noting that, "by abstaining from all interference with the customs of the country" while governor of the Jewish homeland, he "kept the nation at peace" (2.220). But, in the later *Jewish Antiquities*, the report is much less laudatory, noting that the elder Alexander "was also superior to his son Alexander in his religious devotion, for the latter did not stand by the practices of his people" (20.100).

Even that seems such a mild comment, at least from our viewpoint: Alexander no longer followed the traditions of his people. But it is also an important warning at the start of this chapter. Maybe it was possible to keep the ancient traditions of Israel and still refrain from any opposition to Roman domination. Maybe it was possible to maintain the religious practices of the Jewish people and still collaborate with Roman power as an expression of God's will. But, without those covenantal traditions, how could a Jew resist slow but steady Greco-Roman acculturation? Without those religious practices, how could Jewish identity not eventually disappear into the common gene pool of an imperial melting pot? *With* purity rituals, it was still possible to ignore the far greater demands of justice and righteousness in the Torah, but *without* them, would you still bother to try? *With* purity practices, it was still possible to bow before Roman urbanization, but *without* them, would you long hold out for covenant over commerce?

Throughout the rest of this chapter, therefore, understand precisely what is at stake when, for example, Jewish individuals and groups emphatically maintain external rituals of bodily purification distinct and different from those of the pagans who surround them, interact with them, and rule over them. In that situation, Jewish purity is about Jewish identity, about fundamental Jewish resistance to Greco-Roman submersion, and about the future; that is, whether there will be a future, for the Jewish tradition, the Jewish people, and the Jewish God.

Collaborators

Josephus was an aristocratic Jerusalem priest who had "prepared" Galilee for war against Rome in 66–67. After surrendering to the Roman general Vespasian and prophesying his imperial future, he continued as an adviser to Vespasian's son Titus at the siege of Jerusalem in 70 and as an apologist for Romans to Jews in the *Jewish War*. But also, later, he was an apologist for Jews to Romans in the *Jewish Antiquities* and *Against Apion*. Collaborator? Certainly. Traitor? Maybe not. Apostate? Certainly not. According to his *Jewish War*, he believed three things about Rome.

First, God wanted the land of Israel to be, internally, a priest-led theocracy and, externally, a colony of the empire: "God who went the round of the nations, bringing to each in turn the rod of empire, now rested over Italy" (5.367). Second, God had designated Vespasian as Judaism's long-awaited messiah: "an ambiguous oracle . . . found in their sacred scriptures, to the effect that at that time one from their country would become ruler of the world. This they understood to mean someone of their own race, and many of their wise men went astray in their interpretation of it. The oracle, however, in reality signified the sovereignty of Vespasian, who was proclaimed Emperor in Jewish soil" (6.312–13). Third, to rebel against Rome was therefore to rebel against God and God's messiah: "You are warring not against the Romans only, but also against God" (5.378). Tiberius Julius Alexander and Flavius Josephus were both on Titus's staff as Jerusalem fell and its Temple burned, but at least their declared intentions were rather different.

Lest Josephus's imperial theology be dismissed as merely the self-justification of a turncoat or the self-interest of a collaborator, recall that it was also the solution proposed by delegations of Palestinian and Roman Jews after the death of Herod the Great. They begged Augustus, as Josephus's *Jewish War* recorded, "to unite their country to Syria and to entrust the administration to governors from among themselves" (2.91). It was also the later rabbinical position after resistance had almost completely destroyed the Jewish homeland. But, of course, if nonresistance was for some a theological submission to God's will, it was probably for others an opportunistic acceptance of Roman power.

OPTIONS FOR RESISTANCE

Nonresistance or collaboration was a relatively straightforward option. The opposite one of resistance was far more complicated. We can distinguish three separate suboptions within resistance, but remember, as always, that these are somewhat ideal types and that, in practice, there may have been more mix and match than distinction and separation among them.

Bandits

One type of resistance came from those the Romans called bandits or brigands. Some of them may have been common thugs or general criminals, but imperial situations often make it difficult to distinguish between the systemic violence of the conqueror and the individual counterviolence of the conquered. In any case, Josephus's emphasis on the first-century numerical increase in banditry indicates that disposed peasants were choosing to fight in the hills rather than beg in the towns or die in the hedges. When armies marched out against legions, the Romans respectfully called it a *bellum justum*, not so much a *just* as a *real* war. When "bandits" or "brigands" fought a guerrilla war from the hills or the marshes, they contemptuously called it a *bellum servile*, a slaves' war. In general, therefore, quotation marks are usually needed around "bandits" in pro-Roman texts, since "bandits" from the imperial viewpoint could be "liberators" from the colonial one.

Apocalypticists

Another type of resistance came from those termed apocalypticists, and we presume here our discussion in Chapter 2 about the continuum from the covenantal through the eschatological to the apocalyptic Kingdom of God. Apocalypticism proclaimed an imminent act of transcendental power that would make the whole world, but especially the land of Israel, into a space of unhindered fertility and unlabored prosperity, into a Eutopia of perfect justice, idyllic peace, and absolute holiness. Soon. Immediately. Any day. Now. Recall, also and always, that apocalypse then did not mean destruction but transformation, not just the end of the material world of space and time but the end of the social world of evil, impurity, injustice, and violence.

Here then are three sub-options within such apocalyptic expectations. We emphasize them separately while fully aware that, in reality, they mix and match, slip and slide, and move back and forth between one another.

Militant Violence.   The first active suboption is *militant violence*. As an example, think of Judas the Galilean or others like him. His motto or manifesto was "No Lord but God" and in the name of that divine mandate he instigated a revolt when the Romans exiled Herod Archelaus in 6 C.E. and ordered a taxation census preparatory to placing his territories directly under a Roman governor. Not Caesar, but God alone could be called Lord. Indeed, much of what Josephus terms the "fourth philosophy," in order to insist that it was a late and invalid appendage to the three earlier and valid ones of Essenes, Pharisees, and Sadducees, was probably composed of apocalypticists and probably within these militant options. But, of course, if Josephus could find God's will in nonresistance, Judas could just as easily find it in resistance.

Archetypal Symbolism.   The second suboption is *archetypal symbolism*. As an example, recall John the Baptist from the preceding chapter, or think of the so-called Egyptian prophet or others like him in the 50s and 60s C.E. He gathered a multitude of followers at the Jordan River and brought them through it toward the walls of Jerusalem, expecting the walls to collapse at his arrival just as Jericho's had done for Joshua over a millennium earlier. Inaugural enactment would presumably beget apocalyptic repetition. As God had acted then, so God would act now. Beginning and end would coalesce. Those crowds were unarmed, since God alone could bring about the desired consummation. They were slaughtered, since God did not.

Covenantal Community.   The third suboption is *covenantal community*. As an example think of the so-called *Damascus Document*, a community rule now known both in medieval copies from the sacred-book depository of Old Cairo's (now beautifully restored) Ezra Synagogue and in ancient copies from several of the Qumran caves. What is the relationship there between apocalyptic expectation and community commitment? The rule seems to be a deliberate attempt to resist the normalcy of imperial greed by creating intense share-communities attempting to live a covenantal holiness that would actively initiate or proleptically institute that apocalyptic consummation. Those who entered its "new covenant" were "to abstain from wicked wealth which defiles, either by promise or by vow, and from the wealth of the temple and from stealing from the poor of the people, from making their widows their spoils and from murdering orphans." Its command was "for each to love his brother like himself; to strengthen the hand of the poor, the needy and the foreigner; for each to seek the peace of his brother and not commit sin against his blood relation." It required of each "the salary of two days each month at least. They shall place it in the hands of the Inspector and the judges. From it they shall give to the orphans and with it they shall strengthen the hand of the needy and the poor, and to the elder who is dying, and to the vagabond, and to the prisoner of a foreign people, and to the girl who has no protector, and to the unmarried woman who has no suitor; and for all the works of the company." That too, or maybe that above all, was resistance to imperial injustice.

As another example, recall the preceding chapter's discussion of communalism within the James community at Jerusalem and the first chapter's mention of an earlier pro-James and anti-Paul source in *Clementine Recognitions* 1. That text blamed Paul for the failure of the mission to the Jews as well as the death of James himself. That was done, as you will recall, by having an obliquely identified Paul attack James violently at the very moment when authorities and people were ready to convert to Christian Judaism. As literal history, that story is, of course, fantastically incredible, but as metaphorical condensation of the chasm between James and Paul it is highly instructive. But there is also one other aspect of the James community mentioned in that narrative that is of immediate relevance.

The parable in the *Clementine Recognitions* had Paul cast James down from the steps of the Temple and leave him there for dead. "But our colleagues lifted him up. For they were both more in number and greater in strength than the others. But because of their fear of God, they allowed themselves to be slain by the few rather than slay others" (1.71.1). Our point is not that the James community so acted that day in the Temple, but that they took care to insert the comment into their parabolic story about it. Apart from their communal share-life as a mode of resistance to the normalcy of imperial greed-life, there is also their programmatic nonviolence as another aspect of that same resistance.

Protesters

All *bandits* operated with human violence. Some *apocalypticists* expected divine violence, some human violence, some both, and some neither. (We repeat that such violence was always counterviolence to imperial injustice.) *Protesters* are those who worked with nonviolent resistance: not with violent resistance (like Judas the Galilean), and not simply with nonviolent nonresistance (like Josephus the historian), but, precisely and accurately, with nonviolent resistance. It was, however, a form of absolute protest that accepted the logical implications of its position and had determined on martyrdom rather than submission. It deserves, therefore, a special name, perhaps *martyrological protest*. It challenged imperial force to lay bare its own covert violence by the overt slaughter of unarmed and nonviolent resisters. There are two major examples, one from the late 20s against Pilate and the other from the early 40s against Petronius.

Examples of Nonviolent Resistance. A first example concerned Pilate's military standards. It probably dates to 26–27 C.E., on the presumption that it would have happened very early in Pontius Pilate's tenure as prefect. His troops carried standards with images of Caesar into Jerusalem. The result, according to Josephus's *Jewish War* (2.169–74) and

Jewish Antiquities (18.55–59), was that "the indignation of the townspeople stirred the country folk, who flocked together in crowds" to Pilate's base at coastal Caesarea. They stayed before his residence for five days and, when finally surrounded by armed soldiers, "the Jews, *as by concerted action*, flung themselves in a body on the ground, extended their necks, and exclaimed that they were ready rather to die than to transgress the law." Pilate gave in and removed the offending standards.

A second and climactic example is the case of Gaius Caligula's statue. This incident dates to 40–41 C.E., when that emperor attempted to erect his statue in the Temple of Jerusalem. Here we know what happened from two first-century sources, not only the Jewish historian Josephus in both his *Jewish War* (2.185–203) and *Jewish Antiquities* (18.261–309), but also the Jewish philosopher Philo in his *Embassy to Gaius* (203–348). As the Syrian governor Petronius came south with enforcing legions from Antioch, according to Josephus, a popular nonviolent protest greeted him first at the Mediterranean port of Ptolemais ("many tens of thousands of Jews") and again inside Galilee at Tiberias ("many tens of thousands"). Their nonviolence is emphasized as "the Jews assembled with their wives and children" and assured him that "if he wished to set up these statues, he must first sacrifice the entire Jewish nation; and that they presented themselves, their wives and their children, ready for the slaughter." Petronius recognized "that the country was in danger of remaining unsown—for it was seed-time and the people had spent fifty days idly waiting upon him," so he relented and returned to Antioch with his legions. That nonviolent resistance is backed up not only with a willingness for martyrdom, but with, in effect, an agricultural strike.

Philo recounts this same incident with some minor differences; for example, Josephus's agricultural strike at sowing time becomes an arson danger at reaping time. But, if anything, Philo emphasizes even more than Josephus both the nonviolence of the resisters and their willingness for martyrdom. Here are the key sentences in that portion of his account:

> But when the inhabitants of the holy city and of all the region round about heard of the design which was in agitation, they all arrayed themselves together *as if at a concerted signal*, their common misery having given them the word, and went forth in a body, and leaving their cities and their villages and their houses empty, they hastened with one accord into Phoenicia, for Petronius happened to be in that country at

the moment. . . . And the multitude was divided into six companies, one of old men, one of young men, one of boys; and again in their turn one band of aged matrons, one of women in the prime of life, and one of virgins. . . . "We are, as you see, without any arms . . . [and we are] offering our bodies freely an easy aim to any one who desires to put us to death. We have brought unto you our wives, and our children, and our whole families, and in your person we will prostrate ourselves before Gaius [Caligula], having left not one single person at home, that you may either preserve us all, or destroy us all together by one general and complete destruction. . . . And if we cannot prevail with you in this, then we offer up ourselves for destruction, that we may not live to behold a calamity more terrible and grievous than death. . . . We willingly and readily submit ourselves to be put to death."

That long citation underlines its importance for our present argument. If only Josephus described such nonviolent resistance backed by a willingness for martyrdom, it might be dismissed as propaganda, as his wish for what might have been in the past or his example of what should be for the future. But, in this case at least, and even allowing for rhetorical exaggerations, both authors agree on the major points. There are two important footnotes to those stories.

Leaders.   In citing those cases of nonviolent resistance against Pilate and Petronius, backed up, necessarily, by a willingness to let protest escalate into martyrdom, we insist on one element. Such large-scale public demonstrations involved theoretical plans, practical controls, permanent leaders, and consistent managers. They did not simply happen spontaneously. Note, for example, the phrase "as if at a concerted signal," which we italicized in both Josephus and Philo above. Who organized those protests? Who exercised crowd control on those resisters? The following is our best guess, but if it is not acceptable, the question still stands. Who invented, organized, and controlled these public demonstrations of nonviolent resistance and martyrological protest in the first half of that century? Scholars have recently proposed three points that may indicate an answer. First, the Pharisees enjoyed wide popular influence in that period, an influence indicated by how much Josephus directly and indirectly laments it. Second, that leadership did not just involve exegetico-legal debates, but also politico-religious activities. In other words, their piety and politics were always but two sides of the same coin. For example, it was Pharisaic teachers who were executed by Herod the Great for having incited their students to remove the imperial eagle from above a main gate of the Temple. Third, the two major schools of Pharisaic tradition, the Shammaites and the Hillelites, may have diverged not just on severe versus lenient legal rulings, but also on violent versus nonviolent responses to Roman oppression. If all those points are correct, it was probably the Hillelite Pharisees who instigated theoretically and organized practically those nonviolent but martyrdom-ready early-first-century resisters.

Objections.   Here is one objection or question. What exactly is the religious basis or theological ground beneath those dangerous acts of martyrological protest? No answer is given in the texts, but here are three suggestions. Those nonviolent protesters hoped that their martyrdom would motivate God to violent or even apocalyptic retribution. Or they wanted to avoid violence themselves so that, whatever about the blood shed by violent Greco-Roman paganism, they themselves would not pollute the land of God by spilling blood upon it. Pagans would do what pagans had to do, but *they* would refrain from even defensive bloodguilt. Or, finally, those protesters intended to imitate a nonviolent divinity, to act in union with a nonviolent God. Remember, in any case, that twin extremes such as that of Josephus (nonviolent nonresistance) and that of Judas the Galilean (violent resistance) grounded their absolutely opposite programs in the will of the same Jewish God. So, however one explains the divine basis of nonviolent martyrological protest, it was most likely present, even if we are unsure about its content.

A second objection is a very obvious one, and you have probably thought of it already. Is claiming such nonviolent resistance simply an invalid retrojection of Tolstoy, Gandhi, and King from here and now back into there and then? But if such anachronism is always a danger, so also is arrogance, that is, the condescending presumption that only modernity, not antiquity, could have invented nonviolent resistance. But, almost all the imaginable options for colonial resistance were practiced and/or invented in that first-century situation. For example, think about the Sicarii (a *sica* is a short and easily hidden dagger) as one example from the other end of the religio-political spectrum of resistance.

First, those Sicarii, or *sica*-users, did not invent conspiratorial assassination. That was already well established everywhere. But what they invented was urban terrorism, and that term is no anachronism, no retrojection of modernity into antiquity. According to Josephus's *Jewish War* (2.254–57) and *Jewish Antiquities* (20.208–10), the Sicarii killed high-placed fellow Jews, especially ones from the high-priestly family, who were collaborating with Roman rule. But they assassinated them surreptitiously in the midst of urban crowds, so that, as Josephus recognized, "the panic created was more alarming than the calamity itself; every one, as on a battlefield, hourly expecting death." Second, before media coverage was available, "the festivals were their special seasons" not only for protection within the crowds, but also for the maximum public awareness of their activities. Third, they also invented kidnapping for prisoner-exchange purposes: "[they] kidnapped the secretary of the captain [of the Temple] Eleazar—he was the son of Ananias the high priest—and led him off in bonds. They then sent to Ananias saying that they would release the secretary to him if he would induce [the Roman prefect] Albinus to release ten of their number who had been taken prisoner." Fourth, that initial success led to the inevitable result of "greater troubles" as the Sicarii continued regular high-profile kidnappings for successive prisoner releases. Would we have imagined those tactics in first-century Jerusalem without Josephus's precise descriptions? None of that *proves* Hillelite-led nonviolent resistance backed by martyrdom. It just warns us that we did not invent everything for either good or evil in the modern age.

MASADA AND QUMRAN IN THE SOUTH

All those options, from resistance to nonresistance and from violence to nonviolence, are clearly present in the textual remains from that terrible first century. What about the material remains? They may show abandoned sites, blackened stones, charred timbers, battered walls, broken bodies, arrowheads, lance shafts, and abandoned weapons. But is it only violent revolt that can leave permanent traces on the ground, permanent scars on the earth? We begin with another look at those Sicarii, but then go on to consider what else is left for archaeologists to discover and interpret.

The Sicarii at Masada

The Jewish revolt against Rome ended atop the cliffs of Masada some four years after the fall of Jerusalem and the destruction of the Temple in 70 C.E., and a full eight years after it began in 66 C.E. Violent resistance to

Roman domination was finally crushed at the fortress-palace complex Herod the Great had built nearly a century earlier along the Dead Sea.

Stories. According to Josephus, a band of Sicarii and their families committed mass suicide the night before Roman legions burst through a breach in the wall atop Masada. Josephus tells the dramatic story of those defenders who had captured the fortress early in the revolt and survived through its vast stores of wheat, water, wine, and weapons, but who decided in the end to take their own lives instead of dying at the hands of the Romans. Each man put his wife and children to the sword, ten chosen men then killed the others, and of the surviving ten one was chosen by lot to kill the rest, burn the buildings and valuables, and then turn his sword on himself. This way, in words Josephus attributes to their leader Eleazar ben Yair in a dramatic oration, they "chose death rather than slavery" and carried out their resolve "neither to serve the Romans nor anyone else except God." The next morning, the battle cries of Flavius Silva's soldiers were met with complete silence. The Jewish uprising was at an end.

After Yigael Yadin excavated the site between 1963 and 1965, Masada became a metaphor for the State of Israel, and "Never again will Masada fall" a national refrain. Just as some Christian archaeologists, operating from a conservative theological framework, often seek to confirm some biblical story from the material remains, so the Israeli archaeologists, operating from a defensive political framework, sought to ground their national saga in Josephus's story from the ruins atop Masada.

Today, however, considerable doubt has been cast on some of the excavators' initial interpretations. The mass suicide, at the heart of Josephus's story, has been questioned—it is a recurrent theme elsewhere in Josephus and a common literary device in Greco-Roman literature. And the excavators' ready identification of skeletal remains as the defenders of Masada has been questioned. The bones of a man, a child, and a woman found with braided hair and a sandal, along with about twenty skeletons in a cistern, were given a reverent state burial, yet they may have been those of Romans who later occupied the site until 111 C.E. After all, asks Israel's physical anthropologist Joe Zias, why would the Romans who occupied the site for another forty years tolerate decomposing corpses in the northern palace? How does one account for the pig bones among the skeletons in the caves, especially since their sacrifice was a common Roman burial practice? This, coupled with the fragmentary nature of the skeletons and the presence of predatory tooth marks, suggests that instead of the final resting place of Jewish families, excavators may have found the temporary den of a hyena family, who scavenged bones from the Roman garrison's burial site.

The Yadin excavation also readily connected Josephus's narrative with a group of ostraca, or inscribed potsherds, unearthed at Masada. This collection, found together with a single name on each, was publicized as the very lots drawn before the final suicide, and one inscribed "Ben Yair" was equated with Eleazar ben Yair, leader of the Sicarii. But the group consisted of eleven lots and a fragmentary one, not ten as Josephus reported. In fact, over seven hundred ostraca were found atop the mountain terrace, inscribed also with women's names, single letters, foodstuffs, and priestly notations. The ostraca were part of the defenders' rationing system, and no single group can be taken as the lots cast on their final night. The veracity of Josephus's narrative of the mass suicide rests on shaky archaeological ground.

Excavations.   The basic story, however, left unmistakable traces in the archaeological record: a large Roman force of legionaries and auxiliaries besieged and defeated a small band of Jews atop Masada's rock at the end of the nationwide revolt. These facts are undisputed. To this day, the outline of a circumvallation, or siege wall, encircling Masada is visible, along with eight rectangular and square siege camps. The wall, over 6 feet thick and containing on its northwestern side twelve towers spaced at intervals, was built by Roman military engineers of the Tenth Legion (*Fretensis*) to ensure that none of the defenders escaped. Of the camps, two very large ones flanked both the eastern and western side of the diamond-shaped mountain. These had the size and shape of the classic legionary camp, walled minifortresses with four entrances, one in each direction, and, like a Roman city in miniature, they were bisected by two major thoroughfares and hierarchically arranged with the *praetorium*, or commander's post, at the center and smaller units set out on a grid for the soldiers.

The most impressive ruin is that of the massive Roman siege ramp constructed on Masada's western side. The precipitous cliffs on every side of the mountain and the casemate wall along its top made Masada an impenetrable fortress; a winding path snaked up the eastern slope, where a few sentries could easily fend off an entire army. Herod the Great had designed this stronghold with a system for collecting and storing water, and its silos were

VIEW OF MASADA, THE TENTH LEGION'S ENCAMPMENTS, AND THE
ROMAN RAMP
(reproduced with permission from the Israel Exploration Society)

well stocked for a siege. Knowing this and impatient to starve the defenders out or bent on disheartening further revolt, the Romans began a systematic siege whose centerpiece was the ramp on the western side, over 650 feet long, over 650 feet wide at the base of the mountain, and 250 feet at its highest point. Timber scaffolding held rocks, stones, and packed earth together and provided enough stability to roll up a siege machine with both a platform on top for catapults and cover underneath for a battering ram.

Hoards of catapulted *ballista* stones, roughly hewn and the size of grapefruits, were found strewn about the western side around the ramp. These had been pelted onto the fortifications by Roman artillery, and among and around them scores of iron arrowheads lay scattered, evidence of archery barrages flung against the defenders. After a futile attempt by the defenders to reinforce the casemate wall, perhaps with wooden beams that would absorb the blows of the battering ram, the wall was breached and ready for entry.

Defenders. On this, the archaeological record is clear: the Romans entered, were victorious, and occupied the site into the next century. But how, apart from Josephus, would we know that the defeated were Jewish? And is there any way, from the excavated artifacts, to tell whether they were in fact Sicarii? Four sets of artifacts found atop Masada certify their Jewishness: ostraca detailing concern for purity and priestly tithes; cups and goblets made of soft chalky limestone; stepped, plastered immersion pools called *miqwaoth*, or ritual baths; and a newly built synagogue.

Ostraca.   Ostraca are fragments of broken ceramics used for casual written records. The vast majority found by the excavators were in layers associated with the defenders. Most of the over seven hundred ostraca were written in the common Aramaic and Hebrew scripts of the latter half of the first century C.E., and a few in the archaicized Paleo-Hebrew common in biblical scrolls and on Jewish coins minted during the revolt. Many potsherds inscribed in black ink were found in and around storerooms and were tagged with a single letter, perhaps used as a numeral, or a name followed by a single digit, perhaps used in some kind of rationing system by the defenders. The names provide a remarkably personal link to the past, and were all typically Jewish like those of the ossuaries discussed in chapter one; for example, we find here Yehochanan (John), Yehudah (Jude), daughter of Damali, wife of Ya'akov (Jacob/James), son of Yeshua (Jesus). A group found in the western palace was inscribed with names of possible priests, like Yoezer, Yoshayah, and Hezekiah. Other storage jars had been set aside for priests or marked as either appropriately pure or inappropriately impure: "priest's tithe" and "suited for the purity of hallowed things" were written across the shoulders of several storage jars. Some were unsuitable and rejected: "disqualified" or "these jars are disqualified" were written on a few.

Stone Vessels.   Valued especially for its imperviousness to ritual uncleanliness in Jewish rabbinic literature, stone was often carved into cups, mugs, and shallow bowls at Jewish sites during the first centuries B.C.E. and C.E. At Masada, a set of stoneware vessels made from the distinct soft limestone has been found, including cups with handles and some with spouts, often called "measuring cups," which are somewhat crudely hand-carved and chiseled. Other bowls, turned on a lathe, were smoothly polished and incised with simple decorative ridges.

Ritual Baths.   Two *miqwaoth*, or ritual baths, have also been found, one at either end of the complex. These stepped, plastered installations were not part of the original Herodian construction, but were dug into previously existing rooms and sealed with a thick dark gray plaster. These constructions are clearly datable by several Jewish coins found throughout the layers associated with the revolt, with legends stating the year of the revolt—"Year 1," "Year 2," "Year 3," or "Year 4," and usually including the phrase "for the freedom of Zion" or "for the redemption of Zion" in Paleo-Hebrew. Each installation had three pools. One pool, separated slightly from the other two, had perhaps been used as a footbath or basin where one could wash off the dust before ritual purification. Of the other two pools, one had steps on which bathers descended for immersion, and the other was an adjacent reservoir connected to the former by a pipe or channel. That third pool stored additional rainwater, "living water" according to Leviticus, and the channel allowed small amounts of this to enter the immersion pool's water.

Synagogue.   The fourth and final artifact that certifies the defenders' Jewishness is a synagogue in the western casemate wall. The synagogue was built into a previously existing room whose interior dividing walls were knocked out, its pillars rearranged, and around whose sides a set of tiered seating benches were built. The northwestern corner was closed off as an internal storage area, perhaps used as a *geniza* for stowing scrolls too old to use but too sacred to discard. In two pits dug under the floor of the synagogue, fragments from two scriptural scrolls had been placed, preserved by the arid climate until their discovery two thousand years later. These confirm that the building served as a communal meeting place, where, among other activities, the traditions of Israel were read and consulted.

Ideals.   Can we tell from the archaeology whether or not the Jewish defenders were, in fact, Sicarii, as Josephus claims? No. But what they left behind tells a lot about their understanding of what it meant to be Jewish and about the ideals for which they rebelled and fought, lived and died. Think back to the palace on Masada's northern terraces built by Herod the Great. Recall not only its *triclinium* and fresco, baths and mosaics, but the entire architectural blueprint of his kingdom: orthogonal grids implying control and structural styles that reinforce the social hierarchy with himself at the top of its pyramid. These themes permeated Herod's Caesarea and were combined at Masada with massive fortifications to endure a

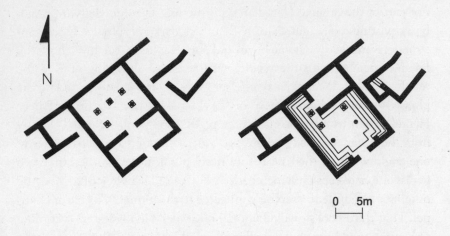

THE SYNAGOGUE AT MASADA, BEFORE AND AFTER (AFTER YADIN)

lengthy siege. The site was eventually besieged as Herod had feared, but protected others than those for whom it was intended.

Herod the Great had superimposed *his* kingdom onto the landscape, but years later Jewish defenders had *their* rebuttal at Masada. They renovated. Instead of some families living in the elegant northern and western palaces, they converted these into administrative centers and defensive posts, tipping over capitals and column drums to fortify their positions. They occupied other, simpler buildings, often erecting crude partition walls to create evenly sized living quarters, and across the plateau they set up what must have looked like squatter camps made of crude stones and mud, covered with canvas, wicker, or thatch shades. They transformed Herod's elaborate storage facilities into a redistributive system rationing goods with ostraca. Special items were set aside not for kings, but for priests. Instead of a Roman *basilica* structure, designed to focus on the oration and judgment of the ruler from an apse, they built a synagogue with circular tiered seating, so that each person could see the others. Where water had been used for pleasure and bathing in Roman style, they constructed *miqwaoth* for purity. Purity is to be understood not in the derogatory sense of some esoteric system of ablutions, but as a physical reminder that God's presence extends into all areas of bodily life throughout a land that, according to the Torah, belonged to God.

A final note on the scroll fragments found in the synagogue. The fragments were from Deuteronomy and Ezekiel. We take this combination to be coincidental—fragments from other scrolls were found a few rooms away—but these two biblical books are somehow programmatic of the revolt. Deuteronomy, the second giving of the law through Moses, reiterates the covenantal stipulations of how Israel was to live in the land. It includes, among other things, a system of checks and balances to ensure a just distribution of the land and its produce since, of course, that land belonged to God, so that all its inhabitants were, as Leviticus put it, but tenant farmers and resident aliens. Herod the Great had imported wine from Italy to Masada, and he evaluated its suitability for aristocratic luxury, but the Jewish defenders evaluated their wine's suitability for the priests, and they doled out grain with inscribed potsherds.

Ezekiel, the first postexilic prophetic book, ended with a detailed revelation of the new, vast, and orderly Temple complex, in which kings and monarchs were relegated to minor roles and God and priests ruled in their stead. Herod the Great put himself and Rome at the top of the hierarchy; the Jewish defenders, as their coins illustrated, hoped for the freedom of Zion and its redemption by God. Atop Masada, there is material evidence for a clash in kingdom types, Herodian-Roman and commercial versus Jewish and covenantal. Recall, of course, that continuum of covenantal through eschatological to apocalyptic Kingdom of God in Chapter 2 as well as that opposition between a commercial and a covenantal kingdom from Chapter 3.

The Essenes at Qumran

Was violence the only means to resist Roman rule, protest foreign influences, or combat perceived internal decay? Just north of Masada, off the shore of the Dead Sea, the site of Khirbet Qumran and the so-called Dead Sea Scrolls found in nearby caves show an alternative to violent resistance.

Debates.   At Qumran the ruins of a monastic center were excavated by Roland de Vaux of Jerusalem's École Biblique et Archéologique Française, between 1951 and 1956, shortly after the discovery of the Dead Sea Scrolls in nearby caves. The site housed members of the Jewish sect called the Essenes, who very likely wrote and copied the Dead Sea Scrolls. That sect is known from Josephus, the Jewish philosopher Philo, and the Roman author Pliny. De Vaux died in 1971 without having published a final report—it is still lacking to this day—so that some of the site's layering

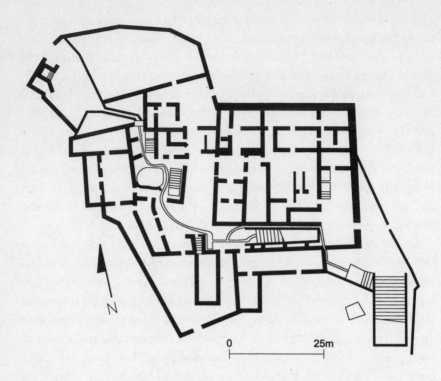

THE ESSENE COMPLEX AT KHIRBET QUMRAN (AFTER DONCELL)

details are disputed. Especially debated is the date of Qumran's initial founding and its original function, the time of the site's transformation into a monastic complex, the extent of earthquake damage and length of the site's abandonment in the latter half of the first century B.C.E., and whether the first phase of monastic settlement involved animal sacrifices or cultic meals.

Excavations.   Regardless of these disputes, by the end of Herod the Great's reign and until its destruction by Roman legions in 68 C.E., the settlement undoubtedly served as a sectarian communal center. Perhaps initially built as a fortified farm during the late second or early first century B.C.E., by the end of Herod the Great's rule, in what excavators label Occupational Phase II, Qumran had been transformed into a monastic settlement that continued for the better part of the first century C.E. Lying on a marl terrace in a remote setting a mile off the Dead Sea, wedged against rocky cliffs to the west and cut off by a *wadi,* a deep, rainy-season runoff, to the south, the site exhibits architecture that is unusual and without close parallel elsewhere. The walls around the complex enclosed a series of water installations including reservoirs, channels, and stepped, plastered pools. There were also buildings with large rooms, a potter's workshop and kiln, a kitchen, a refectory, and a *scriptorium*, a room where scrolls were copied.

Scrolls. That last room most closely connects the inhabitants of the site with the scrolls found nearby. Among the debris from a second floor that collapsed when the site was destroyed at the end of Phase II, fragments of long narrow tables as well as a bronze and several terra-cotta inkwells were found, leading to its identification as a *scriptorium*. The tables may have been used to lay out the lengthy leather scrolls and to mark their columns and lines with a sharp utensil. One of the inkwells still had remnants of the same ink, made from a mixture of soot, resin, and oil, that was used on the scrolls. Nearby, a series of parchment fragments and potsherds were found inscribed with jumbled letters, very likely the random scribbles of scribes as they set about their work and checked their quill or practiced their hand.

The Qumran Essenes may have made their own parchment. There is evidence for animal husbandry at another complex, about 2 miles south, beside the spring of Ein Feshka. Plastered tanks and canals could have been used as a tannery where hides were processed, and several leather strips and tags used to bind and identify the scrolls have been found there.

Ceramics. That the Essenes made their own pottery is obvious. In addition to a kiln and a potter's workshop, many whole or restorable ceramic vessels have been uncovered, over a thousand from a pantry near what is possibly the refectory. The uniformity of the simple, coarse, reddish orange plates, bowls, and goblets stands out, and aside from these, virtually no other serving vessels were found. Noticeably absent are any imported fine wares. But one unusual variation of a storage jar found frequently at Qumran and nearby caves, but virtually absent elsewhere, is the so-called scroll jar, in which many of the scrolls were found. Unlike their bag-shaped counterparts made for water, wine, or oil, these had longer and more cylindrical bodies in which scrolls could fit perfectly.

Finances. Two finds offer a glimpse of the community's financial resources. First, de Vaux unearthed a hoard of 561 silver coins, hidden away in three pots, in the central administrative structure. Some cash was on hand. The silver coins were almost exclusively Tyrian *tetradrachmas*, the most commonly used large denomination in the Jewish homeland, but also the requisite coin for the Temple's half-shekel tax. Perhaps the community collected these many coins for the required payment, or perhaps the Qumran initiates paid the equivalent to the community instead, since they considered the Temple's administration at that time to be corrupt. Either way, this was a substantial sum of money.

The second find is an ostracon found nearby that reads like a draft of a deed, transferring property from an individual to the group. Did the community have wealth and possessions? It did, but it was communal property, not for display, and wealth was not to distinguish the members of the group from each other. Rome, Herod, and his descendants shared a predilection for façades and displayed their wealth as an indicator of their social status, but the Qumran Essenes, in spite of some wealth, neither erected façades nor flaunted possessions that might have differentiated their members.

Lives. The complex had rooms for everything except sleeping. No buildings had such cubicles, but evidence for sleeping arrangements was found in caves along the cliffs next to the complex. There many stubby metal nails or tacks were discovered along pathways, likely relics from members' sandals as they trekked back and forth morning and evening. Other items in the caves, like combs, oil lamps, domestic pottery identical to that of the complex, a tent pole, and even *mezuzot*, tiny cases containing verses from Deuteronomy and affixed to entrances, indicate that members of the community slept nearby, but not in the complex.

Even apart from the scrolls, the archaeology of the complex provides a good indication of what life was like for the one to two hundred sectarians living there at any one time. Sleeping in caves, tents, or huts outside the complex, they strove for self-sufficiency by growing grains on a nearby plateau and dates at a nearby oasis and by herding goats. They made their own pottery and leather goods, including parchment, on which they laboriously wrote and copied. Theirs was a uniform, simple, and modest life. Although Herod the Great had built lavish pleasure palaces just to its north and south, Qumran showed no outward signs of wealth. The Essenes constructed their buildings mostly of rubble with very few square-cut stones, did not set mosaics on their floors, did not cover their walls with plaster or fresco, and displayed no imported or other luxury items. A few expensive stone jars turned on large lathes were discovered, but these indicate their willingness to spend money for the sake of purity, not luxury.

The lives of the Qumran Essenes were austere and communal, and even if wealth was on hand, they had renounced any ostentatious display as evil. Unlike the wealthy in Rome, the Herodians in the Jewish homeland, and even some of the rich priests in Jerusalem, the archaeological record reveals that theirs was a simple life with egalitarian meals.

Rituals.   The Essenes were especially concerned with ritual purification, in spite of the shortage of water and difficulty of transporting it to the site, and they shared common meals. The inhabitants' concern for purity, as exemplified by their efforts at channeling "living water" into their community, is one of the more amazing features of the complex. Any site in the remote Judean wilderness needed a system for collecting and storing water, and Qumran had a very complicated system. A somewhat crudely built dam collected water from the nearby *wadi* after the occasional flash floods in the winter, and channels cut into the limestone brought it into the complex. But there, in addition to reservoirs supplying water for survival in the oppressive heat, about a dozen *miqwaoth*, or ritual baths, were excavated, including some of the largest ever found. Two sizable *miqwaoth* at either end of the complex adjacent to entrances provided opportunity for a large number of people to purify themselves frequently. Over a dozen steps descended into a massive pool on the southern side, with two low partitions separating impure descent from purified ascent. The bathers must have queued at the top as they waited their turn. According to the scrolls, the sectarians purified themselves prior to the "pure meal" served on a daily basis.

The members sat together, in silence according to some of the sectarian scrolls, on woven floor mats according to archaeology, for what they called the "pure meal." A flour mill, baking oven, and room with five fireplaces could feed a large number of people at the community. Once again, eating—what, how, and with whom—is in this case a vital and equal sharing of material food, but also a symbol of their lives and hopes. That meal was not just externally pure because they had purified themselves before consuming it, but internally so because God was present at it, at that equal share-meal of God's own food.

Enemies.   Some of the scrolls detail the Essenes' displeasure with the Temple or, better, with those who were running the Temple, and record

THE ISAIAH SCROLL FROM QUMRAN
(reproduced with permission, copyright John C. Trever; image courtesy of the
Ancient Biblical Manuscript Center)

that they were preparing for God's ultimate victory over the usurpers currently in charge. Well before the Romans arrived, the Qumran Essenes had withdrawn from participation in the Temple and calendar of the priestly leadership in Jerusalem. They refused the legitimacy of the Hasmonean combination of king and priest in one person, and priestly legitimacy hardly got any better when the Herodians and Romans hired and fired high priests as if they were lower-level civil servants. But, for the Qumranites, it was the Jerusalem high-priestly authorities and not the Roman occupiers who were the far older and more hated opponents.

The Romans were not singled out as much in their sectarian documents, although against them, in their so-called *War Scroll*, they were preparing to fight the ultimate apocalyptic battle. This was to take place at the end time, when the Sons of Light, the members of the group, were to clash with the Sons of Darkness, the Romans, code-named the Kittim. A battle against Rome did take place eventually, when the Roman general and soon-to-be emperor Vespasian marched through the area on his way to Jerusalem in the early summer of 68 C.E. But the Qumran Essenes' final battle did not end as the *War Scroll* imagined. What de Vaux labeled and archaeologists still call Phase II of the site ended in a fiery destruction, with Roman arrowheads scattered around the site. In their final desperate act, the members took and hid their sacred scrolls in the nearby caves, rolled up in storage jars with bowls as lids, and they were not discovered again until a Bedouin shepherd stumbled upon them in 1947.

JODEFAT AND GAMLA IN THE NORTH

In the south, Qumran and Masada represent very different responses to Roman occupation and, indeed, two very divergent reasons for any such response. But both sites ended in fiery destruction at, respectively, the start and end of the 66–74 C.E. revolt. In the north, Jodefat (Jotapata in Greek) and Gamla represent exactly the same type of tragically futile response to the Romans at the start of that same rebellion.

In the end, most Jews in Galilee and Golan sided with the revolt and resisted Roman domination. Or, at least, once hostilities broke out and indiscriminate violent Roman reprisals became certain, Galileans fled to fortified sites for temporary safety. And the Galileans were the first to suffer Roman wrath after Vespasian and his son Titus organized their legionary and auxiliary forces at the port of Ptolemais in 67 C.E. and marched inland. Two of the villages destroyed by the Romans in 67 C.E., Jodefat in July and Gamla in October, were never resettled. But recent excavations have yielded finds that make it very clear how suicidal the revolt had been. Topography offered their best defense. The Lower Galilean town of Jodefat sits atop a knoll cut off on three sides by sharp inclines, but is approachable from the more gentle slope to the northwest. Gamla in the Golan is like the camel's hump, from which it takes its name, and has steep ravines on either side, making it inaccessible except from the ridge's tail to the east.

Josephus chronicles the battles at each site. In fact at Jodefat he offered his last assistance to the Jewish cause before surrendering to the Romans and serving them as guide and translator. His accounts are full of brave speeches, heroic acts, and tragic—suicidal—ends. A vivid picture of the village's siege and destruction can be drawn from the archaeological excavations, and they also provide dramatic testimony to the feebleness of the defenses and futility of the revolt. At both places, the Jewish townspeople and refugees from the surrounding villages tried to fortify the walls at their most vulnerable positions.

At Jodefat, a wall and tower dating back over a century to the Hasmonean period were expanded and reinforced. A formidable 30-by-36-

foot tower had been constructed by those early Hasmonean settlers. It was built right on top of bedrock in several courses of hewn limestone ashlars, with the larger stones nearly 6 feet long. The earlier walls defending the tower's northwest side were less sturdy, were in some places dilapidated, and were rebuilt shortly before the Roman attack. The defenders built a casemate wall, not on top of bedrock, but on the limestone chippings from the original wall's construction. They used earth and stone fill along with boulders from the earlier collapsed wall, hardly a secure foundation. The outer wall of the casemate was nearly 6 feet thick with rows of stacked stones, and one of the interior rooms of the casemate was frantically filled in with field and quarried stones in the final days of the defense.

At Gamla, a large round tower at the top of the ridge was linked with a defensive wall running along the slope of the hill. This wall was nothing more than a series of houses on the outskirts of town that had their exterior rooms filled in with debris and walls built in the open spaces between them. The front rows of these walls were more tightly built, with roughly hewn basalt stones and rubble fill as well as larger basalt boulders packed into place behind them.

The walls at Jodefat and Gamla were no match for Vespasian and Titus's highly trained legions, who first weakened them with artillery, probing for the weakest spot, then brought up a siege engine under the cover of archers, and finally opened a breach for the infantry's assault. At Gamla, the breach is still visible to this day, right next to the synagogue whose exterior rooms had formed part of the wall. Evidence of the battle is scattered widely across the ruins of each town. At Gamla excavators uncovered over sixteen hundred arrowheads, several tips of large catapult bolts, and more than a thousand spherical basalt stones that had been hurled by the Roman attackers. At Jodefat fewer were found, and they concentrated in the northwestern portion of the wall, where Josephus says the Romans broke through the defenses. At Gamla, groups of *ballista* stones were discovered right inside the town wall, hoarded there by the defenders to hurl down at their attackers the next day.

The legions left behind bits and pieces of evidence after destroying the towns: armor scales, nails from boots, a helmet's silver-plated cheek guard, the gold-plated tip of a sword sheath, and standard-issue *fibulae* pins that held their tunics in place. The spoils of war went to the victors, and the Roman forces left nothing of value behind. But Moti Aviam, of the Israel Antiquities Authority, the excavator of Jodefat, did find one striking artifact left behind by a defender. Crudely scratched onto a small stone slab were a crab and a mausoleum, the former perhaps the zodiac sign of Cancer for the month of July, the latter symbolic of death. Aviam provides a chilling interpretation of the pictographs, left behind by one of the illiterate defenders who had given up hope: "In July, I die."

Were Jewish purity rituals a weapon in the resistance against Rome? The walls were feeble, and no challenge for the Roman military engineers. The Romans had powerful artillery and accurate archers. They were well trained, well organized, well paid, and well fed. The Jewish defenders at Gamla and Jodefat had none of this, but must have been determined and had some measure of hope to rise up against Rome. Their houses contained many stone vessels, and there were communal *miqwaoth*, or ritual baths, at each site. Even after decades under Herodian and Roman rule, those daily reminders that God was present in their lives and land provided the resolve and determination to stand up to Roman might and occupation. The land belonged to God and certainly not to the Romans. And even if their defenses were outmatched, to know that God was with them gave them some measure of hope.

IDENTITY MAINTENANCE AS COVERT RESISTANCE

In the north, Jodefat in Galilee and Gamla in Golan ended in similar destruction and so, in the south, did the Sicarii at Masada and the Essenes at Qumran. The events at Masada were spectacular and dramatic. Mix archaeology and Josephus and you have the climatic battle against Rome on Jewish soil: heroic speeches by Eleazar, the Sicarii as the most feared urban terrorists, Masada as the most impregnable fortress, and the Roman engineering feats as the most remarkable. And there was also a concern for purity. Life at Qumran was ascetic and pious. Mix archaeology and the Dead Sea Scrolls and you have a tale of withdrawal from this world, communal life, rejection of foreign influences, and the battle between the Sons of Light and the Sons of Darkness. And there was also a concern for purity. Are these two extremes, violence or withdrawal, the only alternatives?

Life, in antiquity as today, was more complicated, more gray and less black and white. In the south, Masada and Qumran make today's headlines precisely because of their catastrophic endings—their violent destruction and abandonment left them relatively undisturbed for archaeologists. Thanks to their remoteness and arid climates, remains were preserved to this day, including the scrolls, which would have disintegrated in a damper environment. In the north, however, Jodefat and Gamla are striking as sites undisturbed since their first-century abandonment. In Galilee there is more rain and damp soil, and most sites were resettled and earlier building materials reused. Less is preserved there, and more of it is fragmentary. The layers are, for the most part, messier, the archaeology more complex. But so too were the Galileans' lives under Roman-backed Herod the Great, under Roman-backed Herod Antipas, and under direct Roman rule. Violent confrontation or complete withdrawal were only the extreme alternatives, but for most of that century, the majority of Galileans managed something between shrewd acquiescence and silent defiance. Two illustrations from excavations in Galilee, one specific and singular, the other general and widespread, reveal the middle ground between the two poles: the city of Sepphoris in the years leading up to the revolt, and the use of stone vessels and *miqwaoth* throughout Galilee. In the former case we look, as it were, from the top down. In the latter, from the bottom up.

Sepphoris as City of Peace

As you will recall, Herod Antipas built his kingdom by first refounding Sepphoris and then founding Tiberias. It was a kingdom he ran with indigenous Jewish elites and in which he preserved an essentially Jewish character. His cities had no statues or images, and his coins did not bear his profile, in contrast with those of his brother Philip, who ruled a mostly pagan population. Antipas imposed a Roman architectural overlay upon his cities and some of the wealthier citizens selectively adopted Roman features in their homes both in those cities and, sometimes, in the larger towns. But theirs was a more guarded or more cautious adaptation of Roman architecture than was Herod's at Caesarea. Antipas was well suited as a Roman client-king in Galilee. He was educated in Rome, but as a Jew he understood Jewish traditional religion and seemed to have an instinct for the fine line between ruthless control and tolerant respect.

Some later coins minted at Sepphoris show how its civic leaders continued Antipas's approach, fusing a Roman veneer onto a Jewish cultural base. During the revolt against Rome, the city minted bronze coins with, on one side, a double, crossed cornucopia, a typically Jewish numismatic symbol of fertility, and, on the other, *Caesar Nero Claudius* in large letters, using a name but not an image. Pro-Rome, yes, but still observant of the Torah's prohibition against images. The legend was more submissive: "Under Vespasian, in *Eirenopolis—Neronias—Sepphoris*." Struck in 68 C.E., the coin announced the city's refusal to rebel against Rome by including its newly adopted names, *Neronias* after the emperor Nero, and *Eirenopolis*, Greek for "City of Peace." The same Greek inscription is found encircled by a wreath on another issue in the same year, whose other side also omits the emperor's image, but instead is imprinted with the large Latin letters "S" and "C," representing "S[enatus] C[onsulto]," "by the decree of the Roman Senate." These coins were aniconic and in that sense were typically Jewish—albeit mostly in Greek and bowing to Roman rule. Herod Antipas had been politically shrewd enough to know where to draw the line with his subjects, and Sepphoris's later civic leaders were prudent enough to proclaim their intentions, bowing to Vespasian and Nero without abandoning Jewish religious sensibilities on their city coins.

Along with these coins, excavation directors Eric and Carol Meyers, of Duke University, have unearthed additional evidence of Sepphoris's acquiescence to Roman rule. Over several field seasons from 1993 to 1997, they excavated the remains of a fortress near the top of the acropolis that had been intentionally and systematically filled in and leveled around the time of the revolt. The fortress was constructed about 100 B.C.E., presumably when the Jewish Hasmonean rulers made Sepphoris an important outpost in the newly acquired territory of Galilee, as attested at its foundation by hundreds of coins from Alexander Jannaeus (103–76 B.C.E.). Eventually Sepphoris developed into a larger settlement, but the imposing walls of the fortress remained in place for nearly the next two centuries. To date, seven walls have been excavated, constructed right on top of bedrock, three of them north-south and four east-west, bisecting each other and enclosing at least three square rooms. The walls were made of large stones hewn from bedrock and were in fact doubled walls, two abutting walls built back to back, measuring together nearly 6 feet. Perhaps one set of walls had been constructed first so that the outlines of the fortress could be in place quickly, and later, maybe right after that was completed, the second set of walls was constructed to buttress its strength.

The finds inside are what one would expect from a garrison: a cistern for water supply, an oven, many small coins lost from soldiers' wages, a few arrowheads in the corners, and two *ballista* stones against a wall. The structure itself is not too remarkable. But what initially puzzled the excavators was the way in which the so-called fortress was abandoned. There was no evidence of fire, destruction, or collapse whatsoever. Instead, the rooms seem to have been tidied and swept up, the walls meticulously dismantled to the same height, and the entire area then filled and leveled. Dirt, stones too small for construction, and thousands of broken pottery sherds were dumped there in a massive earth-moving operation that stacked up in some places 6 feet high.

When was the fortress dismantled, and why? The latest coin found in the fill is of Herod Agrippa II and dates to 53 C.E., so that the fortress could not have been filled in earlier. The mass of ceramic sherds sets the latest possible date, which is less precise but estimated at around 70 C.E. because of the absence of several types of cooking pots and bowls that appear at the site (and elsewhere in Galilee) only after the revolt in 70 C.E. Why would Sepphoris's citizens defortify their city between 53 and 70 C.E.? Most likely, as signs of the revolt drew near or at the beginning of hostilities, they preemptively displayed their antirebel stance to the Romans, or were directed to do so by Herod Agrippa II or by some Roman official. Whether this act was offered as a gesture or obeyed as a command, the city of Sepphoris did not revolt with its fellow Galileans, a consistent point in Josephus's writings on the war. In his autobiography he states that the city "forbade any of its citizens to take service with the Jews" who were preparing to oppose Rome, and then "voluntarily admitted a garrison provided by Cestius Gallus, commander in chief of the Roman legions in Syria" (*Life* 347). Though Josephus's other accounts of Sepphoris during the war are garbled and at times contradictory, the city's avoidance of hostilities against Rome is stressed throughout.

The Jewish leaders at Sepphoris were wary of Roman might and those in the peace party eventually won the day. Perhaps the Roman attack on the city under the Syrian legate Varus after the death of Herod the Great in 4 B.C.E. was still part of their collective memory, and the lessons of Rome's vindictive might were well remembered. Or perhaps the wealthy urbanites had much more to lose by revolting than had their rural counterparts. Either way, they bowed to Rome and betrayed their fellow Galileans, but without, however, abandoning their Jewish traditions. It was a material ambiguity somewhat similar to the textual ambiguity of Josephus's collaboration. They were still undoubtedly Jewish, still faithful to ancestral traditions, but actively collaborating with Roman rule as well as actively imitating Roman style. It was an ambiguous position that, as we say in Chapter 3, made many of the Galilean peasantry seek to burn Sepphoris to the ground at the start of the great revolt.

Stone Vessels and Ritual Baths

The other Galilean strategy for coping with Herodian and Roman rule is more widespread in the archaeological record, but much more complex. Not all Galileans refused revolt and, ultimately, Sepphoris's pro-Roman— or, better, antirevolt—stance saw it through the war, unlike the fate of many Galilean villages that were destroyed. Take a look, but not from above, not from the urban elite's perspective on the Sepphoris acropolis, but from below, from the villagers' perspective across the valleys of Galilee. For this we use fragmentary artifacts found in households and plastered installations found at sites. We consider stone vessels and ritual baths, those two widespread artifacts, already encountered at Qumran and Masada, that typify Judaism in the archaeological record. Both are ubiquitous in Early Roman layers at sites in the Jewish homeland, in Jerusalem, throughout Judea, all across Galilee, and in the southern Golan. But they are virtually absent in neighboring territories.

Stone Vessels. Vessels made from that soft white limestone known geologically as chalk are one of the most characteristic finds at Jewish sites. They are called stone vessels, or sometimes Herodian stoneware, because of their appearance throughout the Jewish homeland beginning with Herod's rule. That, by the way, is an interesting fact. Once again, is a special concern for Jewish purity a covert anti-Herodian and anti-Roman statement? Be that as it may, those assemblages consist of forms for liquids such as bowls, cups, mugs, lids, basins, and large jars. In Jerusalem and its environs during the late Second Temple Period, a veritable industry emerged for their production, and it included other items made of the same material, such as ossuaries (boxes for the bones of the deceased) as well as stands and tops for tables. Several stone-vessel workshops have been discovered and excavated, so that much is known about how the limestone was quarried into blocks, cut into smaller chunks, and shaved on lathes or chiseled by hand. Most recently in June 1999, a construction worker's tractor accidentally broke through a cave in East Jerusalem, opening onto a large underground complex, with stone debris and unfinished stone vessels and wasters cast about, adding to the list one more first-century quarry and workshop for stone vessels.

Production sites were not limited to the south, however, as one has also been found in Galilee at Reina, near Nazareth and Sepphoris, where the geological formation had created a limestone outcropping along a slope in

FIRST-CENTURY STONE VESSEL, A SO-CALLED MEASURING CUP
(collection of the Israel Antiquities Authority, photograph copyright the Israel
Museum, Jerusalem)

the terrain. There, numerous cores were found that had been cut out from
the inside of mugs using a lathe, as were many wasters, vessels that broke
during production and were discarded. Since such limestone outcroppings
are frequent in Galilee, stone vessels could have been manufactured at a
variety of sites there. This whitish chalk is remarkably workable after it has
been soaked in water and can be shaped with a set of simple metal tools
and a hammer. The most common forms in Galilee are hand-held mugs or
cups of various sizes, which are sometimes mislabeled "measuring cups."
These had their insides hollowed out with a mallet and chisel or had their
cores extracted using denticular-type tools and a small lathe. The outsides
had been chiseled vertically, leaving facets and some chisel marks and creating a rough feel and a rugged look. They usually have one or two square
handles and some have a spout, so that they are similar to vessels shaped
from wood. The other common hand-chiseled forms in Galilee are shallow
rectangular basins or tubs, and there are also some finer bowls, cups, and
lids turned on a small lathe and incised with simple decorative ridges along
their sides and rims.

Since the stone vessels will disintegrate only in the most acidic and
damp soils, they are widely found in fill layers of excavations at most
Galilean sites. They are found, notably, in large numbers at every site in
Galilee with a substantial first-century C.E. layer. For example, at the village of Nabratein in Upper Galilee, over fifty fragments have been found

in the Early Roman layer. In a single area of a courtyard house several fragments were discovered accompanied by scores of limestone chippings and chunks, perhaps the remnants left by a local craftsman who fashioned them for his family or the whole village. At Capernaum, each and every house with first-century layer contained stone-vessel fragments; hundreds of them were found at the site. Over a hundred have also been found in first-century contexts at the Lower Galilean town of Jodefat and the southern Golan village of Gamla. And they are also present in each of the first-century houses at the city of Sepphoris.

These uniquely Jewish artifacts are closely connected to the purity system in rabbinic literature, since they were deemed not to contract ritual impurities. Stone vessels were unlike ceramic vessels, which had to be destroyed after contacting impure liquids according to Jewish *halakhah*, or sacred law, since they would then impart impurity to later contents and also to their users. Stone, however, was deemed impervious to ritual defilement, so that vessels made from it were always "clean."

Why stone? At one level, one might think this was because stone was not really fashioned in the same sense as was glass, metal, or clay. It was, as it were, cut out of its surrounding material. It was, as it were, somewhat less a human product than a divine gift. Rabbinic literature implies that stone vessels were clean because they had not been fired, since along with them those made of sun-dried dung and earth were likewise clean (see the Mishnah, *Kelim* 10:1; 4:4). Another reason stands out: most of the stone vessels have close parallels with glass, metal, and ceramic ones, which were imported and more expensive. Uncleanness was easily attributed to glass, metal, and ceramic vessels brought from the "lands of the Gentiles," that is to say imported luxury items. Stone was ritually pure, but it was also a cheap local product, a native material that could be made into vessels with relative ease.

Ritual Baths.   Stepped, plastered pools, or *miqwaoth* (singular *miqweh*), are the second artifact that typifies Judaism in the archaeological record. To date, over three hundred from the Roman Period have been uncovered in the Jewish homeland, in Judea, Galilee, and the Golan, yet they are sparse along the coast and virtually absent in Samaria or on the other side of the Jordan. Though these installations are not entirely uniform, they share several basic features: they are cut or built into the ground; they are heavily plastered and often replastered to prevent leakage; most have some device for leading in rainwater, spring water, or runoff; and

A FIRST-CENTURY
MIQWEH FROM
SEPPHORIS
(courtesy Eric Meyers,
copyright Sepphoris
Regional Project, Duke
University)

they have built-in descending steps. This latter feature distinguishes
them from reservoirs or cisterns, since steps are obviously designed for a
person's immersion and would otherwise subtract from the volume of
water being stored.

Like the stone vessels, *miqwaoth* are a feature that flourished from the
time of Herod the Great through the first century C.E. In urban sites like
Jerusalem and Sepphoris, and in some larger towns, they are often in private homes. At Sepphoris, over twenty *miqwaoth* have been excavated in
the western domestic quarters, where most houses had several, showing
that they too were concerned with purity. But at most Galilean sites they
are found near agricultural installations or synagogues. The site of Gamla,
where its excavators discovered four *miqwaoth*, is typical in this regard.
One is adjacent to the synagogue, and two are next to olive presses. The
synagogue is the oldest excavated in the north to date, and the only one
from the first century C.E. Its main hall was around 100 by 130 feet with
the entrance facing Jerusalem. Like the synagogue built at Masada, there

were tiered stone benches along each of the four walls of the main hall, which needed columns to support a roof across such a large area. Although the *miqweh* was dug outside the synagogue proper and is part of a complex to its west, the two are physically connected by a channel through which the ritual bath was filled with water collected from the synagogue's roof. The size of the immersion pool, at around 13 by 33 feet with seven extant steps, could hold sufficient water for communal use and was no doubt a shared facility used by all of the town's inhabitants.

Another *miqweh* was discovered just to the west, next to a very large oil-pressing facility, with two presses and several collection vats or pools that were likely shared by all of Gamla's inhabitants. The room with the *miqweh* was part of this complex and had both a small bathtublike basin above ground and, next to it, a large oval-shaped *miqweh* cut into the ground and heavily plastered. One could immerse oneself by descending a set of downward-spiraling stairs along the wall. Presumably the bathtub was used first for hygienic washing and the *physically* dirty water let flow out a drainage channel, so that the *ritually* clean water of the *miqweh* would not get too (hygienically) dirty from the sweat and grime of those working the olive press.

Josephus tells the story of how the village of Gush Halav in Upper Galilee shipped kosher oil to Jews living in the larger pagan cities on the coast, and since liquids readily transmit impurity, the production of olive oil was of particularly concern. As it does with stone vessels, rabbinic literature connects *miqwaoth* with purity, and in fact an entire tractate of the Mishnah is devoted to their proper use.

Purity. The obvious question is how these stone vessels and *miqwaoth* were a means of resisting Rome. Certainly dining with stone wares or bathing in stepped pools did not overtly confront Roman rule, Herodian accommodation, or foreign influences. Rome did not fear these implements of purity, but they were not thereby rendered colonially benign. They are the remnant in the material culture of a broader pattern of behavior with which Jews defined themselves over against others; they were a form of covert defiance, a daily reminder of one's tradition and covenant with God, an acknowledgment of God's holiness and of Israel's requisite purity.

There was no unified system of beliefs and rituals with regard to the purity system in Judaism of the first century. They were on a spectrum, or perhaps, like resistance, on a spectrum of spectra. The priests most closely associated purity with their roles in the Temple cult. Their main concern had to do with foods and contacts before approaching the divine presence in the Temple, and they were particularly fastidious in this regard on the Day of Atonement, when the high priest entered the Holy of Holies in the sanctuary.

Though the Temple was the center of Jewish religion, the Pharisees, as popular interpreters of the Torah, not only sought to decide on issues relating to purity for the priests—and in that sense competed with priests for social status—they also appropriated notions of purity typically reserved for the priests and applied them to their own activities. Their activities stood alongside, perhaps at times stood in tension with, the Temple cult, as they extended aspects of the cult into everyday life, in particular by eating their meals in purity. Perhaps they were imitating the priestly meals in the Temple, but certainly they were acknowledging that the divine was present at their meals, which necessitated the same kind of washings before they ate together, and that God was present in other spheres of life. They vigorously debated the interpretation of scripture among themselves, especially regarding purity issues, and these debates were later recorded at the end of the second century in the law code of the Mishnah. Like the Pharisees, the Essenes at Qumran purified themselves before their pure communal meals, since they assumed God's presence to be among them as they ate.

Identity. But why are such "purity" implements so widespread throughout Galilee? Was every house at Sepphoris a priest's home, since stone vessels and *miqwaoth* were found there? Hardly. Did every household at Capernaum participate in Pharisaic meals, since stone vessels were discovered? Unlikely. Were the villagers at Jodefat all Essenes? No. Instead, Jews in the Second Temple Period shared a common concern for purity. We in no way mean by this a set of legalistic rituals, but understand it to be an emphasis on appropriate bodily attitude and proper bodily preparation to stand before God, since God resides in everyday land and is part of everyday life.

How did ordinary people understand purity? There were certainly disputes over details. The Pharisees criticized how the peasantry, "the people of the land," avoided full adherence to their decisions. But they also criticized certain priests. And they argued with each other, for example, the less strict school of Hillel against the more strict school of Shammai. Many

Galileans probably ignored some of their interpretive details. For example, very few of the stepped, plastered pools in Galilee fully adhere to the rabbinic prescriptions found in the later law code of the Mishnah. But they took the issue seriously: stone vessels were everywhere, and *miqwaoth* were widely distributed.

We do not think this implies a widespread legalism or popular externalism, as Christian anti-Semitism has so often insinuated. Instead, it means that the Jews of the first century believed God to be present, knew that God's presence required appropriate bodily behavior, which included not only purity in response to God's holiness, but also righteousness and justice in adherence to God's covenant. What Jewish purity codes emphasize is that a concern for the body's ritual decorum before God is a necessary concomitant for the body's ethical life before that same God.

The use of stone vessels for meals and stepped, plastered pools for purification were neither a symbol of violent resistance to Rome, as at Masada, nor a symbol of outright withdrawal from world, as at Qumran. What each of those extremes shared with those in the middle was a concern for how to live in the land with God's presence and under God's covenant. Their use solidified Jewish identity, in the case of *miqwaoth* by restoring the individual's place in the community of Israel under the covenant, and in the case of stone vessels by preserving one's status before God. These were a concrete means of self-identification, preserved in the soil and commonly recovered by archaeologists, that defined Jews over against others, in addition to their names, dress, circumcision, diet, burial practices, scriptures, and traditions.

It is not coincidental that these implements of purity uncovered by archaeologists challenge two of the main cultural encroachments from the Hellenistic and Roman worlds, modes of bathing and modes of dining. Bathing in *miqwaoth* contrasted with elite Roman-style bathing practices and offered an alternative that reinforced Jewish distinctiveness and strengthened resistance to foreign domination. Similarly stone vessels offered an indigenous and inexpensive alternative to expensive imported glasses, metals, or ceramics. Is continued material and bodily self-definition resistance? In this case, Jewish self-definition was the profoundest act of nonviolent colonial resistance. Summarize it this way. It was certainly possible to observe Jewish purity rules and still collaborate fully with Rome. But, if they did not observe those customs at all, would it have been possible to resist in any way, violently or nonviolently?

RADICAL NONVIOLENT RESISTANCE

Where, across the spectrum of resistance, do we locate Jesus? He is not among the nonresisters, for two overriding reasons. First, it is relatively certain, from his life, that he announced and enacted the Kingdom of God. He and/or his companions may have spoken, out of respect for that sacred name, not of the Kingdom of God, but of the Kingdom of Heaven. That is similar to the modern newscaster who reports not "the president says," but "the White House says." The residence means the resident. Unfortunately, however, the phrase "Kingdom of Heaven" has often been mistaken to mean a kingdom *in* heaven, rather than *from* heaven, and then misinterpreted to mean the next world, or life after death. But, for example, in the Lord's Prayer, Matthew glossed "your kingdom come" as "your will be done, on earth as it is in heaven" and that was exactly correct. Whether it is called the Kingdom of God or the Kingdom of Heaven, it means the divine will for this earth, for here below, for here and now. How, in other words, would God run the world if God sat on Caesar's throne? What would a perfect world of prosperity and fertility, justice and peace, purity and holiness look like? Its meaning, in other words, must be interpreted along that traditional continuum from covenantal to eschatological to apocalyptic divine rule on earth.

Second, it is also relatively certain, from Jesus' death, that Roman power considered him a lower-class subversive, since crucifixion was a publicly placarded and officially hung-up warning against such criminal activity. Before Jesus, Herod the Great was officially appointed "King of the Jews" by Rome. After Jesus, Herod Agrippa I was officially appointed "King of the Jews" by Rome. In between, Jesus of Nazareth died under a mocking accusation that was also a serious indictment, accused as illegal "King of the Jews" by Rome. Rome, and Rome alone, decided who was and who was not King of the Jews. But that title and that fate, in their full religio-political meaning, indicate that Jesus was executed for resistance to Roman law, order, and authority. Where, then, do we locate him along that spectrum of resistance outlined above?

A major debate among contemporary scholars concerns whether the historical Jesus was an apocalyptic or nonapocalyptic figure. Quite often the disagreement gets nowhere, as both sides fail in any detailed analysis of those twin options. If he was apocalyptic, what distinctions and options are necessary to understand his apocalypticism? For example, was his God's solution to evil the *extermination* or *converion* of evil-doers? And

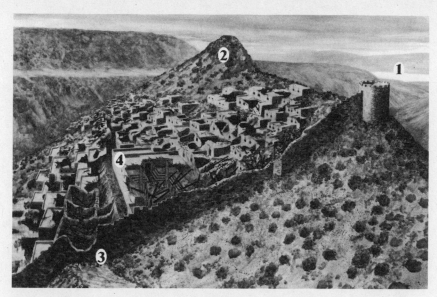

RECONSTRUCTION OF THE DESTROYED TOWN OF GAMLA. *No match for the Roman legions, the walls of the Jewish town of Gamla have lain destroyed since 67 C.E. With the Sea of Galilee in the distance (1), Gamla rises from the surrounding valleys in the Golan like a camel's hump (2), from which it takes its name. Jewish refugees fleeing the Roman advance swelled its population, and although the town offered stiff resistance according to Josephus, Titus breached the wall (3) and successfully conquered its inhabitants. Excavators discovered hundreds of Roman ballista stones and thousands of arrowheads around the breach, which was right next to one of the very few first-century synagogues ever discovered (4), with tiered benches for seating and a ritual bath near the entrance.*

were believers to wait *passively* or participate *actively* in that process? If he was nonapocalyptic, what, apart from that negation, was the content of his Kingdom of God? Our general hope in this book is to get beyond that impasse by insisting on the continuum in basic content from a covenantal through an eschatological to an apocalyptic Kingdom of God. Our specific hope in this conclusion is to locate Jesus and the Kingdom of God movement more accurately among those first-century apocalypticists and/or protesters.

Putting Jesus among the apocalypticists does not mean that he advocated *militant violence*. Even if one accepts Jesus as an apocalyptic prophet, the sayings thereby attributed to him would have to be interpreted against all else in his life and in his death. Militant violence could certainly be grounded in apocalyptic expectation, as was the case, most likely, with

Josephus's so-called fourth philosophy in general or with Judas the Galilean in particular. But if Pilate had considered Jesus that type of threat, many of his companions would have been rounded up along with him and would have died beside him. Neither did Jesus communally enact some *archetypal symbolism*, like the Egyptian prophet marching with his followers around the walls of Jerusalem, or, once again, many others would have died with him. And, if he did so more individually, like John baptizing in the Jordan, no such ritual has come down to us. We must locate him, therefore, on the choice or interface between *covenantal community* and *martyrological protest.*

In Chapter 3 we considered what was termed the Common Sayings Tradition, the earliest selection of oral Jesus materials discernible as such by independent usage in both the *Q Gospel* and the *Gospel of Thomas*. In this present chapter we consider what we will call the Common Sayings Cluster, the earliest cluster of written Jesus materials discernible as such by independent usage in both the *Q Gospel* and the *Didache*. You will recall from this book's Introduction that we accept certain scholarly conclusions about those materials that are presumed but not argued here, namely, that (1) the *Q Gospel* exists, that (2) the *Gospel of Thomas* is independent of it, and that (3) the *Didache* is also independent of the *Q Gospel* or any of the canonical foursome. Those conclusions were among the ten most important textual "discoveries" mentioned in the Introduction. Whether you agree or disagree with them, you must make a decision about them and, thereafter, your conclusions will stand or fall on the accuracy of those decisions.

The Golden Rule Radicalized

We use the term Common Sayings Cluster for a linked set of six sayings that appears at the start of both the *Q Gospel* and the *Didache*, the former a community's gospel about Jesus, the latter a community's rule about life.

In the *Q Gospel* this sixfold cluster of sayings appears in Matthew 5:38–48; 7:12 = Luke 6:27–36, where it is part of Jesus' programmatic and inaugural address. In the *Didache* it appears at 1:2c–5a, where it is inserted into an instruction for converts, especially pagan rather than Jewish ones, since the former's ethical standards might well be in doubt. That insertion is placed at the start of an earlier or pre-*Didache* instruction, which is typically Jewish. It announces Two Ways, one of life and virtue in 1:1–2c and 2:1–4:14 and one of death and vice in 5:1–6:2. That overall instruction is somewhat radicalized (it was already quite radical!) by this cluster's initial insertion at 1:2c–5a. But it is also somewhat softened by the terminal insertion at 6:2, "If you can bear the whole yoke of the Lord, you will be perfect, but if you cannot, do what you can." Notice, by the way, that *The Golden Rule* in 1:2c was present in both the newer insertion and the older pre-insertion text. Its common presence facilitated that process at that place.

Here are the three clusters in sequence as they now appear in those three texts. Notice, immediately, that the cluster's six sayings appear in different arrangements as Matthew and Luke reshape that inaugural address from the *Q Gospel* within their own new compositions. The general scholarly presumption, by the way, is that Luke rather than Matthew is closer to the original *Q Gospel* sequence.

Matthew (*from* Q Gospel)	*Luke* (*from* Q Gospel)	Didache
The Other Cheek	Love Your Enemies	The Golden Rule
Give Without Return	The Other Cheek	Love Your Enemies
Love Your Enemies	Give Without Return	Better Than Sinners
Better Than Sinners	The Golden Rule	The Other Cheek
As Your Father	Better Than Sinners	Give Without Return
The Golden Rule	As Your Father	As Your Father

Before proceeding, it may be helpful to read the full text of that cluster, but focus on general content rather than on precise sequence, since that latter is much less secure:

1. *The Golden Rule:* Do (not do) to others as you would (not) have them do to you.
2. *Love Your Enemies:* Love your enemies, do good to those who hate you, bless those who curse you, pray for those who abuse you.
3. *Better Than Sinners:* If you love those who love you, what credit is that to you? For even sinners love those who love them.
4. *The Other Cheek:* If anyone strikes you on the right cheek, turn the other also; if anyone wants to sue you and take your coat, give your cloak as well; and if anyone forces you to go one mile, go also the second mile.
5. *Give Without Return:* Give to everyone who begs from you; and if anyone takes away your goods, do not ask for them again.

6. *As Your Father:* So that you may be children of your Father in heaven; for he makes his sun rise on the evil and on the good, and sends rain on the righteous and on the unrighteous. Be perfect, therefore, as your heavenly Father is perfect.

One technical footnote. In the previous chapter, the reason for concluding that the Common Sayings Tradition of thirty-seven sayings was derived from oral tradition rather than a written document was that there is absolutely no common order to those units as they now appear in the *Q Gospel* and the *Gospel of Thomas* (which, as a list of sayings, would have no reason to reorder them). On the other hand, in this chapter, the Common Sayings Cluster of six sayings derives from a written document rather than oral tradition, something that is evident in Greek but not in English translation. We no longer distinguish second-person singular ("you") from plural ("ye"), but Greek does. In this cluster, however, both the *Q Gospel* and the *Didache* use a similar mix of "you" and "ye." For example, *The Other Cheek* and *Give Without Return* are singular ("you"), while *Love Your Enemies* and *Better Than Sinners* are plural ("ye"). That striking coincidence convinces us that a written cluster rather than either a memorized oral cluster or a general oral tradition lies behind those twin sets. It is difficult to imagine oral memory retaining and repeating that "you/ye" differentiation.

Focus first on *The Golden Rule* saying. It is positive ("Do to others as you would have them do to you") in the *Q Gospel,* but negative ("Whatever you do not want done to you, do not do to another") in the *Didache.* There is no difference in meaning or emphasis between the positive and negative versions, and both forms are well known in the general tradition. But here is the crucial question raised especially by that combination of *The Golden Rule* and those other sayings in the cluster. Is that rule to be taken only offensively or also defensively? Does it say (only offensively): "Since you do not want to be attacked, do not attack"? Or (also defensively): "Since you do not want to be attacked, do not attack back even when attacked"? Does it admonish you not to attack or not to attack back? Does it forbid initial violence or all violence?

Think, next, of that cluster as a very radical interpretation and very profound motivation for *The Golden Rule.* Imagine it in context in those three sections. *The Golden Rule* is the heart of the cluster. The injunction, taken by itself, can be read either offensively (do not attack) or defensively (do not attack back). But the rest of the cluster, that interpretive commentary, which includes *Love Your Enemies, The Other Cheek* (about face struck, garment taken, and labor forced), and *Give Without Return*, demands that it be taken not only as "Do not attack" another, but also as "Do not defend yourself."

Finally, there is the motivation, on both a human comparative level in *Better Than Sinners* and a divine imitative level in *As Your Father*. The human motivation is to be and do better than the nations, the pagans, the gentile sinners. But the divine motivation is much more important. In the *Q Gospel*, one is to "be perfect" in Matthew or "merciful" in Luke in imitation of "the Father." That *perfection* is commanded by Matthew "so that you may be children of your Father in heaven; for he makes his sun rise on the evil and on the good, and sends rain on the righteous and on the unrighteous." That *mercy* is commanded by Luke so that "you will be children of the Most High; for he is kind to the ungrateful and the wicked." There is nothing parallel to that in the *Didache*, although being "perfect" is mentioned in 1:4. The *Didache* has, however, a much fuller discussion of that *Give Without Return* aphorism, and the motivation is that what we give does not belong to us in any case, but to God; "for the Father's will is that we give to all from the gifts we have received." We are not so much imitating God by the giving of human gifts as we are participating in God's giving of divine gifts. We are, in other words, cooperating as stewards in that divine generosity. What we give is not our own. "It should be noted," as a recent commentary put it, "that the gifts given by the rich to the poor are really God's gifts. Thus the one who gives alms is only a manager, one who distributes the divine gifts." In that case, of course, we are no longer speaking of human almsgiving generosity, but of divine distributive justice.

What we have in this Common Sayings Cluster, as is clear from that comparison with "gentile sinners," is not Christianity against Judaism, but Christian Judaism against Greco-Roman paganism. It establishes a very radical community of resistance based on imitation and participation in the very nature of God. If we had *The Golden Rule* alone, it could be offensive (do not attack) rather than defensive (do not attack back). If we had only *The Other Cheek*, it could be nonviolent existence rather than nonviolent resistance. But the cluster, taken as a whole, links that radical God of distributive justice and egalitarian righteousness from Mosaic law to this radical ideal of nonviolent resistance in the Common Sayings Cluster. Resistance, in this case, is in the very lifestyle of a share-community, which gives from its possessions because they come from such a God and which seeks to avoid even defensive violence for such is the nature of its God.

One final note. Jesus began as a follower of John, since he was baptized by him in the Jordan. For that moment, at least, Jesus must have accepted John's vision of the imminent arrival of an avenging God who would eradicate sin and sinner alike. But, as we saw at the start of Chapter 3, even their common enemies agreed that, although both were weird characters, they were weird in opposite ways. So Jesus did not continue as a disciple, follower, or even as heir apparent to John's position. We suggest one major reason for that change of mind. God did not come in imminent vengeance, did not come, actually, even in time to save John. So, for Jesus thereafter, perhaps that was not how God would ever act because God was not violent, but worked some other way upon this earth, even or especially in apocalyptic consummation.

Jesus, Christians, and Caesar

Apart from isolated units in Paul's epistles or elsewhere, that Common Sayings Tradition of thirty-seven units in the *Q Gospel* and the *Gospel of Thomas* seen representatively in the last chapter and this Common Sayings Cluster of six units in the *Q Gospel* and the *Didache* seen above are the earliest "chunks" of, respectively, oral and written Jesus materials that we can discern at the moment. Both of those complexes go back before the first level of the third layer, before the *Q Gospel*, since they are both examples of its source materials. Our working hypothesis is that both of those complexes derive even earlier from the first layer, that of the historical Jesus himself. Wherever you locate Jesus on that continuum of covenantal to eschatological to apocalyptic resistance, the Kingdom of God is a force for nonviolent resistance to the normalcy of both social oppression by class and colonial oppression by Rome.

There are, however, two rather obvious objections to that interpretation. First, did the earliest companions and later followers of Jesus really maintain nonviolent response even when under attack? Second, did not Jesus himself divide up the world between Caesar and God?

Staff and Sword. There are two very interesting indications that not every member of the Kingdom of God followed that program. But even as they later deviate from it, they witness to its earlier presence.

Recall, from the last chapter, how Jesus sent out his companions to live and act as he did, to share spiritual power (healing) and material power (eating), and thereby to proclaim the presence of the Kingdom of God. That appeared both in the *Q Gospel* and in Mark 6:6b–13. But there is one very striking difference between them. The *Q Gospel* explicitly forbids the carrying of a staff in Matthew 10:10 and Luke 9:3. But it is explicitly permitted in Mark 6:8. The staff was the basic and ubiquitous defensive weapon against dogs and thieves, and one would not have been expected to travel anywhere without it. Indeed, it was so normal and expected that, even if we had only Mark allowing a staff, we could have presumed that there must have been some other prior text that forbade it. Even if one were guaranteed food and lodging on the way, the staff was minimal defensive equipment. Recall, for example, what Josephus says about communal hospitality for Essene travelers: "Consequently, they carry nothing whatever with them on their journeys, except arms as a protection against brigands" (*Jewish War* 2.125). We consider, therefore, that the change from prohibited staff in the *Q Gospel* to permitted staff in Mark is a change from absolutely no protection to normally basic protection, from absolute nonviolence to minimal defensive violence. But the change underlines what was there before it.

The symbolic dress and equipment of those Kingdom messengers in Luke 9:3 (no staff, bag, bread, money, extra tunic) and in Luke 10:4 (no purse, bag, sandals) are explicitly revoked by Jesus himself on the night of his arrest in Luke 22:35: "He said to them, 'When I sent you out without a purse, bag, or sandals, did you lack anything?' They said, 'No, not a thing.' He said to them, 'But now, the one who has a purse must take it, and likewise a bag. And the one who has no sword must sell his cloak and buy one.'" Luke, presumably, rather than Jesus, is literally negating those earlier prohibitions, and that unit is Luke's permission for the defensive sword from now on.

Whether it is a question of the less expensive staff or the more expensive sword, those explicit permissions revoke an earlier defensive nonviolence (no staff, no sword). That both certifies that it was there once and also that it is here no longer. Nonviolent resistance, both offensive and defensive, is quietly changing to allow some degrees of defensive violence.

But the first layer, the layer of the historical Jesus, is that earlier one of nonviolent resistance to injustice in the name of the Kingdom of God.

Caesar and God.   What about that well-known aphorism of Jesus that says, "Render to Caesar the things that are Caesar's and to God the things that are God's"? Does that not separate politics (Caesar) and religion (God)? Does that not forbid resistance to Caesar?

First of all, recall from the start of this chapter that it was impossible to separate religion and politics, ethics and economics, for anyone in that first-century world. Second, if all we had in our texts was that isolated saying, shorn of all context and situation, it would be quite impossible to understand it as coming from *any* first-century Jew. Josephus, who was as pro-Roman as one could find, never divided this world between Caesar and God, but maintained that God had given power to Caesar, a power that, presumably, Caesar had to use as God wanted. For Josephus, in rendering to Caesar, one rendered to God. Similarly, as Paul says in Romans 13:1, "Let every person be subject to the governing authorities; for there is no authority except from God, and those authorities that exist have been instituted by God." How, then, could Jesus possibly divide the world between the affairs of Caesar and of God?

Go back and replace the saying in its setting. Go back and read the whole story. We have two independent versions of that incident, one from the *Gospel of Thomas* and one from Mark:

> *Gospel of Thomas 100:* They showed Jesus a gold coin and said to him, "The Roman emperor's people demand taxes from us." He said to them, "Give Caesar what belongs to Caesar, give God what belongs to God, and give me what is mine."

> *Mark 12:13–17:* Then they sent to him some Pharisees and some Herodians to trap him in what he said. And they came and said to him, "Teacher, we know that you are sincere, and show deference to no one; for you do not regard people with partiality, but teach the way of God in accordance with truth. Is it lawful to pay taxes to Caesar, or not? Should we pay them, or should we not?" But knowing their hypocrisy, he said to them, "Why are you putting me to the test? Bring me a denarius and let me see it." And they brought one. Then he said to them, "Whose head is this, and whose title?" They

answered, "Caesar's." Jesus said to them, "Give to Caesar the things that are Caesar's, and to God the things that are God's."

In Mark, it is clearly a trick question to trap Jesus either for or against Caesar's taxes and thereby to bring against him either Roman dissidents or Roman collaborators. But Jesus himself does not even carry Caesar's coins as they do. When they produce one, his response is beautifully ambiguous (for them). Did he say to throw Caesar's coins rebelliously in Caesar's face or pay Caesar's taxes dutifully into Caesar's coffers? And even in the much shorter version, the core situation is still retained, and they have to show Jesus a coin. The problem is not whether to pay Caesar's taxes, but whether to carry Caesar's coins. And Jesus has already decided on that point. It is unfortunate that we have for centuries misunderstood Jesus' meaning and no longer hear his laughter or that of his companions as they walked away from the trap.

SIX

Beauty and Ambiguity in Jerusalem

In the centuries before the Babylonian Empire destroyed Jerusalem's First Temple and deported its aristocratic, scribal, and high-priestly ascendancy, there was a clear distinction between monarchy and high-priesthood. Both were hereditary, the former descending from David (at least in the southern part of Israel's divided kingdom) and the latter from Zadok at the time of Solomon. In the centuries after the Babylonian exile, the high-priesthood was restored, but the monarchy was not. Internally and successfully, Israel was a priest-led theocracy. Externally and successively, it was a colony under the Persian, Greek, Egyptian, and Syrian empires. But in the second half of the second century B.C.E., the Hasmonean Maccabees revolted against the Syrians and established a Jewish kingdom in which king and high priest were now consolidated in a single ruler. That combination was a profound breach of ancient tradition and raised equally profound questions of high-priestly legitimacy.

The ordinary people may not have cared or even known that there was a problem with the novelty of a royal priesthood or a priestly monarchy. But the Qumran Essenes probably abandoned the sacred space of Jerusalem's Temple and the sacred time of its lunar calendar because they considered the Hasmonean priesthood as no longer valid. Illegitimacy, surely, was the worst impurity, and how could an impure or illegitimate high priest enter the Temple's Holy of Holies to represent the land and people of Israel before God on the Day of Atonement? It was a very pointed rebuke to that Hasmonean novelty when Qumran announced the advent of a dual messiah, one priestly and one royal, separate and in that hierarchical sequence.

The situation did not get better under the Herodians or the Romans. Now, once again, there was a clear distinction between high-priestly authority and royal Herodian or imperial Roman rule. Herod the Great was Idumean, an ethnic group converted to Judaism under the Hasmoneans. But he never made himself the high priest. Still, both the Herodian and, later, the direct Roman rule treated the high priests like subordinate civil servants, playing the major high-priestly families off against one another and appointing or dismissing them at will. That, by the way, was a bad policy for all concerned. An imperial aristocracy always needs the cooperation of its colonial equivalent. At best, the latter mitigates imperial depredation. At worst, it joins in colonial exploitation. Either way, it is usually the first to die if and when the people revolt.

We saw in Chapter 2 that the most basic source of conflict between Rome and the Jewish homeland was the Torah's insistence that the land belonged to God by right of ownership and justice as against the empire's presumption that it belonged to them by right of conquest and power. Here now is another significant contributing factor to that history of escalating discord in the first-century Jewish homeland. Externally, Roman authority involved a prefect-governor who had auxiliary but not legionary troops and who was, therefore, under the legate-governor of Syria and the three or four legions guarding the Euphrates frontier against the Parthian Empire. Internally, on the one hand, the Herodians replaced the Hasmoneans, and, on the other, competing high-priestly families replaced the ancient and hereditary high-priesthood. Maybe disputed land alone would have been enough to make rebellion possible, but disputed authority helped to make it inevitable.

All of that is background for understanding this chapter's title. With regard to high-priesthood, cult, and Temple, there was in that first century a fundamental clash between beauty and ambiguity, between the beauty of antiquity and the ambiguity of legitimacy. It was possible, for example, from a position of most stringent Jewish purity, to reject the contemporary high-priesthood and even the current Temple. Was the high priest legitimate or not? Was that Temple a shrine to be protected or a fortress to be destroyed? Was it, as it were, just the acropolis of Jerusalem? Both Josephus and Tacitus falter in describing its destruction, although that may be rhetorical piety rather than military policy. Beauty and ambiguity, indeed.

We issue a special warning about this chapter's content. We make it not only from ecumenical courtesy or even post-Holocaust sensitivity, but first and foremost from historical accuracy. Criticism of the Jewish high-priesthood and/or the Temple has often been derived from theological anti-Judaism or from racial anti-Semitism. And also, it would appear, some Christian denominations without a priesthood have criticized that ancient Jewish priesthood as a surrogate for more contemporary Christian priesthoods they wished to oppose.

As Christians, we are deeply aware of those prejudicial and unhistorical attacks from outside Judaism. We reject absolutely any such attempt to turn *intra*-Jewish conflicts into *anti*-Jewish criticisms. And we denounce also the unfair strategy of comparing Christian ideals with difficult Jewish decisions made in those harsh first-century realities. In that first century, Judaism was a great religion and an ancient tradition fighting hard against the overweening pride of Greek internationalism and the overwhelming power of Roman imperialism. But empires conquer and divide while colonies bicker and lose. Essene Judaism, Pharisaic Judaism, and Josephus's so-called Fourth-Philosophy Judaism could all debate furiously with one another, but especially with Sadducean Judaism, which held a power monopoly through collaboration with Roman authorities. Any such conflict would be directed especially against that priestly aristocracy since their excessive luxury, their controlling violence, their high-priestly legitimacy, and their Jewish loyalty could all be questioned. And all of that conflict with the Sadducees could spill ambiguously over both cult and Temple.

Think back to what Jesus was doing in Galilee, according to Chapter 3 earlier. In accord with his programmatic itinerancy, he refused to settle down either with the family at Nazareth or Peter at Capernaum, because such a fixed center to which all must come proclaimed a geographical hierarchy not in keeping with the Kingdom of God. His programmatic reciprocity of healing and eating shared the spiritual and material power that belonged ultimately to God alone. The Torah commanded an equitable distribution of a land that belonged to a just God, but amid the Romanization, urbanization, and commercialization of Antipas's Galilee, Jesus could speak only of the food the land produced. But grounded in the Torah's theology of creation, the land had to be shared equitably and justly because its owners were but its stewards. Jesus' vision and program for the Kingdom's presence invited others to do exactly what he himself was doing, not to go out and bring others to him, and not even to go out and act in his name. Most strikingly, Jesus does not pray when he heals and he does not tell his companions to do so either, since those who have entered the Kingdom of God are now within its powerful presence. All or any part of that Kingdom movement set Jesus against Antipas's long-range plans to become, like his father, King of the Jews. That life so lived would have brought Jesus to eventual execution as surely as John's had done before him.

Jerusalem was a much more dangerous place. Instead of a Herodian tetrarch there was both a Sadducean high priest and a Roman prefect. If, on the one hand, Jesus did and said there what he was saying and doing in Galilee, especially if he did so at a festival, which was the most likely time for him to be there, and especially if he did so in the tinder-box atmosphere of Passover, his immediate execution would have been almost a foregone conclusion. But, on the other hand, how could his Kingdom of God not escalate its confrontation with the Kingdom of Rome when cult, priesthood, and Temple seemed less the service of God than the normalcy of collaboration.

No matter what a Jesus of Nazareth said or did in Jerusalem or its Temple, two misunderstandings must be equally avoided. One is to claim that he was attacking Judaism itself. The other is to claim that he was not attacking anything. Jesus was Jewish and had a right to fight his own intra-Jewish battles without Christians either denying he did so or making them anti-Jewish ones. And, on the other hand, if the high priest Caiaphas had been a saint, he would still have had to cooperate with the prefect, Pilate. Eventually, the Syrian legate deposed them both, which means, presumably, that, even from the Roman point of view, they had cooperated not wisely, but too well. Roman and Jew, empire and colony, high-priesthood and Temple. Beauty and ambiguity, indeed.

COLONIAL REVOLT AND CLASS WARFARE

It is not difficult to see the archaeological evidence of colonial revolt, of the two great wars with Rome within the Jewish homeland in 66–74 and 132–35 C.E. Those rebellions destroyed the glory that was the Temple and the grandeur that was the great pilgrimage city of Jerusalem.

The Destruction of Jerusalem

In the first revolt, Jewish resistance to Roman domination was crushed after eight years of fighting. The legionary forces began to quell the revolt in Galilee and ended it at Masada, but the intervening climax was the siege of Jerusalem and the destruction of the Temple. According to

Josephus, the Temple fell on the ninth day of the Jewish month of Av in 70 C.E., although some Jews held out for another month in the Upper City. Those who survived famine and combat were crucified or sold into slavery. The Roman legions celebrated by setting up their standards, crowned by a golden eagle with thunderbolts in its talons and bearing the insignia SPQR, *Senatus Populusque Romanus*. The eagle was the symbol of Rome's divine protector, Jupiter Optimus Maximus; the insignia indicated their service to the "Senate and People of Rome." Herod the Great's Temple was burned and systematically dismantled, although, according to the Roman historian Tacitus, even some battle-hardened officers were reluctant to carry out Titus's demolition order, feeling "that it would not be right to destroy a holy building renowned as one of the greatest products of human endeavor."

Yet its grandeur was destroyed, and nineteenth-century explorers along with more recent excavators have uncovered the large stones and debris cast down by the Romans from the Herodian Temple's walls. From below, the Romans fruitlessly chiseled away at its massive foundations and then, from above, they toppled column drums, collapsed arches, and knocked down the upper walls. The fragments still litter the paved street and steps beneath the Temple Mount. The Romans looted and then leveled much of the rest of the city, and stationed detachments of the Tenth Legion on the hill west of the Tyropoeon Valley to keep a close watch on its remaining inhabitants.

Remains symbolizing Roman triumph and colonization are strewn atop the layer sealed by the war's destruction. Triumphal columns were erected in Jerusalem and inscribed in Latin to honor both the Tenth Legion and Titus, son of Vespasian made emperor in 69 C.E. The victorious Tenth Legion left artifacts scattered across the western hill of the city: roof tiles, drainpipes, and bricks bearing the stamped insignia LXF, *Legio X Fretensis*, and/or a depiction of the legion's emblem, a wild boar.

Later, the emperor Hadrian refounded what remained of the city as a Roman colony, renaming it Aelia Capitolina after himself (Aelius Hadrianus) and his patron god (Jupiter Capitolinus), and forbidding entry into the city to Jews. He Romanized the city by imposing an orderly grid with two colonnaded *cardos* and eradicated all signs of Judaism, going so far as to erect a pagan temple dedicated to Jupiter Capitolinus right atop the ruined Jewish Temple once dedicated to Yahweh. He visited it on his royal tour of the eastern provinces in 129–30 C.E. That itinerary included

Philadelphia, Petra, and Jerash, east of the Jordan, as well as Scythopolis and Caesarea, to the west. At each city, his arrival was marked by a royal *adventus* entrance. In those official entry activities, he wore ceremonial armor, rode a white horse, and was met by local dignitaries and civic officials singing hymns and making speeches, as well as by ordinary citizens lining the streets and waving palm branches as a sign of his victories. In exchange, Hadrian offered sacrifices for the city and granted its citizens privileges, all designed to foster devotion to the emperor and loyalty to Rome. In the course of his imperial journey, he established shrines and temples dedicated to the emperor cult, and in them he dedicated statues of himself as the divine Zeus. That, for future reference, is one way to enter your city as its ruler.

Jerusalem, without natural resources and far off major trade routes, had thrived as a Jewish pilgrimage city that also attracted pagan visitors, but now it was deprived of Jewish visitors or inhabitants. Even its elevation to a colony by Hadrian could not boost its population. It remained somewhat diminutive until Constantine the Great converted the empire to Christianity, which made it again a destination for pilgrims, this time Christian rather than Jewish. The city reverted back to Greek and Latin versions of its Jewish name, Jerusalem, but was transformed into a Christian Holy City, whose centerpiece was no longer the Temple, left intentionally in ruins as a reminder of Christian victory over Judaism, but the Church of the Holy Sepulcher, the supposed site of Jesus' resurrection. Later, Byzantine and Persian armies battled there, Islam made it the third holiest city, constructing the Dome of the Rock atop the Temple Mount to commemorate Muhammad's ascension-visit to heaven. Over the following centuries, intermittent Crusader conquests, Ottoman and Turkish rule, European colonialism, and most recently the Six-Day War in 1967 have left their mark on Jerusalem.

The aftermath of the Six-Day War permitted large-scale excavations south and west of the Temple Mount, which itself remained in Muslim custody, as well as in the Upper City in what today is called the Jewish, or Herodian, Quarter. A Who's Who of Israeli archaeology worked in these areas: Nahman Avigad excavated in domestic quarters of the Upper City, Benjamin Mazar and Meir Ben-Dov worked outside the Temple Mount, where today Ronny Reich is still digging. And a tunnel of some 900 feet was dug along the Western Wall by Israel's Ministry of Religious Affairs, mostly under the supervision of the archaeologist Dan Bahat.

There had been much earlier explorations of the area outside the Temple Mount. In the nineteenth century, two British explorers, Charles Wilson and Charles Warren, working under the auspices of the Palestine Exploration Fund, dug a series of deep vertical shafts along the Western Wall all the way to bedrock, both finding the Herodian street west of the Temple Mount and exposing its lowest courses. Earlier, the Swiss explorer and architect Titus Tobler detected the remnant of an arch protruding from the Western Wall. It is known today as Wilson's Arch because the latter publicized the find. Still earlier, in 1838, the American explorer Edward Robinson had investigated the remains of a stairway at the southwestern corner of the Temple Mount.

A Revolt Within a Revolt

All those excavations of Jerusalem and its Temple clearly depict the grandeur before and the desolation after that first great revolt against the Roman Empire in 66–74 C.E. Those giant fractured stones brought down by the Romans are there forever. But, in the first century, resistance was not just a colony-based rebellion against external imperial control; it was also a class-based resistance against internal aristocratic power. Opposition to Rome, certainly, but also opposition to home. And that is where the ambiguity intensifies. Chapter 4 focused on the spectrum of colonial response to imperial control, from treasonous or collaborative nonresistance to violent or nonviolent resistance. Think of that spectrum as one of multiplying options, of options not always neat and separate, but often mixed and interactive. But recall also the start of Chapter 2. Amos, the peasant prophet from Judean Tekoa, spoke for God against Jeroboam the king of Israel and against Amaziah the high priest of Bethel. That was not colonial protest demanding human freedom, but covenantal protest demanding divine justice.

Prophetic resistance could be nonviolent, as with that eighth-century prophet Amos, or violent, as with the earlier ninth-century prophets Elijah and Elisha. They had brought down the Omri dynasty and replaced it with the Jehu dynasty. But it was no great improvement to destroy Ahab of Omri and get eventually Jeroboam of Jehu. Be that as it may, even before the violence and/or nonviolence of colonial resistance to external imperial injustice, there was already present the violence and/or nonviolence of prophetic resistance to internal royal injustice. The deepest Israelite tradition was not just colonial resistance to foreign domination, but covenantal resistance to unjust oppression whether foreign or domestic. And, as seen earlier, it was always grounded somewhere along that ideal continuum from the covenantal through the eschatological and into the apocalyptic Kingdom of God. Imagine, then, Jerusalem and especially its Temple in the first century of the common era. Imagine, therefore, both beauty and ambiguity.

It was precisely that interacting violence of class warfare *within* colonial rebellion that characterized the great revolt of 66–74 C.E. in both Galilee and Judea. This emphasis does not in any way deny other intra-Jewish tensions within that war. There were deep divisions among priestly aristocrats themselves, but also between aristocrats and retainers. Those Sicarii mentioned in Chapter 4, for example, were learned teachers rather than priestly aristocrats. There were profound tensions between regional groups such as Idumeans, Judeans, and Galileans, but also between individual leaders, whatever their class or region. But, for here and now, we focus specifically on internal socioeconomic revolution within and under the cover of external politico-imperial rebellion.

The Defense of Galilee

At the start of the 66–74 C.E. war, Josephus was sent from Jerusalem to prepare Galilee for the impending arrival of Vespasian's avenging legions. Later, writing under imperial Flavian patronage, he had a vested interest in exalting his own Galilean cohorts into worthy opponents for Rome's best general, who had just become Rome's new emperor. He had, he tells us, "an army, ready for action, of sixty thousand infantry and three hundred and fifty cavalry," and he had trained this army "on Roman lines" (*Jewish War* 2.583, 577). When Vespasian assembled his legionary and auxiliary forces at Ptolemais in the spring of 67, his army also "amounted to sixty thousand" soldiers (3.69). All seemed set for a clash of equal titans. This is what happened. "The troops under the command of Josephus, who were camping beside a town called Garis, not far from Sepphoris, discovering that the war was upon them, and they might at any moment be attacked by the Romans, dispersed and fled, not only before any engagement, but before they had even seen their foes" (2.129). That, of course, was very, very prudent.

What Josephus had actually accomplished in preparing Galilee for the Roman revenge was both militarily unsuccessful and humanely successful. His army was not composed of peasant levies forged in a few winter months into legionary equals. It was composed of brigand bands personally loyal to himself, because he was able to pay them with monies offered by those they would otherwise have robbed. Instead of those sentences just cited from the *Jewish War*, listen to this one from his much later *Life*: "I also summoned the most stalwart of the brigands and, seeing that it would be impossible to disarm them, persuaded the people to pay them as mercenaries; remarking that it was better to give them a small sum voluntarily than to submit to raids upon their property" (77–78). Indeed, that very process of turning brigand-robbers into salaried soldiers was obliquely admitted even in the *Jewish War* itself, although there it is almost lost in fantasies about himself as the very model of a modern Roman general. He mentioned, about his conscripts, that "he should test their military discipline, even before they went into action, by noting whether they abstained from their habitual malpractices, theft, robbery and rapine, and ceased to defraud their countrymen and to regard as personal profit an injury sustained by their most intimate friends" (2.581).

Josephus could never have defeated the Romans in open battle or held out long against them in walled enclave. But he had done something in Galilee. He had prevented class warfare from breaking out within the anarchic situation of colonial rebellion. He had prevented country and town, peasantry and gentry, rural bandit and urban landowner from slaughtering one another before the legions arrived to slaughter them both. We saw above how his forces melted away when the Romans arrived. But if those "Galileans," Josephus's usual term for the peasantry, were not too interested in doing battle with Roman legions, they were very interested in destroying two major regional capitals like Sepphoris and Tiberias, as you will recall from Chapter 3 above. That was where law courts met, tax archives were kept, and absentee landlords lived. That was what Roman control looked like to the peasantry of Lower Galilee. General Josephus did not succeed in winning an externally directed colonial war, but he did succeed in preventing an internally directed class war. In Jerusalem, later, nobody succeeded on either front.

The Zealots and the Aristocrats

As a specific and technical term, the word "Zealots" refers to a loose coalition of peasant fighters (brigands to some, liberators to others) forced inside the protective walls of Jerusalem as Vespasian's scorched-earth devastation swept southward in the winter/spring of 67–68. But from that very summer and into 69, Nero's suicide, the rise of three competing would-be emperors, and Vespasian's eventual accession gave Jerusalem an unexpected respite from immediate siege. Despite that interlude or because of it, class warfare erupted inside Jerusalem as the Zealots instituted a reign of terror against the upper classes. Their usual charge was conspiracy to betray the rebellion to the Romans. Josephus is clearly horrified by what he has to record (*Jewish War* 4.147–48, 153–57).

One action is indicative of the Zealots' ideological motivation. The high-priesthood had been hereditary from Zadok at the time of Solomon until the new Jewish Hasmonean dynasty declared itself a king-priest combination in the second century B.C.E. Later, both the Herodians and the Romans appointed and dismissed high priests at will and used four different families in a divide-and-conquer strategy. The Zealots chose one high-priestly clan, presumably with better Zadokite legitimacy, and used lots to select within it.

Since lottery was understood as divine providence rather than human luck, it replaced human selection with divine choice. For that reason, it was part of a long tradition from the election of Saul as ruler in 1 Samuel 10:21 ("He brought the tribe of Benjamin near by its families, and the family of the Matrites was taken by lot. Finally he brought the family of the Matrites near man by man, and Saul the son of Kish was taken by lot") to that of Matthias as apostle in Acts 1:26 ("And they cast lots for them, and the lot fell on Matthias; and he was added to the eleven apostles"). It was also established by the Qumran Essenes in their *Community Rule*: "Decision by lot shall be made in every affair involving the law, property and judgment."

Within that tradition, then, the Zealots, says Josephus, "summoned one of the high-priestly clans, called Eniachin, and cast lots for a high priest. By chance the lot fell to one who proved a signal illustration of their depravity; he was an individual named Phanni, son of Samuel, of the village of Aphthia." Although the "summons" of that clan indicated a human choice for legitimacy over illegitimacy, those "lots" resulted in a divine option for peasantry over aristocracy. Josephus is almost speechless as he describes a peasant replacing an aristocrat as high priest. But that incident is only the most symbolically obvious part of the Zealot program.

Furthermore, the Zealots imprisoned, judged, and executed "Antipas, one of the [Herodian] royal family" who had "charge of the public treasury" and also Levias and Syphas, "both also of royal blood—besides other

persons of high reputation throughout the country" (*Jewish War* 4.139–
46). Next, strengthened by Idumean peasant forces, they killed the former
high priests Ananus and Jesus, going "so far in their impiety as to cast out
the corpses without burial, although the Jews are so careful about funeral
rites that even malefactors who have been sentenced to crucifixion are
taken down and buried before sunset." Instead, those aristocrats were "cast
out naked, to be devoured by dogs and beasts of prey" (4–317). Then, the
"young nobles" were imprisoned so that they "would come over to their
[the Zealots'] party," and, when all refused, they were tortured and executed, so that "twelve thousand of the youthful nobility thus perished"
(4.327, 333). A further stage of this wider purge was the show trial of
Zacharias son of Baris, "one of the most eminent of the citizens . . . [and]
he was also rich." Seventy judges from "the leading citizens" acquitted him
of conspiracy with the Romans, but the Zealots executed him anyway
(4.335, 336, 343). As Josephus summed up this class warfare: "None
escaped save those whose humble birth put them utterly beneath notice,
unless by accident" (4.365). Finally, Matthias, the current aristocratic
high priest, sent for the messianic fighter Simon bar Giora "as one who was
to rid the city of the Zealots" and, on his entrance into Jerusalem, he was
"acclaimed by the people as their savior and protector." Class warfare and
social revolution were over, but political revolution still continued, and
imperial vengeance was still ahead for a doomed Jerusalem.

There are some important conclusions to be drawn from that interaction between colonial revolt and class conflict. First, you could find resistance to the injustice of Roman domination and/or class discrimination
based at any point along that continuum from the covenantal through the
eschatological to the apocalyptic Kingdom of God. Second, you could certainly have colonial resistance without class warfare. The war of 66–74,
for example, started with a split within the aristocratic high-priesthood
as the daily sacrifices for the Roman emperor were omitted at Jerusalem's
Temple. Third, and most important, you could not have class conflict in
that colonial situation (or probably any other one) without becoming
embroiled in imperial conflict as well. To oppose the colonial Jewish aristocracy was also to oppose its imperial Roman patrons and sponsors.

From all of that preceding history, this most important point must be
emphasized once again. In the first century both Jerusalem's Temple and
that Temple's high-priestly authority had assumed for many a ferocious
ambiguity. For Essene Judaism, concerns for covenantal fidelity and ritual

purity turned it against both Temple and priesthood. Had the Essenes taken over power in Jerusalem, they imagined a much more purified Temple in a much more purified city, according to their own *Temple Scroll* found at Qumran. For Zealot Judaism, class warfare turned it against both Temple and priesthood. For Pharisaic Judaism, how should one put it? When the Pharisees extended priestly purity into their own homes, were they expanding and increasing what they considered to be perfect observance or replacing and relocating what they considered to be imperfect observance? If and when Christian Judaism opposed Temple and/or priesthood, therefore, it would be a very serious historical mistake to read it as an abstract attack on sacrifice or purity, sanctuary or priesthood, let alone as some attack on "Judaism" by "Christianity." For many Jews, within that first century, those questions of excessive luxury, dynastic legitimacy, aristocratic ascendancy, and imperial collaboration shrouded the beauty of the high-priesthood, the glory of the Temple, and even the splendor of Jerusalem under layers of ambiguity that cannot be ignored.

THE GLORY OF THE TEMPLE

Throughout antiquity and long after the Temple's destruction, the sages of Israel insisted that "whoever has not seen Herod's building has never seen a beautiful structure." Josephus, Philo, Tacitus, and other ancient writers chime in with praise of the Temple's beauty. Thanks to archaeological excavations and discoveries, we now have a firm grasp of Herod's achievement, his grandiose design for the entire complex, his construction details, his architectural techniques, and we can now picture the Temple as Jesus would have seen it.

Herod the Great could not significantly alter the Temple's innermost sanctuary from how it had been rebuilt after the Babylonian exile, a reconstruction based on Solomon's precedents and biblical prescriptions. Façades could be renovated or columns plated with gold, but the sanctuary could not be dismantled and enlarged. So Herod set about enlarging its setting by doubling the Temple Mount, on which it stood, a project begun in 19 B.C.E. and not completed until long after his death.

Recall, from earlier chapters, Herod the Great's architectural kingdom building at Caesarea Maritima, his palace there, and those others in the Judean desert. Keep those in mind as we move now to this third component of his kingdom's blueprint, the Temple Mount in Jerusalem. Caesarea bowed to Rome and commerce, those Judean palaces furnished security and luxury, and all of them together maintained and displayed his lavish rule as a *Roman client-king*. Now we look to his crowning achievement as *King of the Jews*. But, as mentioned earlier, all of that is a unity. The massive port at Caesarea was primarily for commerce. But it would also have brought in pagans on their way to Jerusalem's Temple. Why else would Herod have designed the Temple's massive Court of the Gentiles if he did not expect Gentiles to come there as curious tourists and/or pious pilgrims.

The Temple's Geographical Dominance

Since Herod the Great could neither alter nor enlarge the sanctuary, he encased it in a new, splendid, and monumental setting by doubling the platform, or Temple Mount. This was no simple matter, as Jerusalem stood atop hilly terrain with slopes surrounding the Temple on all sides. The Tyropoeon Valley was along the west side, a smaller valley was to the north, and the much deeper Kidron Valley ran along the east side. But Herod the Great imposed his will on the topography and subdued the terrain. He enlarged the platform by filling in the depression to the north and a portion of the Tyropoeon Valley to the west, as well as by constructing a series of vaults along the southern slope to support the plaza above.

Herod then surrounded the entire Temple Mount with a massive retaining wall on all four sides. The eastern wall of the earlier platform was left intact, but extended to the north and south. He thereby created a gigantic platform beneath the sanctuary. It was slightly trapezoidal in shape, but roughly 1,000 feet in east-west width and 1,550 feet in north-south length. To ensure the plaza's stability, some 100 feet above street level, those retaining walls, particularly on the southern and western sides, needed absolutely secure foundations with solid construction and massive stones. Herod's architects cleared the entire area and dug down another 60 feet to bedrock, which was cut and leveled for a bottom course some 16 feet thick. They saved labor by quarrying uphill nearby so that the stones could be hauled downhill either on rollers by oxen or inside a set of large wooden wheels. As each course was set into place, the interior space between the new and old walls was filled in and tightly packed with debris or vaulted, so that the next course could be laid on top of it, eliminating the need to hoist those giant stones from below.

Some of the stones in the lower courses were colossal. The tunnel along the Western Wall dug by Israel's Ministry of Religious Affairs exposed the so-called Master Course, in which a single stone measures a full 40 feet in length and over 10 feet in height and is estimated at 14 feet thick, with an astounding weight of more than 500 tons. That, by the way, dwarfs those megaliths at Britain's Stonehenge. The next stone of the Master Course was 40 feet long, another one 25, and a final one 6, so that those four stones alone extended over 100 feet. Most of the ashlars on the lower courses were not as large as those in the Master Course, being typically 4 feet high, but even the smaller ones weighed 3 to 5 tons. They were all evenly squared and smoothly chiseled so that the entire retaining wall was constructed without any kind of mortar. Each stone stood atop another and fitted against those adjacent to it so tightly that, even today, twenty centuries later, neither a knife nor a piece of paper can be wedged deep between them.

The Temple's Magnificent Façade

The walls of Herod's Temple Mount also created an imposing façade. They rose from street level to a height of 100 feet, and each course was set back by about an inch, giving a slightly pyramidal effect to the whole. Each ashlar's outside face was cut in the typical Herodian boss-and-margin style. In this technique, an outer frame or margin of some 3 to 6 inches was chiseled deeper than the framed internal area, or boss. Both the margin and the boss were smoothly polished, giving the edifice a unique aesthetic: instead of appearing as a monolithic whitewashed façade, the individual stones stood out, and in the course of the day, the sun's rays cast shifting shadows off the boss and into the margins. The retaining wall's rich texture captured a pinkish hue on the sandy-yellow stones at sunrise and sunset. At other times they shone brilliantly as though made of marble, with the outlines of individual ashlars becoming apparent as one drew closer. On some stones, cube-like projections were left, tiny protrusions the size of a lunch pail, around which originally ropes were hitched for transport by oxen or for hoisting by crane. These were removed from most ashlars once they were put into place, but left at random on some others, so that an additional layer of light-and-shadow patterns was cast on the Temple Mount's façade.

The smooth yet rich texture of the retaining wall's lower portions contrasted with the upper portions. None of the upper walls or buildings along the outer platform remain in place, as they were all destroyed and toppled by the Romans. But they can be reimagined by archaeologists and architects from their fragments in the rubble below. The upper portions were made with pilasters and topped with capitals. Set in but standing out from the walls at even intervals, those embedded columns were rectangular half-pillars rather than the round ones used in the palace at Masada. From outside, then, the Temple Mount's façade had two parts, the lower slightly sloped retaining wall and the upper pilastered wall, topped by a rounded parapet and framed by a tower at each corner. From there, priests and Levites could keep watch, and from there, as an inscription tells us, trumpet blasts could ring out.

The inscription was recovered by the late Benjamin Mazar's excavations at the southwest corner of the Temple Mount. Written on an 8-foot-long ashlar that once capped the rounded pinnacle of the wall, the Hebrew inscription in a steady angular hand with slightly unevenly spaced letters translates: "for the place of trumpeting for/to . . ." The final letters of the inscription were broken off, either when the Romans threw it down to the pavement or, more likely, when Charles Warren dug his exploratory shaft. Various suggestions for its ending have been proposed: it was a place of trumpeting "for the priest" or "to the Temple" or "to herald the Sabbath." The slightly crude hand, along with faint traces of plaster, has led to the suggestion that it was inscribed at the quarry to mark the stone's ultimate destination, and once the stone was put into place, it was covered with plaster by the construction workers. Be that as it may, the inscription provides solid evidence of priestly lookouts and confirms the practice of announcing the Sabbath and other festivals by a trumpet blast from the Temple, as Josephus and later rabbinic literature describe.

The architectural energies expended on the Temple's façade developed austerity into a sophisticated aesthetic and probably had two motives. One was that such a stone-only façade saved an enormous amount of plaster, which was produced in part by firing limestone, an expensive task for a city in the Judean desert with very little wood for fuel. Also, by avoiding plaster and building in solid stone, repairs would be few and far between. Herod's Temple was built to last.

The second motive was the result of Herod's thoroughly aniconic guidelines for this project. Save for one exception from Josephus, to be seen below, no text mentions any representation of a living being in or on the Temple, and neither statue nor relief of human or beast has been found by any of its explorers or excavators. Instead, decorations were floral and geometric. And they were mostly inside. If you entered the Temple up the southern staircase, through the so-called Double Portal of the Hulda Gates, passed under the Royal Stoa, and emerged by an opening in the plaza's floor, you would have passed under a series of variously colored and fantastically ornate round-domed chambers. Squares of intricately different geometric patterns were combined with rosettes resembling chrysanthemums, crowfoot, and other local flowers, with vines and grape clusters featured prominently. This entrance is possibly the Beautiful Gate, where Peter is said to have healed a lame beggar, according to Acts 3:1–10.

The Temple's Architectural Hierarchy

Those entering the Temple complex were already differentiated by their approach at the various gates. Most traffic came from the south and entered through one of two Hulda Gates that opened onto the plaza above. To the left, right next to a building housing several *miqwaoth* in which members of the public could immerse and purify themselves, a large staircase led to the Double Portal intended for the laity; to the right, a narrower staircase led to the Triple Portal's smaller entrance reserved for priests. At the southwestern corner, a monumental staircase, now called Robinson's Arch, led directly from the southern plaza below the Temple Mount into the Royal Stoa atop the entire southern wall.

These entrances could be easily controlled, and levitical guards under the high priest's command were stationed at each portal, where they could bar suspected troublemakers and control the flow of the crowds. Once inside, the Court of the Gentiles, comprising about two-thirds of the Temple Mount's plaza, was open to all visitors, Jews and Gentiles, males and females alike. Beyond this court, the so-called *soreg,* a stone barrier or lattice only a few feet high, barred non-Jews from further entry, although, of course, they could peer over it. Two inscriptions from the first century C.E. announcing the death penalty for any trespassing pagan have been found, one in the nineteenth century and another in the first half of the last century. Chiseled in stone with a steady and professional Greek script, one contains the following complete inscription and the other a fragment of it:

> No foreigner is to enter within the balustrade and enclosure around the Temple area. Whoever is caught will have himself to blame for his death which will follow.

The lettering of the fragmentary inscription found in 1938 still had residual red paint designed to stand out against the stone background. On the one hand, pagans could not transgress those borders under pain of death. On the other, they had access to more of the Temple's precincts than all the rest put together. It is surely not correct to claim, as does Mark's Jesus, that the Temple should be but was not a house of prayer for all the nations (11:17).

Thus far archaeology takes us. For the rest of the Temple, we turn to Josephus and rabbinic literature, which agree on the basic outlines. Jewish priests and laity, men and women, could proceed past the *soreg* and into the next perimeter, which was divided into three sections, from east to west the Court of Women, the Court of the Israelites, and the Court of the Priests. Women could not enter the Court of the Israelites, where Jewish men brought their offerings, who in turn could not enter the Court of the Priests, where the priests sacrificed on the altar.

Scholars debate whether or not the laity brought their own animals for sacrifice or purchased them in the Royal Stoa, or what mix of these two options existed and when. There is also some debate over who held the beasts during their slaughter. But there is no doubt that the priests and their levitical assistants were skilled and efficient butchers who sliced the throats of quadrupeds or turned the necks of birds, drained the blood, cut them up, and burned them on the altar's fire. Inside the sanctuary and behind the altar, facing due east and precisely into sunrise on the Day of Atonement, was the Holy of Holies. It once held the Ark of the Covenant, but later stood empty as the aniconic house of God. Only the high priest, only on the Day of Atonement, and only in complete purity, could enter through the curtains that veiled God's presence. It was a hierarchy, to be sure, but it was one dictated by Jewish purity norms rather than by Roman power or royal dignity.

The Temple's concentric arrangement was flanked by two important structures, the Royal Stoa inside its southern wall and the Antonia Fortress outside its northern wall. Architecturally, the Royal Stoa was a giant basilica made up of four rows of forty columns that extended nearly the entire length of the 900-foot southern wall. The southernmost row was a set of pilasters set into the Temple Mount's southern wall, the middle two rows flanking the nave were topped with an additional row of columns to support the upper roof, and the fourth and northernmost row was without a wall but created an open colonnade through which one could go straight into the plaza. The excavators found some toppled columns as large as Josephus had boasted: three men could barely stretch out their arms around one and hold hands. The apse or focal point of the Royal Stoa was at its eastern end.

Functionally, the Royal Stoa served as a place where money for the Temple tax was changed into the required Tyrian half-shekel, where the animals for sacrifice could be purchased, and where, perhaps, the council, or Sanhedrin, met at its eastern end. In other words, it was intended to house the commercial operations on which the Temple's fiscal and sacrificial systems depended.

Herod named the Antonia Fortress after his erstwhile patron Mark Anthony before the latter lost to Octavius and Herod moved smoothly to obey that new Roman power. The site had earlier been the location of the Baris Fortress at the time of the Hasmoneans, but, archaeologically, we know much less about it during the Herodian period, since Hadrian rebuilt much of his new Aelia Capitolina on top of it. It contains a large-stoned pavement that has been shown to tourists and pilgrims from the time of the Crusades up until today as the *lithostroton* where Pilate sat in judgment on Jesus according to John 19:13. It dates however, from the second-century time of Hadrian rather than the first-century time of Pilate. But the very location of that military fortress, whether for Herodian monarch or Roman prefect, emphasizes the importance of overseeing regularly, intervening immediately, and thereby controlling completely whatever went on in the Temple courts below. The Roman Empire and the Herodian kingdom each kept a careful eye on the Temple, the priests, and the crowds. One example: the high priest's vestments were often kept by the Roman procurators and prefects in the Antonia Fortress and given back to him for the festivals only after it was understood that the crowds were under proper control.

The Temple's Golden Eagle

Archaeology confirms the aniconic politics and imageless aesthetics of Herod's Temple. And, indeed, why build such a wonder of the world for your people's faith and provoke their anger in the process? But we know of one striking exception to that aniconicity not from material, but from textual data. This incident happened just before the death of Herod the Great and was an immediate prelude to the Passover slaughter executed by his son Archelaus inside the very Temple itself. We return to that latter case below, but here is how *Jewish War* (1:650–55) and *Jewish Antiquities* (17.151–67) record the story of the Temple's eagle:

It was, in fact, unlawful to place in the temple either images or busts or any representation whatsoever of a living creature; notwithstanding this, the king had erected over the great gate a golden eagle. This it was which these teachers [of the law named Judas, son of Sepphoraeus, and Matthias, son of Margalus] now exhorted their disciples to cut down. . . . At mid-day, accordingly, when numbers of people were perambulating in the temple, they let themselves down from the roof by stout cords and began chopping off the golden eagle with hatchets. The king's captain . . . with a considerable force, arrested about forty of the young men and conducted them to the king. . . . Those who had let themselves down from the roof together with the doctors he had burnt alive; the remainder of those arrested he handed over to his executioners.

Where was the "great gate" over which the golden eagle was placed? Josephus does not tell us clearly and may not even have known himself. What follows, then, is our best educated guess. The raised walkway from the Upper City's wealthy quarters across the Tyropoeon Valley led to the Temple Mount's wall immediately at the back of the sanctuary itself. That royal bridge is how Jewish elites from the Upper City entered the Temple and how Herod and visiting pagan dignitaries entered from his fortress-palaces. Most likely, Herod placed the golden eagle above that bridge's gateway in the western Temple wall. On the one hand, it could not be seen from inside the Temple or from any of its southern approaches used by the masses. On the other, it could be seen from the way pagan power entered the Temple.

But why place an eagle anywhere? Why do it at all? It was certainly not for provocation, and it was likely there for years before anyone decided that God demanded its removal. But forget for a moment about the beauty of brilliant white paint, shining gold sheathing, and intricate geometric decorations. Think instead of the ambiguity of those giant ashlars, those monumental foundations. Was Herod building a magnificent shrine, the Romans might ask, or constructing an impregnable fortress? So it was absolutely necessary to place atop that edifice an unambiguous symbol of submission to Rome, to locate between sanctuary and city the golden eagle representing Roman domination and Jewish submission. Just as Herod's Caesarea bowed to Rome through the Augustan Temple, so too Herod's Jewish Temple acknowledged Roman rule. That, at least, is one very probable reconstruction of the eagle's location and of Herod's intention.

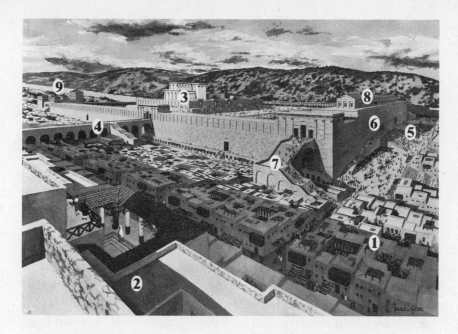

RECONSTRUCTION OF THE TEMPLE MOUNT LOOKING TOWARD THE
MOUNT OF OLIVES.   *The beauty of the Temple towered over Jerusalem's Lower
City (1) on an artificial mount built by Herod the Great, seen here from the Upper
City (2). At the center of the largest sacred precinct in antiquity was the white and
gold sanctuary (3), in front of which priests sacrificed. The Temple Mount was
accessible to the aristocratic priests living in the Upper City via a causeway over the
Tyropoeon Valley (4); most pilgrims entered from the south at the plaza that
housed ritual baths (5) and through either the Double Gate (6), which led to the
esplanade above, or up and around a stairway (7) leading to the Royal Stoa (8), a
basilica-like portico where presumably Jesus drove out the money changers. At the
far left, at the time of Jesus the Antonia Fortress (9) housed Roman troops, who
kept a careful watch over the crowds at Passover and other feasts.*

THE HIGH-PRIESTLY QUARTERS

We talked earlier about the beauty and ambiguity of Jerusalem's Temple as
it stood between the Jewish colony and the Roman Empire. It was both the
house of God and the seat of collaboration. It was both magnificent shrine
and impressive fortress. It was controlled by an aristocratic priesthood who
cooperated, perforce, with imperial occupation. In the end colonial revolt
destroyed that Temple and its priesthood forever. But think now not just
about colonial revolt, but about class warfare, about what happened when
the Zealot peasants took over Jerusalem during that revolt in 66–74 C.E. We

have not found Jerusalem's Zealots in the archaeological record as fully as we have found Masada's Sicarii. But we look next at what archaeology can tell us about the high-priestly quarters in Jerusalem. We do not presume that their occupants were more venal or evil than any other colonial aristocracy whose destiny is collaboration with imperial power. But if the Zealots can be found only by exegesis in the texts of Josephus, what can we find out about those whom the Zealots opposed so virulently and rejected so violently?

In the first century, as just mentioned, a large overpass served as a walk-way and aqueduct from the Upper City of Jerusalem to the Temple Mount. It led from Wilson's Arch on the Mount's western wall, crossed the Tyropoeon Valley, and linked the Temple courts to the Upper City, where the upper classes and wealthy priests lived. Nahman Avigad, of the Hebrew University of Jerusalem, began systematic excavations in 1969 on the western hill of Jerusalem's Old City, in what today is called the Jewish, or Herodian, Quarter, which overlooks the Temple Mount. What he found almost immediately, under the surface and with few intervening layers, were houses from the Herodian or Early Roman Period that had been destroyed by the disaster of 70 C.E. The houses he excavated were part of the affluent Upper City, where the high-priestly families lived, according to our literary sources. Their beauty and wealth are remarkable, paralleling those of the luxurious villas frozen in time at Pompeii or Herculaneum. Take a look at one example, almost a palace according to Avigad, and today described as the Palatial Mansion.

The Palatial Mansion

The house was arranged around a square courtyard, though, unlike those of Galilean Capernaum, it was paved with smooth, squarely cut flagstones. To the west, where the first floor survives and some walls to a height of 3 meters, a vestibule led from the courtyard to a large hall (a reception hall or *triclinium?*), and to the east, where only the basement levels of the house survive, a series of water installations and storerooms were cut into bedrock. The mansion covered an area of over 6,000 square feet—about the size of the Dionysos villa at Sepphoris or the larger urban villas in the Roman world. It dwarfed other residences in the Lower City below and, by employing building techniques, materials, and styles similar to those in the Temple, created a sophisticated ambiguity between public and private, sacred and profane space.

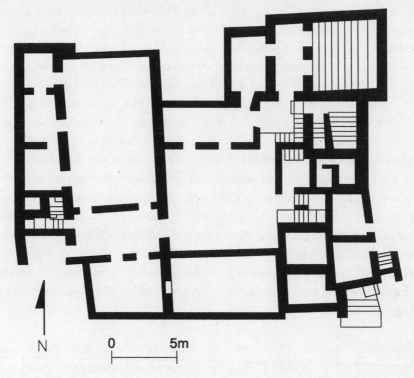

THE FIRST-CENTURY PALATIAL MANSION IN JERUSALEM'S UPPER CITY
(AFTER AVIGAD)

Fresco. The house was well constructed on bedrock with evenly hewn ashlars. Almost all of the walls from its earlier phase, around the first half of the first century, were covered with colorful frescos akin to the Second Pompeiian style: some had flora including garland strands, pomegranates, and apples; others imitated marble panels or had geometric designs in bright red, ochre, and green; and, at one place, painted remains of a fluted Ionic column were found. The frescoes of the Palatial Mansion, and indeed all those of the Upper City, were entirely aniconic—only a single and therefore exceptional depiction of a bird was found on nearby Mount Zion. The mansion's walls were painted in true fresco, done while the plaster was still wet, unlike the inexpensive and technically less demanding *al secco*, or dry method, used in the Insula II of Sepphoris, which easily chips, flakes, or peels.

Stucco.   In the final phase of the house, the owners chipped away at the frescoes in regular intervals and plastered a new layer onto the walls, this one not painted, but in ornamental stucco. The walls were smoothed and grooves cut in patterns that imitated ashlar masonry very similar to the Herodian boss-and-margin stones of the Temple. Though the ceiling was of course destroyed, stucco fragments found on the floor below betray its one-time splendor: egg-and-dart motifs surrounded a series of triangular, hexagonal, and octagonal geometric patterns. Somewhat oddly, by replacing the earlier wall's vibrant colors with somber pseudo-ashlars, the owners reversed the trend sweeping the Mediterranean world in which geometric reliefs and simple panels were giving way to colorful and illusionist natural realism. Perhaps the owners grew weary of the latter's garish kitsch and replaced it with a more artistically conservative and minimalist style. Or, more likely, by privatizing architectural features from the Temple, they sought to evoke an aura of Jerusalem's public and religious life inside their home, and to place themselves on top of the social pyramid by linking their residence with that of the divine.

Mosaic.   Several of the rooms' floors were covered with mosaics. Though these were mostly of plain white stones, a few ornamental mosaics in simple red-and-black geometric designs were found: a red-and-black tessaraed rosette with six simple petals, and a basic black-and-white checkerboard surrounded by a red frame. More ornate stone floors have been found in nearby houses, from a complicated maze bordered by wave crests, guilloche, and triangles to *opus sectile* flooring like that found at Herod's palaces in Jericho and Masada, where larger triangular and square stones were set in patterns and polished. The floors—like the frescoes—show the owners' traditional conservatism as they avoided depicting human or animal figures, but also established their owners among the wealthy elite.

The small finds inside the mansion and other houses in the Upper City likewise marked their owners' wealth. They acquired the most exquisite wares from abroad, seldom seen elsewhere locally and valued precisely because of their inaccessibility for the lower classes. Together, the artifacts below clearly articulated their place atop the social strata of Jerusalem.

Pottery.   The Palatial Mansion had its fair share of local, everyday cooking pots and storage jars, and many dropped into cisterns were found whole. But what sets the houses of the Upper City apart from, say, those of Galilean villages, is the quantity of fine serving vessels, both elegant imported wares and locally made bowls of the highest quality. The imports included shiny red decanters and bowls from the west, a rare Megaran bowl made in a mold with decorations in relief, and locally made shallow bowls, thin and delicate with ringed floral patterns in red, brown, or black paint.

Glass.   Much glass was found, including molded bowls with ribbed sides, ointment or perfume bottles, and fragments from a rare vaselike jug. This latter item, though deformed in the blaze that destroyed the house in 70 C.E., is almost fully reconstructable. Under its handle a Greek inscription set in a frame reads *Ennion epoiei*, "Ennion made this" or "Made by Ennion," a well-known Phoenician glassmaker from Sidon, some of whose wares today grace places such as the Metropolitan Museum of Art in New York.

Lamps.   Most of the lamps were common Herodian lamps, made on a wheel, with a spatulated nozzle to hold the wick. But several rarer and finer examples were also found, such as "Ephesus lamps," finished with a gleaming black or red slip and having a (sometimes double) nozzle flanked with volutes, which could be held with an often exaggerated loop handle.

Alongside the wealth contained in that Palatial Mansion and other houses of the Upper City, and alongside their owners' eagerness to put it on display, those homes always contained those artifacts we most closely associate with Jews and Jewish purity concerns: stone vessels and *miqwaoth*. In fact, each of the houses excavated in the Upper City by Avigad had several *miqwaoth* and scores of stone vessels. But even in these items, a closer look reveals the families' wealth.

Stone Vessels.   Of the many stone vessels, some were the hand-chiseled mug variety, or "measuring cups," so common in Galilee. But many others were made on a small lathe, such as finely polished spherical bowls with simple incised-line decorations. But most outstanding were the many quite large jars, found in each house of the Upper City. Over a foot in diameter and up to 3 feet in height, they could hold many gallons of water and are of the sort presumed in the story of the wedding in Cana, in which Jesus turned water into wine, according to John 2. They were fashioned from huge chunks of stone and achieved their nearly perfect circular shape by having been turned on a large lathe operated by at least three people. They are smoothly polished internally and externally, and some had

LARGE LATHE-TURNED
STONE VESSEL
(collection of the Israel
Antiquities Authority,
photograph copyright the
Israel Museum, Jerusalem)

simple lathe-incised lines near the rim or at the base, while others were decorated with more ornate egg-and-dart motifs or vertical fluting. These large lathe-turned vessels are virtually absent in Galilean villages. None have been found at Nabratein, and very few if any at Gamla, Jodefat, or Capernaum, although some do appear in the aristocratic houses in the domestic quarters of Sepphoris. They may have been modeled after bronze or even ceramic kraters common in aristocratic houses of the Greco-Roman world. They show, no doubt, their owner's concern for purity, but also that they maintained purity in cosmopolitan style.

Ritual Baths.   The case is similar with *miqwaoth*, or ritual baths. Recall how in the Galilean villages, *miqwaoth* were mostly in communal settings, for example, at Gamla around an olive press or next to the synagogue. Think of the large communal pools at Qumran that served the entire community. And remember the *miqweh*-building on the Temple Mount's southern side, along with the many found in the Lower City's houses where rentable rooms with *miqwaoth* accommodated pilgrims. Only in the wealthier houses of the Sepphoris acropolis did we encounter stepped, plastered pools inside private houses. But the houses of the Upper City had many *miqwaoth*, and some of them were elaborate complexes.

In one example, a plain white mosaic-paved vestibule led to three distinct baths. You entered the vestibule, used as a changing room, and to your left was a room with a bathtub—incidentally just like the one at Masada—perhaps again for hygienic cleaning. Straight ahead from the vestibule five steps descended down into a *miqweh* some 6 feet wide and 9 feet long, holding well above the Mishnah's requirements of 40 *seahs*, or about 200 gallons. A third and smaller pool, linked by a channel to the former, may have served for storing additional water, but, with descending steps spiraling downward, it may also have been used for purification.

Digging into bedrock, plastering and sealing the cavities, covering them with arches, and paving the changing room with mosaics were expensive and technically complex undertakings, and so especially was conducting rainwater from the roofs to the basement pools. But such efforts kept the wealthy from having to bathe with their plebeian and public counterparts. They immersed in elegance and privacy, unlike the communal baths in some villages, or the open waters of the Sea of Galilee at Capernaum. And they certainly contrasted with John the Baptist's political and apocalyptic immersion of others in the Jordan. The *miqwaoth* of the Upper City show, no doubt, their owners' concern for purity, but also that they could afford to purify themselves in the luxury of their own homes.

Somewhat ironically then, at the very time that the Pharisees were extending notions and practices of purity beyond the Temple to their meals and daily lives, wealthy priests were making luxury items out of some of the implements of purity. Ordinary Jews were also democratizing the presence of the divine beyond the Temple, and the masses were using stone vessels and *miqwaoth*, but the wealthy modified some of the very implements of purity to indicate social status.

Taxes and Tithes, Priests and Sacrifices

Anthropologists have suggested that the priestly class in a typical agrarian society often owned as much as 15 percent of the land, which was, of course, the basic capital of an ancient economy. It was very striking, then, that in Israelite tradition the land was divided between all the tribes except, precisely, the priestly tribe of Levi. Their inheritance was not land, but God. Here, for example, is Deuteronomy 18:1–5:

> The levitical priests, the whole tribe of Levi, shall have no allotment or inheritance within Israel. They may eat the sacrifices that are the Lord's portion but they shall have no inheritance among the other members of the community; the Lord is their inheritance, as he promised them. This shall be the priests' due from the people, from those offering a sacrifice, whether an ox or a sheep: they shall give to the priest the shoulder, the two jowls, and the stomach. The first fruits of your grain, your wine, and your oil, as well as the first of the fleece of your sheep, you shall give him. For the Lord your God has chosen Levi out of all your tribes, to stand and minister in the name of the Lord, him and his sons for all time.

The Torah's clear intention was that the priests would obtain their share of the land only indirectly through taxes, tithes, and sacrifices. The ideal was that all of those portions were divided equitably among the priests. The just distribution of land to and among the tribes included the just distribution of food to and among the priests. Food without land was perfectly adequate for the priests in the scriptural ideal. But the reality was that already shortly after the Babylonian exile some priests owned fields, according to Nehemiah 13, and by the first century many had acquired considerable estates. Josephus, himself an aristocratic priest, tells us that he was compensated by his imperial patron Titus for the land he lost around Jerusalem in the revolt with more land on the rich coastal plain (*Life* 422). The scriptural ideal was the just distribution of food, but the inevitable reality was an unfair hoarding of wealth. Some priests became far wealthier than their colleagues, let alone the peasantry. Think, then, about how the process worked.

First, and most important, the sacrifices and tithes offered by the people were scripturally prescribed, but lacked any real enforcement mechanism under Roman rule. No one was forced to sacrifice, and certainly Galilean peasants did not make the three major pilgrimages to Jerusalem on an annual basis. Many of the offerings were entirely burned before God, with nothing at all left over to eat. Some of the sacrificed animals went to the priests, so, obviously, they ate more meat than most ordinary people did. Some of the sacrifices were remarkably flexible: Leviticus 5 requires a lamb, but two birds could be substituted, and even grain could be offered by those unable to afford birds. People sacrificed to God, the priests obtained their share, and that was how, in the absence of their own tribal land, they were supposed to survive.

Their protein-rich diet had the likely by-product that priests were larger and more muscular. But meat without refrigeration also posed a danger, and children of meat eaters in antiquity were particularly susceptible to food poisoning. Indeed, interred in the ossuary of the high priest Caiaphas, to be discussed in the next chapter, were the skeletons of a child and two infants. Even wealth was no guarantee of longevity.

Second, the tithes of agricultural products supported the priests, who otherwise could not work outside the Temple. The tithing system was complex, with Leviticus differing from Deuteronomy, and Josephus interpreted them differently from the rabbis. In any case, it is unclear to what extent the people knew about these differences, and the priests hardly measured accurately or accounted fully for each family. Instead, people brought what they thought was a tenth of their agricultural produce to the Temple for distribution to the priests, or pious Galileans who could not make a pilgrimage gave directly to local-dwelling priests. According to Deuteronomy 14, some of the tithe was to be taken to Jerusalem to be sold, and the proceeds spent by the pilgrims in the city on virtually anything, including "wine or strong drink." This supported Jerusalem financially, but also allowed the pilgrims to celebrate at festival time.

Third, the Temple tax was only a half-shekel, about two days' work for a common laborer. Again, the sources are rather confusing: Exodus 30 requires a half-shekel of each Israelite male over twenty, but apparently only once in a lifetime. Nehemiah 10 requires a third-shekel, but every year. By the first century, the common practice attested in Philo, Josephus, and rabbinic literature was a half-shekel each year, which went for the maintenance of the Temple and especially the costs of communal sacrifices. Vespasian, by the way, expanded this tax as a punishment to every Jewish man, woman, and child after the revolt of 66–74 C.E. but made it payable to the temple of Jupiter Capitolinus in Rome.

As a whole then, the taxes and tithes would not account for the opulent lives of the wealthy priests in Jerusalem. Even the strictest and most generous observers of the law would give no more than 15 percent of their income to the Temple, and many more probably made only nominal or occasional gifts. And very likely some Galileans, living farther from the

Temple, which made travel more cumbersome or unrealistic, tithed only haphazardly, a practice that seems to have annoyed the rabbis. But these were not the taxes that the Galilean peasants were most concerned about. They worried about the taxes collected through Herod Antipas for Rome, which were carefully monitored and extracted under the threat of imprisonment, extreme violence, or land confiscation. These tax rates were most likely around 25 to 40 percent of all produce and income.

There seems to be little resentment recorded in the literary sources against either the Temple taxes or tithes in general on the part of the Jewish laity, but the wealthier priests are sometimes accused of usurping too much from their poorer priestly colleagues. Josephus details two occasions of such enmity, one of them under the high priest Ismael in 59 C.E. and one under Ananias shortly before the revolt:

> At this time King Agrippa conferred the High Priesthood upon Ismael the son of Phabi. There now was enkindled mutual enmity and class warfare between the high priests, on the one hand, and the priests and the leaders of the populace of Jerusalem, on the other. . . . Such was the shamelessness and effrontery which possessed the high priests that they actually were so brazen as to send slaves to the threshing floors to receive the tithes that were due to the priests, with the result that the poorer priests starved to death. . . .
>
> But [the High Priest] Ananias had servants who were utter rascals and who, combining operations with the most reckless men, would go to the threshing floors and take by force the tithes of the priests; nor did they refrain from beating those who refused to give. The High Priests were guilty of the same practices as his slaves, and no one could stop them. So it happened at that time that those of the priests who in olden days were maintained by the tithes now starved to death. (*Jewish Antiquities* 20.179–81, 206)

But these were abuses, and no one attacked tithing itself as a support for those who served God. The Christian Jews in the first-century community rule known as the *Didache*, for example, encouraged the community to tithe to their prophets, "both of your vine-fat and threshing floor, of your oxen and sheep . . . for they are your chief priests" (13:3).

There was, on the other hand, a clear resentment against the theft of

Temple wealth by the Romans. The Roman general Crassus looted the Temple's treasury in 54 B.C.E. of some ten thousand talents of coins and valuables (a talent being about 88 pounds). Pontius Pilate caused riots when he took some of the Temple's funds to pay for the construction of an aqueduct. Another Roman procurator, Gessius Florus, stole seventeen talents from the Temple treasury on the pretext that Caesar needed it, resulting in civil unrest directed against his rule of extortion and robbery.

Still, the example of the Zealots shows how a militant peasantry could conduct a bloodbath against some of its own priestly aristocracy as soon as it got the chance. In that pogrom they fused class warfare with colonial revolt; because of high-priestly wealth and power, actual past collaboration, and potential future treason, the Zealots create a reign of terror against their aristocracy. It is a warning that at least some of the peasantry found problems not so much personal and individual, as systemic and structural, with their aristocratic and especially with their high-priestly families. It was not just, or maybe not at all, a question of wealth from participation in the Temple, but a question of wealth from collaboration in the empire. It was the beauty of an ancient priesthood and the ambiguity of a colonial aristocracy.

The Burnt House

Whatever collaboration with Rome existed and whatever wealth it generated came to a crashing end for all those aristocratic families. The Temple fell, though the Upper City held out for another month. The entire priestly quarter was destroyed, and nowhere is the destruction captured more vividly than in the so-called Burnt House, discovered by Nahman Avigad in January 1970, almost exactly nineteen centuries after its destruction. Charred ashlars and burned beams from the upper stories had all collapsed onto the house's lower story and basement. Two finds vividly capture the final moments of the house. A bronze spear tip still leaned against the corner of a wall. And the skeletal arm of a woman in her twenties reached upward toward the stairs, a vivid and tragic indication of her attempt to flee the Romans or escape the inferno.

The date of the house's collapse and the woman's death is clear: ceramic finds approximate it to the second half of the first century, and coins pin it precisely to 70 C.E. Some coins in the debris were minted by the Roman procurators of Judea, but most were minted during the revolt by Jerusalem's

Jews. Their legends read, "Year Two/The Freedom of Zion" and "Year Three/The Freedom on Zion," and the last ones found read, "Year Four/Of the Redemption of Zion," that is to say, 69/70 C.E.

Some artifacts in the house were reminiscent of a kitchen, but there were so many ovens, basalt mortars and pestles, grinding stones, and large stone vessels scattered through several rooms that it must have been some kind of workshop. Small glass perfume bottles, numerous weights, and the varied and unusually shaped stone vessels led Avigad to suggest that the workshop produced spice or incense for the Temple, something that needed to be produced in ritual purity.

Among a series of squat cylindrical stone weights, one of under 3 inches in diameter was clearly inscribed in square Aramaic script as "of Bar Kathros" or "of the son of Kathros." The House of Kathros is one of the four well-known high-priestly families who held offices in the Temple under Roman rule. Their evil reputation is preserved from centuries later in the Babylonian Talmud. Rather than respected and esteemed, they were derided and shamed, along with other priestly families in an ode (*Pesahim* 57a):

> Woe is me because of the House of Beothus
>   woe is me because of the staves.
> Woe is me because of the House of Hanan,
>   woe is me because of their whisperings.
> Woe is me because of the House of Kathros,
>   woe is me because of their pens.
> Woe is me because of the House of Ishmael, son of Phiabi,
>   woe is me because of their fists.
> For they are the high priests,
> and their sons are treasurers,
> and their sons-in-law are trustees,
> and their servants beat the people with staves.

That poem preserves mid-first-century reality in a mid-sixth-century document. A very harsh judgment on all those ancient priestly families was held in very memorable format for over half a millennium. The House of Ishmael, son of Phiabi, was rebuked by Josephus, and the House of Hanan, Annas, or Ananias, is well known from the New Testament for an opposition to Christian Jews extending across thirty years from Jesus of

RECONSTRUCTION OF A WEALTHY PRIEST'S HOME IN JERUSALEM'S UPPER CITY. *Looking out toward the Mount of Olives (1) and the Temple's sanctuary (2), the Upper City was home to Jerusalem's rich as well as the leading priests. This reconstruction is a collage from various excavated houses, including the spectacular Palatial Mansion. The artifacts unearthed in these homes include large stone vessels (3), stone cups or mugs (4), and stone tables (5), each of which was deemed impervious to ritual impurity in Jewish law. Signs of wealth include a bronze lampstand (6), hanging lamps (7), and three-footed tables (8). The ornate mosaic (9) is a replica from the Upper City, as are the well-executed frescos (10), while the ceiling (11) is a hypothetical reconstruction from stucco fragments. In contrast to contemporary houses of the Roman world, those of the Upper City were thoroughly aniconic in adherence to Mosaic law.*

Nazareth to his brother James of Jerusalem. Those high-priestly families were remembered for their tight control of debts and nepotistic selection of various officials. We presume that the workshop found in the Burnt House, the House of Kathros, was one of the profitable monopolies granted to an aristocratic priestly family, this one to produce incense or spices for the Temple. Among the artifacts were two pottery inkwells nearly identical to the ones found at Qumran. But those of the Kathros house remind us that writing in antiquity was not just for sacred scrolls. It was also for contracts and legal agreements that were carefully guarded: "woe to me because of their pens." Notice, above all, those twice-mentioned "staves," framing that poetic attack at its beginning and end.

A PILGRIMAGE TO THE TEMPLE

Josephus, an eyewitness who had also seen Caesarea and Rome, describes the Temple Mount's façade with awe. He does it, tragically enough, at the very moment he is describing how the Temple was burned to the ground:

> The exterior of the building wanted nothing that could astound either mind or eye. For, being covered on all sides with massive plates of gold, the sun was no sooner up than it radiated so fiery a flash that persons straining to look at it were compelled to avert their eyes, as from the solar rays. To approaching strangers it appeared from a distance like a snow-clad mountain; for all that was not over-laid with gold was of purest white. (*Jewish War* 5.222–23)

Imagine yourself a pilgrim arriving for the first time in Jerusalem and getting your first glimpse at the Temple. Come to the Temple Mount not from an Aegean city or Rome, but from Galilee or the Golan, from Jodefat or Gamla, Capernaum or Nazareth. Approaching Jerusalem from the East, past Bethany and within view of the Mount of Olives, you would enter the city through its southern gates in the Lower City. Passing by the Siloam Pool, where many pilgrims washed after an arduous journey, you walked up the Kidron Valley past markets, houses renting rooms—some with *miqwaoth*—and pilgrim hospices housing Jewish visitors from the diaspora. One inscription in Greek, from an inn built by and for the Jews of the island of Rhodes, reminds us of the many foreign languages and dialects the pilgrims would have heard.

Approaching the southern plaza under the Temple Mount, you first see the massive arch and overpass ahead and behind it the bridge spanning what remained of the Tyropoeon Valley. It led directly to the wealthy houses of the aristocratic priests, who along with the rest of the nobility had easier admittance from their quarters.

Once on the plaza under the Temple Mount, you could, if you needed, immerse in a crowded public *miqweh* right by the Hulda Gates. Then, the unevenly spaced steps about 8 inches high, but alternating in width between 12 and 35 inches, required a slow and deliberate approach to the Double Gate. Already dazzled by the size of the great stones, you are even more astonished by the vivid colors and geometric illusions of the round-domed vestibule inside the portal. As you pour out with the crowd at the end of the staircase and up onto the Temple Mount's esplanade, you are met by the sights, smells, and sounds of sacrifice, something you take absolutely for granted as the normal way that all people worship the divine. Sights included plumes of smoke ascending to heaven from the altar. Smells included the sweet aroma of burning fat and meat, of wine and oil, of frankincense and other exotic spices (coupled, of course, with the smell of defecating oxen, goats, sheep, and birds!). The sounds included the bleating of sheep mixed with the lowing of oxen. As a Galilean peasant you are used to living your life with and through animals and, of course, you expect to meet God with and through them as well.

If you were Jewish, you could pass through the *soreg* partition and circle around to the east to enter the sanctuary's precincts—there, its axial arrangement afforded a glimpse through the Court of the Women, past the circular-tiered steps leading into the Court of the Israelites and next to the altar, where steps led up into the sanctuary, at whose recess was the Holy of Holies covered by a thick curtain.

If you were a Jewish woman, you stopped in the Court of the Women. If you were a Jewish man, you could continue with your sacrifice and hand it over to the corps of priests and Levites. They were skilled and hard working, sweaty and bloodied, busy slitting throats, hanging carcasses, cutting and slicing meat to be tossed on the altar. Some brought wood for the fire, others prodded the coals, and a few tossed on incense. Your offering was consumed in fire as the smoke ascended upward before God.

Awe at the Temple mixed profoundly and almost ecstatically with joy at the festival. During Passover, for example, you first sacrificed your lamb in the Temple, giving its blood to God through the priests, and then received back its flesh to eat with your family and friends that very night and still in the presence of God. The Passover feast recalled what God had done for your people long ago but, in a way, it was in once and future time. God stood with a small people, enslaved and condemned to death, against the might and power of the Egyptian empire.

Your Passover ritual correlated past and present. Did it also equate the Egyptian empire then with the Roman Empire now? Maybe you never even thought of that equation? Maybe you never even thought about priestly legitimacy, colonial submission, or imperial collaboration? Maybe, as you walked through the Temple courts that very morning, you never looked to your right and saw soldiers looking down at you from the ramparts of the Antonia Fortress? They were local pagan auxiliaries and not foreign legionary forces, but they watched you from the north and it was from the

north that the Roman revenge would always arrive. Maybe you were so
focused on family and friends, sacrifice and feast, God and Passover, that you
saw only the awesome beauty of the Temple and missed the dangerous ambiguity of celebrating liberation in an occupied country? Maybe.

Still, that dangerous ambiguity was always present. It was there at any
festival with large numbers of people in one crowded place. It was there
especially at Passover as those crowds celebrated freedom from a past
empire in the colony of a present one. Here, for example, from Josephus,
are two cases across fifty years of that first century.

In 4 B.C.E., according to both *Jewish War* (2:10–13) and *Jewish
Antiquities* (17.204–5), Herod the Great's son Archelaus unleashed his
troops against protesting crowds during "the feast of unleavened bread,
which the Jews call Passover . . . an occasion for the contribution of a multitude of sacrifices" when "a vast crowd streamed in from the country for
the ceremony." Furthermore, "Passover [is] a commemoration of their
departure from Egypt." Shouting protests escalated into throwing stones,
until finally:

> Archelaus, however, now felt that it would be impossible to restrain
> the mob without bloodshed, and let loose upon them his entire army,
> the infantry advancing in close order through the city, the cavalry by
> way of the plain. The soldiers falling unexpectedly upon the various
> parties busy with their sacrifices slew about three thousand of them
> and dispersed the remainder among the neighbouring hills. The her-
> alds of Archelaus followed and ordered everyone to return home; so
> they all abandoned the festival and departed.

That was a Herodian prince not yet confirmed in rule by Augustus, but
an even worse slaughter took place just over a half century later when the
Roman procurator Ventidius Cumanus governed the entire Jewish homeland. In Josephus's twin accounts the numbers vary but it is still a slaughter at Passover:

> The usual crowd had assembled at Jerusalem for the feast of unleav-
> ened bread, and the Roman cohort had taken up its position on the
> roof of the portico of the temple; for a body of men in arms invariably
> mounts guard at the feasts, to prevent disorders arising from such a
> concourse of people. Thereupon one of the soldiers, raising his robe,

stooped in an indecent attitude, so as to turn his backside to the Jews, and made a noise in keeping with his posture. Enraged at this insult, the whole multitude with loud cries called upon Cumanus to punish the soldier; some of the more hot-headed young men and seditious persons in the crowd started a fight, and, picking up stones, hurled them at the troops. Cumanus, fearing a general attack upon himself, sent for reinforcements. These troops pouring into the porticoes, the Jews were seized with irresistible panic and turned to fly from the temple and make their escape into the town. But such violence was used as they pressed round the exits that they were trodden under foot and crushed to death by one another; upwards of thirty thousand perished, and the feast was turned into mourning for the whole nation and for every household into lamentation. (*Jewish War* 2.224–27; *Jewish Antiquities* 20.106–12 says 20,000 died)

Archaeology cannot record such incidents as those and we know them only from Josephus. Referring to a date about midway between those two Passover disasters, Luke 13:1 mentions "the Galileans whose blood Pilate had mingled with their sacrifices." Luke is very fond of historical allusions, and sometimes his enthusiasm outstrips his accuracy. But if that is not some conflation of Archelaus and/or Cumanus with Pilate, it is one more incident, maybe at Passover or maybe at some other festival, when the blood of protesters and the blood of animals mingled together in the Temple of Jerusalem. Beauty and ambiguity, once more, but now at the level of the ordinary Jewish peasant.

TWO DANGEROUS ACTIONS

Jesus was not executed by the Jewish tetrarch Antipas in Galilee, but by the Roman prefect Pilate in Judea. Why not and why? Jesus opposed Antipas's Romanization and urbanization in Lower Galilee, challenged his building of a commercial kingdom there by both word and deed, by both vision and program. He grounded that opposition in the covenantal Kingdom of God. He incarnated it in the lifestyles of alternative share-communities. That Kingdom movement of Jesus was at least as subversive as the Baptist movement of John. But Antipas ruled for over forty years, and he must have acted if not correctly, then at least carefully to have lasted so long. He had, however, executed John, and one popular prophet per decade may have been all Antipas judged to be prudent. Jesus was probably saved by John's martyrdom. But that was in Galilee. Judea was different. Galilee had only the Herodian Antipas. Judea had both the Sadducean Caiaphas and the Roman Pilate. Double jeopardy there.

Jesus may have gone up to Jerusalem *only once*, as in Mark's parabolic scenario. He may have gone up *more than once*, as in John's equally parabolic but opposite scenario. In any case, we can be quite sure that he went there *at least once*. And never returned. The Roman historian Tacitus says that Jesus "had undergone the death penalty in the reign of Tiberius, by sentence of the procurator Pontius Pilate." Josephus writes that "Pilate, upon hearing him accused of men of the highest standing amongst us, condemned him to be crucified." Both writers locate that condemnation within a sequence of movement-execution-continuation-expansion. The execution, one gathers, was to finish off a movement, but that movement not only continued despite it, but expanded after it. Neither author mentions any specific and immediate cause for that supreme penalty.

Some warnings before continuing. Even if we can never know for sure what *immediate* cause resulted in crucifixion, Jesus' incarnated enactment of the Kingdom of God as a program of resistance (whether it was covenantally and/or eschatologically and/or apocalyptically derived) must eventually have resulted in a fatal collision with official authority. It was only a matter of at what time and in what place. It was only a matter of whether his general attitude or some specific incident would lead finally to that inevitable martyrdom. Further, it is not necessary to make monsters out of either Caiaphas or Pilate to understand their collaborative action against him. If you announce a Kingdom of God, it could easily be taken as claiming that you yourself are its king and, although neither Jewish nor Roman authorities saw Jesus as a military danger, since they did not round up his followers, they clearly saw him as a social one, since they did not execute him privately. Finally, in this section more than anywhere else, the problems of exegetical strata and textual layers become well nigh intractable. What, for example, is from the first layer of the historical Jesus around the year 30 and what is from later layers in or even before the first level of that third layer in the historical Mark around the year 70?

The Entry into Jerusalem

As already mentioned, any subversive action was especially dangerous at Passover, when an ancient tradition of liberation from imperial slavery combined with large crowds in the same confined space of sanctuary and city. There are two major *actions* from Jesus' last week in Jerusalem either of which could have brought down on him the combined wrath of high priest and prefect, of Caiaphas and Pilate. The incidents are usually entitled the *Entry into Jerusalem* and the *Cleansing of the Temple*. Both events are completely in keeping with Jesus' Galilean activity as seen earlier. With regard to violent injustice, they emphasize, respectively, those elements of *nonviolent* resistance from Chapter 4 and of nonviolent *resistance* from Chapter 3. There are also striking similarities and significant differences between them.

Both incidents are recorded in all four gospels. That, however, may mean no more than that Mark narrated them and the others copied from him. That is relatively certain for Matthew and Luke, but also entirely possible for John as well. But is it equally possible for both units?

Both incidents combine deed and word, action and interpretation, incident and scriptural citation. In the *Entry*, however, that scriptural fulfillment appears only in the written context and then only in Matthew and Luke. In the *Cleansing*, it comes from Jesus himself.

Both incidents, therefore, are certainly *in* the first level of the third layer, that is, in Mark. But are they *from* earlier layers? Does either go back to the historical Jesus? There are good arguments that both stories came to Mark as traditional narratives, because you can glimpse his changes upon that received basis.

In the *Entry*, Mark avoids any scriptural allusions to Zechariah 9:9–10: "Rejoice greatly, O daughter Zion! Shout aloud, O daughter Jerusalem! Lo, your king comes to you; triumphant and victorious is he, humble and riding on a donkey, on a colt, the foal of a donkey. He will cut off the chariot from Ephraim and the war horse from Jerusalem; and the battle bow shall be cut off, and he shall command peace to the nations; his dominion shall be from sea to sea, and from the River [Euphrates?] to the ends of the earth." Instead, Mark uses the story as one more negation of Jesus as Son of David. First, in a passage preceding the *Entry*, 10:46–52, Mark describes a blind man who hails Jesus as "Son of David" and who must be healed before he can "follow him on the way." Next, in a succeeding passage, 12:35–37, Mark argues that he who is David's Lord cannot at the same time be David's son. Finally, it is the Kingdom of God that Mark usually connects with Jesus and not the Kingdom of David. From all of that we judge that the proclamation in Mark 11:10, "Blessed is the coming kingdom of our ancestor David," is intended in context to be quite wrong. The crowd erroneously prefers the coming Kingdom of David (triumphant and/or militant messiahship?) to the present Kingdom of God. In such a negative usage, any explicit or even implicit allusion to Zechariah 9:9–10 must be muted entirely.

It is possible, in other words, to locate the *Entry* in a pre-Markan layer, one earlier than the third or evangelical layer's first level. But is it the first and original layer of the historical Jesus? On the one hand, if it was a historical incident enacted by Jesus, it would probably have been enough to entail very serious consequences. It was almost a lampoon, a satirical antitriumphal entry into Jerusalem. A general entered his conquered city in a war chariot or on a ceremonial steed, using the symbols of violent power, but Jesus entered on a donkey. In the tightened security of a Passover celebration, the authorities would not have found that amusing. That public action would have been enough for public crucifixion. On the other hand, if it was not a historical incident, but a parabolic story, although it would not explain what happened, as a narrative-in-character, it would tell us how Jesus' kingship was understood by his early companions or later followers as nonviolent antikingship.

The *"Cleansing"* of the Temple

In the *Cleansing* a similar editorial adaptation of a pre-Markan unit seems evident. Jesus performs not so much a ritual cleansing as a symbolic destruction of the Temple. The scriptural citation from Jeremiah 7:11 ("You have made it a den of robbers") fits perfectly with that action (more on this below). But the preceding one from Isaiah 56:7 ("My house shall be called a house of prayer for all the nations") interrupts that close unity and is, in first-century historical context, unfairly inaccurate. Jerusalem's Temple was, in fact, a house of prayer for all the world. Its huge Court of the Gentiles was not just ornamental, but indicates how many pagans made pilgrimages and/or tours to visit Herod's monumental reconstruction, one that would have justified calling it the Third Temple.

A comment on that *Cleansing* title. It was certainly possible, completely within Judaism, to criticize the Temple because of dynastic illegitimacy or imperial collaboration on the part of the high-priestly families. It was even possible, absolutely within Judaism, to withdraw in protest from any participation in its calendar or cult. If, for example, the Qumran Essenes had ever taken over control of Jerusalem and its Temple, they would probably have "cleansed" it first from ritual impurity. Granted all of that, there has often been a subtle anti-Jewish or even anti-Semitic taint to describing Jesus' action as "cleansing" the Temple, especially as it focused almost exclusively on "overturning the tables of the money changers." Herein, therefore, always read it with quotation marks indicating its inaccuracy.

In any case, Mark 11:15–17 does not describe a symbolic cleansing, but a symbolic destroying of the Temple. That is clear, first, from its fig-tree frames, when that tree is cursed beforehand at 11:12–14 and found withered afterward at 11:20. For Mark, destroyed tree means destroyed Temple. It is clear, next, from the fact that Jesus does not simply attack those who changed foreign currencies into the acceptable coinage for Temple taxes and donations. He stops all the fiscal, sacrificial, and logistical operations of the Temple. "Destroys" or "stops" are, of course, prophetic and symbolic rather than actual and factual (like a minister pouring red paint on draft-office files in the American 1960s). It is clear, finally, from the appended saying of Jesus about a "den of thieves."

Think, for a moment, about that phrase. A "den" (hideaway or safe house) is not where thieves do their thieving, but where they flee for safety after having done it elsewhere. That is both the commonsense meaning for "den of thieves" and the precise meaning it has in that scriptural quotation from Jeremiah 7:11. The context there is part of an ongoing tradition of prophetic warnings against presuming that divine worship in the Temple can be separated from divine justice for the earth. How can they "oppress the alien, the orphan, and the widow," against the law of God, and think to escape by fleeing back to the Temple of God? How can you come here to "this house, which is called by my name, and say, 'We are safe!'—only to go on doing all these abominations? Has this house, which is called by my name, become a den of thieves in your sight?" (Jer. 7:6, 10–11). How dare you turn my Temple into a safe house for injustice?

Against that prophetic background and with that scriptural citation, Jesus' action consummates God's warning about the Temple's destruction in Jeremiah 7:14. If you continue to separate divine Temple sacrificial worship from divine distributive justice, "I will do to the house that is called by my name, in which you trust, and to the place that I gave to you and to your ancestors, just what I did to [the ancient sanctuary at] Shiloh."

Of those two dangerous incidents, the *Entry* and the *Cleansing*, the latter is more likely to be historical event rather than parabolic story. Why? One reason is that there is a better possibility that John 2:13–17 has an independent version in this case rather than simply a very creative rephrasing, reinterpretation, and relocation of it. Another is that there is an independent version in the *Gospel of Thomas* 71: "Jesus said, 'I will destroy [this] house, and no one will be able to build it [. . .].'" If, therefore, there was one specific event that led to Jesus' crucifixion, we think this the most likely recoverable incident. In summary, if either of those stories (let alone both) is historical, it would have led to public execution as an immediate Passover warning. If neither of them is historical, we can no longer determine the specific event in Jerusalem that led to Jesus' execution. But, then, as noted above, his vision and program, his life in and enactment of the Kingdom of God, placed him on a deliberate collision course with the Kingdom of Rome, whether in Galilee under Antipas or in Jerusalem under Caiaphas and Pilate. But that discussion, however decided, introduces the far wider question of historicity of the trials of Jesus.

THE HISTORICITY OF THE TRIALS OF JESUS.

We are not raising questions about the basic fact of Jesus' crucifixion under Pontius Pilate (as in Tacitus), nor about collaboration between the highest Jewish and Roman authorities in effecting that execution (as in Josephus), nor about *some* conjunction of Jesus' death with the feast of Passover (as in the gospels). Those are as secure as historical facts can be. But neither are we simply asking whether every minor he-said-this, they-said-that, he-did-this, they-did-that element is factual. We ask primarily whether those trials took place at all or whether execution was accomplished at a lower level of standard police procedures for Passover crowd control. We ask especially about the historicity of the seemingly incidental elements that together have helped forge Christian anti-Semitism over the centuries.

These questions include: Was there an open Passover amnesty? Could "the crowd" annually get whomever it wanted freed? Was there a choice between Barabbas and Jesus? Did Pilate want to release Jesus, deeming him innocent? Did he argue for his release and did he, eventually and reluctantly, give in to the counterdemands of Judaism's high-priestly authority and Jerusalem's shouting crowd? The question is not whether all of that is compelling drama or exciting narrative. Of course it is. The question is not whether one can conduct engrossing biographical analyses of Pilate's outer political insecurity or inner psychological tension. Of course one can. But did it happen? Is it history? Because of space limits, we focus here on the central elements in that ancient scenario, on the crowd(s) and Barabbas, on Jesus and Pilate.

The Roar of the Crowd and the Choice of Barabbas

Was an open Passover amnesty historically plausible? It was possible, of course, but was it likely? We are not speaking of lower-level criminals in general or even some upper-level one released by festive concession as a result of some governor's own decision. It is a question of whether a Passover amnesty, open to whomever was requested, was a likely custom anywhere and especially in Pilate's Judea.

In writing his attack on Egypt's governor Flaccus, the Jewish philosopher Philo of Alexandria described what a normal governor might do for a condemned person on a festival occasion. Since "the sacred character of the festival ought to be regarded," a good governor would opt for postponement, but not remission, of a condemned person's crucifixion. For example, "with all rulers, who govern any state on constitutional principles, and who do not seek to acquire a character for audacity, but who do really honour their benefactors, it is the custom to punish no one, even of those who have been lawfully condemned, until the famous festival and assembly, in honour of the birth-day of the illustrious emperor, has passed." That is his best example of what governors usually do when "the very time itself gave, if not entire forgiveness, still, at all events, a brief and temporary respite from punishment" (*Against Flaccus* 81–84). Philo can imagine at best a temporary delay rather than an open amnesty.

Another question concerns that crowd shouting for Jesus' execution. For the moment, let there be such an open Passover amnesty and such a just and decent governor. But why is there such a crowd demanding crucifixion? What have they against Jesus? What has Jesus done against them? Watch how that story unfolds and develops from one to another source across its transmission.

In our earliest account, Mark 15:6–8 records the crowd's arrival this way: "Now at the festival he used to release a prisoner for them, anyone for whom they asked. Now a man called Barabbas was in prison with the rebels who had committed murder during the insurrection. So the crowd came and began to ask Pilate to do for them according to his custom." They come, in other words, *for* Barabbas and not *against* Jesus. But Pilate attempts to release Jesus instead and thereupon, at high-priestly instigation, they insist that Jesus be crucified (and Barabbas released). That arrival *for* Barabbas is found only in Mark. Here, Barabbas is mentioned first and Jesus only later.

As Matthew rewrites his Markan source, the "crowd" in 27:15 expands into the "crowds" in 27:20 and becomes "all the people" in 27:25. We are not told that they came for Barabbas, but that, on arrival, Pilate presented them with an immediate choice; "So after they had gathered, Pilate said to them, 'Whom do you want me to release for you, Jesus Barabbas or Jesus who is called the Messiah?'" Thereafter, once again, priestly instigation dictates their choice. Here, Barabbas and Jesus are first mentioned together, in that order.

In Luke's rewriting of Mark, there is a similar change. In 23:13–18 Pilate declares Jesus' innocence to "the chief priests, the leaders, and the people," but "they all shouted out together, 'Away with this fellow! Release Barabbas for us!'" There is nothing about a "crowd" coming up before Pilate to get Barabbas released and Jesus is rejected even before Barabbas is demanded. Here, Jesus ("this fellow") and Barabbas are first mentioned together, in that order.

Finally, in John 18:38–40, the crowd has become "the Jews," they do not come to Pilate for Barabbas, but Pilate addresses them: "'You have a custom that I release someone for you at the Passover. Do you want me to release for you the King of the Jews?' They shouted in reply, 'Not this man, but Barabbas!' Now Barabbas was a bandit." Jesus alone is offered by Pilate and rejected by "the Jews" in favor of Barabbas, who only appears at that point. Here, Jesus is mentioned first and Barabbas only later.

Across those texts, across those levels of the third layer from Mark through John, there is a steady escalation. It moves, first, from "crowd" to "crowds" to "all the people" to "the Jews." It moves, second, from an understandable situation, in which they come to get Barabbas released and are therefore against any Pilate-proposed release of Jesus, to an ununder-standable one, in which they are against Jesus and therefore for the release of Barabbas.

Understanding those twin processes is vital for deciding whether *any* of that story comes from the first layer at the time of the historical Jesus or was created by the historical Mark for the first level of the third layer. Recall that the Evangelists write gospel and not history, biography, or jour-nalism. Gospel is good news, and good news, to remain good for new hear-ers or readers, must be updated, actualized, and made relevant always to new places, times, experiences, and communities. That, for example, is the logic that determines how later writers deliberately change and adapt their Markan source, change and adapt the very words and deeds of Jesus that Mark recorded. Thus as Christian Jews are more and more marginalized within their own people in the present experience of gospel authors, the animosity against Jesus expands accordingly in the past representation of his execution. Hence that steady escalation just mentioned. It is the inevitable result of narrative *actualization*, of making the past story fit present reality. Who are our friends and enemies right here and now? Those, then, were the friends and enemies of Jesus at his execution long ago. If the author and community of John's gospel experience "the Jews" (all other Jews except us few good ones) as their present enemies, those will be retrojected as the enemies of Jesus. But, finally, if actualization is the root principle of gospel narrative, was Mark's own actualization one of adaptation or creation? Once again: is it history from the first layer or parable from the third layer's first level?

Mark writes in the immediate aftershock of that great revolt in 66–74 and especially of Jerusalem and the Temple's destruction in 70 C.E. Recall from earlier in this chapter how various bands of brigands (freedom fighters or guerrilla rebels) were forced inside the city's protective walls by Vespasian's advance. There they formed the loose coalition known technically as the Zealots. Mark's Barabbas is exactly such as they, a rebel using counterviolence against Roman imperial control. In this parable, Mark confronts the ruined city with its fatal choice of the wrong savior, the wrong "son of the father." You made that once and future choice, says Mark, of trusting yourselves to a violent Barabbas instead of to a nonviolent Jesus. That was your terrible mistake, claims Mark. The Barabbas or Jesus selection is parable, not history, but it is, as Mark intends it to be, a past parable about Jerusalem's recent history.

The Reluctance of Pilate and the Innocence of Jesus

What about Pilate as fair, decent, and just, but caught between internal ethics and external politics, vacillating between private conscience and public pressure? We are not just asking about that (in)famous contrast found only in Matthew: "When Pilate saw that he could do nothing, but rather that a riot was beginning, he took some water and washed his hands before the crowd, saying, 'I am innocent of this man's blood; see to it yourselves.' Then the people as a whole answered, 'His blood be on us and on our children!'" (27:24–25). That formally, officially, ritually passes responsibility for the execution from Roman to Jewish hands. That is clearly a Matthean addition to his Markan source, but it does no more than focus what the whole passion story emphasizes: a reluctant Pilate who acknowledged Jesus' innocence was forced, for various reasons, to acquiesce in demands for his execution.

There are early-first-century governors about whom we know only their names, others about whom we have only a passing comment. But we know about Pilate from two separate first-century Jewish sources, from Philo once again, but also from Josephus. And precisely what they choose to criticize is his way with unjust condemnations and protesting crowds.

Philo describes him as "a man of very inflexible disposition, and very merciless as well as obstinate," castigates "his corruption, and his acts of insolence, and his rapine, and his habit of insulting people, and his cruelty, and his continued murders of people untried and uncondemned, and his never ending, and gratuitous, and most grievous inhumanity," and summarizes him as "being at all times a man of most ferocious passions" (*Embassy to Gaius* 301–3). Even if that is rhetorical overkill, it was Pilate he chose to receive it, Pilate he chose as the personification of bad government.

As you will recall from Chapter 4, Josephus recorded how, having brought imperial standards within the walls of Jerusalem, Pilate backed down before an unarmed but protesting crowd ready for general martyrdom. But the next time they tried the same procedure, he infiltrated out-of-uniform soldiers among the unarmed protesters, started a riot, and "large numbers of the Jews perished, some from the blows which they received, others trodden to death by their companions in the ensuing flight. Cowed by the fate of the victims, the multitude was reduced to silence" (*Jewish War* 2.177; *Jewish Antiquities* 18.62). Finally, of course, Pilate was dismissed from office by his immediate superior, the Syrian governor Vitellius, and remanded home to explain his "slaughter of the victims" from among another crowd, this time a Samaritan one (*Jewish Antiquities* 18.88). Pilate was neither saint nor monster, but everything else we know about him renders the gospels' story implausible as actuality.

Incidentally, as part of Vitellius's post-Pilate restoration, he remitted Jerusalem's taxes, restored the high-priestly vestments to sacerdotal control, and deposed Caiaphas as high priest. It must be presumed, since Vitellius was "received in magnificent fashion" at the feast of Passover in Jerusalem, that all those changes met with general approval. Caiaphas and Pilate, apparently, stood and fell together.

We come back, then, once again, to ask about the origins of this scenario. Is it the first or original layer from Jesus or the third layer's first level from Mark? And, if it is a Markan creation, what would have been its purpose? The usual answer is that Mark and the later Evangelists are playing the Roman card. They know that Jesus was crucified by Pontius Pilate even if with some high-priestly collaboration. But, this explanation claims, they deliberately transferred the responsibility from Roman to Jewish shoulders by creating a shouting crowd under sacerdotal control and a Pilate who knew Jesus was innocent but had to give in to avoid a worse result. They did that to make their movement more palatable to imperial power, to cloak the fact that they were the followers of a condemned criminal.

There is, however, a better explanation. The layer in which that decreased Roman and increased Jewish/Jerusalem responsibility originated was one after the first, but before the third layer. Our proposal is that the basic passion story was created in the early 40s in a very special situation. First, the Romans were no longer in direct control of the Jewish homeland by means of an imperial governor. Second, the Jewish monarch Herod Agrippa I was "King of the Jews," a title not granted since the death of Herod the Great. Third, Agrippa had appointed a high priest of the house of Annas. Fourth, none of that boded well for a dissident group of Christian Jews. Josephus reports that Agrippa "enjoyed residing in Jerusalem and did so constantly; and he scrupulously observed the traditions of his people. He neglected no rite of purification, and no day passed for him without the prescribed sacrifice" (*Jewish Antiquities* 19.331). And the Acts of the Apostles reports that Agrippa "laid violent hands upon some who belonged to the church. He had James, the brother of John, killed with the sword. After he saw that it pleased the Jews, he proceeded to arrest Peter also" (12:1–3).

Think of a passion story first created against that background. The Romans look very good because it would be safer for Christian Jews to have them rather than Agrippa in charge. The high-priestly authorities (especially the house of Annas) are the implacable enemy, but the Jerusalem people are also more likely to be on the side of Agrippa. It was contemporary actualization from the early 40s that determined the friends and enemies of Jesus in that story. It was not created to play falsely to Roman power. It was not created to tell a deliberate lie about Pilate. It was created to mirror closely and thereby console fully the situation of Christian Jews in the new and very dangerous situation of the 40s in Jerusalem. It was, once again, parable, not history, gospel, not journalism. In this book's Introduction, the second to last of the ten key exegetical "discoveries" for

FRAGMENT OF
THE GOSPEL OF PETER
(copyright the Egypt Exploration
Society, photograph courtesy of the
Ashmolean Museum, Oxford)

excavating Jesus proposed that such an early passion story could still be
seen in the fragmented remains of the so-called *Gospel of Peter*. In that earlier passion story Pilate has nothing at all to do with the crucifixion, an
unspecified Herod is in total charge, and there is eventually a serious split
between the authorities of the Jews and "the people of the Jews" over the
crucifixion and resurrection of Jesus. Not factual history of course, but fictional dream, still, a dream from early rather than late in that first century.

All of that points to how much work must still be done in understanding the intention, clarifying the situation, and thereby assessing the historicity of those passion stories. No matter how we explain their origins,
we know that they bear a heavy freight of responsibility for directly

encouraging Christian anti-Judaism and indirectly fostering racial anti-Semitism. Think, for example, of the Oberammergau Passion Play, a reenactment of Jesus' execution portrayed dramatically by the Bavarian village of Oberammergau in vowed thanksgiving for deliverance from plague. It had been staged since 1634 every tenth summer on the decade—but with some necessary omissions, as in 1940, and some special occasions, as in 1934. On July 5, 1942, Adolf Hitler, who had seen the Oberammergau Passion Play twice, in August 1930 and August 1934, concluded that

> It is vital that the Passion Play be continued at Oberammergau; for never has the menace of Jewry been so convincingly portrayed as in this presentation of what happened in the times of the Romans. There one sees in Pontius Pilate a Roman racially and intellectually so superior, that he stands out like a firm, clean rock in the middle of the whole muck and mire of Jewry.

Even apart from Hitler's prejudicial language, is that juridical contrast factual? Was there ever a Pilate struggling for innocence and justice against implacable Jewish opposition? Indeed, from Pilate's Roman viewpoint could Jesus have ever been seen as completely innocent and unjustly accused?

Even if everything about those trials happened exactly as narrated in the gospels, it would have been as invalid to extend responsibility to all Jews of all time because of Caiaphas as to all Italians of all time because of Pilate. But, to repeat from this chapter's opening, apart from ecumenical courtesy or even post-Holocaust sensitivity, there is this fundamental question of factual accuracy. What is our best historical reconstruction of what actually happened long ago in Jerusalem amid the beauty and ambiguity of Jewish feast under Roman rule?

SEVEN

How to Bury a King

Two themes interact with one another in this final chapter. One theme is aristocratic sepulchers. Graves and tombs, sepulchers and mausoleums, death rituals and burial practices tell us about views of the afterlife, but, as anthropologists remind us, monuments for the dead are also ciphers for present social life. Archaeologists have uncovered a broad spectrum of first-century Jewish burials that not only indicate attitudes toward the afterlife, but also emphasize locations in the society. In death, perhaps even more than in life, funerary architecture and luxurious expenditure mark the deceased's status in society and distinguish between haves and have-nots, rulers and ruled. How do you bury an emperor, a king, or a high priest? Even better, how did each prepare for his own burial? We focus not so much on what their burials tell us about their views of the afterlife, but on what their monuments tells us about their kingdoms. How did they prepare for death, and how did they want to be remembered? If you were a ruler and were in charge of your own burial preparations, what would that burial announce about your kingdom?

The other theme is Jesus' sepulcher. Jerusalem, the city of holiness and peace, is also the city of division and strife. There are tensions between Christian groups atop the burial place of Jesus, within the Church of the Holy Sepulcher itself. That great shrine, built and rebuilt since the first quarter of the fourth century, is the spiritual capital of Christianity. Yet, first of all, neither Anglican Catholicism nor Protestant Christianity has an assigned place in the cenotaph of Christ. The strife that divides the church's territorial marble comes from an even earlier period in the sad history of Christian divisiveness. Next, six groups, Catholic Latins, Orthodox Greeks, Copts, Armenians, Ethiopians, and Jacobite Syrians, have divided up the church between themselves and struggle, sometimes pettily, sometimes seriously, to hold and defend their marbled turf. Finally, the most striking point is not just that they have covered over the tomb of Jesus with marble and then quarreled over its control. What is most striking is the church's very name, the Church of the Holy Sepulcher. If this is where Jesus was buried from the cross by human agency, then it is also where Jesus was raised from the dead by divine power. The former is a matter of historical debate, the latter is a matter of Christian faith. It is, in fact, the heart of Christian faith. Still, that church is called only the Holy Sepulcher and not the Blessed Resurrection. Is not that the most disconcerting element about Christianity's most sacred shrine? We know, it would seem, how to bury emperor, king, or high priest and adorn the sepulcher appropriately. But how do you bury a crucified criminal and celebrate his resurrection? What sort of place, tomb, or shrine does that?

THE MAGNIFICENT MAUSOLEUM OF AUGUSTUS

Shortly after his military victory over Mark Anthony and Cleopatra in 31 B.C.E., Octavius, the soon-to-be Augustus, commissioned the construction of his Roman mausoleum. Having visited Alexander the Great's tomb in Alexandria and anticipating the adoption in Rome of Hellenistic-style divine kingship, Augustus built a mausoleum that copied in name and shape one of the seven world wonders, the tomb of Mausolus at Halicarnassus in Asia Minor. But some forty years before his death he was not just contemplating the afterlife and preparing for his soul's eternity. At the very beginning of Augustus's reign, that mausoleum announced to his contemporaries what emperor and empire, Caesar and kingdom meant. That monument articulated three themes in the here and now.

First and quite expectedly, Augustus's mausoleum placed him atop the pinnacle of the social pyramid. No Roman family and no Roman individual had as magnificent a tomb. He began construction of his sepulcher in the Campus Martius, which was then on the outskirts of the city and where several illustrious Romans were already interred. During his lifetime Augustus systematically developed the Campus Martius from south to north, that is to say, from the city toward his mausoleum, so that, at the time of his death, it stood in a prominent and often visited spot. He enhanced the main road, which passed his tomb as it led north out of

Rome, and had civic structures for public enjoyment and benefit constructed nearby. Those included his son-in-law Agrippa's magnificent baths, the dazzling Pantheon shrine to all the gods and goddesses, and especially the *Ara Pacis,* or "Altar of Peace," which celebrated the *Pax Romana,* or "Roman Peace," Augustus had bestowed upon the empire.

Augustus was cautious and did not directly violate Roman tradition with a burial inside the city proper, yet he meticulously and steadily expanded the city toward his grave. By placing his mausoleum near the Pantheon, that equally round and marble-sheeted rotunda built as a temple to divinity, he elevated himself into the realm of the divine. The mausoleum of Augustus became, then, not just a crypt interring a corpse, however important, but a templelike public memorial honoring the divine ruler and crowning him— even in death—at the very peak of Roman society.

Second and closely related to the first point, Augustus put up a spectacular façade of monumental proportions on his sepulcher. As just noted, it approached that famous Mausoleum of Halicarnassus in shape and size. Like that more ancient tomb, it was a rotunda, rising in concentric circles, but it also integrated a garden and took on a moundlike shape, so that it was similar to earlier, traditional Etruscan mound burials around Rome. The outer cylinder had a diameter of nearly 300 feet and was an imposing 25 feet high, constructed internally of brick and concrete, but covered externally with a splendid travertine façade, which the geographer Strabo describes as "a lofty foundation of white marble." Inside and extending above the outer cylinder, cypresses and other evergreens grew on a cone-shaped mound of soil, at whose nucleus a cylindrical cone of travertine marble shot up to give it a total height of 150 feet. The top was capped with a large bronze statue of Augustus. Underneath, vaulted circular corridors and several radial chambers led to the inner sepulchral chamber, where an urn held the cremated ashes of Augustus.

Third, and perhaps most obviously, Augustus's mausoleum immortalized his legacy and dynasty in Rome. The mausoleum was not only his final resting place, but also that of his royal family and scions—he envisioned the continuity of his reign through a dynastic succession even after his own death. The long-standing ideal in the Mediterranean world was family burial. One hoped to rest in death with one's ancestors and to be remembered there by one's descendants. Augustus's nephew was the first interred there in 23 B.C.E., and the ashes of five others were deposited there before his own in 14 C.E. After him, and apart from others later,

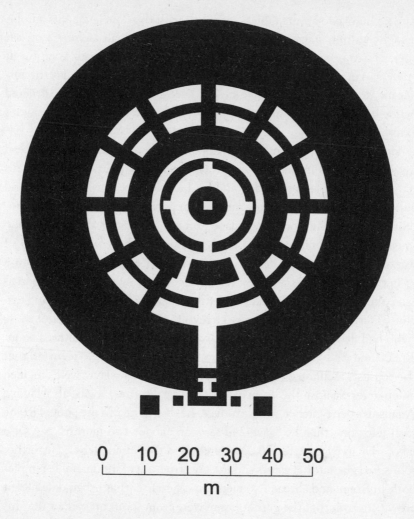

AUGUSTUS'S MAUSOLEUM IN ROME

three Julio-Claudian Caesars followed: Tiberius, Caligula, and Claudius. Some relatives were deliberately denied the privilege of family burial, shamed by exclusion even in death, and banned from the family crypt; Augustus's daughter Julia and the later emperor Nero.

Along with his family, Augustus also enshrined his legacy by fastening the so-called *Res Gestae Divi Augusti*, the "Achievements of the Divine Augustus," inside the tomb. He flanked the entrance of the mausoleum with two granite Egyptian-style obelisks, and on twin pilasters inside the

gate he hung two bronze tablets inscribed with the *Res Gestae*, his autobiography written at age sixty-six. Those Roman originals are now lost, but
copies have been recovered from the Temple of Rome and Augustus at
Ancyra in northern Galatia, now Ankara in central Turkey. Today the earlier mentioned *Ara Pacis Augustae* has been relocated and reconstructed
beside his mausoleum, and the *Res Gestae* are inscribed around the altar's
external base.

How did Augustus want his kingdom and rule to be remembered? Read
his achievements in his own words. He lauded his military victories, his
establishment of law and order, and his benevolence. His many wars and
battles, bloody and violent, are sanitized as pacifying the seas, keeping stability at home, and spreading peace abroad: "As victor I spared all who
sought pardon as citizens. The foreign nations—those which in safety I
was able to forgive—I preferred to preserve rather than to kill." His sense
of law included three censuses: the first counted 4,063,000 Roman citizens, the next 4,233,000, and the third 4,937,000. He kept order and dispensed justice by suppressing a slave revolt, of which he says that of those
"who had fled their masters and . . . had taken up arms, I captured about
30,000 and gave them to their masters for punishment." No mention that
the censuses facilitated taxation, no mention that the slaves were crucified
as enemies against the Roman order. The bronze tablets also lauded
Augustus's benevolence and patronage: he distributed to the poor of Rome
cash gifts; one time he "gave 240 *sesterces* [about two months' pay for a
laborer] man by man, to 320,000 members of the urban plebs." He further
sponsored gladiatorial games and the construction of innumerable temples
both in Rome and abroad. No mention, of course, that urban dole meant
crowd control, that the gifts at home were from spoils abroad, or that his
own statue was placed in imperial temples around the empire.

His achievements, in his own words, were permanently inscribed in
bronze and affixed to the entrance of his monumental and splendid mausoleum. This imperial monarch wanted later generations to understand his
legacy correctly, that is, as he wrote it, as he sought to control the future
even in death. That is how you bury a king.

THE DESERT TOMB OF HEROD

After but also imitative of his patron Augustus, Herod the Great built his
own mausoleum well before his death. It was no mere Augustan copy, but
bore the marks of his own kingdom-building enterprise, Roman in minia-

ture, Jewish in approach, but uniquely Herodian in final synthesis. Every bit a sepulcher for the afterlife, it was at the same time a fortress to protect his present life, a pleasure palace to celebrate it, and a signal to Jerusalem about who was in charge at society's pinnacle.

As seen earlier, Herod the Great named construction projects, from Caesarea and its harbor Sebastos, through the city of Sebaste, to the Jerusalem fortress Antonia, in order to honor Roman power and protection. He also named places after family members—the city of Antipatris after his father, the hilltop fortress Cypros after his mother, and the Jerusalem tower Phasaelis after his brother. But one site he named after himself, calling it the Herodion. Josephus tells us that he built it for his burial on the very spot in the Judean wilderness, some 8 miles south of Jerusalem, where he had earlier fought off Parthian and rival Hasmonean soldiers on his flight to Arabia in 40 B.C.E. With his family escaping to Masada and himself on his way to solicit Nabatean aid, he was attacked by the forces of his adversary Antigonus, and, according to Josephus, he "routed and crushed [them] as if he were in no such helpless and difficult position but were excellently prepared for war and had a great advantage. And later when he became king, he built a wonderful palace on the spot" (*Jewish Antiquities* 14.359–60).

The Herodion was a two-part complex, with a fortress-palace on the hilltop and a palace-garden-pool complex on the plain. It is a fitting tribute to his personality and kingdom building, combining the architectural themes seen in his other projects. He subdued and conquered the topography, on the one hand, by raising a massive artificial mound for his rotunda-like fortress, which he "rounded off in the shape of a breast," as Josephus puts it. On the other hand, he leveled the area to its north and created a plateau for a pool-and-garden complex. And, of course, he built an aqueduct to turn the barren wilderness into a desert oasis. The elevated hilltop fortress made the Herodion a prominent landmark and emphasized the eminent position of Herod himself. By raising the artificial mound, he not only gave its visitors a panoramic view, but perhaps more important, he allowed the monument to be seen from nearby Jerusalem. Josephus says he intended this personal memorial "for all so see." He even cut down a hill east of the Herodion to aid the new mound's identification from afar and to make it look higher than it really was.

Visibility was also heightened by the shape and façade of the fortress. It was round and built with two concentric circular walls, the inner with a

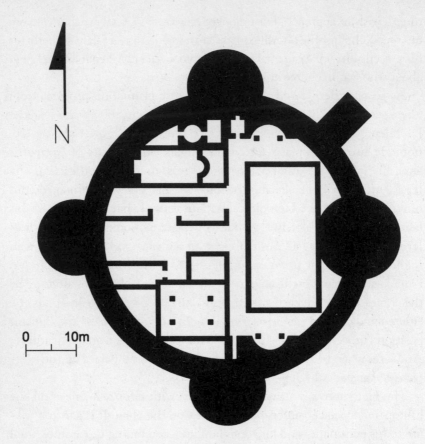

0   10m

THE FORTRESS-TOWER AT THE HERODION (AFTER NETZER)

diameter of 175 feet and the outer with one of some 200 feet, and held four towers, one in each cardinal direction, with the eastern one towering cylinder-like above the rest. The rotunda-like shape of the Herodion soared above the Judean hills and was made more noticeable by its façade, which was either smoothly polished in appearance like the Temple Mount or, possibly, plastered and whitewashed. Although Josephus describes the prominent and massive "white marble" steps leading up to the fortress, no marble has been found by its long-time excavator and veteran Israeli archaeologist, Ehud Netzer. Even if Herod brought no marble into the desert, and even if Josephus did not use the term in a technically correct sense, Herod finished his monument with a glistening façade.

In many ways, Herod's mausoleum copied that of Augustus. It was rotunda-like and prominently visible and had greenery as a prominent part of its design. But Herod did not slavishly copy Augustus. Instead, he built the Herodion in his unique style, making it suitable to his own unique kingdom. It typified Herod's career. It commemorated not a great military victory, but a bloody fight for personal and political survival as he fled a civil war for Roman aid. And though the mausoleum had a rotunda, it needed to be a fortress to protect him from a popular uprising, and perhaps, therefore, he also built it a safe distance from the crowds in Jerusalem. In fact the tomb itself has not been found; it may not have been in the upper fortress, but in the lower complex, where a rectangular mausoleum-like building at the end of a long corridor was built akin to monumental Jewish burials in Jerusalem's Kidron Valley, which had pyramidal and conical roofs. But everywhere around it, Herod built pools and gardens with this life in mind. Finally, unlike Augustus, Herod was not buried with his family, many of whom he killed out of jealousy or paranoia. His surviving sons were not united with him in death: Archaelaus was stripped of his ethnarchy and exiled to Gaul, Antipas was stripped of his tetrarchy and exiled to Spain, and Philip was buried in his own territory to the north.

Josephus records that on his deathbed Herod ordered many eminent Judeans locked up, commanding his sister to have them all killed upon his own passing, so that he could be mourned even if "on other people's account." Then, he said, "all Judea and every family will weep for me— they can't help it." His sister rescinded the order, but his son Archaelaus gave him a regal burial. The corpse of Herod the Great, King of the Jews, was carried on a golden bier studded with precious stones and draped in royal purple; it was accompanied by his kinsmen and mercenaries from Thracia, Gaul, and Germany, and it was brought to the Herodion for burial. There were also five hundred servants carrying spices. Those, of course, were to counter the smell of decay. That is how you bury a king.

THE SPLENDID OSSUARY OF CAIAPHAS

Primary and Secondary Burial.   Unlike the Roman tradition of cremation, which was one of the common customs alongside interring the deceased in body-sized sarcophagi, Jewish tradition strictly forbade the burning of bodies. Instead, Jewish burial practices included the long-standing Semitic tradition of secondary burial, in which the body was laid in the tomb for about a year and then the bones were gathered up and

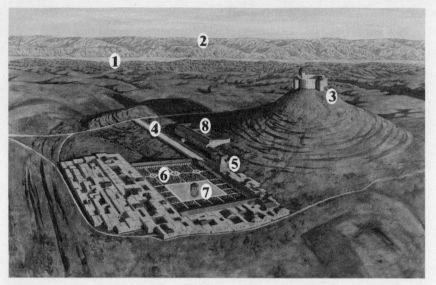

RECONSTRUCTION OF THE HERODION.   *Herod the Great, King of the Jews, built his monumental tomb complex some 8 miles south of Jerusalem in the Judean wilderness. Overlooking the Dead Sea (1) and modern-day Jordan (2), the Herodion was a memorial that also combined elements of a fortress and a pleasure palace. The upper fortress (3) capped an artificial mound and resembled the mausoleum of Caesar Augustus in its rotunda-like form. However, Herod's tomb was likely located in the lower complex, at the end of a long corridor (4) in a more traditional Semitic style. (5). The Herodion offered Herod safety and enjoyment long before his death, as gardens (6), a pool and gazebo (7), a lower palace (8), and quarters for servants and guests had transformed the barren desert into a plush oasis resort.*

redeposited. For nearly a millennium the custom had been to place those bones along with others from the family or clan in a pit or cavity, called a charnel pile, within the burial chamber; hence the biblical desire and phrase "to be gathered with my fathers." But around Jerusalem by the first century, bones were collected in ossuaries, those bone boxes discussed in Chapter 1 and made of the same soft limestone or chalk as those stone vessels described in Chapter 5.

At the time of Jesus, bodies in the primary burial phase were laid out in one of two ways. The most common was to place them in deep burial niches, fingerlike shafts called *kokhim* that protruded some 6 feet from the chamber into the walls, were about 1¹/₂ feet wide, and commonly had an arched ceiling. The other way was to place them on wide indented shelves, called *arcosolia*, cut into the walls of the chambers, some 6 feet wide and 2 feet deep. In the secondary burial phase, during the first century, the bones were less frequently collected in charnel piles, but were almost always deposited in ossuaries, those small-lidded and often decorated boxes just long enough to hold a femur and other large bones. About a quarter of the thousand or so known bone boxes were inscribed with the names of the interred, and many of the excavated ossuaries were found placed back in one of the *kokhim* shafts or atop one of the *arcosolia* ledges.

Why did the practice of ossuaries develop then and there, around Jerusalem and in the first century? It is possible that burial in ossuaries reflects the widespread theological belief in bodily resurrection among some Jews, a belief especially advocated by the Pharisees. It is also possible that depositing individual skeletons in discreet containers reflects the heightened psychological sense of individuality of the Hellenistic Age. It is even more likely that the social and political pressures felt by Jews living under Roman rule also affected their burial practices. Just as the stone vessels and *miqwaoth* seen in Chapter 5 can been seen as identity markers, and purity as a form of resistance, so, too, enclosing the bones in ossuaries might have been a way for Jews to reinforce their social boundaries even after death. Ossuaries not only very clearly distinguish Jewish from Roman burial, they mark in a very concrete sense this boundary and protect the individual even in death from the disorderly outside world. But it is hard to press the archaeological evidence in those directions and, below, we consider objections to some of those interpretations.

It is perhaps easier to see the broader pattern that accounts for ossuaries in the environs of Jerusalem during and after the reign of Herod the Great. Look at the socioeconomic factors at work in the adoption of ossuaries. The economic activity accompanying Herod's commercial kingdom dramatically increased the population of Jerusalem, making burial space near the city sparser. Burial chambers could no longer be added as easily in the crowded necropolises. Ossuaries saved space as skeletal remains could be packaged in boxes and reinserted into the shafts.

But more important, Herod's Temple project not only brought an influx of funds into the city, it also trained a professional cadre of local stonemasons. In several tombs, the abandonment of charnel pits and the addition of ossuaries can be dated to a decade or two before the common era, the very time when construction of the Temple began. The decorations on the more elegant ossuaries are almost always those same geometric and floral motifs seen in the Temple's architecture, with rosettes particularly common. Further, architectural motifs like columns, colonnades, and margin-and-boss faces resemble those of the Temple, and imitative ashlar walls look like those of the Palatial Mansion, all elements seen in the preceding chapter. Two inscriptions are more intricately linked to the Temple. In an elaborate and wealthy burial chamber on Mount Scopus an ossuary was found inscribed in Greek with "Nicanor of Alexandria who made the gates," presumably the very donor who funded the Temple's Nicanor Gates mentioned in literary sources. Another more modest burial in Givat Hamivtar contained the ossuary of one "Shimon the Temple-Builder," presumably one of the foremen or masons employed on the Temple.

We conclude that belief or theology alone cannot explain the phenomenon of ossuaries. Ossuaries *may* reflect a common belief in the resurrection, a heightened sense of individualism, or a subconscious desire to maintain identity and be protected in death, but their use was made possible by the Herodian-initiated Temple economy in Jerusalem and a well-trained stonemasons guild. And their distribution was not common but more upper class. A plain ossuary would not have been too expensive—an inscription prices one at a *drachma* and four *obols*, or just over a day's wages for a skilled laborer, and the style, decorations, and workmanship of the James ossuary in no way imply that extraordinary wealth was available. The more prohibitive factor was the plot of land for the burial chamber. Not everyone could afford a funerary chamber with primary burial in shafts and secondary burial in ossuaries.

A brief cautionary aside on ossuaries and Hellenistic-style individuality: very few of the ossuaries found contained a single individual—the vast majority held several skeletons. The inscriptions tell us that family burial was still the Jewish norm, and endearing family terms like the Aramaic *Abba* ("Daddy") or *Emma* ("Mother") are commonly scratched on ossuaries. In fact, most of the names are noted by some family relation, not only by the frequent and obvious Aramaic *bar* x or "son of x" that indicates paternal lineage, but by a host of other family relations such as "wife of," "father of," or "mother of." Though the formula of the James ossuary—*akhui di*, "brother of"—occurs on only one other ossuary, more frequently brothers were interred together and identified with the inscription "sons of x"; in one case Mathai and Simon, brothers and sons of Yair, were buried together even though Mathai's wife, Maryame, was laid to rest separately. Charnel rooms or pits with anonymous multiple interments were abandoned, but

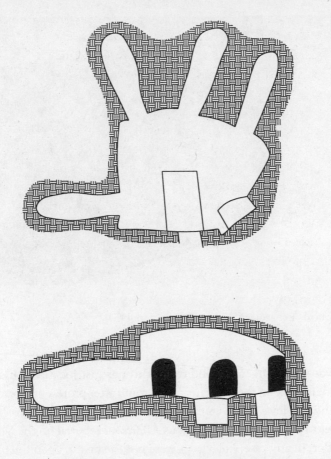

THE CAIAPHAS FAMILY BURIAL CHAMBER (AFTER GREENHUT)

ossuaries do not imply an absolute individuality, since individuals in death were still related to their family and combined together in bone boxes.

The Caiaphas Ossuary.   In November 1990, an accidental but spectacular discovery in a Jerusalem cave turned out to be the final resting place of Caiaphas, the high priest who participated in the crucifixion of Jesus. We consider his ossuary and tomb in some detail not just because it is a direct link to a prominent figure in the gospels, but because it is so typical of upper-class burial in first-century Jerusalem.

The tomb was discovered during work on a park and roadway in the Peace Forest, south of Jerusalem's Old City and facing Mount Zion. Its

THE JAMES OSSUARY
(courtesy Biblical Archaeology Society, Washington, DC)

chief excavator, Zvi Greenhut, and the anthropologist Joe Zias could not complete their work on the contents of the tomb after protest and pressure by ultraorthodox Jews led to its resealing and its human remains being handed over to the Ministry of Religious Affairs for reburial on the Mount of Olives. But, in any case, excavators were not the first to open the tomb. Sometime in antiquity grave robbers looted it and took everything of value, and modern construction workers also moved some of the ossuaries, leaving only two of the twelve ossuaries undisturbed in their original place. The rest had been broken or scattered inside.

The single burial chamber had been cut into the soft limestone hill in the Early Roman Period, and four *kokhim* shafts extended fingerlike from the chamber. The chamber had been unevenly cut in the crumbly rock on all but two sides, which were more smoothly worked. A low and narrow rectangular opening forced entrants to crawl into the chamber, but, inside, a depression was cut to create standing room under the chamber's 5½-foot-high ceiling. A repository pit had been cut in the eastern corner, very likely as a charnel pile. The four *kokhim* shafts extended some 6 feet out from the chamber; only in one shaft were two ossuaries undisturbed, and one of those was that of the high priest Caiaphas.

THE CAIAPHAS OSSUARY
(collection of the Israel Antiquities Authority, photograph copyright the Israel Museum, Jerusalem)

Most of the ossuaries were decorated and many were inscribed with typical Jewish names. The decorations were professional and well executed, and the ossuary inscribed with the name Yehosef bar Caiapha was of exceptional beauty, the finest in the tomb, and even one of the finest ever found. It exceeded, in each and every way, that simple and slightly trapezoidal ossuary of James with its crude and faded rosette. The front of the ossuary was framed by branch patterns on the top and both sides and displayed two circles formed of six rosettes each. The rosettes are very delicately made, with unique and alternating petal-and-whirl combinations, and a few of them were painted orange. The lid was vaulted and decorated in front with ashlarlike zigzag frames and had also been painted with a slightly orange wash.

However intricately fine were the decorations of the ossuaries, the inscriptions had been crudely etched onto their sides, perhaps by family members, and likely with the two iron nails found inside one of the ossuaries and one of the *kokhim* shafts. The writing was certainly not the work of professionally trained masons or scribes, but had been etched onto the ossuaries after they had been deposited inside the shafts. In some cases they were written from bottom to top instead of right to left by a hand wedged between the ossuary and wall. The names served to remind survivors whom they had interred and where. The names were etched in a cursive Jewish script similar to that on other first-century ossuaries. The women's names were quite common at the time, Miriam (Greek, Maria) and Shalom (Greek, Salome), as were the men's, Shimon (Greek, Simeon) and Yehosef (Greek, Joseph). But the rare Aramaic nickname Caiapha (Greek, Caiaphas), otherwise unattested on ossuaries or any inscriptions, was written three times in this tomb, twice specified as Yehosef bar Caiapha (Greek, Joseph son of Caiaphas), the high priest so-named in Josephus. It contained bones from six different skeletons, two infants, a child between two and five years, a male teenager, an adult woman, and a male around sixty years old. There should be no doubt that the chamber was the resting place of the family of the high priest Caiaphas named in the gospels for his role in the crucifixion, and it's very likely that the elderly man's bones were those of Caiaphas himself. That certainty, by the way, stands in stark contrast to the questionable James-Joseph-Jesus ossuary, and is due not so much to the statistical rarity of the name Caiaphas but to the archaeological integrity of the find.

Three final thoughts on Caiaphas's burial. First, in spite of the ossuary's beauty, the tomb chamber itself is relatively modest. This serves as a reminder that Herod and the Roman procurators advanced certain priests into the high-priesthood above more popular and prominent families. We know that Caiaphas left his family home in Beth Meqoshesh, where presumably most of his family remained and where the family tomb was located, and married the daughter of Annas, who was both the high priest from 6 to 15 C.E. and the founder of the Annanide high-priestly dynasty, which dominated much of pre-70 C.E. Jerusalem. Joseph Caiaphas advanced not through heredity but through marriage and, though well connected, may not have come from a very wealthy family himself. But he had acquired enough personal wealth to purchase one of the most ornate ossuaries ever discovered, even though the outward and publicly visible monument was less prominent.

Second, in spite of difficult working conditions and ancient looting, which left skeletal remains strewn about, Joe Zias was able to identify sixty-three individual skeletons in the chamber. The demographic distribution of the dead is a grim reminder that even the wealthy were not impervious to rampant disease and infant mortality. Take a look at the age distribution of the people buried in the chamber:

Age	Skeletal Remains
0–1 years	10
2–5 years	16
6–12 years	14
13–18 years	3
19–25 years	1
26–39 years	1
40+	6
adult (age unknown)	13

Some 40 percent never made it past their fifth birthday and 63 percent never reached puberty. The death rates are shocking by today's standards, but common in Jerusalem and throughout the Roman Empire.

Third, a final and perplexing issue arises from the tomb. Think about how hard it is to reconstruct the *beliefs* of Caiaphas and his family from the traces their burial *practices* left in the ground. Consider these two ironies. Remember that the high priests at the time of Jesus were Sadducees, who, unlike the Pharisees, did not believe in the resurrection of the dead. Another ossuary of a known Sadducean family has been found, inscribed with "Yehochana daughter of Yehochanan, son of Thophlos, the high priest." Were ossuaries really intended to collect and preserve the bones for the resurrection? We think it unlikely that Caiaphas purchased an ossuary in anticipation of the resurrection, but we know for sure that he adopted the common burial practice among the wealthy Jerusalemites and did so in grand style. Furthermore, a bronze coin of King Agrippa I (42–43 C.E.) was found inside one woman's skull from the Caiaphas family tomb, having dropped from mouth into cranium after her flesh decayed. This was a long-standing custom in the Greek world and is also sometimes found in Jewish burials. Coins were placed in the mouth or hand of the deceased as payment to the ferryman Charon, who brought the souls of the dead across the River Styx. Had the high-priestly family adopted a pagan belief? Hardly. More likely, a family member had simply adopted a popular custom of the Hellenistic world.

In any case, a splendid ossuary in a cut-chamber was far beneath what an Augustus or a Herod had designed for memory and mausoleum. Still, their bones have not survived and those of Caiaphas probably have. That is at least one way to bury a high priest.

THE HOLY SEPULCHER OF JESUS

But not every family in first-century Jerusalem had a parcel of land with a burial chamber, nor could many afford an ossuary. For every one of the hundreds of ossuary and *kokhim* burials examined by archaeologists, we must assume thousands of bodies were deposited in shallow graves without any protection from decomposition and disintegration in the soil.

The Burial of Ordinary People

In spite of their unlikely survival, many simple graves have been found around Jerusalem. In the Jerusalem suburb of Beit Safafa, only a few miles farther outside the first-century city than Caiaphas's tomb, fifty simple vertical-shaft graves were found. These were accidentally discovered during road construction; they would otherwise have escaped notice since nothing like a tombstone or even a heap of stones marks them as burials. No inscriptions were found anywhere, and nothing of value was found inside. These were rectangular shafts sunk between 5 and 7 feet into the ground, with a lengthy burial niche at the bottom where a body could be laid out horizontally, similar to those found in the cemetery at Qumran. The niche was then covered with a limestone slab and the shaft filled in with rocks and dirt. Almost all of the burials had one body in each, though a few had two-storied niches. Of the fifty tombs only one contained a rather plain and simple ossuary. Of the identifiable bones of forty-seven individuals, forty-two were from adults and only five were from children between five and eighteen years of age. One suspects that infants who had died prematurely were simply cast aside in even less permanent graves.

Even simpler burials for the poor have been found around Jerusalem. Shallow field graves have been discovered at several sites just west of the Old City, some were cut about a foot into bedrock and then covered with soil, others simply used natural depressions in the rock. At Mamilla, fifteen rock-cut troughs covered with stone slabs protected the bodies and those were accompanied by the very smallest of Hasmonean coins and glass vials from the first century C.E. Also, hollows dug into the ground had been lined with rocks and covered with slabs in the Hinnon Valley. Again, nothing notable marked them, and nothing valuable was interred within them.

Leave Jerusalem and return briefly to Galilee. There several first-century burials have been found, not nearly as many as around Jerusalem, but enough to sketch this pattern. There are, around villages like Nazareth and Cana, several *kokhim*-shaft burial chambers, many of which were shielded with the round rolling stones or square sealing stones typical for Jewish burials in Jerusalem. But most were crudely hewn into the side of hills and not finely smoothed. More important, within first-century contexts in Galilee, ossuaries, and therefore ossuary inscriptions, are rare. Instead, charnel piles or repositories were used. This suggests, once again, not a distinct Galilean burial practice as much as the lack of wealth and the absence of a local stone-carving industry in Galilee.

The Burial of Crucified Criminals

What, finally, about crucifixion? How do you bury the body of a crucified victim? Keep in mind that crucifixion was not the punishment of citizens and aristocrats, but of slaves and servants, peasants and bandits. Those former cut chambers and left ossuaries all around Jerusalem, and those latter who died of natural causes dug shallow and elusive graves, but the thousands of victims of crucifixion left no traces save one. The norm was to let crucifieds rot on the cross or be cast aside for carrion. The point was to deter lower-class violations of Roman law and order.

Josephus speaks of thousands crucified by the Romans around first-century Jerusalem, from two thousand after the death of Herod the Great in 4 B.C.E. to five hundred a day after the destruction of the Temple in 70 C.E. But those are textual references, and we have archaeological evidence of only one single victim, found in an ossuary in the northern Jerusalem suburb of Givat Hamivtar. Vassilios Tzaferis, of the Israel Antiquities Authority, excavated several burial caves there in June 1968. Within a first-century rock-hewn tomb, within one of the five ossuaries, were the skeletal remains of two men and a young child. The right heel bone of one of the men, 5 feet, 5 inches tall and in his mid-twenties, had been pierced by a 4^1/$_2$-inch nail at whose head was still attached a small olivewood board. The man's legs had been spread and nailed to the side of the upright beam, and the wooden board nailed to the outside of his heel to prevent him from tearing his leg off the nail's small head. But the nail had bent as it was hammered into the hard, knotty upright beam and could not be removed after his death. So a piece of the beam was cut off, and ankle, nail, and wooden board remained together after his body was taken down from the cross, and some time later his bones were deposited in the ossuary with heel, nail, and wood still connected to one another.

Because there was no evidence of violent trauma to the forearm or the hand's metacarpals, the victim had presumably been tied to the crossbar

Copy of a Crucified Ankle
(collection of the Israel Antiquities Authority, photograph copyright the Israel
Museum, Jerusalem)

instead of being nailed to it as crucifixion is popularly imagined. His legs
had also not been broken to accelerate his death. Without that, the victim
died a slow and painful death by asphyxiation, as the diaphragm's muscles
slowly gave out and the victim stopped breathing. Scratched onto the
ossuary's side was the name of the deceased, Yehochanan, now known as
the Crucified Man of Givat Hamivtar.

Archaeologists had thus the coincidental discovery of a crucified victim
who in spite of crucifixion received a family burial. They also had the good
fortune of recovering that one rusty nail, which had bent going into a
gnarled olivewood beam and was still in his heel. But, despite his terrible
death, Yehochanan had the good fortune of coming from a wealthy family
(as the ossuary indicates) and presumably from a well-connected one that
was allowed to recover his body from the cross. Keep in mind how exceptional were both his fate and his discovery. As a rule, crucified victims were
left unburied. Without minimizing the extended and excruciating pain,
which was temporal, the shame of nonburial, which was eternal, was
equally feared. In the ancient mind, the supreme horror of crucifixion was

to lose public mourning, to forfeit proper burial, to lie separate from one's ancestors forever, and to have no place where bones remained, spirits hovered, and descendants came to eat with the dead. That is how Jesus died. According to the gospels Pilate affixed atop his cross a plaque inscribed *Jesus of Nazareth King of the Jews*. What, if any, kind of burial did Jesus receive? What, eventually, did his sepulcher look like? Did burial and tomb show clearly how he differed from Augustus, Herod, or even Caiaphas? And were they as appropriate to the Kingdom of God as each of theirs was to the Kingdom of Rome they had created, copied, or obeyed?

An Appropriate Mausoleum for Jesus?

The Burial. The burial of Jesus in John's gospel is appropriate not only for a royal funeral, but even for a divine one. But that is, far from the first layer of the historical Jesus, the third level of the third layer, the creative imagination of the gospel of John. What the first layer actually was, may be too horrible for followers then as well as now to acknowledge. According to John 19:41, "there was a garden in the place where he was crucified, and in the garden there was a new tomb in which no one had ever been laid." A new tomb in a garden setting befits a monarch, as with the kings of Judah "in the garden of Uzza," according to 2 Kings 21:18, 26, or Augustus beneath that artificial garden of cypresses atop the Julio-Claudian mausoleum, or Herod the Great next to that pool and garden of the Herodion. But Jesus was also buried, according to John 19:39, by Nicodemus using "a mixture of myrrh and aloes, weighing about a hundred [Roman] pounds." Calculated as a volume measurement, 4 gallons of ointment would leave the body swamped in liquid spices. Calculated as a weight measurement, 75 pounds would leave the body smothered in dry spices. In either calculation, the amount is deliberately excessive. (Strange, however, to emphasize spices, since burial spices were there to offset the smell of decomposition.) John intends to emphasize that Jesus received not just a royal, but a divine burial. How, that gospel asks, do you bury not just royalty, but divinity? And what would be a proper mausoleum?

Herod the Great died in 4 B.C.E., Caesar Augustus in 14 C.E., and Jesus was crucified around 30 C.E. Some three centuries later and twelve years after Constantine the Great took control of the entire Roman Empire, the first Christian archaeological expedition was launched to find the site of Jesus' resurrection. Led by local Christian authorities to a pagan temple, imperial officials ordered "the building to the impure demon called Aphrodite, a dark shrine of lifeless offerings," knocked down, and then proceeded to dig through the earthen fill atop which the temple platform had been built. Eusebius, the bishop of Caesarea and later biographer of Constantine, describes the work carried out under imperial Constantinian decree: "as layer after layer of the subsoil came into view, the venerable and most holy memorial of the Savior's resurrection, beyond all our hopes, came into view" (*Life of Constantine* 3.38).

The Site.   Did they find the site of Jesus' burial? We think that along with St. Peter's House in Capernaum, the Holy Sepulcher in Jerusalem is one of the few Christian holy sites with any credibility. The Constantinian church may well sit atop the site of Jesus' crucifixion and the spot where his body was left. It was inside the third northern wall of Jerusalem, built by Herod Agrippa I (41–44 C.E.) to the north, but outside the second wall, which demarcated the city at the time of Jesus. It was, as Jews would demand of both crucifixion and burial, outside the first-century city. And those Constantinian archaeologists did eventually find the tombs of a cemetery when they dug beneath the temple of Aphrodite. The layers peeled away by Constantine have been corroborated by recent stratigraphic excavations. Walls were found from a monumental structure dating to the time of Hadrian and that was probably Aphrodite's temple. Underneath them tombs have been discovered from the first century and earlier. Before that the rocky area was uninhabited and served as a quarry.

Constantine's Church of the Holy Sepulcher is atop a cemetery and very likely near where Jesus was crucified. It may even accurately mark the spot, but we ask whether it adequately preserves the memory. We are here less interested in whether this was the spot of Jesus' burial than we are in what was done with the spot of his burial. Think of the meaning of his life, death, and resurrection, and then read the following from the letter Constantine sent to Makarios, bishop of Jerusalem:

It is my wish, then, that you should be especially convinced of this, which I suppose is clear to everyone, that of all things it is my chief concern how we may *splendidly adorn* with buildings that sacred place which, under divine direction, I freed. . . . Not only shall this basilica be the *finest* in the world, but that the details also shall be such that all the most *beautiful* structures in every city may be sur-

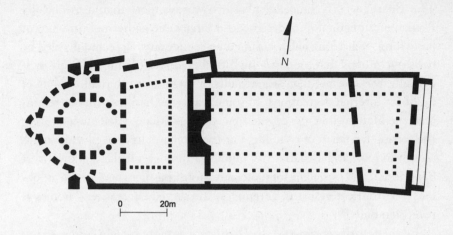

N

0   20m

THE CHURCH OF THE HOLY SEPULCHER (AFTER GIBSON)

passed by it. . . . As for the *columns* and *marbles*, have a care to tell us in writing, after you have inspected the plan, whatever you judge to be most *precious* and serviceable, so that those materials, of whatever sort and in whatever quantity, may be procured from every quarter. (Eusebius, *Life of Constantine* 3.29–32, italics added)

The temple to Aphrodite was torn down and the one-time quarry that had become both execution site and cemetery was transformed into a magnificent sacred precinct. The Church of the Holy Sepulcher was built with four interconnected structural elements from east to west: an *Atrium* forecourt; a basilica called the *Martyrium*; a court known as the Holy Garden, containing the rock of *Golgotha* protruding from the ground; and finally the colonnaded rotunda called the *Anastasis*, encasing the tomb of Jesus itself.

What do we know of the complex? Much can be pieced together from early-twentieth-century architectural surveys, from limited late-twentieth-century archaeological probes, from the depiction in the sixth-century mosaic Madaba Map in Jordan, and from descriptions by Eusebius and early pilgrims. To understand the complex, we take a close look at two of the four architectural elements commissioned by Constantine, the inclusion of a basilica in the complex and the construction of a rotunda over the crypt.

The Basilica.   Technically, a basilica was no more than a specifically Roman architectural form designed for large civic gatherings. In its most basic form, it is a long hall focusing on a semicircular apse and divided by rows of columns that support a high timbered and tiled roof. That, incidentally, was cheaper than stone vaults or arches, and thus allowed more funds for internal decorations. In some ways, the basilica's format resembled the Hellenistic city's covered but open porticoes (*stoa*), which were the setting for much of civic life, but the Roman city moved them completely indoors and used them for public gatherings, regular markets (as at Sepphoris), and especially for judicial sessions. Basilicas also served as lobbies next to theaters, baths, or temples, and served elite citizens' homes as reception halls.

By the fourth century C.E., the basilica was more closely connected to its name as a *royal building*. Leave the Jewish homelands and travel across the Mediterranean and over the Alps to Roman Trier on the German Mosel, seat of Constantine as Caesar of the divided Roman Empire before his victory in 312 and before the Edict of Milan in 313, which declared Christianity an acceptable state religion. Between 305 and 312 Constantine built there an enormous basilica adjoining his palace, still standing 100 feet high today. Its hall's width is 100 feet and is cut by two rows of columns, and its length is 200 feet and terminates in an apse. High-set windows let in ample light, which radiated off walls that were once multicolored with marble inlays and glass-tessaraed mosaics and glistened off black-and-white slabs of marble pavement. There, Constantine sat on the *sedes iustitiae*, the "seat of justice," where as divine majesty he received homage and as law incarnate he dispensed justice.

From Augustus to Constantine, the basilica had developed from a simple structure for public gatherings into a powerful instrument of imperial politico-architectural propaganda. It encapsulated the splendor of Rome and the divinity of its Caesar. Inside its decorated walls justice was dispensed, commercial activities conducted, and public edicts issued under the watchful eye of the emperor in the apse, either in person, by representative, or in effigy. At the very pinnacle of society, emperors required official buildings that had to fit the grandeur and splendor of their position.

This setting never divided between Caesar and God, state and religion, and as a sanctuary of God on earth, the basilica effectively obliterated any boundaries between the sacred and the profane, civic and personal, judicial and commercial. After centuries of the Roman emperor cult and by the time of Constantine, the presence of the emperor in person, through a representative, or by representation had become the characteristic feature of the basilica. This was Constantine's choice for a church model when he made Christianity an acceptable and imperially sponsored religion. By 320 he completed the Lateran Basilica in Rome, today known as San Giovanni, which under Constantine became the throne hall for Christ *basileus*, Christ the King. And, then, in 325–26 he began construction on a new basilica as part of the Holy Sepulcher in Jerusalem.

This basilica, what Eusebius calls the *Martyrium*, was almost 200 feet long and 130 feet wide with a double set of colonnades lining each side of the nave. Galleries on either side provided additional space for crowds to stand and gaze at the apse, which was unusual in that it extended the height of the basilica to enhance the acoustics and amplify prayers or hymns through the entire structure. The apse was surrounded by twelve marble colonnettes on which stood silver bowls donated by Constantine himself. Windows high atop the side walls cast light on the coffered and gilded ceiling, the walls' colorful glass-tessaraed mosaics, marble revetments, and gold-bordered silken textiles, a foretaste of heaven according to some pilgrims, but perhaps too shiny, garish, and kitschy for modern sensibilities.

The Rotunda. The focal point of the Constantinian complex was the rotunda encasing the Holy Sepulcher itself. To construct around it, the sloping bedrock had to be cut and leveled, and even the knoll in which the cave's original *kokhim* shafts or *arcosolia* shelves were cut had been chiseled away so that only the ledge on which Jesus' body allegedly lay remained; all else had been cut to a lower level. An imposing colonnaded rotunda called the *Anastasis*, Greek for "resurrection," was then constructed around the tomb's shelf.

The focal point of the rotunda was the site of Jesus' resurrection. Tossed aside were elements of a pagan temple above that Jewish tomb and quarried away were rocks beside and below it. Around it, in circular arrangement, twelve columns were interspersed in threes between three pillars that held up the high domed roof. The inner concentric circle surrounding the sepulcher had a diameter of nearly 70 feet, and around it the portico added another 16 feet on all sides. Two of the large columns have survived to this day, each nearly 4 feet in diameter. Large portions of the circular

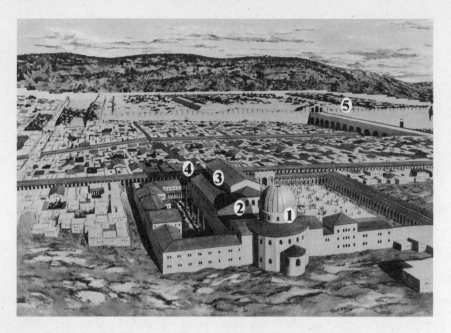

RECONSTRUCTION OF THE CHURCH OF THE HOLY SEPULCHER.   *The Church of the Holy Sepulcher, traditional site of Jesus' crucifixion, burial, and resurrection, was the dominant feature on Jerusalem's landscape after the fourth century* C.E. *The four-part structure consisted of a rotunda built over the tomb of Jesus (1) called the* Anastasis, *Greek for "resurrection," an atrium around the rock of Calvary, or Golgotha (2), an enormous basilica called the* Martyrium *(3), and a forecourt behind the basilica that opened onto the cardo (4). Built by Constantine the Great with imperial and personal finances, the church was to be the most beautiful public structure in the new Christian empire. In the background the remains of the Jewish Temple Mount (5), atop which a pagan temple had been built in the second century and then dismantled, were intentionally left dilapidated and abandoned as a sign of Christian victory over both Judaism and paganism.*

portico's external walls likewise stand today; one of the three walls of the apse is 35 feet high, and still visible are the dowel holes in which marble slabs were hung. Read Eusebius again on the rotunda: "Royal generosity made it radiant with all kinds of adornment, as if this was the chief part of the whole. He embellished the holy cave with choice columns and with profuse decoration" (*Life of Constantine* 3:34–39).

The rotunda was much like the mausoleum of Augustus and resembled even more so the one Constantine later built for himself in Constantinople. But note this significant difference between Jesus' and Augustus's sepulcher: the *Anastasis* rotunda was roofed with timber and tile, like contemporary basilicas, which could be held up by slender walls. No massive walls supporting arches or vaults were needed. That was not just a point of architectural minutiae, since narrower walls opened more space and created the wide outer portico and roomier inner sanctum around the crypt. This accommodated large visiting crowds of pilgrims to circle around the crypt and enter or exit at will.

The Question. Centuries later, therefore, after the Roman Empire became a Christian one, Constantine's marble church fulfilled John's gospel story. On the one hand, it seems unfair even to hint at criticism for such an action. That is how one buries a king or, at least and however belatedly, that is how one commemorates and celebrates the site of burial, the place of sepulcher, and Constantine's rotunda did not just celebrate the burial, but the resurrection of Jesus. On the other hand, and leaving aside how the present church is divided up among opposing Christian groups, there is still this question. Why should Christianity's central shrine be named for the Holy Sepulcher and not for the Blessed Resurrection? And, since that question is not just about a name or a title, we rephrase it like this. What is the proper sepulcher for one believed by Christians to have been raised by God from the dead? If we know full well how to celebrate a human king's burial, how does one celebrate a divine king's resurrection? Or, finally, what does resurrection mean?

THE JEWISH RESURRECTION OF JESUS

Anyone who reads the gospel stories about Easter Sunday is struck by their diversity on several fronts. First, there are no risen apparitions in Mark, but several in Matthew, Luke, Acts, and John. Second, the scribes who copied and transmitted Mark found that absence so disquieting that they appended three different endings, all containing risen apparitions. Third, the resurrectional visions differ in almost every way imaginable. In *number:* how many happened? In *place:* inside and/or outside a house, in Judea and/or in Galilee? In *time:* all on one day, over forty days, or somewhere in between? In *content:* who said what to whom? Fourth, even the final climactic meeting, in which Jesus announces the community's missionary program and leadership structure, is extremely diverse. Still, maybe it is all substantially the same Easter experience, but refracted through the vagaries of memory and the intensity of excitement? If that were so, is everything explained?

The Problem of Meaning

Paul wrote to the Corinthians from Ephesus in the early 50s C.E. But he says in 1 Corinthians 15:3a that "I handed on to you as of first importance what I in turn had received." The most likely source and time for his reception of that tradition would have been Jerusalem in the early 30s when, according to Galatians 1:18, he went "up to Jerusalem to visit Cephas [Peter] and stayed with him fifteen days." That received tradition, therefore, is an example of the second layer on the resurrection of Jesus. It says, in 1 Corinthians 15:3b–7, "that Christ died for our sins in accordance with the scriptures, and that he was buried, and that he was raised on the third day in accordance with the scriptures, and that he appeared to Cephas, then to the twelve. Then he appeared to more than five hundred brothers and sisters at one time, most of whom are still alive, though some have died. Then he appeared to James, then to all the apostles."

First, for the present discussion, we will bracket historical debates and *stipulate* that Jesus was buried beneath what is now called the Church of the Holy Sepulcher. Let that place be, for the present discussion, actually and factually, geographically and historically the correct location. Then why, returning to this chapter's opening paragraph, is the central shrine of Christianity not called the Church of the Blessed Resurrection? Put that question another way. Ancients knew, just like moderns know, how to bury a ruler. They, like we, knew how to prepare a magnificent sepulcher and celebrate a famous burial. But how do you celebrate a resurrection? What shrine or temple is appropriate for that event? Are Christians right not to call that church by its obviously more important name?

Second, historical questions about Jesus' resurrection usually concern the burial (whether or how?), the finding of an empty tomb (if or when?), and those diverse postresurrection visions (here or there?). Did some or all of that happen? Is all, some, or any of that history? Is all, some, or any of it parable? There are, however, some much more fundamental historical questions and, in order to focus on them here, we will bracket those ones just mentioned. We will again *stipulate*, for the present discussion, that everything happened the way the gospels describe Easter Sunday morning (however you correlate and reconcile those various accounts). Let that stand for here and now. We do this to make certain that debate is about the heart of the matter, which is (granted that all happened as told): why did those first recorders call it "resurrection"?

So here, then, are the two most fundamental *historical* questions that take us back to the first or original layer of the Jesus tradition. First, what did first-century Jews mean when they used the term "resurrection"? For example, before Jesus or Christianity ever existed, what did Pharisees and Sadducees mean when they argued for and against "the resurrection"? Second, against that background, what did first-century Christian Jews mean when they announced the resurrection of Jesus, when they proclaimed that God had raised Jesus from the dead? In other words, we bracket debates over the historicity of gospel accounts or church locations to focus on first-century meanings. And before you affirm or deny, believe or disbelieve in Jesus' resurrection, you must know what that claim meant and means. That is why the adjective "Jewish" appears in this section's title. We are asking a historical question about what Jews meant by "resurrection."

The Maccabean Martyrs

For around a millennium of its earliest history, Israel did not believe in an afterlife, not in the immortality of the soul and not in the resurrection of the body. The dead went down to Sheol, a place that was simply the grave writ large, as if all the tombs were somehow connected into one great subterranean never-never land. The grandeur of the Law, the challenge of the Prophets, and the beauty of the Psalms all derived from a faith based on life among the people of God and a hope that one's family and one's memory would live on among that people. It was not a faith ignorant of afterlife possibilities, since Egypt was always next door. But it may well have considered human afterlife claims as simple usurpations of an exclusively divine prerogative. An afterlife, in other words, was not worth serious discussion.

Sanctions for good and evil, therefore, were necessarily this-worldly, were enacted here, not hereafter. When, for example, Deuteronomy 28:2 promises that "all these blessings shall come upon you and overtake you, if you obey the Lord your God" and 28:15 adds that "if you will not obey the Lord your God by diligently observing all his commandments and decrees, which I am commanding you today, then all these curses shall come upon you and overtake you," the long list of benefits or disasters refers to internal fertility or infertility and external victory or defeat. Here below, here on earth, here and now.

Then came the crisis. In the 160s B.C.E., the Syrian monarch Antiochus IV Epiphanes, squeezed by the old northward pressure of Egypt and the new eastward pressure of Rome, tried to consolidate Israel politically, socially, and economically into his weakening empire. But although he got support from some Jews for commercializing Jerusalem into a standard Greek-style city, others resisted out of ancient religious tradition. So he invented something radically new—a religious persecution. Deny your religion and you live, affirm it and you die. How, on earth, could Deuteronomic theology explain the fate of martyrs? Where was the justice of God when obedience to God meant death and disobedience to God meant life?

That religious or theological problem was not erased by the Maccabean revolt, by its victory over the Syrians, and by a hundred years of Jewish independence under the indigenous Hasmonean dynasty. How could God's rule of justice be reconciled with the torture of those who had died for that very same God? How could one speak of the justice of God when confronted with the battered and brutalized bodies of martyrs? There were several options and four different ones are mentioned in 2 Maccabees, from the late second century B.C.E., and 4 Maccabees, from the middle of the first century C.E.

You could, for example, explain the heroism of the aged Eleazar in the Greco-Roman tradition of the noble death: "Welcoming death with honor," as 2 Maccabees puts it, in order to "leave to the young a noble example of how to die a good death willingly and nobly for the revered and holy laws" (6:19, 28). The classical model for accepting execution rather than defection was, of course, the death of Socrates. You vindicated the integrity of your life by your death; you justified all you had said and done by refusing to change under threat of execution.

You could also explain it in a completely different manner as a voluntary and vicarious atonement in the Jewish tradition of Isaiah's Suffering Servant. "Be merciful to your people, and let our punishment suffice for them," as that same Eleazar said in 4 Maccabees, "make my blood their purification, and take my life in exchange for theirs" (9:29). Christian theology has not been as careful as is necessary with vicarious atonement. It has converted a gift offered upward and graciously accepted by God into a demand coming downward and implacably demanded by God. But divinely *demanded* vicarious atonement is a theological obscenity.

That same book explains the martyrdom of the mother and seven sons as a triumph of divine reason over human emotion, for "how then can one fail to confess the sovereignty of right reason over emotion in those who were not turned back by fiery agonies?" (4 Macc. 13:5). And there may also be an allusion to the immortality of their souls in 4 Maccabees 9:8:

"For we, through this severe suffering and endurance, shall have the prize of virtue and shall be with God, on whose account we suffer."

But for other Jews a noble death, a vicarious atonement, or an immortal soul was not an adequate response to the question of God's justice. Those martyrs had died not in their souls, but in their bodies. They had been tortured and branded not in spirit, but in flesh. How did the justice of God vindicate the *bodies* of the martyrs? Another and different answer is very clear in 2 Maccabees and it is asserted without argument, as if it were known all along rather than something completely new. Someday, somehow, someplace in the future God would restore, publicly and visibly, the bodies of those martyrs. Listen to these dying statements from the mother and her seven sons in 2 Maccabees.

First: "You accursed wretch, you dismiss us from this present life, but the King of the universe will raise us up to an everlasting renewal of life, because we have died for his laws" (7: 9). Second: "When it was demanded, he quickly put out his tongue and courageously stretched forth his hands, and said nobly, 'I got these from Heaven, and because of his laws I disdain them, and from him I hope to get them back again'" (7:10–11). Third: "One cannot but choose to die at the hands of mortals and to cherish the hope God gives of being raised again by him. But for you there will be no resurrection to life!" (7:14). Fourth: "The Creator of the world, who shaped the beginning of humankind and devised the origin of all things, will in his mercy give life and breath back to you again, since you now forget yourselves for the sake of his laws" (7:23). Fifth: "Do not fear this butcher, but prove worthy of your brothers. Accept death, so that in God's mercy I may get you back again along with your brothers" (7:29).

There is even a rather gory combination of noble (suicidal) death and bodily resurrection in the death of Razis in 2 Maccabees. "Being surrounded, Razis fell upon his own sword, preferring to die nobly rather than to fall into the hands of sinners and suffer outrages unworthy of his noble birth. . . . Still alive and aflame with anger . . . he tore out his entrails, took them in both hands and hurled them at the crowd, calling upon the Lord of life and spirit to give them back to him again" (14:41–46). The overheated rhetoric makes the understanding of *bodily* resurrection quite clear. It is not adequate to speak of punishment for the persecutors. There must also be a time and place of justice for the persecuted. They must receive back from God what they lost for God. Someday, somehow, sometime, someplace, there had to be a general bodily resurrection when the martyrs would receive justice from their God. And from the martyrs, as it were in rippling circles, that hope went out to all the just, to all those who had lived for justice or suffered from injustice.

At this point the general resurrection connects to what was said about that spectrum of hope from covenantal through eschatological and into the apocalyptic Kingdom of God in Chapter 2 earlier. Resurrection is an utterly eschatologico-apocalyptic concept. It is, in fact, the last moment and the grand finale of that hope. And it is not about the survival of us, but about the justice of God. It's question is not: am I eternal? But: is God just? Its chant is: God will overcome, someday.

GOD HAS RAISED JESUS FROM THE DEAD

When, then, in the 30s of the first common-era century, anyone within that Jewish background proclaimed that God had raised Jesus from the dead, what exactly did that person mean? Irrespective, once again, of agreement or disagreement with that claim, what exactly was its content? Three negatives first, and then the positive conclusion.

The Content of the Resurrection Claim

Resuscitation.   Resurrection is not the same as resuscitation. It did not mean that an almost-dead Jesus had been revived once taken down from the cross. Individuals could survive an interrupted crucifixion, as Josephus mentions in his *Life*. He begged Titus for three acquaintances already on crosses after the destruction of Jerusalem in 70 C.E. and, although "two of them died in the physician's hands, the third survived" (421). So also could criminals hung by strangulation be taken down from London's eighteenth-century Tyburn Tree and resuscitated ("resurrected" as they put it). But the Christian tradition's insistence on "after three days" or "on the third day" is its way of emphasizing that Jesus was really and truly dead. Only a visit to the tomb after such an initial period could certify for sure that the person was actually dead. That is why John 11:17 notes that "when Jesus arrived, he found that Lazarus had already been in the tomb four days." He was, in other words, certainly and securely dead.

Apparition.   Resurrection is not the same as apparition. The question is not whether apparitions and visions occur or how they are to be explained. The ancient world presumed their possibility; for example, the slain pears to Anchises at the end of the Trojan War and the start of *neid*. The modern world does too; for example, *The Diagnostic tical Manual of Mental Disorders-IV* judges them not as mental but as common characteristics of uncomplicated grief. That e especially so, then and now, after the sudden, tragic, or terrible death or disappearance of a beloved person. Even if, therefore, no Christian texts had mentioned apparitions or visions of Jesus after his crucifixion, we could safely have postulated their occurrence. But, and this is the point, apparition is not the same as resurrection or anything like enough to invoke its presence.

Exaltation. Resurrection is not the same as exaltation. Within Jewish tradition, certain very holy persons were taken up to God rather than being consigned to an earthly tomb, for example, Enoch from among the patriarchs or Elijah from among the prophets. The Greco-Roman equivalent was apotheosis; for example, Augustan coins showed Julius Caesar's spirit ascending like an upward-shooting star to take its place among the heavenly divinities. Those were uniquely individual cases and had no general relationship to the fate of others. If one wanted to say that about Jesus, the proper terms were *exaltation, ascension,* or *apotheosis,* not *resurrection*. Put another way, with regard to Jesus, you could not have resurrection without exaltation, but you could have exaltation without resurrection. Jesus could be at the right hand of God without ever mentioning resurrection.

Resurrection. The positive answer should now be obvious. *To say that God raised Jesus from the dead was to assert that the general resurrection had thereby begun*. Only for such an assertion was "resurrection" or "raised from the dead" the proper terminology. That is very clear from a reading of 1 Corinthians 15, a commentary by Paul on an earlier and presumably second or traditional layer text.

One example. Paul can argue consistently in either direction: if there is no Jesus resurrection, there is no general resurrection; if there is no general resurrection, there is no Jesus resurrection. Notice, for example, how both directions appear in 1 Corinthians 15:12–13, "if Christ is proclaimed as raised from the dead, how can some of you say there is no resurrection of the dead? If there is no resurrection of the dead, then Christ has not been raised." That last argument is repeated in 15:16, "if the dead are not raised, then Christ has not been raised." The Jesus resurrection and the general resurrection stand or fall together. Paul could never imagine one without the other, never imagine Jesus' resurrection alone and by itself. Such an event would have been exaltation, ascension, apotheosis, but never resurrection as that term was used in first-century Judaism.

Another example. Jesus' resurrection and general resurrection stand or fall together because they are the beginning and end of a single process. That is clear from the metaphor Paul uses in 15:20, "Christ has been raised from the dead, the first fruits of those who have died" (literally, "of them that sleep," a technical term for those below awaiting liberation from Sheol). The first fruits are those first parts of the harvest that are taken and set aside for the Temple. They are not the promise of future harvest, but the start of present harvest. With them the harvest has already begun. *The resurrection of Jesus is the start of the general resurrection, that is to say, with Jesus' resurrection the general resurrection has begun.* That proclamation is stunningly creative and profoundly original on four counts, each involving a crucial choice between alternatives.

First, it is profoundly original in its distinction between *general imminence* and *specific finale* for apocalyptic consummation. It is not particularly stunning or even unusual for an individual or group, sect or religion to announce that apocalypse is imminent. That has happened already too often to be surprising. Neither is it particularly stunning to claim that apocalypse has already begun. It was always presumed that wonders and terrors, persecutions and catastrophes, wars and rumors of wars would inaugurate that final process. And such horrors were always available to render at least plausible assertions of apocalyptic beginnings. But the general resurrection was, as it were, the grand finale of apocalypse, the final moment when a God of justice publicly and visibly justified the world, turned it from a place of evil and violence to one of goodness and peace. To announce the resurrection of Jesus was to claim that such an event *had already started.* It was to claim that God's long-awaited vindication of all those who had lived, suffered, and died for justice and all those who had lived, suffered, and died from injustice *had already begun.*

Second, it is profoundly original in its distinction between *within Judaism* or *against Judaism* in apocalyptic consummation. Jesus' resurrection as start of the general resurrection is not a claim for Christianity over Judaism, nor is it a claim that here at last is what ultimately divided Christianity from Judaism. It is, instead, an absolutely original move within the possibilities and options of Judaism itself. For example, within Judaism it was quite possible to imagine apocalypse under God alone and without any messianic leader; then, to imagine a messianic leader as angelic or human; and, finally, to imagine a human messiah as prophetic, royal, or priestly. Essene Jews proclaimed a single coming of a double messiah, separate and hierarchical, one priestly and one royal (most likely to criticize the Hasmonean combination of those two roles in one person). Christian Jews proclaimed a double coming of a single messiah and that was no more and no less creatively original, no more and no less inside rather than outside Judaism than was that preceding Qumran creativity. So also with Jesus' resurrection—it is an utterly possible even if unexpectedly original option within its contemporary Judaism. But it is also a quite astounding claim: not the start but the end of the world's justification has begun.

Third, it is profoundly original in its distinction between the general resurrection as *instantive moment* or *durative process* in apocalyptic consummation. There were unseen and unseeable implications in that change. It was one thing to imagine the general resurrection as God's terminal act of apocalyptic conclusion, as a divine instant and moment that ended all human instants and moments. But apocalypse now became durative rather than instantive, an ongoing process in time and not just a terminal flash of time. Maybe that was easier to imagine for Paul, since the end of that beginning, the termination of apocalyptic climax, was imminent for him. He thought of weeks and months at least, years and decades at most. But, thereafter, we Christians would have to think about decades, centuries, and, finally, millennia. It was no small step to change the general resurrection from instantive to durative time. One thing it did, for example, and immediately, was to raise this next question.

Fourth, it is profoundly original in its distinction between *passive nonparticipation* or *active participation* in apocalyptic consummation. The general resurrection as God's final act of cosmic justification transforming our world from unjust normalcy to just Eutopia hardly allowed much scope for human assistance of any kind. At best, humans could pray for it, wait for it, hope for it, maybe even lead lives of great holiness or accept deaths of great persecution to hasten its advent. That is what is meant by passivity or nonparticipation. Those terms may be inadequate for such lives and such deaths, but they are clearly different from the active participation in the following example.

Recall what was said in Chapter 2 earlier about conversion rather than extermination of the pagans in certain strands of Jewish apocalyptic tradition. Those Christians who proclaimed an apocalyptic climax once the resurrection of Jesus started the general resurrection easily concluded that now was the time for pagan conversion to Judaism's God of justice. But it was quite another step to conclude that a Jewish mission to convert those pagans was demanded by God even within that apocalyptic interpretation. Was that not a matter for God's direct action? Should they not remain in Jerusalem praying and waiting for the Temple's huge Court of the Gentiles to be flooded with God's eschatological Gentiles, God's apocalyptic pagans?

It was quite possible, for example, to agree with Paul that Gentiles must now be included within the community of Judaism's apocalyptic present without having to follow the rituals of Judaism's ancient tradition (for example, circumcision for males). It was also quite possible for those very same people to disagree strongly with his general missionary program and especially with his particular claim of a personal vocation not just to Christian Judaism, not just to missionary activity within Judaism, but specifically to missionary activity among pagans. That was quite a further step, and some or even many of those who opposed Paul did so from within a Christian Judaism that found a proactive pagan mission in no way included within God's apocalyptic plan. In any case, such human participation in a divine solution created an absolutely new situation and a radically novel understanding of this general resurrection as instant became duration, as a moment of time became a process in time.

The Evidence of the Resurrection Claim

But how on earth (literally!) could anyone ever make such a claim? Where was the evidence? Unlike a future prophecy, it made a present challenge. Where, then, was the evidence, the proof, the indications of a divine Eutopia on an earth as normally evil, violent, and unjust as ever? How, for example, could Paul of Tarsus argue that claim to a first-century pagan and how could James of Jerusalem argue it to a first-century Pharisee? This is not a question of undeniable proof or irrefutable evidence. It is simply one of what a Paul or a James would have indicated to open-minded listeners in minimal defense of their claim that God had *already* started the vindication of the martyrs and the justification of the world.

Paul to a Pagan.   Imagine Paul arriving at any city for the first time. He carries his tools with him and can find employment in any leather workshop needing a skilled extra hand. Where, he asks, is the street of the leather workers? There, somebody replies, is the shop of a freed slave, still capitalized by his former master, proud of his patron, proud of his newly bought freedom, proud of the Roman citizenship that accompanied manumission from a Roman citizen, and proud that his future children will be freeborn Roman citizens.

Paul is of immediate interest along the workbenches. He has been everywhere to the east, from Jerusalem to Antioch to Corinth. He can tell of all those places, but must also tell why he moves around so much. Is he perhaps a runaway slave? What if Paul announces, without preamble or prelude, that God has raised Jesus of Nazareth from the dead over there in Judea? (He would hardly have done it just like that, but let it stand for here and now.)

"So, Paul, is Jesus' resurrection like what happened to Julius Caesar after he died? See, here is a coin showing his spirit ascending like an upward-shooting star to take its place among the heavenly divinities. And if you do not believe that story, Paul, how do you explain the fantastic successes of the imperial Julio-Claudian dynasty? I can see what Caesar has done for our business, but what has your Jesus ever done for anyone?"

Faced with that question, Paul would have to explain all the specific content of resurrection in Jewish tradition and how Jesus' resurrection meant that God had *already* begun to make just an unjust world. And then would come, however politely put, the obvious question. "Where, Paul? How, Paul?" What could he answer? Something like this?

"There is a small group of us who meet for prayer in a shop near here before it opens each day. And once a week we meet there to share half of all we have from the preceding week's work. We call that meal the Lord's Supper because we believe that all creation belongs to the Lord and that we must share the Lord's food equally among us. We hold ourselves as equal in the sight of the Lord, Jew and Greek, slave and free, female and male, poor and rich. Food is the material basis of life and life belongs to God. We share what is not our own—that is the Lord's type of meal, the Lord's style of supper. So, I invite you. Come and see if God is not already making a more just world right under the very noses and against the very plans of Rome. If you do not see it, leave, but if you do see it, stay. And, by the way, we have small groups like the one here in every city of the Roman Empire. It is not just how many we are, but how everywhere we are. And whenever one of you turns from Caesar, who crucified Jesus, to God, who raised Jesus, you participate in this justification of the world. It is a choice between the divine Caesar and the divine Jesus. It is a choice between divinity incarnate as violent power or divinity incarnate as distributive justice (or, as we call it, *agape*). Come to the sardine seller's shop the day after tomorrow to see and decide for yourselves."

Paul, of course, would also say something like this: "Since we believe that Jesus died and rose again, even so, through Jesus, God will bring with him those who have died. For this we declare to you by the word of the Lord, that we who are alive, who are left until the coming of the Lord, will by no means precede those who have died. For the Lord himself, with a cry of command, with the archangel's call and with the sound of God's trumpet, will descend from heaven, and the dead in Christ will rise first. Then we who are alive, who are left, will be caught up in the clouds together with them to meet the Lord in the air; and so we will be with the Lord forever" (1 Thess. 4:14–17). That, however, was similar to what his hearers had heard from the contemporary mystery religions, from, for example, the devotees of Isis of Egypt. It was not unimportant but, for some, how a god operated here below in this life might be most persuasive for how that god would operate in the next one. So, maybe, a god establishing a just world was worth investigating. For some. And some were enough to begin with.

James to a Pharisee.   If James of Jerusalem explained Jesus' resurrection to a Pharisee, all the Jewish background would be known and taken for granted. And, once again, the question would be the same. "Show me how God has already begun to justify an unjust world, how God has already begun to vindicate the sufferings of the just and the deaths of the martyrs." Like Paul, James would invite the Pharisee to come and see how his community lived its life. But he would also have to speak of something that Paul never mentions. It was not enough, not nearly enough, to speak of an individual resurrection of Jesus as start of a soon-to-be-consummated general resurrection. Jesus was not the first Jewish martyr, nor would he be the last. Neither was he the first Jew to die on a Roman cross, nor would he be the last. What about all those others who had gone before him? Jesus' resurrection must have been a corporate one. He could not have risen alone, but only with, maybe at the head, or even as the cause of a corporate resurrection of all those who, having suffered and died unjustly, now slept in Sheol awaiting vindication.

That *corporate* resurrection does not appear anywhere in Paul's theology. It appears, of course, in the Apostles' Creed as "he descended into Hell," with Jesus descending into Sheol to liberate all those who, like him, had lived, suffered, and died unjustly. That phrase, by the way, is not present in the Nicene Creed. The very idea of a corporate resurrection is almost lost completely to the present New Testament. And with that loss is also lost the full meaning of Jesus' resurrection as God's inaugural justification of the world—and our necessary cooperation in that process.

You can still see a forlorn and truncated residue of that corporate understanding of Jesus' resurrection in Matthew 27:51b–53, where, at the crucifixion, "the earth shook, and the rocks were split. The tombs also were opened, and many bodies of the saints who had fallen asleep were raised. After his resurrection they came out of the tombs and entered the holy city and appeared to many." You can find it, outside the New Testament, in the *Gospel of Peter* 10:39–42, where God asks the risen Jesus, "Have you preached to them that sleep?" that is, have you proclaimed liberation to the just awaiting you below in Sheol. And the answer is, "Yes."

But you can see it most clearly in a very beautiful hymn from the end of that first common-era century, as Jesus speaks in the *Odes of Solomon* 42:10–20:

> I was not rejected although I was considered to be so,
> and I did not perish although they thought it of me.
>
> Sheol saw me and was shattered
> and Death ejected me and many with me. . . .
>
> And those who had died ran toward me;
> and cried out and said, "Son of God, have pity on us. . . .
>
> And open for us the door
> by which we may go forth to you,
> for we perceive that our death does not approach you.
>
> May we also be saved with you,
> because you are our Savior."

Then I heard their voice,
and placed their faith in my heart,

And I placed my name upon their head,
because they are free and they are mine.

You could easily argue that the corporate Jesus resurrection is a later expansion of the individual Jesus resurrection, that it comes from somewhere in later and post-third layers of the tradition. Yet it seems as likely that it was eliminated early but survived in some hymns and prayers. But it raised a profound question. If, apart from the future, Jesus' resurrection was for him alone, where in that was the justice of God, how in that was the justification of the world inaugurated? Was that not what we might call nepotism (or filiotism, as it were), a special dispensation for a special person, a particular privilege for the Son of God? What about all those who had gone before him?

Paul could certainly omit any mention of a corporate Jesus resurrection in speaking to pagans who would not, in any case, have worried too much about Jewish martyrs. But James could not have omitted it in speaking with a Pharisee. The more Christian Judaism was Jewish, the more it would have spoken of a corporate and not just an individual resurrection, and when Christianity ceased to speak about the former, something profoundly important was lost. The resurrection was no longer primarily about the justice of God, but about the survival of us.

A MONUMENT OF MARBLE OR JUSTICE?

Return to the Church of the Holy Sepulcher. There and then, the Kingdom of God had come to rest. Jesus' covenantal Kingdom was no longer a moving center that went out to all alike, but had found its central place to which all must come. And the Kingdom of God had a marble façade. Jesus' covenantal Kingdom was no longer an alternative community sharing freely the spiritual power of healing and the physical power of eating. It had tapped into the imperial marble trade and ate off silver bowls.

This circular rotunda of the Holy Sepulcher resembled in shape that already discussed mausoleum of Augustus in Rome and fortress-palace-tomb of Herod the Great in the Judean desert. They bore a family resemblance: circular shapes imposed on the landscape with imposing façades of marble or polished stone. Christians had finally given their king an appropriate burial, like that of Herod the Great or Caesar Augustus and, although they did not know it, far better than that of Caiaphas.

But the Christian Holy Sepulcher was made possible as much by Hadrian's erasure of Jewish Jerusalem as it was by Constantine's imperial finances. The great irony and tragedy is this. The one who rebelled in every way against a Roman-backed commercial kingdom in Galilee, Jesus the Jewish peasant, was now Christ the imperial king. To build a regal burial place for the Jewish Jesus, Constantine cut away the *kokhim* shafts or *arcosolia* shelves of a Jewish tomb beyond any recognition. But over time Christianity also cut away and forgot the Jewish roots of its covenantal Kingdom. Read again Eusebius's description of the building of the New Kingdom:

> So on the monument of salvation itself was the New Jerusalem built, over against the old one so famous of old which, after the pollution caused by the murder of the Lord, experienced the last extremity of desolation and paid the penalty for the crime of its impious inhabitants. Opposite this the emperor raised, at great and lavish expense, the trophy of the Savior's victory over death. (*Life of Constantine* 3.33)

We do not ask whether Constantine constructed the Holy Sepulcher on the right spot. Yes, probably. We ask whether his construction was appropriate to Jesus' Kingdom of God, to that Jewish ideal of a covenantal Kingdom *on earth* as in heaven. No, probably. Above all, we ask and question not so much how Constantine celebrated the sepulcher of Jesus, but how Christianity celebrates the resurrection of Jesus.

It is sometimes claimed in contemporary Christian thought that only the stupendous miracles of empty tomb and risen apparition(s) can explain *historically*, first, how the companions of Jesus recovered their faith in him lost at the crucifixion and, second, how others came to faith in him despite his crucifixion. There are two problems, one minor and one major, with that oversimplified understanding.

First, it was the male and not the female companions of Jesus who fled, since they were much more likely to be arrested along with Jesus. But to lose your nerve is not to lose your faith. Even Mark's story of Peter's triple denial so formulates it that he loses not his faith but, as it were, his memory. It might have been braver to stay and confess, but it was cowardice and not disbelief to deny and run.

Second, we are retrojecting our own post-Enlightenment rationalism into a pre-Enlightenment world. Imagine a contemporary debate along these lines. *Nonbeliever:* "All those stories about virginal conceptions, divine births, miraculous events, wondrous deeds, risen apparitions, and heavenly ascensions never did and never could have happened. They are myth at best and lie at worst." *Believer:* "It is true that such events do not happen regularly, but they all happened to our Jesus once and for all, long ago." In that post-Enlightenment contradiction, impossibility battles with uniqueness.

Both those positions, however, are equally irrelevant for a pre-Enlightenment world, equally unusable in such a cultural milieu. In a world where anything from divine birth to heavenly ascension was a possible part of the transcendental landscape, *impossibility* was not an available argument for polemical attackers, but neither was *uniqueness* an available argument for apologetical defenders. In the free market of religious ideas that was the Greco-Roman world, one had to enter a spiritual free-trade area and argue for one's God or one's Son of God without using either of those post-Enlightenment moves.

For example, in the middle of the second century Justin is arguing for Jesus in his *First Apology* directed toward pagan readers. He never suggests uniqueness. "When we say also that the Word," he begins, "who is the first-birth of God, was produced without sexual union, and that He, Jesus Christ, our Teacher, was crucified and died, and rose again, and ascended into heaven, we propound nothing different from what you believe regarding those whom you esteem sons of Jupiter." He then lists many examples and concludes by referring to divine emperors and especially Julius Caesar. "What of the emperors who die among yourselves, whom you deem worthy of deification, and in whose behalf you produce someone who swears he has seen the burning Caesar rise to heaven from the funeral pyre?" Finally, however, Justin is certainly not ready to say that all such claims are equal. But notice that his criterion of discrimination is not uniqueness in event, but superiority in action. "As we promised in the preceding part of this discourse, we will now prove Him superior—or rather have already proved Him to be so—for the superior is revealed by His actions" (21–22). That is an utterly appropriate pre-Enlightenment argument. Of course there have been many sons of God around, but Jesus is best of all because of certain very specific arguments.

Similarly, about a quarter century later, when a pagan polemicist named Celsus is attacking Christianity, he uses exactly the same pre-

Enlightenment type of argument. He never mentions impossibility, but counters that Jesus has never done anything for anyone. The argument for superiority is met by one for inferiority. "After all, the old myths of the Greeks that attribute a divine birth to Perseus, Amphion, Aeacus and Minos are equally good evidence of their wondrous works on behalf of mankind—and are certainly no less lacking in plausibility than the stories of your followers. What have you done [Jesus] by word or deed that is quite so wonderful as those heroes of old?" *(On the True Doctrine)*. Both pro-Christian apologist and anti-Christian polemicist use the same argument, but in opposite directions. Impossibility and uniqueness are not imaginable as absolute claims (maybe, of course, as hyperbolic overclaims), but superiority in action is where the debate occurs. *Justin:* "Jesus has done more than all those others like him." *Celsus:* "Jesus has done less than all those others like him."

Paul and his audience lived in a first-century pre-Enlightenment world. That precluded those two arguments of uniqueness versus impossibility that present-day believers and nonbelievers use against one another. To assert empty tomb and/or risen apparitions(s) is not enough to explain anything, let alone everything in that ancient world. But that full content of Jesus' resurrection just outlined above would make for debate in that world. It was the content and implications of your miracle that mattered there. "Wow" was not enough, because there were too many "wows" around. Ancients might declare Jesus' resurrection unbelievable, but never impossible. What that audience would say to Paul is not an impolite "We do not believe you," but a polite "How nice for Jesus, but why exactly should we care about that?" Or, more bluntly, "What's in it for us?" And that is exactly when Paul would have explained willingly and in great detail, for example, the sociocosmic and religio-political difference between Julius Caesar's ascension and Jesus Christ's resurrection, and how it was time to choose one or the other.

Recall the discussion of Jewish and of Christian-Jewish "resurrection" above. Those who claimed Jesus had begun the terminal moment of apocalyptic climax would have to present some public evidence of a world transformed from injustice and evil to justice and peace. It would not and could not suffice to claim one or many empty tombs and one or many risen apparitions. That might all be well and good, but where was the evidence, any evidence, of a transformed world? For that they had only their own communal lives as evidence. This is how we live with God and on this basis we seek to persuade others to do likewise. This is our new creation, our transformed world. We in God, God in us, and both together here below upon this earth.

Paul claimed in 1 Corinthians that, "if Christ has not been raised, then our proclamation has been in vain and your faith has been in vain" (15:14). As stated, that comment is true for Christianity, but so also is its reverse. If Christian faith has been in vain, that is, has not acted to transform itself and this world toward the justice of God, and if Christian proclamation has been in vain, that is, has not insisted that such is the church's vocation, then Christ was not raised. Christianity could certainly still claim that Jesus was exalted and had ascended to the right hand of God. But resurrection, to repeat this chapter's argument, presumes the start of cosmic transformation, not just the promise of it, not just the hope of it, not just talk about it, and not just theology about it. The Church of the Holy Sepulcher can be easily seen in all its marbled past and disputed present within today's Jerusalem. But the Church of the Blessed Resurrection can only be seen in a world under transformation by Christian cooperation with divine justice and by Christian participation in divine justice.

Ground and Gospel

Since the present always knows the future of the distant past, it is hard not to consider that future inevitable, that it had to happen as it did, that it could not have worked out in any other way. To admit how differently it might have happened demands some therapeutic counterfactuals, some remedial thoughts about nodal moments, alternative choices, and divergent outcomes. It demands above all that we acknowledge our own utter ignorance about the future and that we appreciate how that blindness links us to them in common humanity. Two questions, then. First, what are our conclusions about the time, place, vision, and program of the historical Jesus from this book's dialectic of archaeology and exegesis? Second, granted that understanding, what future might one have imagined for the Jesus so reconstructed? Could one have predicted, for example, two separate and even inimical worldwide religions?

ROME AND JUDAISM

Stones and texts, material remains and textual remains, ground and gospel, archaeology and exegesis. But, since the second half of that dialectic has so often dominated the process of integration, step back and join in an act of counterfactual imagination. What if we had no textual materials about that first common-era century in the Jewish homeland? A conceit, of course, and one that avoids facing the fact that archaeology has not only dug up inscriptions, it has also dug up documents. But try the experiment just for a moment.

Imagine, for example, that we no longer have the following documents. We no longer have the Roman historian Tacitus recording the many times imperial legions marched southward from their Syrian bases to avenge colonial uprisings in the Jewish homeland with fire and sword. And we do not have his assurance that, under the emperor Tiberius, all was quiet there and the legions did not move. We no longer have the Jewish historian Josephus telling us about John the Baptist, Jesus, and James of Jerusalem. And we also lack his assurance that under Tiberius's Pilate all was not quiet even if the legions remained in camp. We no longer have the Christian Jewish gospel writers telling us all of that and much more from a very different viewpoint. What would we, could we, should we see if we had only the ground itself?

First, we would recognize throughout Galilee and Judea a complex of artifacts from a people different than those who lived around them and even among them. We would have in their towns and villages those stepped-plastered pools that do not seem appropriately functional as either baths or cisterns, those many small and exceptionally large stone vessels, those burial chambers with wall-shaft fingers for initial bodies and floor-pits or ossuaries for final bones, and the absence of pig bones among meal refuse or kitchen midden. Next, we would see, and recognize from Mediterranean parallels, that Roman imperial power came, at a certain point in time, to dominate those people. In one generation, we would see it at work in the south of this country both inland and on the coast. On the coast, for example, we would recognize not just a Roman-style city but a magnificent port, an all-weather harbor on a difficult shore. We would know, once again from elsewhere, that the Roman Empire did not commercialize its territories by sending out traders on horseback or merchants with wagons. Like Alexander's Greek Empire earlier, it planted cities where aristocrats built lavish homes and reorganized the countryside to maximize its productivity. In the next generation, we would find that same process at work in the north of this country where, within about twenty years and twenty miles of one another, one city was rebuilt and expanded, another was built from scratch, and both of them bore the hallmarks of Roman urbanization and commercialization. Finally, within the next generation or so, a terrible layer of destruction covered that entire country with rubble and arrowheads, charring and soot—an indigenous revolt against Roman control that left towns ruined, walls destroyed, and people, presumably, slaughtered.

That is, of course, a very artificial act of imagination but it is useful to try it every now and then. What if we had *only* the ground, the material remains, the archaeologist's data? What would we see? But we have not only the ground but all those other textual remains as well and, for this book on *excavating Jesus*, we have both ground and gospel, archaeologist and exegete. What have we obtained by their careful conjunction?

First, those artifacts of ethnic difference were from the purity codes of covenantal law and were not just the residues of popular habit. Jews, to be sure, could observe those purity rules and still disagree profoundly on resistance or nonresistance, violent or nonviolent resistance, to Roman control. But, if one abandoned them completely, would not Rome prevail absolutely? You will recall from earlier that Josephus described Tiberius Julius Alexander's abandonment of Judaism for paganism by saying simply that he "did not stand by the practices of his people." To abandon those purity rules could mean abandoning all else as well. But no first-century Jew would have said that covenant was *only* about those artifacts or even *primarily* about those observances. It was, however, *also* about them. To retain them could be a form of resistance to the evil and injustice of imperial oppression. Furthermore, those artifacts were tied to a people who attempted to live in covenant with a God of justice and righteousness, that is, with a divine power for whom to do what was right was to do what was just.

That justice was not only personal and individual, but also structural and systemic, not exclusively retributive, but primarily distributive. Torah, or divine law, the fine print of that covenant, demanded the fair and equitable distribution of land as the material basis of life because, as that God said in Leviticus 25:23, "the land shall not be sold in perpetuity, for the land is mine; with me you are but aliens and tenants." Since land was life, it could not be bought and sold, mortgaged and foreclosed, like any other property. Hence covenantal law focused often on *land and debt* in a continual attempt to forestall the steady growth of inequality as the few got ever more land and the many got ever less. If the land could not be bought and sold like any other commodity then neither could it be mortgaged and dispossessed. Hence all those laws about the forbidding of interest and the controlling of collateral, the remission of debts and the liberation of enslavement every seventh, or Sabbath, year, and the reversal of dispossession every fiftieth, or Jubilee, year. But such covenantal laws would have seemed like bad jokes to the Roman conquerors, in whose eyes the land belonged to them, or, if one wished to wax theological about it, to Jupiter now and to Yahweh no longer. And it would be administered not in terms of Yahweh's distributive justice, but in terms of Jupiter's imperial power, not in terms of maximum theoretical equity, but in terms of maximum practical productivity. It is that fundamental clash between "the land belongs to me" and "the land belongs to us" that explains the terrible failure of Roman policy in the Jewish homeland. Three rebellions there, in 4 B.C.E., in 66–74 C.E., and in 132–35 C.E. (not to speak of the one that destroyed Egyptian Judaism in 115–17 C.E.) emphasize that failure (even from the Roman point of view). No doubt there were other contributing factors such as Roman jurisdiction split between Jerusalem and Antioch or Jewish jurisdiction split between Herodian royalty and priestly aristocracy. Those were soluble problems but whether land (that is life) was ruled by justice or power was not soluble except by the choice of one over the other.

Second, then, the continuity from Jewish Torah to Jewish Jesus is seen most clearly from two connections. One connection is that, in the first century, "the Kingdom" meant simply the Roman Empire. Theirs was the kingdom, the power, and the glory. When, therefore, Jesus spoke of the Kingdom of God, he chose the one expression most calculated to draw Roman attention to what he was doing. Not the "people" or the "community" of God but the "Kingdom" of God. That very phrase was an immediate confrontation with the Kingdom of Rome, which had arrived forcibly with Herod the Great in Judea at Jerusalem and Caesarea Maritima in the generation before Jesus and then arrived with Herod Antipas in Lower Galilee at Sepphoris by 4 B.C.E. and at Tiberias by 19–20 C.E. in the generation of Jesus. That is why, to answer the question posed in the Prologue, two popular resistance movements, the Baptism movement of John and the Kingdom movement of Jesus started in the territories of Herod Antipas in the 20s C.E. The power of the Kingdom of Rome, miniatured in the tetrarchy of Antipas in Galilee, was confronted by the Kingdom of God, which asked quite simply this: How would this world be run if our God sat on Caesar's throne or if our God lived in Antipas's palace? It was not a military confrontation, or else, as mentioned earlier; many of its protagonists would have died alongside John under Antipas and alongside Jesus under Pilate. It was, instead, a programmatically nonviolent resistance but, emphatically, it confronted present economic, social, and political realities. Pilate got it exactly right, from the point of view of his imperial responsibilities: Jesus and his Kingdom were a threat to Roman law and order, and his Jewish God was a threat to the Roman God.

The other connection is the line from *land and debt* in Torah to *food and debt* in the prayer of Jesus. When the Lord's Prayer says "may your kingdom come," it is glossed by Matthew as "may your will be done on earth, as in heaven." That is precisely correct. The Kingdom of God is about God's will for this earth. Heaven is in great shape; it's the earth that is problematic. The prayer then continues with a request for enough food for today and no debt for tomorrow. Land and debt has become food and debt, but the underlying basis is the same. How is *life* itself to be fairly distributed among all the people on earth if one believes that it all belongs to a just God? The underlying basis is still a theology of creation that does not only ask who made the earth (we have seldom said that we did), but especially who owns it (we usually think that we do). To accept divine ownership in all its radical implications meant a new creation.

One could argue that land always meant food and that nothing has changed in that transition. But maybe it had, in Antipas's Galilee. Were covenant-based demands for divinely mandated equitable distribution of land no longer possible or credible by then and was food all one could talk about to dispossessed peasants? Or, conversely, would any such demands about land necessarily lead to violent confrontation with Roman-backed Herodian power?

Third, whether one speaks of land and debt or of food and debt, it is always a question of active life and specific program, not just of abstract law or general prayer. The Kingdom of God, in other words, was not just a vision but a program, not just an idea but a lifestyle, not just about heaven hereafter but about earth here and now, and not just about one person but about many others as well. Recall from earlier that Jesus told his companions to go out and do exactly what he was doing, to share the spiritual power of healing and the physical power of eating and to proclaim that in such open reciprocity one entered the Kingdom of God because God willed the world to be shared equitably and justly among all. That was actually the decisive moment when the future became not yet inevitable, but now possible. Jesus did not settle down at Nazareth with the family or Capernaum with Peter and send his companions out to bring everyone to him. Neither did he tell those companions to go out and do everything in his name. He said: do it, just do it. And at that moment, the future of the Kingdom movement could not be simply foreclosed by Pilate's execution of Jesus as the Baptism movement had been by Antipas's execution of John.

Finally, remember this. In that first century it was absolutely impossible to separate religion and politics, politics and economics. Coinage, the only mass medium of antiquity, said that Caesar was *divi filius*, Son of God, and *supremus pontifex*, the supreme bridge-builder between heaven and earth, the high priest of Roman state religion. Only religio-politics or politico-religion was possible in that situation, and confrontation was always double, never against one or the other, but always against both inextricably together. Only the justice of the Kingdom of God could take on the power of the Kingdom of Rome, which was, of course, simply the normalcy of civilization in that time and place. It was not as if the Kingdom of God stood against the Kingdom of Rome because the latter was particularly cruel or exceptionally evil. It was not its cruelty but its normalcy that cost Jesus his life.

Judaism and Christianity

Accept, for here and now, that this book's understanding of the historical Jesus is fundamentally correct (which, of course, it is). Could you stand at the moment it has reconstructed, including the proclamation of Jesus' resurrection, and predict what was going to happen? Would you have guessed that Judaism and Christianity would become separate and even inimical religions? What had to happen to render that future actual? What could have happened to render another future possible?

We concentrate, in conclusion, on three key decisions without which that separation would not have happened. They represent nodal moments when we can imagine crucial alternative routes through history's garden of forking paths. We focus on three key moments when one road taken meant another road not taken, but with no presumption that the former option was inevitable. But from these three events came eventually *the parting of the ways* between Judaism and Christianity. Without any one of them let alone all of them, it becomes impossible even to imagine what might have happened, and it is good to emphasize that impossibility. In the process of considering those three nodal moments, we return once more to James the Just of Jerusalem and to his very great importance in early Christian Judaism, an importance not created, but only emphasized by his disputed ossuary.

The Cities. Within a few years of Jesus' execution most of the followers of Jesus whose names we know left the rural surroundings and village environs of Galilee to live in Jerusalem. The best explanation is their fervent expectation of Jesus' imminent apocalyptic return, which would surely happen, as they thought, in the holy city itself. That move was in no way inevitable. Think, for example, of the two sources used independently by Matthew and Luke. The *Q Gospel* was apocalyptic but those behind it stayed in Galilee despite woe curses against Capernaum, Bethsaida, and Corazin. Mark was also apocalyptic, but insisted programmatically that Galilee was where Jesus would imminently return, that Jerusalem was the place of opposition and persecution, and that those named disciples who moved there had failed Jesus utterly.

Those named followers, such as James, the brother of Jesus, or Peter the leader of the Twelve, were already in Jerusalem when Paul visited there six or seven years after the crucifixion. Three years after his conversion, as he writes in Galations 1:18–19, "I did go up to Jerusalem to visit Cephas [Peter] and stayed with him fifteen days; but I did not see any other apostle except James the Lord's brother." Furthermore, Jerusalem was a pilgrimage city from which contacts were easily made with other cities. Thus, within three or four years, we have followers of Jesus in Antioch and Damascus. In the latter city, for instance, they had a high enough profile for Paul to persecute them. Had they all stayed in the north, the Kingdom movement could have died out in one or two generations among the hills and hamlets of Galilee. From whom came that insistence on a move to Jerusalem? Maybe from Peter? But he eventually left in 41 C.E. Maybe from James who never left but was martyred in 62 C.E.?

The Pagans. Jews spoke of the nations, or the Gentiles, and we translate it as the pagans. But that is not exactly correct. Jews did not spend much time thinking about pagans as an abstract classification of those distinct from themselves as Israelis today might think of themselves as distinct, for example, from the Irish or the Chinese. The nations, or the Gentiles, meant those great empires that one after another had conquered, oppressed, and persecuted them over half a millennium.

When, then, Jews hoped for that great future act in which God would finally clean up the unjust mess that was the earth and establish here below a perfect world of justice, peace, and holiness, a major question was, What would God do with those evil empires? As seen in our first chapter, there were two contradictory answers to that question. These were the alternatives: either extermination *or* conversion, either the Great Battle *or* the Great Banquet, either Mount Megiddo (Armageddon) *or* Mount Zion. And, most important, conversion was not to Judaism but to God; not, for example, to circumcision and kosher but to justice and peace.

At Jerusalem, James, Peter, and the others clearly chose that second option since they accepted male pagan converts into the community without circumcision. As with their move to Jerusalem, their acceptance of uncircumcised male converts represented aspects of their apocalypticism, their belief in God's eschatological operation. On that uncircumcision, Luke's Acts 15 and Paul's Galatians 1–2 agree. They also agree on the fundamental importance of James in that process. And the only way James could have accepted that position was from an apocalyptic perspective. With that decision, of course, a second problem arose immediately. How could *unity* be maintained in a community composed of both Christian Jews and Christian pagans? How, especially, would they eat together when such commensality programmatically proclaimed and progressively established that unity?

It was one thing to imagine in prophetic ecstasy or announce in apocalyptic rhapsody that God would end the reign of evil by hosting a great banquet at Jerusalem for all peoples made newly just and peaceful on an earth made newly fertile and prosperous. Nobody, for example, would have interrupted that magnificent vision to ask if the apocalyptic banquet was to be kosher or nonkosher. Or exactly how long it might last. But that was exactly the problem that arose at Antioch according to Galatians 2. If Christians Jews and Christians pagans ate together, said James, they should *both* observe kosher traditions. No, said Paul, they should not; they should continue the earlier solution at Antioch in which *neither* observed such rules. Those were the obvious alternative options for unity, but Peter, Barnabas, and the others agreed with James, while Paul went westward away from them all. It is long, long overdue to consider whether James was right and Paul was wrong in that dispute.

The Wars.   There was a time when it was easy to explain why "Christianity" broke away from and/or was rejected by "Judaism." Christians believed Jesus was Messiah, Lord, Son of God, and Jews did not. Those were the reasons. Or again: Christians refused Sabbath, circumcision, kosher, and Jews did not. Those were the reasons. And those sounded like plausible explanations since Christianity and Judaism did eventually become separate religions and there were then those recognizable differences between them. They now, however, seem totally anachronistic. There were many diverse strands of Judaism in that first-century Jewish homeland, all vying for leadership in the crucible of Greek cultural internationalism and Roman military imperialism. Christian Jews took, therefore, their place alongside Pharisaic Jews, Sadduceean Jews, and Essene Jews, Fourth-Philosophy Jews, Sicarii Jews, and Zealot Jews, as well as many other types, options, visions, and programs. They were no more and no less that one group disputing against other groups, but within the same politico-religious community, that is, *within* Judaism and not *against* Judaism. That, however, only makes even more pressing the question why, eventually, all other Jewish groups came to reject the Christian Jewish option for their future. The basic reason, we suggest, was not so much theological theories, ritual practices, or even legal observances as simply this third element, namely, wars

The first Roman war started under Nero in 66 and was concluded under Vespasian in 74. In the late summer of 70, Jerusalem was destroyed, the Temple burned, and its annual tax was punitively relegated to Jupiter's Temple on the Roman capitol. The second Roman war took place under Trajan from 115 to 117 and centered in Egypt, Cyrene, and Cyprus, but with uprisings in Mesopotamia and possibly in Palestine as well. It resulted in the destruction of Egyptian and especially Alexandrian Judaism. The third Roman war took place under Hadrian from 132 to 135 in the Jewish homeland, with its leader, Simon bar Kochba, acclaimed by Rabbi Aqiba as the Messiah. It resulted in the complete paganization of Jerusalem and in the empirewide if temporary suppression of all Jewish observances (Sabbath, circumcision, Torah study).

The Parting of the Ways. If you phrase the question properly, the answer becomes immediately evident. We do not ask: Why did Christianity break away from Judaism as a rebel daughter from her mother? We do not ask: Why were two daughters, rabbinic Judaism and early Christianity, born to a common mother, second-Temple Judaism? We ask: Why did all other Jewish groups slowly but surely reject the Christian Jewish option? Our answer is not theology, ritual, or tradition but war, devastation, and horror. The Christian Jewish group maintained that pagans and Jews would now live together under God in Christ. They maintained that belief despite three terrible wars in which pagans looked exactly like they always had and behaved exactly like they always did. The *parting of the ways* arose because, for most other Jews, that Christian Jewish claim was incredible. The inclusion of pagans and the devastation by pagans were irreconcilable.

It was sad that both James and Paul wanted unity and agreed on a collection of money from the Christian pagan communities for the communalist, share-all, Christian Jewish mother-community at Jerusalem. It was sadder that, if Paul "caused" James's martyrdom, James may have just as well "caused" Paul's. It was James, as you will recall from the first chapter, who asked Paul to vindicate his law observance by paying for certain rites in the Temple. He was there accused of bringing pagans past the barrier into the Court of the Jews, was attacked, captured, and sent on his long road to Rome and death. In other words, the scenes in Acts 21 and *Clementine Recognitions* 1 are almost inversions of one another. It was saddest of all that neither James nor Paul held the key to the future. The unity of Christian Jews and Christian pagans in one community would not endure either with Paul's nonkosher commensality or with James's kosher commensality. Both hopes were equally doomed, not by theology, but by history. It would be good to rethink that fact. It would be even better to mourn it. The historical Jesus who lived, died, and rose as a Jew would surely have done so.

ACKNOWLEDGMENTS

We are profoundly grateful to the staff and volunteers of those many past and present excavations without whose work this book could not have been written. We are especially grateful to those archaeologists who explained their sites to us in June 1999: Vassilios Tzaferis and John Wilson at Banias, Rami Arav and Elizabeth McNamer at Bethsaida, and Moti Aviam at Jodefat. We are equally grateful to those others with whom we had conversations in preparation for this book that same month, especially Eric and Carol Meyers, of the Sepphoris Regional Project, and the forensic archaeologist Joe Zias. We are also very grateful to Doug Brooks for the architectural drawings and to Kevin Holland for the scanning operations. We particularly thank Balage Balogh for his illustrations reconstructing life in antiquity. He brought together archaeological publications, plans, and artifacts, our description and imagination, along with his own careful research and keen eye to create valuable portrayals of that first-century Jewish world.

ARCHAEOLOGICAL SOURCES

PROLOGUE

For general archaeological background and wider references, see Jonathan L. Reed, *Archaeology and the Galilean Jesus: A Re-examination of the Evidence* (Harrisburg, PA: Trinity Press International, 2000). For fuller discussion and contemporary debates on the historical Jesus, see John Dominic Crossan, *The Historical Jesus: The Life of a Mediterranean Jewish Peasant* (San Francisco: HarperSanFrancisco, 1991) and *The Birth of Christianity* (San Francisco: HarperSanFrancisco, 1998). In this bibliographical appendix, we concentrate on archaeological rather than exegetical resources.

INTRODUCTION

Information on many of the archaeological sites and discoveries treated in this and subsequent chapters is available in the *New Encyclopedia of Archaeological Excavations in the Holy Land,* ed. Ephraim Stern (Jerusalem: Israel Exploration Society, 1993) as well as in *The Oxford Encyclopedia of Archaeology in the Near East,* ed. Eric M. Meyers (New York: Oxford University Press, 1997), which also contains useful articles on archaeological method and theory.

CHAPTER 1

The world-exclusive report on the James ossuary was by André Lemaire, "Burial Box of James the Brother of Jesus: Earliest Archaeological Evidence of Jesus Found in Jerusalem," *Biblical Archaeological Review,* vol. 28, no. 6 (November/December 2002), pp. 24–33, 70. The most comprehensive collection of ossuaries, with an excellent introduction, is in Levi Y. Rahmani, *A Catalogue of Jewish Ossuaries in the Collections of the State of Israel* (Jerusalem: Israel Exploration Society, 1994); for Jewish burial in general, see Byron McCane, *Roll Back the Stone: Death and Burial in the World of Jesus* (Harrisburg, PA: Trinity Press International, 2003). For Eusebius see G. A. Williamson (ed.), *Eusebius: The History of the Church* (New York: Penguin Books, 1965). Our quotations are from pp. 99–102. For the source in *Clementine Recognitions* 1, see Robert E. Van Voorst, *The Ascents of James: History and Theology of a Jewish-Christian Community*, SBLDS 112 (Atlanta, GA: Scholar Press, 1989); and F. Stanley Jones, *An Ancient Jewish Christian Source on the History of Christianity: Pseudo-Clementine Recognitions* 1.27–71, SBL Texts and Translations, 37: Christian Apocrypha Series, 2 (Atlanta, GA: Scholars Press, 1995). Our quotations are from the Latin version translated by Van Voorst, pp. 73–75. The *Gospel of Thomas* and the *Gospel of the Hebrews* are from Wilhelm Schneemelcher (ed.) and R. McL. Wilson (trans. ed.), *New Testament Apocrypha*, 2 vols., rev. ed. of the Collection initiated by Edgar Hennecke (Louisville, KY: Westminster/John Knox Press, 1991–92). Our quotations are from vol. 1, pp. 119 (*Thomas*) and 178 (*Hebrews*).

CHAPTER 2

The peasant culture of Galilee and the Mediterranean in general is described in the two books by John Dominic Crossan mentioned above, and the archaeological evidence for the Jewish character of Galilee in the first century is presented in the work by Jonathan L. Reed cited in that same location. A series of important articles on Galilean history, culture, and religion appear in Sean Freyne, *Galilee and Gospels: Collected Essays*, Wissenschaftliche Untersuchungen zum Neuen Testament 125 (Tübingen: Mohr Siebeck, 2000). The excavations at Nazareth are reported in Bellarmino Bagatti, *Excavations in Nazareth, Volume I: From the Beginning till the XII Century* (Jerusalem: Franciscan Printing, 1969). On the origins of the synagogue and the general lack of synagogue structures in the first century, see Lee Levine, *The Ancient Synagogue: The First Thousand Years* (New Haven: Yale University Press, 2000).

CHAPTER 3

A fascinating and readable characterization of Herod the Great and his rule is available in Peter Richardson, *Herod: King of the Jews and Friend of the Romans* (Minneapolis: Fortress Press, 1996). The present descriptions of the ancient city and Roman urban architecture rely on the work of John Stambaugh in *The Ancient Roman City* (Baltimore: Johns Hopkins University Press, 1988) and Paul Zanker in *The Power of Images in the Age of Augustus* (Ann Arbor: University of Michigan Press, 1990). A well-illustrated (but now outdated) summary of the excavations at Caesarea is Kenneth Holum, *King Herod's Dream: Caesarea by the Sea* (New York: Norton, 1988); more scholarly and up-to-date analyses are found in *Caesarea Maritima: A Retrospective After Two Millennia*, ed. Avner Raban and Kenneth Holum (Leiden: E. J. Brill, 1996). The relevant evidence from the numerous excavations at Sepphoris is summarized and collected in *Sepphoris in Galilee: Crosscurrents of Culture*, ed. Rebecca Nagy et al. (Raleigh: North Carolina Museum of Art, 1996). The archaeological finds from Capernaum and their relation to historical Jesus research are presented in Reed, *Archaeology and the Galilean Jesus*, and a detailed report on the "Galilee boat," its excavation, and its content was authored by Shelly Wachsmann in *The Excavations of an Ancient Boat in the Sea of Galilee*, Atiqot [English Series] 19 (Jerusalem: Israel Antiquities Authority, 1990).

CHAPTER 4

The pottery around the grotto at Banias has been analyzed by Andrea Berlin, in "The Archaeology of Ritual: The Sanctuary of Pan at Banias/Caesarea Philippi," *Bulletin of the American Schools of Oriental Research* 315 (1999): 27–45. On the palaces of Herod the Great, the work of Ehud Netzer is especially important, such as "The Promontory Palace," in *Caesarea Maritima: A Retrospective*. Herod's palace atop Masada is well documented and credibly reconstructed by Gideon Foerster in *Masada V: The Yigael Yadin Excavations 1965 Final Reports* (Jerusalem: Israel Exploration Society, 1995). The Dionysos Villa excavated by Eric and Carol Meyers and Ehud Netzer at Sepphoris is reported in Nagy et al., *Sepphoris in Galilee*. The excavations by Leroy Waterman were published as the *Preliminary Report of the University of Michigan Excavations at Sepphoris, Palestine, in 1931* (Ann Arbor: University of Michigan Press, 1937), and James F. Strange's reexcavation of the villa appears in "Six Campaigns at Sepphoris: The University of South Florida Excavations, 1983–1989," in *The Galilee in Late Antiquity*, ed. Lee Levine (New York: Jewish Theological Seminary, 1992), 339–55. The presentation of elite domestic architecture and dining during the Roman world relies heavily on Andrew Wallace-Hadrill, *Houses and Society in Pompeii and Herculaneum* (Princeton: Princeton University Press, 1994); for houses in the Jewish homeland in antiquity, see Yizhar Hirschfeld, *The Palestinian Dwelling in the Roman-Byzantine Period* (Jerusalem: Franciscan Printing, 1995).

CHAPTER 5

Yigael Yadin published a popular book on the excavations titled *Masada: Herod's Fortress and the Zealots' Last Stand* (New York: Random House, 1966). Thorough final publications have appeared recently in a multivolume work edited by Joseph Aviram, Gideon Foerster, and Ehud Netzer, *Masada I–V, The Yigael Yadin Excavations 1963–1965 Final Reports* (Jerusalem: Israel Exploration Society, 1989–95). Very much has been written about the Dead Sea Scrolls and the excavations at Khirbet Qumran in light of the still pending final publication, but the soundest summary of the archaeological evidence is by Jodi Magness, "Qumran Archaeology: Past Perspectives and Future Prospects," in *The Dead Sea Scrolls After Fifty Years: A Comprehensive Assessment, Vol. 1*, ed. Peter W. Flint and James C. VanderKam (Leiden: E. J. Brill, 1998), 47–77. The excavations at Jodefat as well as the extent to which the archaeological evidence overlaps with Josephus's account of its siege are detailed in David Adan-Bayewitz and Mordechai Aviam, "Iotapata, Josephus, and the Siege of 67: Preliminary Report on the 1992–94 Seasons," in *Journal of Roman Archaeology* 10 (1997):131–65. Whether or not the many stepped, plastered pools were in fact *miqwaoth* has been much debated, but, for a concise statement on the archaeological evidence within the context of Hellenization and Romanization in the Jewish homeland, see Ronny Reich, "The Hot Bath-House *(balneum)*, the Miqweh, and the Jewish Community in the Second Temple Period," *Journal of Jewish Studies* 39 (1988): 102–7. A complete catalogue of the archaeological evidence for stone vessels was compiled by Jane C. Cahill, in "The Chalk Assemblages of the Persian/Hellenistic and Early Roman Periods," in *Excavations at the City of David 1978–1985 Directed by Yigal Shiloh III: Stratigraphical,*

Environmental, and Other Reports, ed. Alon de Groot and Donald T. Ariel, Qedem 33 (Jerusalem: Hebrew University Press, 1992), 190–274.

CHAPTER 6

The best description of the archaeology of the Temple is by Leen and Kathleen Ritmeyer, *Secrets of Jerusalem's Temple Mount* (Washington: Biblical Archaeology Society, 1998); an account of the excavations and summaries of the finds are found in Meir Ben-Dov, *In the Shadow of the Temple: The Discovery of Ancient Jerusalem* (New York: Harper & Row, 1985). Nahman Aviam reports on the excavations in the Herodian Quarter and of the Palatial Mansion in the lavishly illustrated *Discovering Jerusalem* (Nashville: Thomas Nelson, 1983). A summary of the literary sources' description of priestly activities in the Temple is given by E. P. Sanders, in *Judaism: Practice and Belief 63* B.C.E.–66 C.E. (Philadelphia: Trinity Press International, 1992).

CHAPTER 7

The most recent archaeological description of the Holy Sepulcher is Shimon Gibson and Joan Taylor's *Beneath the Church of the Holy Sepulchre, Jerusalem,* Palestine Exploration Fund Monograph Series Maior 1 (London: Palestine Exploration Fund, 1994). Reports on the burial of Caiaphas were published by Zvi Greenhut, "The 'Caiaphas' Tomb in the North of Jerusalem," Ronny Reich, "Ossuary Inscriptions from the 'Caiaphas' Tomb,'" and Joseph Zias, "Human Skeletal Remains from the 'Caiaphas Tomb,'" in *Atiqot* [English Series] 21 (1992): 63–80; summaries along with reports on other burials around Jerusalem are also found in *Ancient Jerusalem Revealed,* ed. Hillel Geva (Jerusalem: Israel Exploration Society, 1994). The tomb and ossuary of the crucified man were first reported by Vassilios Tzaferis, "Jewish Tombs At and Near Giv'at ha-Mivtar, Jerusalem," *Israel Exploration Journal* 20 (1970): 18–32, and the remains by Nico Haas, "Anthropological Observations on the Skeletal Remains from Giv'at ha-Mivtar," *Israel Exploration Journal* 20 (1970): 38–59, which were reevaluated by Joseph Zias and Eliezer Sekeles, in "The Crucified Man from Giv'at ha-Mivtar: A Reappraisal," *Israel Exploration Journal* 35 (1985): 22–27.

Index